P. Markopoulos
P. Johnson (eds.)

Design, Specification
and Verification
of Interactive Systems '98

Proceedings of the Eurographics Workshop
in Abingdon, UK,
June 3–5, 1998

Eurographics

Springer-Verlag Wien GmbH

Dr. Panos Markopoulos
Prof. Dr. Peter Johnson
Department of Computer Science, Queen Mary
and Westfield College, London, U.K.

© 1998 Springer-Verlag Wien
Originally published by Springer Vienna in 1998.

Graphic design: Ecke Bonk

Printed on acid-free and chlorine-free bleached paper

SPIN: 10684775

With 119 Figures

ISSN 0946-2767
ISBN 978-3-211-83212-7   ISBN 978-3-7091-3693-5 (eBook)
DOI 10.1007/978-3-7091-3693-5

Preface

This book is the formal proceedings of the Eurographics Workshop on Design, Specification and Verification of Interactive Systems, DSV-IS '98, which was held in Abingdon, UK, from June 3 to June 5, 1998. The workshop took place at Cosener's House in Abingdon, situated at a picturesque Thames-side position, in the grounds of the medieval abbey of Abingdon. The long sessions of the program were followed by informal discussions over dinner at Cosener's house, during a boat trip on the river Thames and late in the evening at the local pubs. This was the fifth event in a series of workshops which have studied formalisms, tool and methodologies to support the design of interactive systems. The previous events of this series were held at Pisa, Toulouse, Namur and Granada.

The theme of this year's workshop was 'Modelling and Design'. Presentations and discussions focused on models, e.g., of devices, users, tasks, etc., their representations and their role in supporting the design and development of interactive systems. As in previous years, papers and discussions concerned the use of formal representations and their role in supporting the design, specification, verification, validation and evaluation of interactive systems. The workshop aimed to encourage an exchange of ideas and to focus discussion upon the strengths and weaknesses of various modelling approaches.

This book includes the papers of the invited speakers, seventeen papers accepted for presentation out of the thirty five papers submitted and the proceedings of the working group discussions. A further 6 papers were accepted for short presentation and discussion. These papers are reported in a separate volume which shall be published by the Eurographics Association as part of their Eurographics Workshop Proceedings series, under the title "Supplementary Proceedings of the 5th Eurographics Workshop on Design, Specification and Verification of Interactive Systems, DSV-IS'98".

The format of the workshop aimed to mix formal paper presentations with informal discussion sessions. Two invited talks set the tone for the workshop.

Dan Olsen in his invited talk 'Interacting in Chaos' described how the diversity of technological artefacts and information forms that surround people and the wide range of uses for these devices, limit the utility of abstractions made by software engineers. He then described his vision of the way to master this chaos of technological and informational artefacts: Provide people with tools to exploit the regularity that is inherent in surface representations of the information they use.

John McCarthy in his invited talk 'The viability of modelling socially organised activity' described technology as an intervention in socially organised activity. Characterising the activity after this intervention and evaluating its consequences, brings us to the realm of the social and the experiential, what he called the 'messy stuff'. His recommendation for a way forward: analysis of the accountability of work focusing on the information and technological artefacts used, making explicit the interdependency of technology, activity and accountability.

Paper presentations were grouped into the following sessions:

- Modelling for the Design of Interactive Systems (2 sessions)

- The Role of Representations in Designing Interactive Systems

- Formal Support for the Design of Interactive Systems

- Advances in Model Based Design

- Specification and Verification of Interactive Systems

Participants were split into three 'working groups' which discussed three problems given to them. The specification of these problems and the reports from the working group discussions are included in the third part of this volume.

We wish to thank the authors of the papers and the participants of the workshop and to wish success to DSV-IS'99 which will be held next year at the University of Minho, Braga, Portugal. Information about this series of workshops can be found in the Eurographics web site (http://www.eg.org), under the description of special-interest groups. Acknowledgement is due to ERCIM and Eurographics for sponsoring the event.

Finally, we would like to express our gratitude to David Duce for organising the workshop. Special thanks are due also to Michael Harrison and Juan-Carlos Torres for their contribution to the organisation, Lilian Valentine for her administrative work, and all the members of the programme committee for their work in reviewing the papers submitted.

The programme chairs

Panos Markopoulos and Peter Johnson

Contents

Working Group Discussions

Organising Committee

D. Duce (local organisation), Rutherford Appleton Laboratory, UK

P. Johnson (co-chair), Queen Mary and Westfield, University of London, UK

M. Harrison, University of York, UK

P. Markopoulos (co-chair), Queen Mary and Westfield, University of London, UK

J.C. Torres, University of Granada, Spain

Paper Review Committee

M. Apperley, Waikato, New Zealand

J. Coutaz, CLIPS-HCI, Grenoble, France

D. Duke, University of York, UK

P. Gray, University of Glasgow, UK

R. Jacob, Tufts University, USA

D. Olsen, Carnegie Mellon, USA

P. Paternó, CNUCE-CNR, Italy

G. Reynolds, CSIRO, Canberra, Autsralia

P. Szekely, Universityof Southern California, USA

J. Vanderdonckt, FUNDP, Namur, Belgium

R. Bastide, LIS-University of Toulouse I, France

A. Dix, University of Staffordshire, UK

G. Faconti, CNUCE-CNR, Italy

M. Green, University of Alberta, Canada

C. Johnson, University of Glasgow, UK

P. Palanque, LIS-University of Toulouse I, France

A. Puerta, Stanford, USA

S. Schreiber, Siemens, Munich, Germany

C. Stephanidis, ICS-Forth, Greece

M. Wilson , RAL, UK

S. Wilson, QMW, University of London, UK

Interacting In Chaos

Dan R. Olsen Jr.
Human Computer Interaction Institute, Carnegie Mellon University
Computer Science Department, Brigham Young University

In considering which research problems to work on next, one must consider the key uses for future computing technology. To such roles are the support of interpersonal communication and the management, analysis and synthesis of massive amounts of information. When one considers the Macintosh and the impact it has had on computing it is important to understand that it was fundamentally not a computing engine but a communications device. The medium for communication was paper rather than electronic but the Mac was and is all about creating paper artifacts for communication among people. Even today when one examines a software catalog for Windows or the Mac, more than 90% of the software offered is focused on internet or paper-based communications. There is very little that computes or calculates in the classical sense.

Personal computers as information engines are a rather more recent phenomenon. The first personal computers had no network and very little disk space. The advent of the internet has radically changed the role of the personal computer as an information management device. The information management approaches that worked for centralized mainframes are not appropriate for personal internet computing. The personal computer environment was not designed for mass information management. These issues must be rethought.

Before addressing the information and communication problems, we must first consider the key forces that will shape computing for the next ten years. These forces fall into three broad categories 1) exponential growth in digital technology, 2) market driven diversity, and 3) limited human capacity. The exponential growth in processor power, memory capacity, network bandwidth and the shear size of the internet a key story of the late 20th century. Such exponential growth will continue through the next decade and cannot be ignored when developing interactive technology for the future. We must work on problems which will still have relevance in an era when every individual has an order of magnitude more computing interacting with several orders of magnitude more information resources. We must also consider the fact that diversity rather than uniformity will rule computing. There is no way that top-down uniformity will solve any of the key problems that face us. In the face of this explosive growth in technology and diversity, human capacity to absorb it all will not change. Human capacity is the limiting factor and technologies that leverage those capacities are the key to the future.

1. Differing views on the creation of software

Assuming that digital hardware will continue to progress and will continue to be general purpose in its nature, the key to solving problems using computers is in software. Software is the malleable medium that has shaped the digital revolution. The classical view for how to create new software is what I will call the *modeling* approach to problem solving. Using this approach one first attempts to understand the problem being addressed. One then identifies the necessary information and actions which will help to solve the problem. There are various techniques for doing this ranging from entity relationship diagrams through object oriented design. In all such approaches the goal is to create an abstract model of the problem at hand. This abstract model is then encoded in some form that can be analyzed, checked, discussed and ultimately implemented in a working program.

The modeling approach to software problem solving is rather different from what actually happens in the world. A more interesting and common approach is what I will call the *chaotic* approach. In a chaotic world stuff just happens. Problems arise daily and the knowledge workers of the world must face and conquer these problems as they arise. When a problem arises the knowledge worker assembles information that is relevant to the problem. There is always a tradeoff between the relevance of information and its availability. There are constant choices between what is important and what can be obtained with reasonable effort. Such workers then identify strategies that have worked in similar situations. Having obtained information and arrived at a plausible strategy, they muddle through with sufficient precision to get the job done. A key insight occurs when similar problems recur with some regularity. As problems repeatedly arise for an individual or among similar workers, there is then an attempt to proceduralize. By imposing some uniformity such recurring problems can be dealt with more efficiently and problem-specific technology can be developed. If the recurring problems are sufficiently important to a broad enough class of people, then a software development project is begun. There is an information usage cycle of the form.

```
Repeat
{
        1) Chaotic state with a variety of kinds
                of information and problems
        2) Regularity and repetition is discovered
        3) Uniformity is imposed
        4) Software is developed around
                the uniformity
}
Until the end of the world as we know it
```

Traditional computer science is focused on steps 3 and 4. In the centralized world of mainframe computing this was possible and necessary for the technology to even work. In the internet world step 1 is the dominant state. In fact it is argued here that the growth of technology will increase rather than decrease the dominance of chaos.

2. Chaos will rule

The term chaos is used here by analogy to the mathematical definition of chaos. It is not meant that there is random disordered behavior in the world. Quite to the contrary the behavior is highly ordered. However, the existence of this order does not provide a reasonable prediction of the future beyond the next few steps. Chaos theory is actually based on rather simple formulas which can be clearly understood in the very near term. Minor perturbations, however, can produce wildly different long term outcomes. Chaotic models diverge rather than converge. Convergence, however, is essential to the creation of helpful tools. What follows here are three informal discussions which point out the chaotic nature of the future of computing.

2.1 The WWW problem

The modeling approach to computer science assumes that there exists a well defined set information artifacts which are necessary to the user's problems and a well defined set of actions that a user can take. This information and action space is embodied in a set of applications which have been carefully designed for this user and all users with similar needs.

This is not the approach that dominates the World Wide Web. Each web site is not open to a well defined and well understood set of users but rather to the entire internet community. The set of ways in which the information and services of a web site can or may be used is unknowable because of the diversity and functional anonymity of the web community. Web site developers must design for some niche of users whose characteristics may or may not be understood and who may or may not in fact be the real users.

From the web user's point of view there are a functionally infinite set of services and information available. Each user has almost no impact on the design of more than a few of these sites and yet the user is faced with the task of exploiting such opportunities in completing their job. In this situation the site developers are faced with an essentially unknowable user base and the users are faced with resources whose nature they cannot influence but must exploit. This situation is inherently chaotic. As the web grows it will become more chaotic rather than less.

2.2 The stock advisor problem

Consider the role of a stock advisor (a good one), which is to turn information about the economy, markets and individual companies into accurate predictions of what the market or a stock is about to do. Those predictions are then translated into buy/sell strategies which if based on accurate predictions will produce wealth. Suppose there were a world where all stock advisors used the same 327 pieces of information and the same 114 models of the market. If this were so then all stock advisors would produce similar predictions which would lead to similar buy/sell strategies with similar results. Share holders may acquire wealth in such a world, because the market increases, but the advisors themselves will suffer. Stock advisors only succeed by achieving competitive advantage relative to each other. Each such advisor is constantly seeking new information and new models which will offer such an advantage. In such a world, uniform use of information is death. Only by new uses of new information is advantage achieved. In such a world the advantage lies not in uniform and regularized information but in the chaos that lies beyond.

2.3 The market diversity problem

Consider the software market itself. In an ideal world one would create the optimal product, sell it and thus build a large wealth producing company. In actuality this is not possible. Once the "optimal" product has been sold to a sufficiently large body of users there is no more demand for the product. Software never wears out. In fact wealth producing software companies must continually resell to the same users every few years or they will go out of business. Since software never wears out, they must develop new capabilities, add new features, integrate with changes made to other relevant software and so on. Such companies must continue to change their products to justify continuing sales.

This drive to improve and change is exacerbated by the competitive need to differentiate themselves from the competition. If two products are the same then the consumer has no substantive reason to choose one over the other. If company X produced a word processor that was exactly like MS Word, they would fail because there is no compelling reason for users to leave the Microsoft product line. The competitive market is inherently a divergent force. With diversity comes chaos.

3 The impact of chaos

A linchpin of modern computing is communication of information. This not only includes the communication among people in collaborative situation but communication between people and information services as well as communication among components of systems. Consider a community that must share information in order to accomplish some task. In order for digital communication to be effective the information must be shared in standard formats which all members of the community must be capable of utilizing. Almost every time there is an upgrade in the software that the members use, all users must upgrade simultaneously to prevent incompatibility. The larger the community the less likely this simultaneous upgrade will occur. The larger the community the less likely they are to have uniform goals and purposes. If a part of the community upgrades while the rest do not, the community membership is automatically fragmented.

In the face of the forces of diversity, the necessary uniformity to maintain communication compatibility can only be achieved by a centralized force. The larger the community the less likely such centralized control will be effective. Suppose, however, that a large organization was able to enforce uniformity on all of its employees, the problem will not be eliminated. Enforced uniformity to eliminate chaos can only extend to the limits of the organization. Any effective organization must deal with the rest of the world. There is no rational way for an organization to enforce its uniformity on all other groups and individuals with which it might at any point want to do business. Computing never exists in a closed universe and therefore will always be subject to chaotic forms of digital information.

4 Mastering chaos

In order to succeed in digitally supporting truly large communities we must rely upon forms of information that are convergent rather than divergent, otherwise the task is fundamentally hopeless. These are forms that by their very nature will tend to standardize on a few rather than increase in type and variety. In this search for convergence, consider the application architecture in figure 1. Every interactive application has an underlying semantic model which represents all of the information being manipulated by the application. One of the major roles of the application software is to translate that model into one or more surface representations that can be directly presented to the user. All user interaction is defined in terms of such surface presentations.

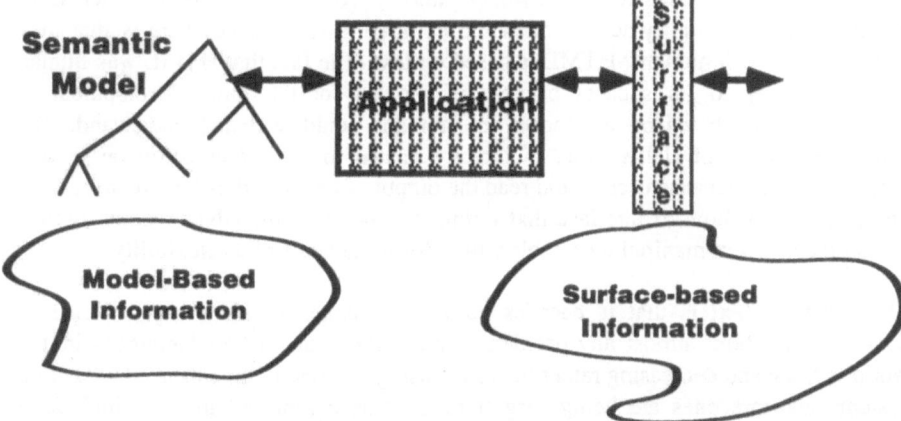

Fig 1. Application Architecture

Most architectures for sharing information are based on the semantic model because it is designed for effective use by a computer. As has been pointed out, such semantic models are highly divergent for large communities. There is no stability to be found here. On the other hand the surface representations are inherently convergent and stable because they are bounded by the capabilities of the users being served.

The capability of human beings is the primary unifying and stabilizing force in all of computer science. The only divergent forces in surface representations occur when the technology has less fundamental capability than the range of human perception. Once a technology exceeds the range of human capability, there is no longer any advantage to be gained by divergence and the diversity of representations disappears.

To understand the role of surface representations, we need to consider a few examples. These show the convergence of surface representations and their value in communicating information.

4.1 Text

Text is a primary surface representation. In the early days of computing there were a variety of encodings some of which conserved the number of bits and others which optimized the hardware interfaces to punched cards. As memory capacities increased and microprocessors simplified hardware interfaces there was no functional need for the diversity. All converged on ASCII and its extension into the Latin character set. Once technology limitations were removed the representations converged to one. The exception to this is that the Latin set cannot encode all written languages. There arose a variety of encodings for non-Latin characters. UNICODE subsumed them all and when memory space became cheap, all other formats are disappearing. In the case of text convergence has already occurred.

Text has proven its value as a communication medium. Email works because it is based on text. Whenever email branches out into attachments (which are model-based) the communication starts to break. Many internet protocols are defined in terms of text because they simplify development and compatibility. The key here is that they communicate with humans. HTML is based on text. The fact that HTML was human readable is key to its success because it allowed for the rapid development of supporting tools based on a standard the humans could read and understand. The component nature of UNIX tools is directly related to their foundation on textual representations. Because users could read the output of one tool they had the necessary understanding of how to interface that output to another tool. UNIX comes with a standard set of text manipulation tools which form the heart of its flexibility.

The power of text is that it encodes human language and thus can be used to communicate about almost any problem. The number of written languages in the world is finite and decreasing rather than increasing. No one is inventing new writing systems and rare ones are being forgotten. Text as a representation is inherently convergent. In spite of the convergence, the space of problems that can be addressed by human language is potentially infinite.

4.2 Audio

The most successful communication medium is the phone. The underlying system of switches and communications lines undergo continuous change and yet the users are not impacted because the surface representation (real-time voice grade audio) is unchanged. The key to success here is that humans communicate with each other by speaking. There is a physical limit on the dynamic range and frequency of the human ear. Once that range is exceeded there is no competitive advantage in divergent representations. Once again we have an convergent medium which can be used to communicate an infinite variety of information.

The majority of the internet users in the world use audio as the means for communicating information. Most users use a modem which converts digital information into audio signals because the only convergent and stable electronic communication available to them is audio. This is clear evidence that conversion into an inefficient but convergent surface medium is preferable to not communicating at all.

4.3 Images

Paper is an excellent medium for communication. There are few problems that are incompatible with paper. Paper, if undamaged, always communicates. Paper encodes any 2D image and therefore subsumes text and a variety of other communication forms. A 2D image works directly with the eyes which provide the highest bandwidth input for humans. The versatility and generality of 2D images is the driving force behind the transition from textual interfaces to graphical ones. 2D images are an obvious success in communications as evidenced by letters, advertising, books and FAX. It is interesting to note that over all of the years that we have printed with Postscript, it is only on version 2. This stands in stark contrast to other software of similar age. The reason is that there is no 2D image that Postscript cannot represent. Once that threshold is met there is no advantage to extending the representation. Note that when the WWW was introduced there were several image formats supported (some badly). At this point nobody considers formats other than GIF and JPEG. These two were enough to meet the capabilities of today's displays. Once the visual threshold is reached diversity is a vice not a virtue.

4.4 Video

The conflict between VHS and Beta is an example of the convergence of surface representations. To the consumers there was not sufficient visual difference to prefer one over the other. The marketplace converged on one. When technology can deliver images that obviously present a visually more desirable presentation, then there will be another standards war and convergence will occur again.

5 Interacting in Chaos

Having considered the new chaotic order that internet based information and collaboration has brought us, we then must decide what to do about it. My contention is that we should concentrate on human consumable data types and the fundamental media for representing information. I believe that the key data types are:

> text / language
> images and pictures
> audio
> video
> 3D environments
> tactile information

Each of these constitutes a fundamental way in which experience is communicated to human beings. The key problems related to such data types are finding appropriate artifacts with such data, organizing what has been found, analyzing information, synthesizing new information in one or more of the data types and interrelating information into a new structure. We need to develop the capability of working in pictures, audio and video that are as facile as EMACS is when working with text. Hardware technology is crossing a threshold that will make such tools possible. Basic algorithms have been studied for some time. As yet these tools are not accessible to ordinary computer users in a facile form.

The reason for focusing on surface representations is that they communicate with human beings. If a service can communicate with people then it can have value. Having communicated with people we would then like to automate, regularize and manipulate what is communicated. This requires highly adaptable tools. This is made tractable by the fact that the information we receive is not random. Consider all of the paper that has arrived in your office in the last year. Consider how many of those printed images at one time existed on a computer before they were printed. Most of the surface information that we receive is computer generated. If we cut out the printing and scanning steps we could receive that information in a noise free form. Consider also that much of the WWW information is generated by an algorithm rather than by people. There is inherent regularity in such output that is waiting to be exploited by other tools. All that remains is for us to design them. This, I believe, is where the future of interactive technology lies.

The viability of modelling socially organised activity

J.C. McCarthy

Department of Applied Psychology
University College Cork, Ireland

Abstract. Research into socially organised activity provides insights which should not be ignored by interactive system designers. At the same time, the emergence of social context as a salient factor in the design and use of information technology poses problems for the activity of modelling in design. By highlighting the informal, tacit, contingent, and relational aspects of technology use, it raises issues which test the technical scope and practical value of model making. In this paper, attempts to use activity-based insights in design are reviewed and their implications for the relationship between model and activity are considered.

1 Introduction

There is a growing interest in HCI (Human Computer Interaction), CSCW (Computer Supported Cooperative Work) and Cognitive Science in conceptualisations of activity as socially organised and situated and in conceptualisations of information and information structures as inescapably embedded in social activity. For the early stages of design, requirements analysis and specification, this has brought with it immersion in, what at first appears to be, the 'messy stuff' of the social and experiential. Despite the messiness, interactional studies of socially organised activity provide observations on the organisation of activity which seem to point to requirements. Examples include: the role of tacit coordination in accomplishing cooperative work; the distribution of representations across a functional system; and the transactional nature of the reliability and safety of a system. These observations have opened up spaces originally opened by the sociotechnical systems movement which were in danger of being closed off by overly technical characterisations of work, interaction, and technology.

The turn to social and experiential not only opens up spaces for enquiry in requirements analysis but also points to significant problems in modelling any such requirements. It questions the possibility of producing veridical representations of activity and requirements [4, 14]. For those who would brush aside this argument with a "we always knew our models were approximate and partial, it would be naive to think otherwise", questions are posed about who chooses which parts to highlight and which to exclude, what do claims of precision or accuracy mean if they are to be dissociated from truth, and what purposes do approximate models play in design. I rehearse some of the difficulties again, not to teach anybody how to suck eggs, but to demonstrate that the gap between requirements and specification can be a chasm.

In this paper, the gap is the starting place. Articulating requirements for design is difficult and we seem to be the kind of species (or at least culture) that builds models and representations to reason about those things that are difficult. But building models is also difficult. Dix goes so far as to suggest that some requirements may be "inherently unformalisable" [4, p.10]. The social and experiential turn opens up spaces but also problematises the relationship between the activity of modelling and the socially organised activity being modelled. The most important question, at this stage, is a pragmatic one: given that some requirements cannot be formalised and that verification of mappings from informal requirements to specification is at least problematic, and given that models are an important part of design practice and that informal requirements are to be addressed in design and evaluation, what do we do?

Any attempt to answer that question is likely to be best served by an immersion in the social and experiential. Therefore, some aspects of socially organised activity are considered in section 2. Attempts to use these insights in design will be reviewed in section 3, particularly efforts between Cork and York based on developing frameworks for describing activity in context. Finally, in section 4, we draw some conclusions about the kinds of modelling that is viable for socially organised activity.

2 Socially organised activity

Interactional studies of the use of information technology focus on intact multi-person, human-technology systems with a view to describing how such systems function. Some use ethnographic and discursive methods to show how activity is socially organised [8]. Others focus on participants' accounts of socially organised activity to show the kinds of conceptual resources used by those organising [11]. The rationale for using interactional studies as part of the design process is that technology constitutes an intervention in socially organised activity and the activity is capable of facilitating or frustrating the effectiveness of any technological system. Thought of this way, these studies are at least capable of raising awareness and sensitising design to aspects of the organisation of activity.

Suchman, [17] Lave [10] and others have demonstrated that performance of a wide range of activities, including photocopying, tailoring, and doing mathematics is highly situated. For instance, a number of studies have demonstrated that people's use of mathematics is contingent upon the activities in which the mathematics are embedded, technological mediation, and particulars of the situation. That is to say that maths performance by shoppers in a supermarket can differ in material ways from maths performance by carpenters on a building site, even if the shopper and carpenter is the same person. Schliemann and Nunes' [16] study of fishermen at work demonstrated that their use of mathematics related in quite sophisticated ways to the material substance of fish, the technology for weighing and processing fish, and the social practices which give salience to proportions in the activity of commercial fishing (i.e. the relationships between weight and price and between processed and unprocessed). These relationships are not necessary, material or universal, rather they reflect socially organised practices which have as much to do with specific notions of trade and commerce as with fishing. Likewise, the context for school maths and maths in science includes the material and technological factors in the situation (e.g. computers, calculators, graphical representations, etc.) and the social organisation of school and scientific activity which promotes certain procedures and routines over others, certain interpretations over others, and certain ways of thinking over others. It seems that even an activity as apparently formal and abstract as doing mathematics is itself difficult to abstract from the context of socially organised activity in a way which does justice to the data on qualitative differences.

But abstractions are possible and meaningful. We know this not from any particular theoretical approach but from the pragmatics of use of abstraction in context. We develop abstractions, such as task models of people doing mathematics, to inform interactive systems design and instructional design and they seem to be useful. The purpose of contextualising mathematics activity as socially organised activity is not to diminish the role of analyses of the individual performer or the task being performed, rather to draw attention to the kind of organisational factors that make the individuation possible in practice.

CSCW has attended to organisational factors in a range of work settings including air traffic control, London Underground, and radiography departments in hospitals. In a joint project between Cork and York, we carried out field research on the work of two ambulance control centres [12]. The research involved a series of visits to the control centres stretching over a 15 month period, the focus of which was to examine how the staff dealt with emergency calls and, in particular, how they located the scene of an emergency. Research methods included: sitting-in with ambulance control staff while they carried out their duties; collecting and transcribing tapes of a number of calls; and open-ended interviews to follow up issues which arose during the sitting-in periods.

The two centres differed in a number of respects. While ACC1 (Ambulance Control Centre 1) served a very large, predominantly urban population with a team that included ambulance despatchers, radio operators, telephonists, and a team leader, and a high technology support system, ACC2 served a modest, predominantly rural, population with a single controller and a low technology support system. However in both centres, acquiring a complete and precise address is a crucial part of locating the scene. In ACC1 this process is constrained by the interaction between the call receiver and the gazetteer, which can offer suggested addresses and point up ambiguities in addresses entered. In contrast, in ACC2 more reliance is placed on acquiring and using local knowledge through collaboration with the caller and controllers tend to rely on their own knowledge of the area and the general characteristics of an adequate description to detect ambiguities in the address and description offered by the caller.

There is also a greater reliance in ACC2 on physical and geographical cues and landmarks, such as public or painted building and people or vehicles at cross-roads, to elaborate and verify the initial description.

Personnel in both centres record elements of the description of the location given by the caller. The ACC1 call receiver enters them into and electronic form linked to the gazetteer and the despatchers' system. The ACC2 controller writes them on a notepad and subsequently transfers them to a call receipt. Although superficially similar, these representations perform different work in the two centres. For example, in ACC1 the description is propagated through the system to provide a resource for the activities of the despatcher and crew. In ACC2 the controller deals with both receipt and despatch and the notes they make are primarily a reminder of what they achieved with the caller and, as such, are first and foremost a representation of the call rather than the location. Finally, a salient feature of call processing in ACC2, which is far less common in ACC1, is the way in which a wide range of individuals are recruited to provide additional checks during the processing of a call. In examples we observed, this included an ambulance driver with local knowledge of the relevant region who happened to be in the control centre, a doctor, and other hospital staff.

My aim in briefly reviewing parts of the ambulance control work here is to reinforce the characterisation of work as socially organised activity. It is clear that ambulance control in both centres is socially distributed across a range of personnel. A great deal of collaborative work is also carried out between the caller and call receiver, though there appears to be more in ACC2 and the nature of the collaboration differs between the two centres. Technology and other material particulars are also implicated. Finally, the ambulance crew are involved to the extent that call receivers are aware that they are developing a representation of a location which has to be adequate for the crew's purpose of getting an ambulance to the scene. This can also differ between the centres and is most apparent in ACC2's use of landmarks.

Analyses of the organisation of work suggest that, for those performing the work, it is only possible to carve the work into discrete tasks on the back of a detailed understanding of what is expected of them as members of a social collective performing work which interrelates with the activities of others. This draws attention to work as concrete, answerable, performed activity and away from abstract possibilities. Any model of 'locating the scene' which focuses on the work or knowledge of individuals or on individual tasks misses the social organisation that makes those individual aspects of the individual work and tasks possible in the particular context in which they happen. The argument here is that the social context is not just noise to be dismissed or background details of little importance to actually accomplishing the work, rather it is seminal in specifying which individual tasks are relevant.

The turn to socially organised activity is more than a turf war about the primacy of individual or collective perspectives. It is not just a turn to the social but even more importantly a turn to the experiential which draws attention to the emotional-volitional character of concrete, answerable, performed work [1]. Ambulance controllers, concerned for the welfare of ambulance crew and convinced of the value of local knowledge in getting ambulances to the scene quickly, despatch the ambulance which has spent the longest time in station, from those available at the station nearest to the scene (known as First In First Out or FIFO). This decision runs counter to policy which requires that the ambulance nearest the scene of the emergency is despatched. Faced with a dilemma reflecting different kinds of concerns, controllers favour the welfare of their colleagues and their appraisal of the value of local knowledge over management concerns for general resource management. They make a decision which has consequences for them no matter which option they take, as they find themselves answerable to both colleagues and management.

The dilemma also finds expression in a design choice. One of the main official resources available to controllers is an electronic display screen that records the history of communications with each ambulance including calls to indicate return to station. In an effort to discourage FIFO despatch, management decided that this screen should not explicitly represent order of return to station. Controllers work around this constraint by using a notepad divided up into boxes for each station on which the controller has recorded: ambulances in station, stood down, despatched and the time at which it arrived in station, stood down, or despatched. Management discourage the use of personal notepads but have not stopped the practice. The dilemma, its technological manifestation and its practical resolution reflects the concerned character of persons-in-activity. Work gets done by concerned workers making contingent decisions. The social and institutional context of activity in those situations casts problems as dilemmas which concerned participants have to resolve as best they can.

3 From social activity to design?

As a perspective, socially organised activity points to concerned workers doing concrete, answerable, performed work and away from work or activity as abstract possibility. It says that it is not advisable to arbitrarily select out the worker, the work, the rules, the procedures, or whatever for decontextualised, individual attention because they all constitute each other. In terms of requirements, it says that we should pay attention to the emergence of organisation from local practices, to the affective responsiveness of people acting, with some discretion, into social structures, and to the tensions and contradictions experienced by people resolving the everyday dilemmas with which they are faced.

One way is to develop a design process in which system development, prototyping and tailoring occurs in parallel with requirements analysis built on social science methodologies, with the two streams of activity interacting in formal and informal ways throughout the process [2]. Social scientists suggest ways of seeing for the development team who in turn constrain the search space of the social scientists. It is sometimes seen as a continuous design dialogue between the designers and users with the users either directly involved or represented by the social scientists [15].

Even when user or social scientist is part of a design team, interpretations of observed activity or of a putative system are inevitably part of the discourse. Representations can facilitate this dialogue, at least as stepping stones in the gap between requirements and specification which encourage movement from one side to the other. From the discussion of socially organised activity, we can make some demands on these representations. For example, that design representations should:

1. be sensitive to the local context of activity i.e. the material and social particulars that make all the difference
2. recognise the concerned, concrete, answerable dimensions of activity

Demands are also suggested by consideration of the use and problematics of representation suggested in the foregoing discussion. For example, that design representations should:

3. Be recognised and accepted by those engaged in the activity
4. Point beyond themselves and not become an end in themselves
5. Reframe activity, not depict it

Distributed cognition [9] provides a means of addressing the first point, retaining a cognitive task-oriented disposition while responding to the salience of local particulars. In the case of our ambulance control work, we developed accounts in terms of the propagation and maintenance of representations of an address through a series of transformations constrained by particular coordinations and communications [12]. This distributed cognitive account of the work of locating the scene in the two ambulance control centres paid particular attention to the work of linking representations of an address (in ACC1) and of a call (in ACC2) to a location, the scene of the emergency. As such, it provided some interesting insights for design and evaluation. However, this kind of interpretation of the work takes no account of the answerable performance of work.

Scenarios, if written as rich descriptions of particular dilemmas, choices, and consequences, can occupy positions between concrete, answerable experience and the social and technical future being designed [3]. They are a means for referring back to answerable practice while imagining future technologies. They also satisfy some of the other demands. They are likely to be acceptable to a wide range of participants. They speak to both social and technical aspects and are more likely than many other representations to be recognised by the people who will use the technology. As used by Bodker, they also have a feel about them of pointing beyond themselves. At least in the senses of looking forward to what might be as well as back to what is and of using grounded particulars to look out.

In order to provoke a dialogical design process, Bodker has argued that scenarios should be complemented by the use of a range of other design tools and representations such as work-oriented checklists, technical-checklists, and prototypes. Our contribution to Bodker's design toolbox is a simple framework for generating analyses of accountability at work [13]. This framework is an attempt to maintain as much as possible of the character of concrete answerable work while, at the same time, enabling us to analyse tasks, activities, and the use of artefacts at the juncture between work and accountability.

The framework operates as a two dimensional space in which we position artifactually mediated activities of interest. One dimension describes a continuum on which work practices are placed. The other describes a continuum on which accountability is placed. In previously reported work we have used a range of dimensions including: explicit-implicit; global-local; stable-transient; and dependent-independent. *Explicit-Implicit* refers to the extent to which organisational and work processes are presented in forms which are available for external inspection, for example, standardised training, written job specifications, task descriptions, and documented procedures, or emerge from the activities, knowledge and understanding of the participants in an organisational process. *Global-Local* refers to the extent to which structure is imposed by people other than those involved in the work activity and to whom those involved are accountable. *Stable-Transient* refers to the extent to which tasks and their allocation remain the same or change across situations. *Interdependent-Independent* refers to the extent to which tasks are separable from one another or are contingent on one another. Tasks which are wholly independent can be carried out with no reference to other tasks even though they are part of the same work domain. Tasks which involve high interdependencies involve actions being carried out with reference to each other, often by more than one person. This set of dimensions is not intended to be a complete set, just a set of dimensions that we have found useful in describing the connectedness of work activity and accountability for a number of areas of work including aviation and radiography.

Figures 1 exemplifies use of the framework to analyse aspects of the design choice whether to represent order of return of ambulances to station on the electronic information display. It highlights a number of organisational issues which both have a bearing on the use of information technology in the control room and are affected by its design and implementation. Broadly speaking, we can see a clash of concerns between management and controllers, ambiguity about accountability, and a degree of tolerance of controllers working around what they would consider to be a limitation of the new electronic display. It would be possible to develop this kind of 'broad brushstrokes' account from observation or from reading a detailed description without developing the framework at all. What the framework offers over and above the broad brushstrokes is an attempt to unpack aspects of these organisational developments,

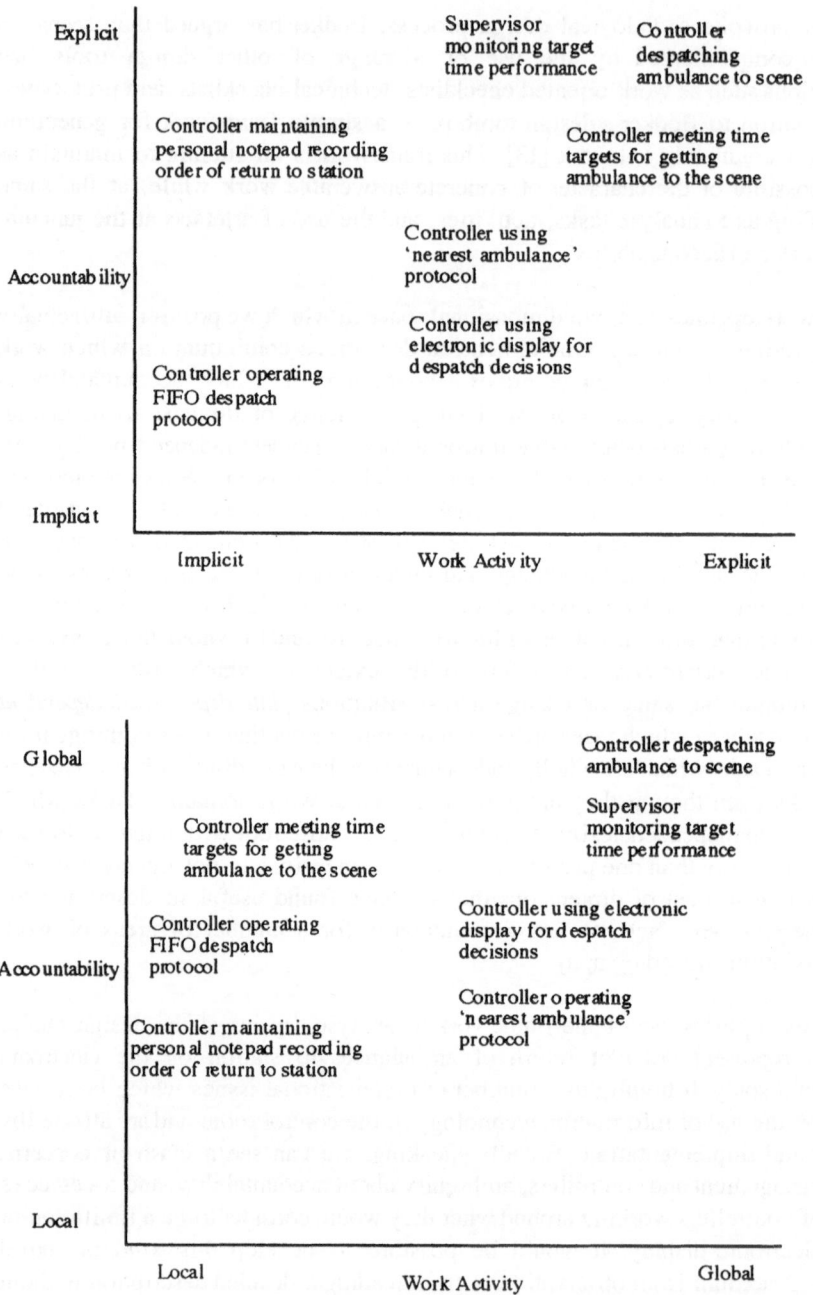

Figure 1: Analysis of ambulance despatch on the explicit-implicit and local-global dimensions

which may be relevant to design, specification and evaluation. It does this in terms of the relationships between artefacts, activity, and accountability.

We can use the framework to explore aspects of the organisation of work that create the dilemma for controllers about their decision concerning which ambulance to despatch. In practice, the decision is made implicitly and locally, that is, it is not supported by any formal (explicit, global) mechanisms such as procedures. However, accountability for this practice is highly ambiguous. For example, and this is only indirectly expressed in the framework, the controller is accountable in different ways to management, colleagues, and patients. In using the framework, we try to express something of the controller's experience of accountability and, given its polyphonous nature in this case, we represent it as more or less implicit and as undecided with respect to the global-local dimension. There is a global accountability to management but local accountability to colleagues and therein lies the dilemma. This can be seen as a process of making hidden relationships visible and explicit for design dialogue.

In making relationships visible, our use of the framework demonstrates the interpenetration of technology, activity and accountability. Management's decision not to represent order of return to station and controller's workaround by employing notepads to maintain an up-to-date representation of that information is an example. Therefore, although we use the framework to make relationships visible for dialogue about the design of artefacts, we consciously represent relationships beyond the artefact itself but somehow constituted by use of the artefact (which is in turn constituted by those relationships). In exploring the dilemma constituted by the decision not to include order of return information, we have already set this analysis in a broader political context to indicate that in socially organised activity, design choices always have a political flavour to them. The framework, by supporting a process of making visible potentially hidden relationships, allows us to explore a range of implications of this choice and alternatives.

One way it does this is by allowing us to explore particular juxtapositions in the space provided by the dimensions. For example, juxtaposing 'Controller meeting time targets' with 'Controller using nearest ambulance protocol', on the one hand, or 'Controller using FIFO protocol', on the other, has significantly different implications. Making controllers explicitly and globally accountable for meeting time targets while enforcing a protocol on them is an incoherent design strategy. Design options include not presenting the information required by the controller to take responsibility for meeting time targets and removing the responsibility from them or providing the information they require and enforcing the responsibility.

Another way in which the framework supports design dialogue is by supporting a process of redescription in terms of contexts for work. For example, in earlier work [13] we have observed similar configurations to those observed in the ambulance control example. There we characterised implicit, local organisation of work practices with ambiguous accountability as a Context for Collusion. The use of the notepad workaround in this analysis supports that earlier interpretation. In that earlier paper, we described a range of configurations of work practice and accountability as particular contexts for work. Although these interpretations need further checking, a number of them have now been useful in aviation, radiography and ambulance control and are beginning to feel somewhat robust. They are intended to be useful concepts that support design dialogue at the organisational level, much as Green [7] intended Cognitive Dimensions to support design dialogue at the cognitive level.

Following Green and others, a third way in which the framework supports design dialogue is by enabling us to consider trade-offs occasioned by any particular decision. Whereas earlier work looked at trade-offs at the cognitive level, our work looks at trade-offs at the organisational level. For example, a designer could consider the option of making accountability and work practice explicit as a way of avoiding Contexts for Collusion. This could be achieved by automating decisions about which ambulance to despatch. In principle, this could reduce the need for a controller. But, knowledge of local circumstances, traffic, crew expertise, and resource requirements would be likely to be lost. The trade-off would be explicit for implicit, control for discretion, a Context for Collusion being replaced by a Context for Loss of Control. Would this be a good thing? In socially organised activity, all design choices are choices in context (and of context). Neither Context for Collusion nor Context for Loss of Control is good or bad per se. One or other might be preferable in particular circumstances. Given, the complexity and uncertainty of ambulance control, Collusion seems to be the preferred option at the moment. Of course, Context for Collusion could be replace by a Context for Responsibility by making accountability less ambiguous.

We have used these representations to meet, in a limited way, the fifth requirement on representations of socially organised activity, that the representation helps to reframe rather than depict. The very space suggested by our framework, a space which accommodates relations between artefact use and accountability in the context of work activity is a form of reframing. Moreover, we have used the dimensions as a means for continually reframing an issue or a problem: once we have framed it in terms of the explicit-implicit dimension, we reframe it in terms of one of the other dimensions. Therefore, as well as the overall socio-organisational perspective to which the framework is committed, we develop a range of reframings of that perspective.

Using the framework to develop lose informal representations enables us to contribute to the dialogue between requirements and specification. We have already demonstrated how it supports us in redescribing context. It could be argued that the overall process is more than that, that it is an act of *reframing context*. Reframing context is a very particular act of expression which involves both uttering, writing down, inscribing and squeezing out or eliciting by applying pressure. We make tractable the rich, detailed description that comes from ethnographies and other field research by squeezing something out of it, aware that if we sever it from the detailed enactment of work, it may be the life itself that we have squeezed out of it. The framework can also be used to *unpack a design philosophy*. If ambulance management opted for automatic selection of the ambulance to be despatched to a scene, this could be seen as characteristic of a particular design philosophy. Our analysis of the dimensions of work practice, by introducing the relation between accountability and work practice into the dialogue, helps to identify design implications of such a philosophy for the organisation of the work.

Our use of the framework can also make a contribution to *creating a philosophy* by making explicit some of the options available. In previous analyses and to some extent in analysis of ambulance control we have expressed a property of work organisation where the worker is 'damned if he does and damned if he doesn't'. One of the primary characteristics of this kind of organisation is a disjunction between responsibility and control: responsibility to achieve a particular outcome with limited control over the means to achieve it. We could take this further by attempting to build a system where responsibility and control are balanced[1]. This is the beginning of a particular philosophical approach which our framework allows us to express informally but which probably contains at least one or two concepts of the type that Dix suspected were inherently unformalisable. It follows that we can also use the fruits of these representations to *evaluate a system* when it has been deployed. Once technology is seen as an intervention in socially organised activity, we need some way of characterising the activity after the intervention to evaluate consequences of the intervention.

Referring back to the initial question posed in this paper, we have argued that, although a lot is lost when a representation of socially organised activity is created, representations of socially organised activity are viable. By viable I mean that, at least for a time and for particular purposes, these representations support our efforts to work with and in socially organised activity. There are no claims of correctness here, just usefulness and limited usefulness at that. We have also argued that when used in a particular way with scenarios, the representations developed in our framework can satisfy the demands on modelling socially organised activity outlined earlier in the paper. As such they support a position on bridging the gap between requirements and specification which argues that the gap is bridged by reconstructing requirements analysis and design as a process of critical reflection in practice rather than transformation of representations depicting the 'reality' of work into representations depicting the 'reality' of the technology being designed. The representations are not depictions of work or of imagined technology, they are supports for continuous reframing of work practices and for looking forward to possible technological futures in a dialogical design process.

---

[1] Ideas in this area are largely due to a conversation with Alan Dix on developing work systems which balance responsibility and control.

4 Modelling itself as a 'messy' activity

When we develop any kind of representation of socially organised activity, we move from the workings of activity as it happens to the study of forms or patterns of activity that has already happened. In modelling, we are talking about the activity, not doing it and even that transformation involves a distancing from the activity. By focusing on pattern and form we inevitably ignore the living reactions and responses which are the workings of socially organised activity as it happens. But we have argued that our representations try to express something of the concrete, answerable performed character of socially organised activity, in other words something of the reactions and responses. In trying to sustain this claim, we trade on the informality of these representations together with an explicit account of the properties we have tried to embody in them. In this regard, the framework has the following properties.

Sparseness: The framework is deliberately sparse as a complement to the richness of scenarios and as a way of opening dialogue with them. There is so much going on in socially organised activity that it is difficult to penetrate. These representations are a deliberate attempt to create a space in the denseness wherein we can ask questions and engage in dialogue. The denseness can be used as a slippery surface which never allows us to get a foothold. The sparseness of the representations is a deliberate attempt to provide footholds in what is a dense and slippery area.

Dampness. The frameworks present an opportunity, especially when used in conjunction with scenarios, of expressing aspects of both the social and technical aspects of information use, what Goguen [6] refers to as the wet and dry aspects of information. In our case we have focused more on artifacts than information but the point holds. Artefacts have formal technical and informal social properties. One of our objectives has been to provide a means for bridging the gap between them. Goguen's notion of reconciling the wet and the dry seems, at this stage, too optimistic to us. Therefore we will settle for providing the kind of steps formalists and social scientists can use to move from one to the other engaging in dialogue with each other. What this requires at the moment is a viable damp representation, one with an eye to formal and informal, one that allows users to see it as wet and dry.

Discretion. As part of the effort to bridge the formality gap, Dix argued for a structural coherence or correlation between informal requirements and formal specifications which is achieved by close structural correspondence between the abstract model and the informal concepts. Our aim, in this regard, has been to squeeze out a representation which has about it a great deal of fluidity, discretion and contingency.

Dialogicality: Different, even conflicting, readings of a situation can be inscribed onto the framework. It does not invite a single (veridical) reading, rather a certain playfulness in considering ways of looking at what is and what might be. By dialogicality, we mean that it offers scope for these different reading to be placed alongside each other. Different opening questions might result in different readings of the same observations. Design should be informed by a range of such readings and the energy or dialogue that results from placing them next to each other.

All representations are partial and ambiguous. They embody within them a choice to focus on a particular characteristic and to ignore others, at least for the moment. As such, all models are ambiguous and any work done with the model, for example to prove correctness, completeness or whatever points to the correctness of the model which may in turn point to the correctness of the machine but, in the context of socially organised activity, which is discretionary, contingent, and messy proves very little about the whole system. The model is not the system.

Those limitations notwithstanding, we use representations in all kinds of dialogue, not least in design dialogue. Moreover as long as we do not confuse the representation with the activity represented, models of socially organised activity, of the kind we have outlined above, can be useful. Their use however is not for specification purposes but for dialogue purposes. The kind of models that stay close enough to the activity to be recognisable by participants tend to be informal and to play on ambiguity rather than trying to reduce it. Socially organised activity tends to involve a range of people with a variety of viewpoints. An accessible representation has to accommodate divergent viewpoints.

Green sees his Cognitive Dimensions as 'discussion tools'. His intention is to provide concepts which are neither too detailed nor too woolly and which capture aspects of something that makes it much easier to talk about that thing. Our framework of dimensions is also a tool designed to promote and support dialogue around socially organised activity. An important difference, however, is that while Green's discussion tends to be about properties of artefacts and notations, the dialogue we are interested in promoting is about activity, particularly technological interventions in socially organised activity. So while Green tries to improve discussion by pinning down concepts and perhaps restricting the lexicon, we try to open up dialogue by providing a space for participants to play with alternative conceptualisations.

In creating this space, we have of course created an artefact, which Cognitive Dimensions helps us characterise. For example, if we could talk about the socially organised activity itself, we would argue that it tends to be viscous, with many hidden dependencies, and poor visibility of components. But we can't talk about the activity itself, as soon as we do we are talking about some kind of representation of the activity, an abstraction in natural language if you like. Even the anthropological 'thick description' [5] is not the activity itself. Despite best attempts to retain as much of the detail as possible, it is a description, an interpretation, an abstraction. And it is difficult to work with this kind of representation in an activity such as design where the objective is weighing up options to make decisions. Nonetheless, as we have argued earlier in the paper, we cannot get away from the messy stuff of thick description, we need to keep going back to it to test our interpretations. However we can develop representations that can work in tandem with thick descriptions to help elucidate choice points and possible consequences. Scenarios do this and our framework tries to do this also. Both do it by reducing viscosity and focusing on some of the dependencies at the cost of ignoring others. Our framework is one of a set of tools for supporting design dialogue by transforming what is at first description a viscous, high dependency, low visibility representation into more fluid representations which make some aspects of the activity more visible and play down some of the dependencies for the purpose of making the subject matter tractable.

Thinking about it in this way, suggests that the activity of modelling has parallels with the activity of ambulance control. Both can be seen as processes of developing, maintaining and transforming representations. But while ambulance controllers have developed practical representations for practical purposes, we often struggle with theoretical representations which have become disconnected from the practical purposes of the activity being modelled but not from the practical purposes of model makers. It might be time to turn the focus on our own socially organised activity to reflect on the practical purposes of our own representations.

Acknowledgements

Pat Healey collected the ambulance control data and Michael Harrison and Peter Wright have been stimulating collaborators on attempts to work from contextualised data to requirements.

References

1. Bakhtin, M.M. Towards a Philosophy of the Act. Austin, Texas: University of Texas Press, 1993.

2. Bentley, R., Hughes, J.A., Randall, D., Rodden, T., Sawyer, P., Shapiro, D., and Sommerville, I. Ethnographically informed systems design for air traffic control. Proc. CSCW'92, 115-122, New York: ACM Press (Toronto, November, 1992).

3. Bodker, S. and Christiansen, E. Scenarios as springboards in CSCW design. In Bowker, G.C., Star, S.L., Turner, W. and Gasser, L. (Eds.), Social Science, Technical Systems and Cooperative Work. New Jersey: Lawrence Erlbaum, 1996, pp. 217-234.

4. Dix, A. Formal Methods for Interactive System Design. London: Academic Press, 1991.

5. Geertz, C. The Interpretation of Cultures. New York: Basic Books, 1973.

6. Goguen, J.A. Towards a social, ethical theory of information. In Bowker, G.C., Star, S.L., Turner, W. and Gasser, L. (Eds.), Social Science, Technical Systems and Cooperative Work. New Jersey: Lawrence Erlbaum, 1996, pp.27-56

7. Green, T.R.G. and Petre, M. Usability analysis of visual programming environments. Journal of Visual Languages and Computing, 7, 131-174 (1996).

8. Hughes, J.A., Randall, D., and Shapiro, D. Faltering from ethnography to design. Proc. CSCW'92, 115-122, New York: ACM Press (Toronto, November, 1992).

9. Hutchins, E. Cognition in the Wild. Cambridge Mass: MIT Press, 1995.

10. Lave, J. Cognition in practice. Cambridge: Cambridge University Press, 1988.

11. McCarthy, J. And O'Connor, B. Integration and dis-integration: situated practice and the structure of hospital information. Proc. ECCE'9 (Limerick, August, 1998)

12. McCarthy, J., Wright, P., Healey, P., Dearden, A. and Harrison, M.D. Locating the scene: The particular and the general in contexts for ambulance control. In Hayne, S. And Prinz, W. (Eds). Proc. Group'97, SIGGROUP conference on supporting group work. pp. 101-110, (Arizona, 1997).

13. McCarthy, J, Wright, P., Healey, P. and Harrison, M. Human error in context: Accountability of work activity in high-consequence work systems. International Journal of Human Machine Systems, 47 (6), 735-766 (1997).

14. Robinson, M. "As real as it gets...." Taming models and reconstructing procedures. In Bowker, G.C., Star, S.L., Turner, W. and Gasser, L. (Eds.), Social Science, Technical Systems and Cooperative Work. New Jersey: Lawrence Erlbaum, 1996, pp. 257-274.

15. Rogers, Y. Reconfiguring the social scientist: shifting from telling designers what to do to getting more involved. In Bowker, G.C., Star, S.L., Turner, W. and Gasser, L. (Eds.), Social Science, Technical Systems and Cooperative Work. New Jersey: Lawrence Erlbaum, 1996, pp. 57-78.

16. Schliemann, A.D. and Nunes, T. A situated schema of proportionality. Journal of Developmental Psychology, 8, 259-268 (1990).

17. Suchman, L. Plans and situated actions: the problem of human machine communication. Cambridge: Cambridge University Press, 1986.

Deriving Business Object Definitions from User Work Process Models

Keith A. Butler, Chris Esposito, Ron Hebron

The Boeing Company
Seattle, WA 98124
keith.a.butler@boeing.com

1   Introduction

When software is developed to support user work processes (WPs) it's purpose is to improve their quality by making them faster, cheaper, more accurate, reducing variance, etc. But across industry this purpose has not yet been met in any conspicuous manner for information workers [4].

There is an industry-wide need to improve internal processes continuously, and in some cases to re-engineer them completely. Often an interactive information system will be the means to implement the desired process. In effect, the information system serves as a major part of the implementation plan to achieve the new process.

In current practice, however, the design of the WP and the design of the supporting software actually proceed as independent activities. It should not be any surprise that the resulting pieces are often a mismatch, disappointing users, frustrating computing support people, and failing to produce a worthwhile WP improvement in return for the computing investment.

Early research on software engineering identified a number of breakdowns in joint problem solving as a likely cause of difficulties in creating usable applications [3]. Our own analysis shows that a major obstacle to better coordination between the people who are responsible for WPs and those who create software lies in the difficulty of translating between WP models and software models. Currently, making the connection from WP to useful software requirements is slow, unreliable and expensive. Our focus here will be on the tools to make that translation more systematic and reliable, and far less labor intensive.

2   The Architecture for BOCs

In order to explain our approach we must first define business-oriented components (BOCs). BOCs are software object classes that model business rules, processes, and data from the end-user's perspective. They have a clear mapping to the process which they are intended to support, and provide function and data that are reusable in tasks throughout that process.

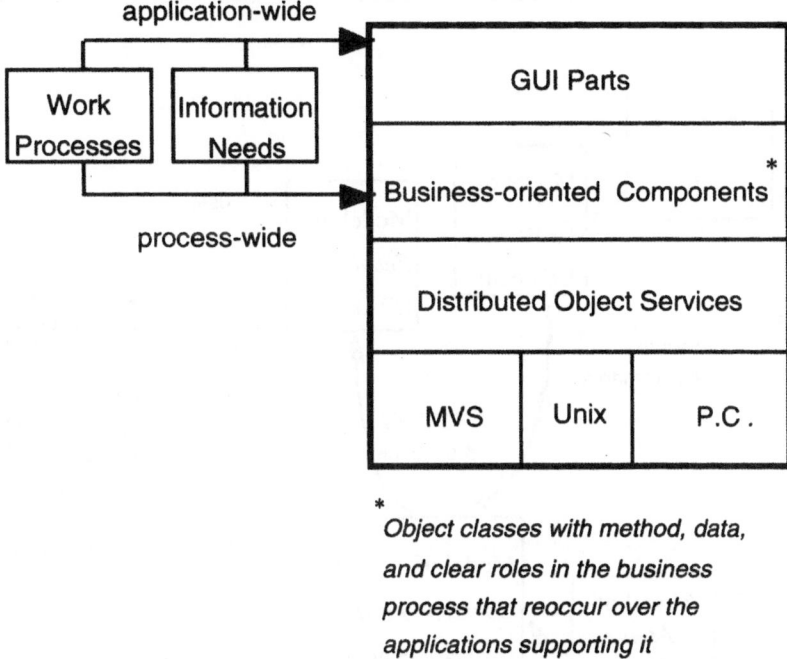

Fig.1. Software Architecture for Business-Oriented Components

Although they should have conceptual meaning to end-users, BOCs are not typically visible to end-users. As shown in Figure 1 they are not necessarily applications by themselves. In the context of the model-view-controller programming paradigm, BOCs are models. BOCs are computational elements of the work process that should be implemented in software, and can then be reused as components to assemble much of the needed applications. BOCs are built to enable rapid application assembly, such as in a visual programming environment. They may integrate heterogeneous, distributed data via distributed object services, such as object request brokers or Java remote method invocation. This capability allows BOCs to satisfy data requirements that are *user-centered*, as opposed to accepting technology-centered constraints. Our earlier reports have described the technical feasibility of visual programming for rapid application development using BOCs [1] and progress towards object-request brokers for distributed BOCs [2].

Rapid development of applications from BOCs as depicted in Figure 2 involves linking the needed components to one another and to a graphical user interface (GUI). Creating the GUI takes on a defining role for implementing the WP since it determines what, when and how information is provided to workers. BOCs play a critical role in this architecture because they provide the needed flexible computing for getting the right information to the right place and time.

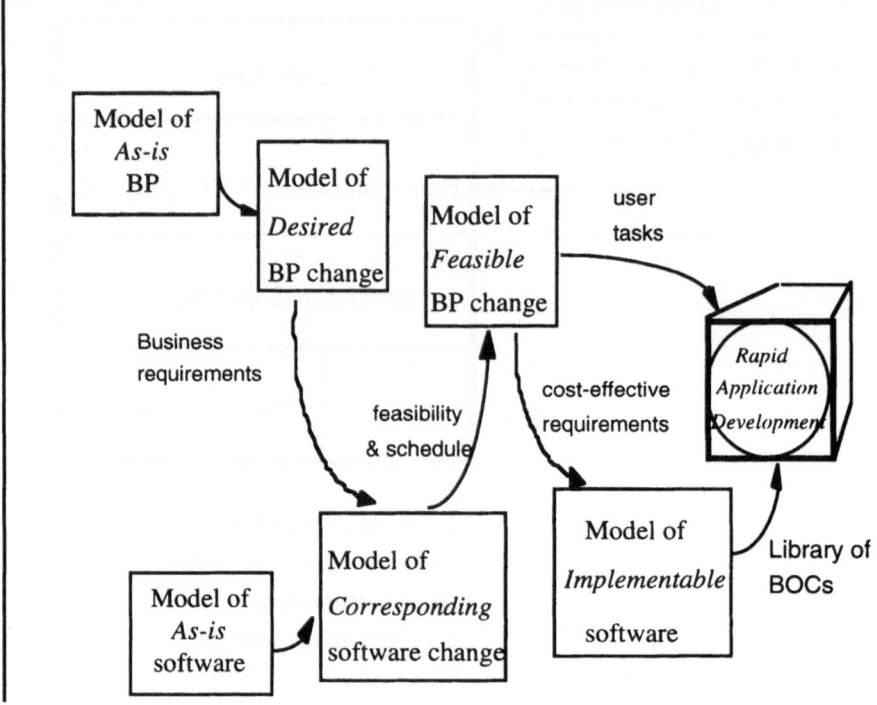

Fig. 2. The Life Cycle for BOCs.

3 The Life Cycle for BOCs

Our overall goal is to demonstrate how software methods for internal information systems can function as the implementation arm of WP quality improvements. Consequently, the life cycle of BOCs begins with modeling an existing WP and continues through BOC re-use for WP revisions for later improvements. Figure 2 shows how the parallel tracks for WP design and software design interact to converge. Initially the *As-is* WP is modeled in terms of user tasks and data to understand what improvements are needed and how they may be accomplished. The *As-is* software is also modeled, by developing event sequence diagrams to document how it currently works to support the user tasks.

The WP analyst then determines how the WP should be changed by developing a *Desired* model. This WP model's database can be queried to obtain usage distributions of user data over all user tasks. The distributions provide the input to develop a cluster analysis on user data. As will be shown in section 4.2, the clusters provide candidate BOC definitions as requirements that are fed to the software designer. The software designer takes the BOCs as preliminary requirements in the form of classes to develop a *Corresponding* object-oriented (OO) model. The OO model is developed enough to analyze the technical feasibility of the BOCs. The analyst re-creates use-cases from the

WP model as event sequence diagrams that include the necessary middleware, legacy functions or data.

The results of the feasibility analysis on the Corresponding OO model provide feedback to the WP designer how much and how long it will cost for the software to implement the *Desired* WP. The WP designer can then perform a cost-benefit analysis and a sensitivity analysis to determine priorities for *Feasible* changes. We expect this decision will actually require several iterations between WP and software, while several possible pairs of designs get developed and analyzed.

The results of the parallel, interactive design activities is a matched pair of designs: A WP design that is valuable and *Implementable*; A software design for BOCs that is feasible and cost-effective. When implemented the library of BOCs support rapid application development through reuse since the BOCs' definitions were literally derived from the user tasks that make up the WP.

4 Tools Enable the BOC Life Cycle

We will now describe in more detail the software tools that support the analysis and design parts of the BOC life cycle. Here we will focus on the tools for modeling and analyzing WPs, for deriving BOC definitions from WP models, and for downloading BOC definitions to a Unified Modeling Language (UML , see ref. 13) modeler. Our general approach is to integrate user task analysis, business work process (WP) simulation, and object definition for an integrated method of software engineering.

4.1 Modeling User Work & Data

Several alternate views of how the same work gets performed are valuable for different aspects of design. We assert that a WP is actually some aggregation of user tasks. User-centered models focus on a higher level of description than technology-centered models, which describe how the technology will work or how it will be implemented. Historically it has been very difficult to integrate the two views.

Figure 3 shows the first of several screen dumps for a model of the WP for employee time-keeping. The existing system is the Employee Time-keeping System (ETS) which is currently used by approximately 86,000 employees for review, recording, and approval of hourly work time. The examples given here resulted from a successful project to redesign the time-entry process and develop a corresponding web front end to the existing IMS database application.

Figure 3 shows the top level flow of events that make up the WP for collecting work time. The event Begin Week triggers the WP. The rest of the events in the flow diagram represent the completion of user functions.

The screen dumps are from OPAL, an enterprise modeling tool from DMR. In the specifications of the Workflow Management Coalition [8] this type of model corresponds to a process definition tool, in which the WP is represented by a hierarchy

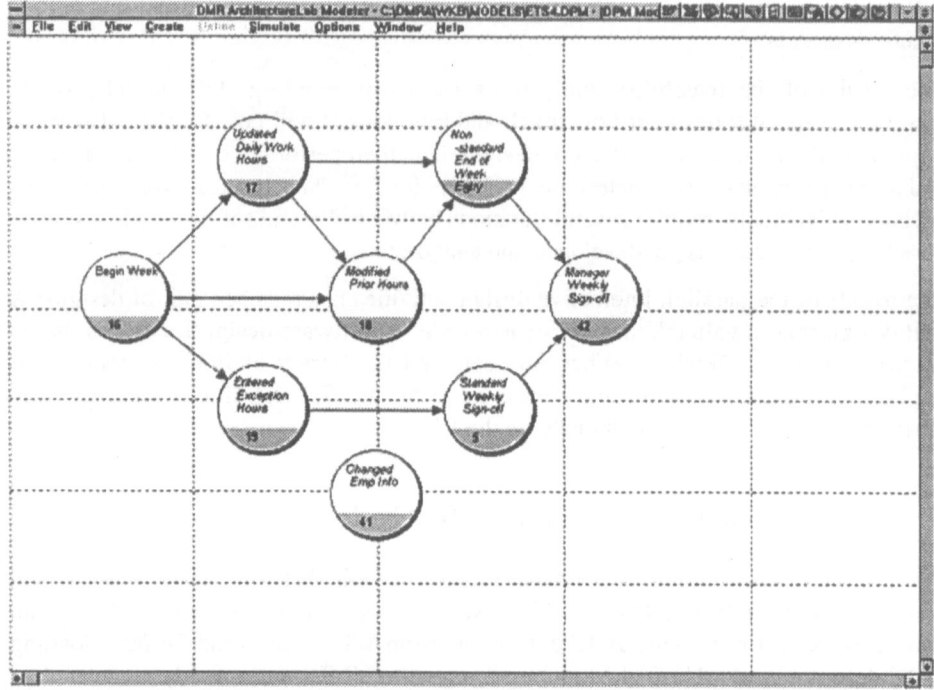

Fig.3. Top-level Process for *Employee Time-Keeping*

of event sequences. The lowest level of event is a user task, where users interact with data to accomplish work goals.

Events whose titles are in italic font can be further decomposed. In Figure 4 we show how the routine user function for Updated Daily Work Hours is, in turn, made up of lower-level events that are triggered by the End of non-standard Task. There is also an alternative path if the user needs to use a charge number, instead of the usual project number, to enter work time.

For our main interviewing technique we applied Jacobson's concept of use-cases to provide input for building the work model [9, 10]. A use-case describes an instance of how users actually accomplish a work goal, We asked our domain experts to identify each type of worker who will interact with the WP and to list their work goals that are either frequent or critical.

Figure 5 is a further decomposition of how the Entered Hours event is performed. It is also an example of how two resources, User and ETS, interact to change one anther's' states to accomplish the Entered Hours task.

In figure 5 the user and the ETS (Employee Time-Keeping System) interact to change one another's states until the goal state (I'm done) is reached for the user.

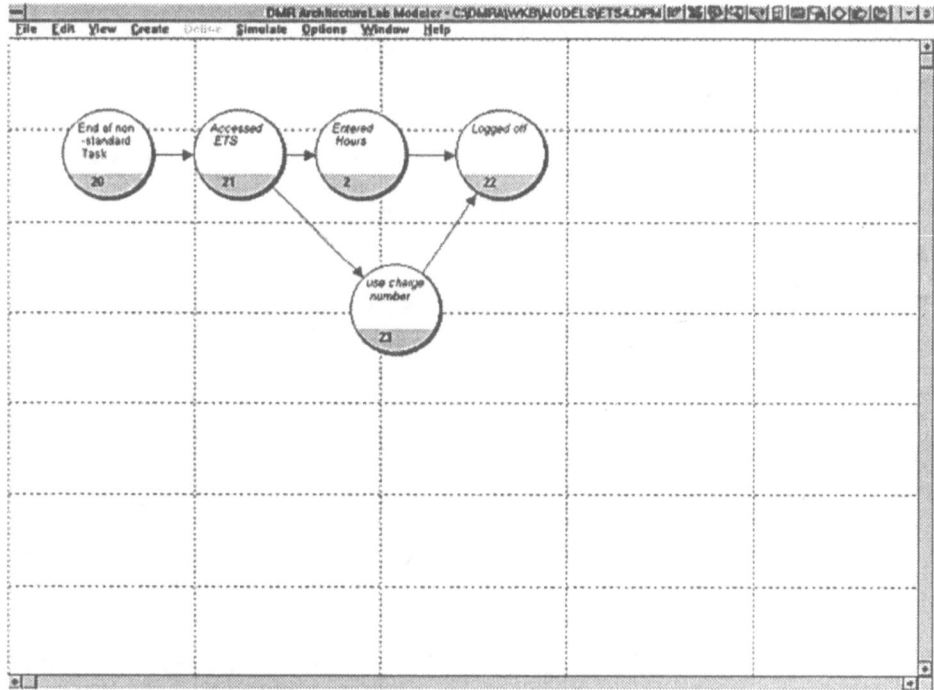

Fig. 4. Decomposition of *Updated Daily Work Hours*

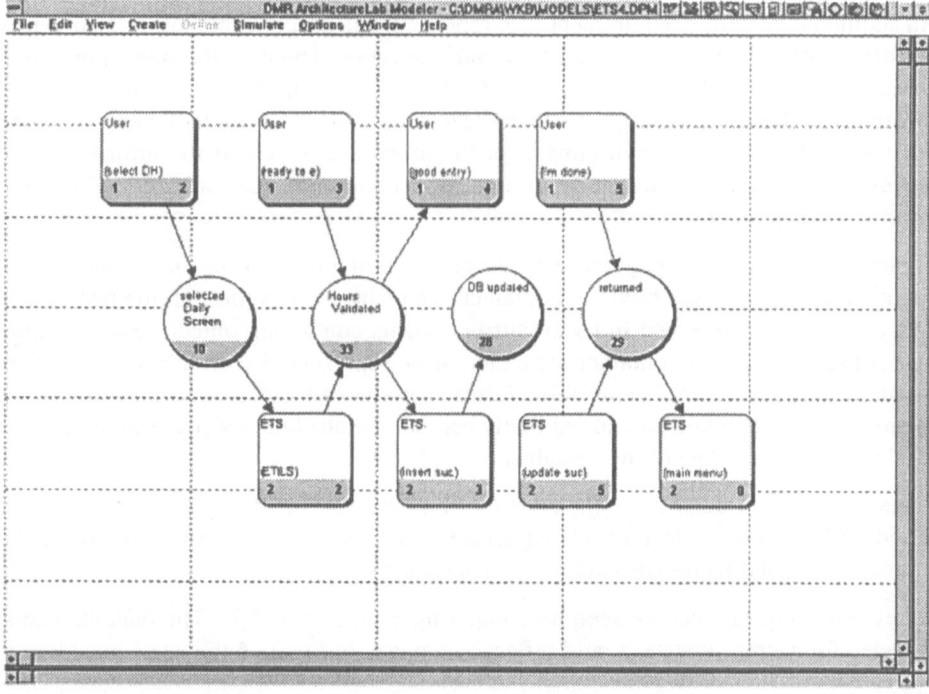

Fig. 5. User and System change one another's state to accomplish the *Entered Hours* task

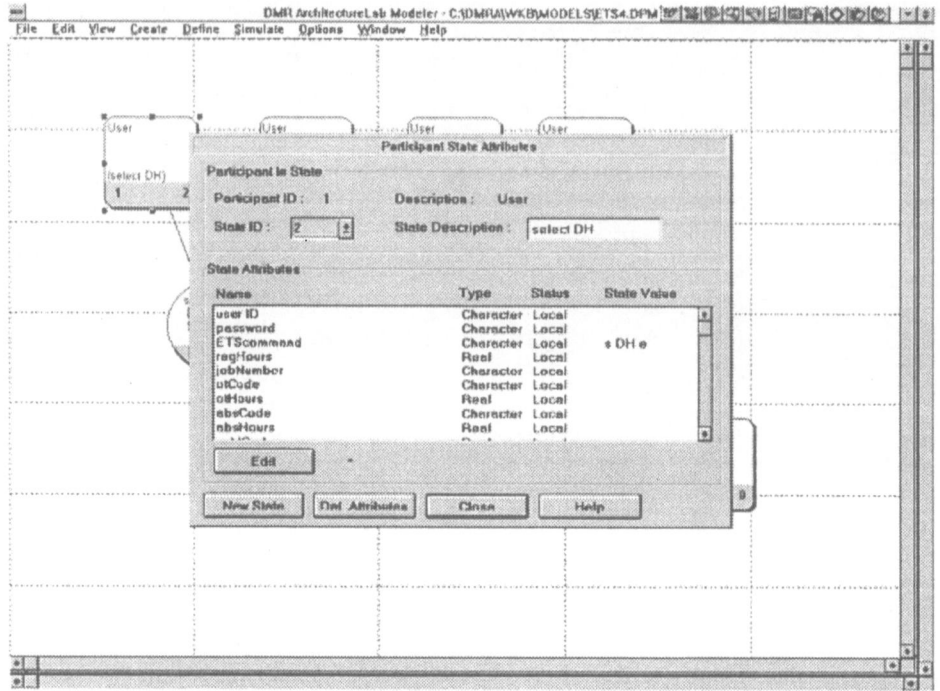

Fig.6. *User* state for *Select DH* is determined by attribute values

An additional modeling requirement is to represent data usage within tasks. In order to perform work a WP needs resources of various types. Three of the more important types in this model are Users, Electronic Information Systems, and Manual Information Systems. Examples of non-electronic sources are other people, paper documents, the physical environment, or the user, him/herself, if the information is retrieved from personal memory. Information containers may also contain other information containers.

Figure 6 shows a user may serve as a container of information that is needed to complete a sub-task, and how the container can change states through the task. Each data concept is represented in by an attribute of its containing object. Every datum that is used in a given container state should be represented with a non-null value, whether or not its source is currently electronically stored and accessed. As shown in Figure 6, the association should explicitly capture the attribute values required by the user's task for each state of the container.

Since containment determines the source of an attribute, this feature is also valuable for identifying re-usable portions of legacy systems. By explicitly modeling data sources we can define re-use potential for legacy systems

A key modeling rule can be seen by comparing Figures 6 and 7. The data elements modeled for each task-state should reflect actual use. In Figure 6 the users must know

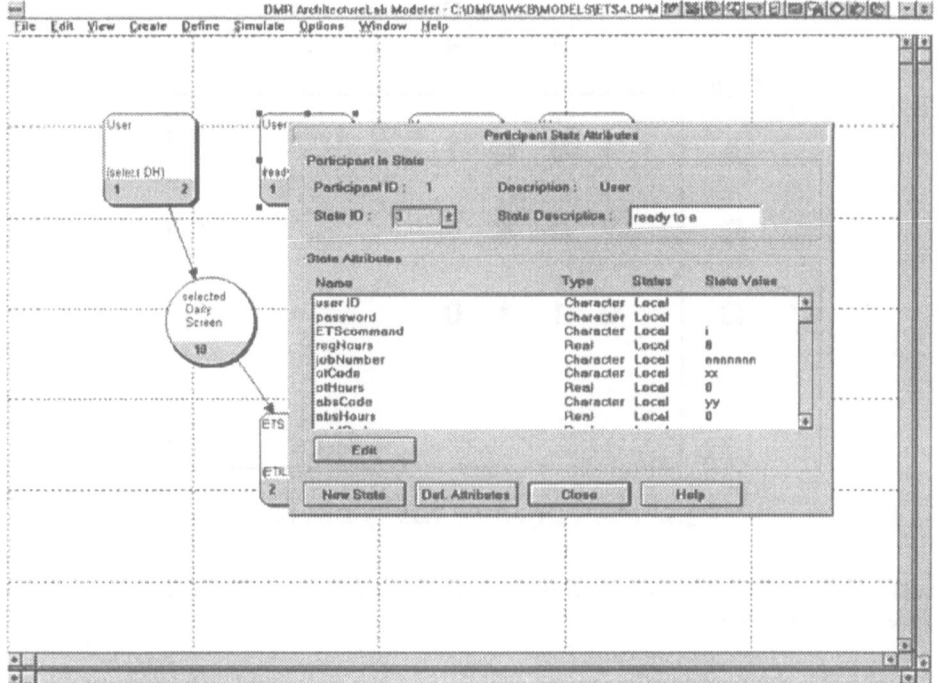

Fig.7. *User* state for *Ready to Enter* is determined by new attribute values

the value for ETScommand when they are in the state Select DH. The same attribute has a different value in Figure 7 when the user is in state Ready to Enter. But users must also know values for attributes that were null in the previous state, such as regHours, jobNumber, etc.

We use this technique to accumulate the state-dependent data requirements for each information container incrementally, as we model the use-cases in the WP modeler. This capability allows us to capture the association between each datum and any of the tasks where it is used. These associations provide the basis of the cluster analysis of data elements into preliminary definitions of components.

Figure 8 shows a conceptual matrix of data occurrences distributed over tasks. The list of data names are on the top axis. The task names are listed down the left. The usage of a data concept in a given task is represented as a "1" in the row of "1"s and "0"s following that task name. A "0" indicates no usage in that task. The co-occurance (or non-occurrence) of data elements with one another within tasks is of particular interest in the design of software to support a business process made up of those tasks. This matrix allows us to begin investigating their co-occurance.

We obtained a database extract from the modeling tool in a similar format to that shown in Figure 8. The matrix is actually a set of distributions of data usage over

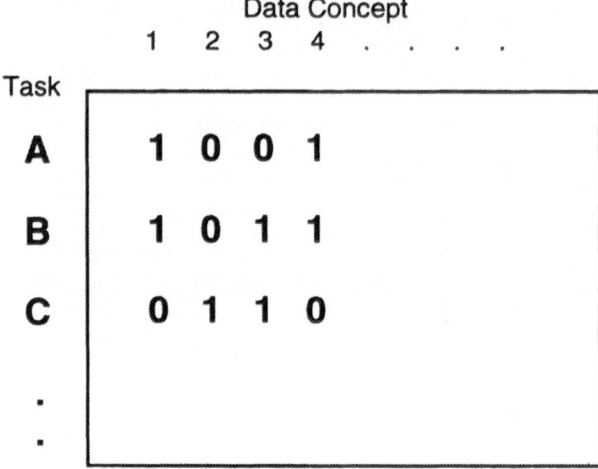

Fig.8. Matrix Layout for Task by Data Usage

tasks, which provide input to a cluster analysis on data usage. The cluster analysis procedures will be described next.

4.2   Analyzing Clusters of User Data

One of the defining features of a good, high-level object is that it should contain information attributes that need to be used in conjunction with one another. These clusters can be derived by analyzing the distribution of data elements over the tasks where they occur. We used a graph-theoretic approach called PathFinder [14]. This section gives the steps for the PathFinder procedures we used for performing cluster analysis on the data usage distributions.

The results of our PathFinder cluster analysis are shown in several steps in Figures 9-12, along with the user-interface controls of our ClusterVis tool that performs the PathFinder analysis. ClusterVis was built by Dr. Chris Esposito using the Amulet GUI builder, and the Graphics Layout Toolkit from Tom Sawyer. ClusterVis screens shown here are running on IRIX 5.3.

Figure 9 shows the results of a graph-theoretic representation which displays a network structure or arcs for the strength of associations among all pairs of data elements. The spatial layout in Figure 9 is only an aid to understanding. Unlike multidimensional scaling, the spatial relations are not usually significant in themselves. The network structure of the arcs is of greatest interest. Some research has shown that interesting clusters appear as cliques, near-cliques and stars [5]. These patterns are sub-graphs that can be identified using the ClusterVis cluster finding algorithms, which are available in the Analysis pulldown menu. Algorithms have been implemented for stars, cliques, and perfect correlation.

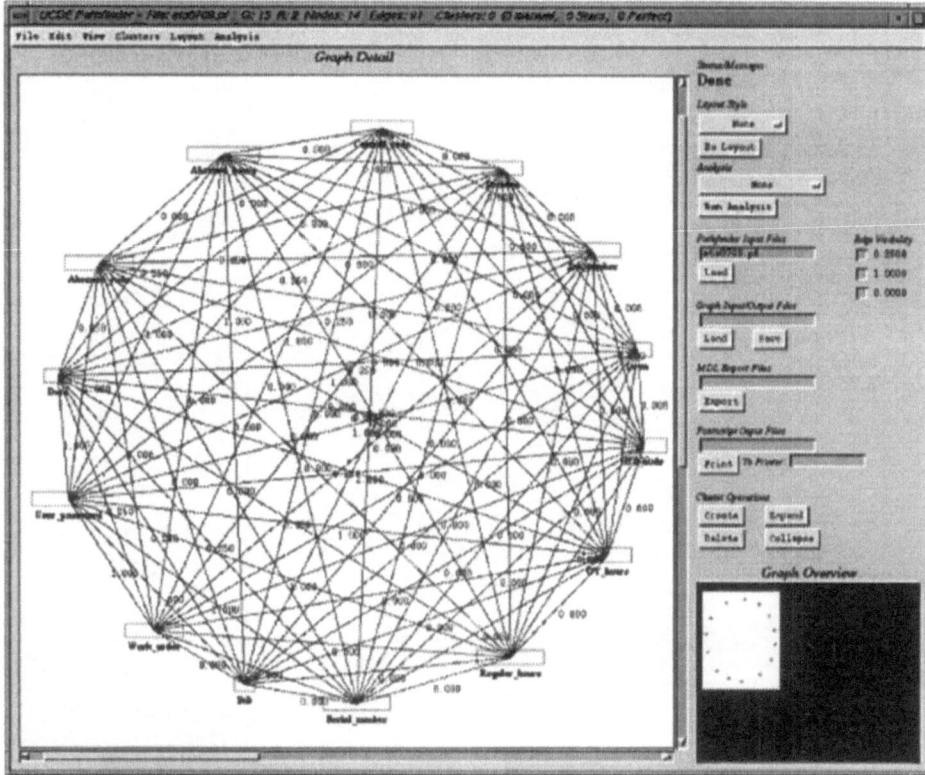

Fig.9. PathFinder Graph-Theoretic Representation of Proximity Data

Figure 9 shows the graph-theoretic network which represents the strength of association among all pairs of data concepts for employee time-keeping. A circular layout is shown. Two alternative layouts to the circular are also available, orthogonal and symmetric.

The construction of PathFinder networks requires three pieces of data for input:

1. **An N x N distance matrix**, where N is the number of data elements. Coefficients that vary in value from 0 to 1.0 can be calculated to measure the strength of co-occurance of any pair of data elements with one another from a matrix such as such as shown earlier in Figure 8. There are several formulas for association coefficients. Following the guidelines in Everitt [6] for a sparse matrix input to cluster analysis, we chose the Jaccard coefficient. The matrix of coefficients was calculated for exhaustive pairings of data elements to represent the strength of user need to use them together in common tasks.

2. **A value for Q**, from 1 to N-1. Increases in the Q value result in fewer edges in the final network. Usually, the selection of a good Q-value is not deterministic and requires some investigation.

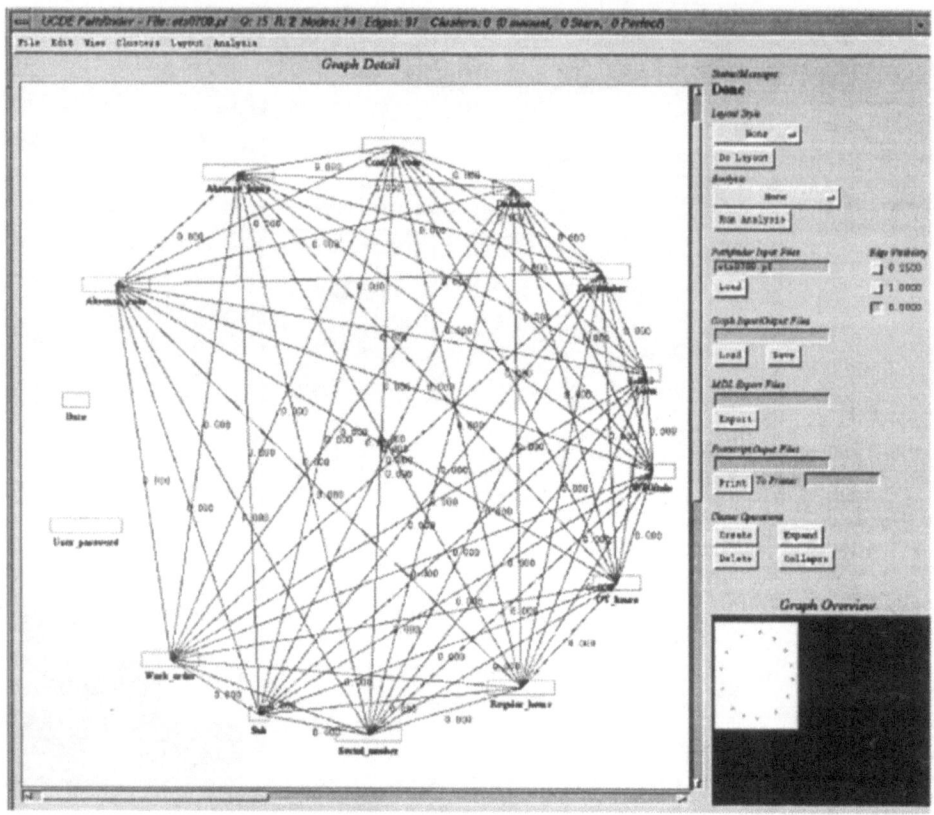

Fig.10. Only Perfectly Correlated Edges

3. **A value for R**, from 1 to infinity, with infinity requiring only ordinal assumptions about the N x N distance matrix.

The standard Pathfinder algorithm examines every pair of nodes i, k (data elements) and keeps their direct connecting edge E_{ik} in the final network if $D_{ik} <= DSP_{ik}$, where:

D_{ik} is the distance associated with E_{ik}

P_{ik} is an Allowable Alternative Path from i to k if it has <= Q edges

SP_{ik} is the shortest of all P_{ik}

DSP_{ik} is the length of SP_{ik}

The length of SP_{ik} will be calculated using the Minkowski [7] metric:

$$DSP_{ik} = (D_{ia}^{R} + D_{ab}^{R} + D_{bc}^{R} + ... + D_{jk}^{R})^{(1/R)}$$

The sparsest network results from Q = N-1 and R = infinity. This network is the union of all minimal cost spanning trees for the complete graph represented by the input matrix. Reducing either Q or R adds additional edges into the network.

Once clusters have been identified ClusterVis has a node editor them to be placed into a higher-level node. For example, Figure 12 shows how the node editor can collapse the cluster of perfectly correlated items into a higher level node.

A perfect correlation among large portions of data can be a characteristic of mainframe applications. The term "monolithic" has also been used for this characteristic. It can be seen in the current example by using the Edge Visibility control on the far right side, and setting it to display only those arcs with a distance = 0.0 in Figure 10.

The contrasting network in Figure 11, without any arcs = 0.0 shows how much of the network they occupy.

Our analysis tells us that the existing support application is very monolithic, and that we should investigate a software design that will be more flexible. The nodes in Figure 12 represent clusters of user data which were distributed over As-is user tasks in correlated manner. Since they tend to be utilized at the same times and in the same tasks, we will use them as a starting point to analyze how a web front-end could be added to increase flexibility.

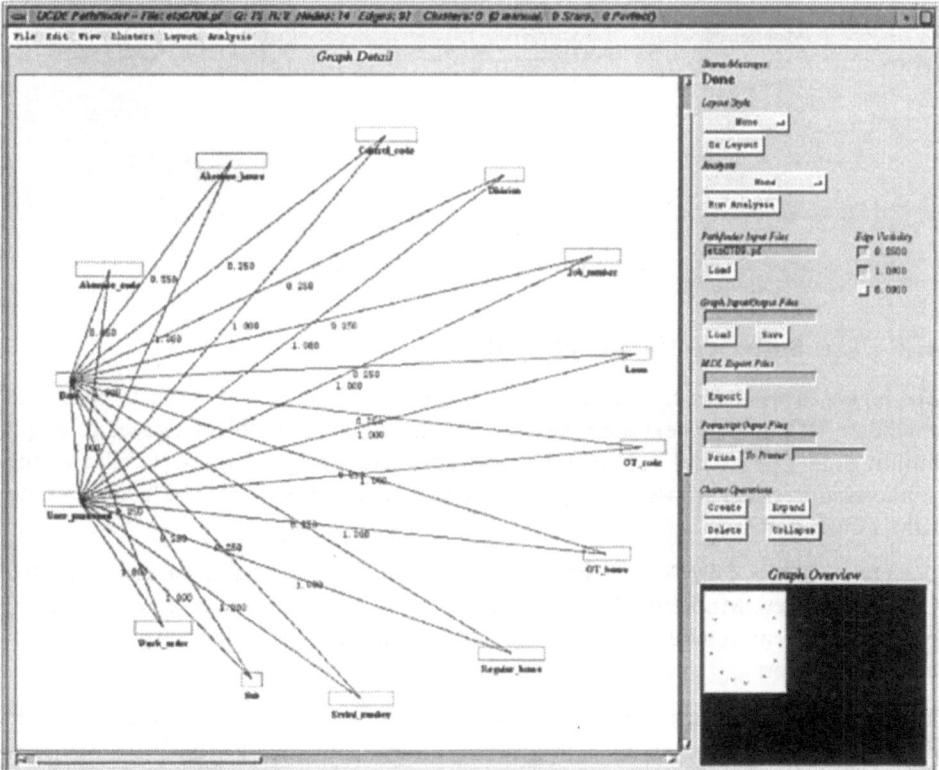

Fig.11. Perfectly Correlated Nodes Removed

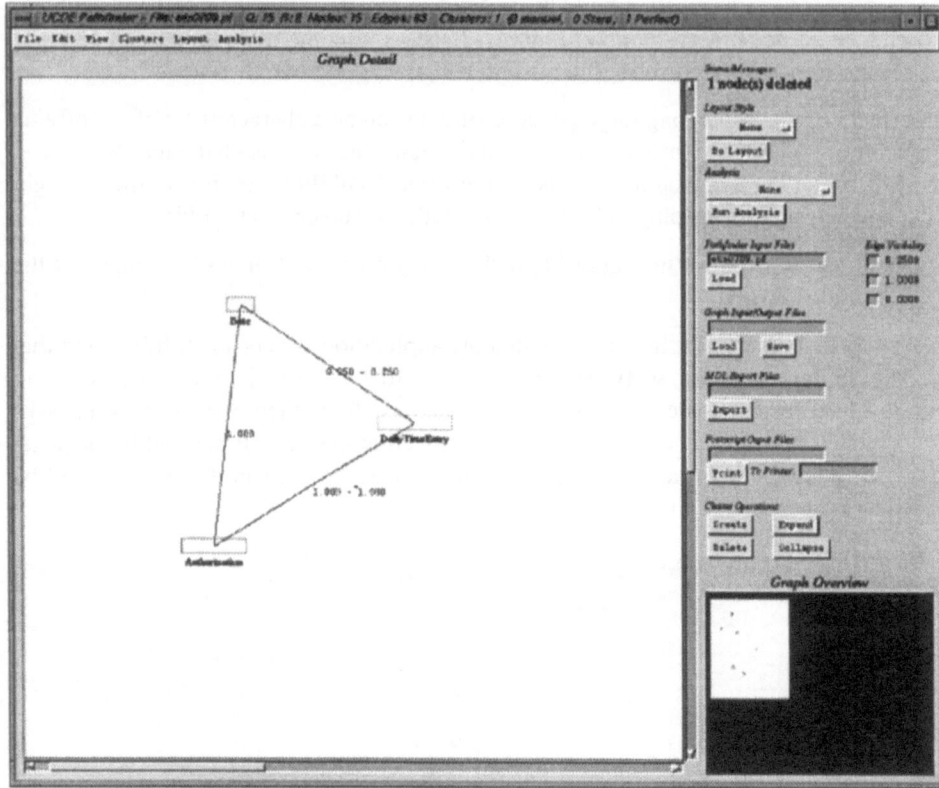

Fig.12. Collapsed Cluster Node

4.3 The Software Design of BOCs

The higher-level nodes can be viewed as clusters of attributes and, as such, constitute candidate BOCs. The next step was to treat the clusters as object classes to begin building an OO model for analysis and software design. Figure 13 shows the Authorization class, whose definition was downloaded directly from ClusterVis onto IBM's OBJChart.

We chose IBM's OBJChart because its development is centered on satisfying the OMG's Unified Modeling Language (UML), it interfaces with a strong visual programming environment, and the file specification was provided to us, along with excellent support.

The ClusterVis analysis program is display oriented; it formats its data for screen display. So we built our own program for interfacing with OBJChart. We first modified ClusterVis to capture the cluster definitions for processing. The output for each cluster is the name of the cluster and the names and types of the attributes it contains.

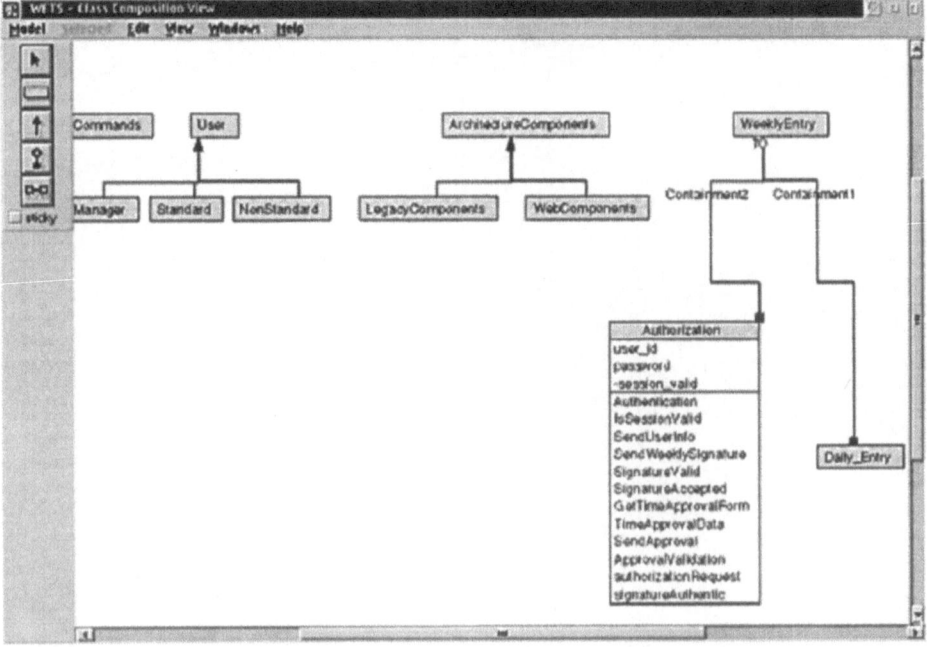

Fig.13. UML Class Diagram

The OBJChart input requirement is for a file in the .mdl format. OBJChart is object-oriented, so several types of data are used by it. However, the scope here is limited to classes containing objects which are data items. A cluster becomes a class and a data attribute becomes an object.

The translation program is called UCDE Filter. It is a filter to translate cluster terminology into the object terminology expected by OBJChart while keeping the structure essentially the same. The translation program is a straight-forward filter, translating syntax terms into the target environment, while keeping the same basic structure.

In Figure 13 the software designer has also added a number of other new classes for software ArchitectureComponents and for the different types of Users of the system.

In Figure 14 the designer is using objects from each of the classes to develop an event trace diagram that will satisfy the meta use-case for EnterDailyTime. As can be seen a key aspect of the BOC design is to exploit the existing mainframe databases, ims_DB and db2_DB. In this manner the software designer can determine the feasibility for building a web front end that will implement the BOCs and support the required use-cases.

38

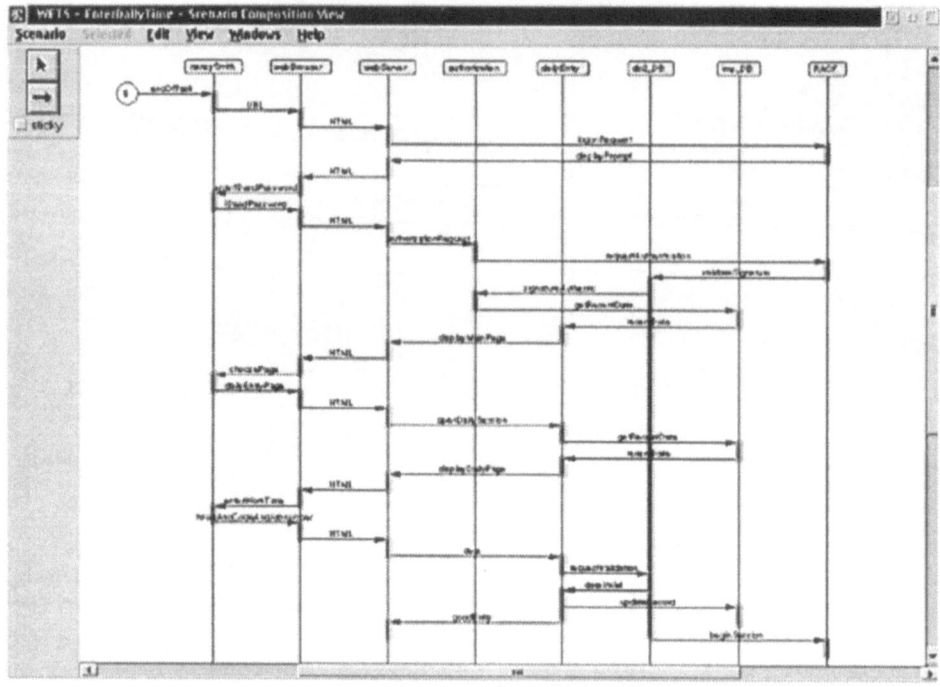

Fig. 14. UML Event Sequence Diagram

The resulting UML model serves as a feasibility analysis that can be feed back to the WP designer. Our intent is to support a technical engineering dialog between WP design and OO design, based on quantifiable value to the WP and technical feasibility for the software.

5   Near-term Plans for Further Technology Development

It could be very valuable during the dialog with the domain expert if the OO designer could talk about a credible estimate of development costs and time schedules for the software.

To support cost and schedule estimation we are currently investigating an interface to download the UML model to a project estimation tool, such as Price-S. Recent development of the POPS method for estimating software complexity appear to have good predictive validity [12] and there is preliminary work on an interface from UML to Price-S.

To support WP value estimation we have begun developing modeling and simulation techniques for the IDEF3 Process Description language [11]. IDEF3 is complete and consistent enough for powerful discrete event simulation engines. The results of simulation can not only provide insight about how to improve a WP, but also generate estimates for performance variables such as mean cycle-time, variance in cycle-time, and error rates, which are often sensitive to information distribution and quality. Improvement in these variables can be quantified in terms of costs.

We have also begun investigating how our tools can be applied to estimate re-use. One way to view re-use is in terms of how much a WP can change and still be supported by the same set of BOCs. We have begun developing metrics and algorithms to compare the amount of change between several PathFinder networks. We will take a WP model through several versions that anticipate changes in business requirements, such as increased production rate, cost reduction, etc. Then derive the corresponding PathFinder networks. If the metric shows that the network is insensitive to changes in the WP, it may mean that set of BOCs have good re-use expectancy.

References

1. Butler, K. A. (1995) Designing Deeper: Towards a User- Centered Development Environment. Proceedings of DIS'95. ACM.

2. Butler, K.; Esposito, C.; & Klawitter, D. (1997) Designing More Deeper. Proceedings of DIS'97. ACM.

3. Guindon, R. & Curtis, B. (1988) Control of Congitive Processes During Software Design: What Tools Are Needed? In: Proceedings of CHI'88, ACM.

4. Dertouzos, M. L. (1990) Redefining Tomorrow's User Interface. Plenary Talk CHI'90 (Seattle, WA, April 2, 1990).

5. Esposito, C. (1990) A Graph-Theoretic Approach to Conceptual Clustering. Pathfinder Networks. In: (14).

6. Everitt, Brian. (1980) Cluster Analysis, 2nd Ed. Halsted Press.

7. Hakimi, S. L. & Yaw, S.S. (1964) Distance of a Matrix Graph and its Realizability. Quarterly Journal of Applied Mathematics, 22 pp. 305-317.

8. Hollingsworth, D. (1995) The Workflow Management Coalition Specification. Workflow Management Coalition Document No. TC00-1003, January 19, 1995.

9. Jacobson, I., Christerson, M., Jonsson, P, & Overgaard, G. (1992) Object-Oriented Software Engineering- A Use Case Driven Approach. Reading, MA: Addison-Wesley.

10. Jacobson, I. (1995) The Use-Case Construct in Object-Oriented Software Engineering. In: J. Carroll (Ed.) Scenario-Based Design. Wiley.

11. Mayer, R,; Cullinane, T.; deWitte, P.; Perakath, B.; Wells, M. (1992) Information Integration for Concurrent Engineering (IICE): The IDEF3 Process Description Capture Method Report. USAF Armstrong Lab.

12. Minkiewicz, A. (1997) Predictive Object Points, Measuring the Size of OO Applications. Paper presented at the Software Technology Conference (Salt Lake City, Apr. 29, 1997)

13. Rational Software Corporation. (1997) Unified Modeling Language Notation Guide, version 1.0. Rational Software.

14.   Schvaneveldt, R. W. (1990) Pathfinder   Associative Networks: Studies in Knowledge Organization. Norwood, NJ: Ablex.

Inference and Information Resources:
A design case study

R.E. Fields and N.A. Merriam*

Human-Computer Interaction Group
Department of Computer Science
University of York, York, YO10 5DD, U.K.
Email: { Bob.Fields Nicholas.Merriam } @cs.york.ac.uk

Abstract. Much attention has been paid in HCI to techniques for designing systems that conform to the tasks users wish to carry out. It is often the case that such approaches rely on identifying the combinations of commands a user will be expected to issue and information they will need to access, and designing an interface with appropriate temporal behaviour. Many fields of activity, however, are highly information intensive, and the way in which a human-machine cognitive system makes inferences and reasons and makes decisions is far more important than the way it carries out actions. In this paper, therefore, we explore an approach to design that places much more emphasis on the form and structure of a display than it's temporal properties, and the role it plays in cognitive activity.

1 Introduction

Much attention has, quite justifiably, been paid in HCI to techniques for designing systems that conform to the *tasks* users wish to carry out, see for example (Elwert and Schlungbaum 1995; Palanque 1996). Task descriptions allow work to be described as a collection of sub-tasks to be performed; see, for example, (Kirwan and Ainsworth 1992). Some approaches to task-based design typically rely on identifying the combinations of commands a user will be expected to issue and information they will need to access, and designing an interface with appropriate temporal behaviour.

Task analysis was devised in order to find out what experts did and what knowledge they relied on so that training could target the acquisition of these capabilities, see (Annett and Duncan 1967). Perhaps for such historical reasons, task analysis approaches seem to focus more on what actions are *done* by an operator than on *how* an operator makes judgements about what actions to do; within a particular task, an operator would simply know what to do next because they had been trained in systematic procedures. Of course the the method of choosing actions can, in theory, be expressed within a task description, and we can express the possible procedures through which those choices are made. However the emphasis appears to remain on systematic procedures.

In domains where reasoning is of primary interest and where behaviour is frequently opportunistic, it can be hard to adequately capture the reasoning processes as simple procedures. In the present paper we explore, through a case study, an approach which

---

* Employed on EPSRC grant GR/K09205

focusses on the reasoning processes that a human-machine system jointly accomplishes in order to determine what actions to carry out. Rather than thinking about reasoning in terms of reasoning procedures, this approach encourages us to think in terms of how information is collected and co-ordinated in order to support decision making. In particular we will consider the form and structure of a display as a provider of such information. The case study here is a real example from a safety-critical aviation domain.

The case study started out as an example application of a "human error analysis" method that is described elsewhere (Fields et al. 1997). This method involved conducting interviews with engineers, flight deck designers and aircrew in order to construct scenarios of a particularly critical and challenging nature. These scenarios were then used to explore the consequences of different system re-design options within an ongoing aircraft upgrade programme, with a focus on identifying potential human error problems. In the course of this exercise, it became clear that one of the scenarios showed that a simple error analysis method, that concentrates on tasks and how they can be carried out wrongly, did not reveal all the interesting aspects of how humans and interactive artefacts conspire together to produce a system, error-prone or not. This highlighted the need for another approach to understanding the scenario, concerning the diagnosis of a problem in an aircraft's hydraulics system, and which is described in the present paper.

The point of departure was the recognition that the interesting thing about this particular scenario is not so much what the humans and machines *do*, but the *inferences* that the combined human-machine system makes.

This leads us to shift our attention away from actions and events, and towards information and representation. A framework that helps us to make this move is the distributed cognition perspective popularised by Ed Hutchins (1995a, 1995b). In this view, the appropriate unit of analysis for understanding work is the *cognitive system* – a network of human actors, artefacts, and distributed representations that act in concert to achieve computational goals. The activity of such a system can be understood on three levels: a *computational* level of information, algorithms and computational objectives; a *representational* level at which the form and media in which information is represented is described, as is the way representations are distributed and move around the system; and the *implementational* level, where the manipulation of representations is reified in the work practices of humans.

It is interesting to compare our work with the automatic presentation designer described in (Casner 1991), which critiques possible displays with respect to task descriptions. However, the reasoning described there only includes look-up and comparison of values and simple optimisations.

We begin by looking (in Section 2) at the nature of the hydraulics system, and (in Section 3) at the computational work of making diagnoses about problems in it. This can be used as a basis for establishing requirements for the design of information displays to support the trouble shooting activity (Section 4). Some properties of a particular representational scheme, embodied in an interface design, will be explored on the basis of how closely the interface matches the diagnostic inference, and the way in which, in order to make inferences, representations in the interface must be co-ordinated with those in the practitioner's head (Section 5).

Our approach to this design problem will involve us in the construction of a number of models that range from the abstract and formal to the detailed, specific, and relatively informal. The subjects of the model will span a broad range too, covering not only the interface itself (indeed, formal models of the interface figure only in a minor way in this paper), but also the external, physical environment, the kinds of knowledge possessed by the distributed cognitive system, the perceptual structure of the interface, and so on. This is precisely the loose federation of models and notations advocated in an earlier DSVIS paper (Fields et al. 1997).

2 Modelling the compútational system

This paper looks in some detail at the inferential processes involved in the diagnosis of failures in a scenario where leaks occur in a hydraulics system. The diagnostic activity involves a pilot or flight engineer trying to achieve two goals: fixing the problem (i.e., maintaining hydraulics power to the control surfaces), and, in the course of doing this, discovering as much information as possible about the causes of the problem. In this section, we look at what is involved in achieving these goals, and what information is required to do so. A subsidiary (though important) aspect of this is to look at how external representations, mediated by particular display format designs, can help to make the process of inference more reliable.

The kind of activity carried out here seems to be typical of diagnosis of problems in process control settings. Here the practitioner performs actions that may change the behaviour of the controlled process in a way that is closely coupled with the ongoing diagnostic reasoning. This is in contrast to medical diagnosis where it would seem that few actions will be taken until the practitioner has arrived at a diagnosis; see (Lindgaard 1995) for a review.

2.1 A generic model of aircraft hydraulics

Before we enter into any discussion of diagnostic activity, formal modelling or HCI, it is important to make a brief detour to explain the domain we are going to be working in. Vital to the safe operation of any modern aeroplane is its hydraulics system, the mechanism by which control inputs from the pilot or autoflight systems are conveyed to the control surfaces (primarily the rudder, ailerons and elevators). The actuation or movement of control surfaces is performed by hydraulic *servodynes*, piston systems relying on hydraulic *fluid*. Servodynes are supplied with fluid from hydraulics *reservoirs*, via a series of valves that determine which reservoir is supplying fluid to which servodyne, and therefore is responsible for maintaining power to which control surface. The hydraulics system can fail in a number of ways, and here we will consider only two: leaks in servodynes, and leaks in reservoirs. On the flight deck a decrease may be observed in the readout showing the quantity of fluid remaining in one or more of the reservoirs. Although the reliability of hydraulics technology is improving all the time, it still remains a safety-critical area of concern; indeed it appears that one of the main diagnostic skills possessed by flight engineers is the ability to discover and mitigate against hydraulics leaks, a work practice that is being supplanted by new computer technology and associated changes in crew complement and work organisation.

Our starting point for the analysis and design study will be an exposition of the functionings of the hydraulics systems and the computational work of carrying out hydraulics diagnosis. To begin with we can construct a formal presentation of the physical hydraulics systems, as a precursor to looking at the knowledge a flight engineer may employ to make the necessary diagnostic inferences and actions.

The model, at Hutchins' computational level, is not only abstract but is also generic, in the sense that it describes a whole class of hydraulics systems. Specialisations of it will define precisely how many reservoirs, servodynes, etc., there are, how they're interconnected, and so on. The discussion of inference and designs to support it later in the paper will all be based on a particular, very simple, instantiation. For the moment, though, it is sufficient to use two relations to capture the static structure of the hydraulics system. A simpler, less general model was arrived at following a series of interviews with aircrew and engineers, together with information from manuals, standard operating procedures, incident reports, and other documentation. The resulting model was then presented to the pilots and engineers through diagrams and explanation to confirm its veracity. The model makes a number of abstractions (e.g., that other parts of the physical system, like cross feeds and pumps are irrelevant for current purposes). The purpose of this part of the exercise was to validate these assumptions, as well as those evident in the discussion of goals and inference later on. We then attempted to generalise this to arrive at the model described below, which has been validated in the sense that it can be specialised to precisely the less general "validated" model.

The interconnection, the physical pipework, between servodynes and valves is modelled by the relation sv, and the interconnection between valves and reservoirs by vr.

$$sv : Servodyne \leftrightarrow Valve$$
$$vr : Valve \leftrightarrow Reservoir$$

The "dynamics" of the system – in other words the variable things that can cause observable effects are captured by three functions: *open* records whether or not a valve is open, and *leaky* and *leakyR* are real valued functions giving a measure of the rate of leakage from the servodynes and reservoirs.

$$open : Valve \rightarrow \mathbb{B}$$
$$leakyS : Servodyne \rightarrow \mathbb{R}^+$$
$$leakyR : Reservoir \rightarrow \mathbb{R}^+$$

We can now say that it is possible for fluid to flow from a reservoir r to a servodyne s if there is an open valve that connects r to s:

$$flow(r,s) = \begin{cases} 1 & \text{if } \exists v \cdot s \text{ sv } v \wedge v \text{ vr } r \wedge open(v) \\ 0 & \text{otherwise} \end{cases}$$

The picture can be completed with a description of how the fluid quantity in a reservoir changes over time.

$$-\frac{dq_r}{dt} = leakyR(r) + \sum_{s \in Servodyne} flow(r,s) \times leakyS(s) \tag{1}$$

where q_r is used to denote the fluid quantity in reservoir r.

Two observations can be made about this abstract model. First, although it describes completely (in generic terms) the relevant properties of the hydraulics systems, it says nothing about a procedure by which diagnosis can actually be done. Second, it can (and indeed has been used to) form a starting point for an implementation of a simulation of the hydraulics system for exercising different interface prototypes.

2.2 A specialisation of the general model

Rather than deal with the full complexity of a realistic hydraulics system, we will base the rest of the discussion on a simpler instantiation of the generic model, with only two control surfaces (rudder and aileron), and two hydraulics reservoirs (blue and green). Each control surface system has two servodynes: primary, connected to the blue reservoir, and secondary, connected to the green, which convey hydraulic power to the control surface actuators under the direction of the flying controls. The operation of the valves is such that each surface is connected to exactly one reservoir at any one time. Figure 1 shows how this example system is configured.

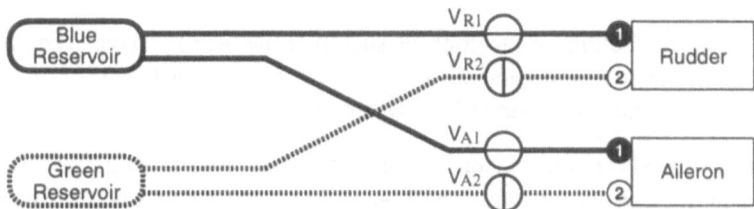

Fig. 1. Schematic hydraulics system — both control surfaces being fed from the Blue reservoir

Since either the primary or the secondary servodyne of each control surface (but not both) may be in use at any particular time, the pilot has two control switches — one for each control surface, each with a blue position and a green position, as shown in Figure 2(a). The switches can be operated independently, but when both are at the same setting, their physical arrangement allows both to be moved together as a single action. Typically, the switches will be located on an overhead panel on an aircraft flight deck, and so are somewhat distant from the information displays.

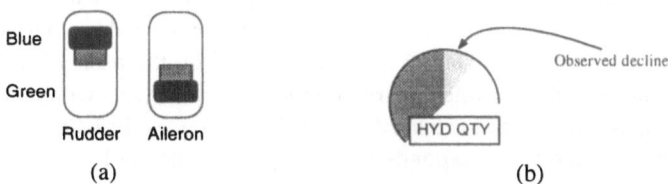

Fig. 2. Hydraulics system controls (a) and quantity display (b)

Two indications of the health of the system are available: the quantity of fluid in each of the two hydraulics reservoirs. By monitoring these and detecting changes, it is possible to gain information about the presence of leaks, which can occur in either the blue or green reservoirs, or in any of the four servodynes. The fluid quantity in a single reservoir is shown by a "piechart" dial as in Figure 2(b). Note that the decline, shaded grey in the figure, isn't shown in the actual display; the pilot must observe the change over a period of time. The fact that (due to limitations in sensing and monitoring devices) it is the pilot, and not the computer system that is responsible for noticing the decline means that all the inference described in the next section will also be the responsibility of the pilot, and cannot be "automated away". The detail of how these indications are presented, in particular an overall display organisation that supports the diagnosis, will be a central problem for the remainder of this paper.

2.3 Computational goals

The presence of leaks must be discovered by the pilot by monitoring the quantities in the two hydraulic reservoirs. The exact format of the displays that present this information are not considered here, but will be discussed in more depth in a later section. When a leak is noticed, the pilot begins an interaction with the system, with two goals in mind:

Goal 1: to select a setting of the controls such that the leak is "fixed" (i.e., hydraulic power to surfaces is maintained with minimum loss of fluid), and
Goal 2: to determine which parts of the system are leaky.

Note that these goals are not satisfiable in all situations (e.g., leaks in both reservoirs), but for the purposes of this example, we consider only situations where they are.

Typically, in a real aircraft, the whole process will be initiated by the occurrence of an alarm, possibly triggered by the detection of hydraulic mist in an underfloor compartment. In this example, we're ignoring all issues to do with the occurrence and recognition by the pilot of warnings. Another simplification is to assume that the pilot can fairly directly perceive the presence of a leak from one or other of the hydraulic reservoirs. In reality, this might be more complex and could involve monitoring the fluid quantity to check whether it reduces over a period of time.

3 A computational view of inference

The specific scenario we shall to look at now is the series of diagnostic inferences made for a complex failure situation where two leaks are present at the same time: one in the primary rudder servodyne and one in the secondary aileron servodyne. The scenario was identified by our informants as being interesting partly on the basis of its complexity, and partly because such multiple-failure situations do occur in reality (as evidenced in formal incident reports) and are used as training exercises. In fact the nature of the failures which we describe corresponds exactly to a "complex failure" training exercise and the inferences listed are just which, according to written notes, practitioners are trained to achieve. Of course, in the real world (and the training) a larger network is involved but our small, example network is still large enough to suffer this particular failure pattern.

Before thinking formally about this episode and the structure of the inferences that drive it forward, here's what happens.

(*i*) Initially, both rudder and aileron are operating on the blue (primary) system. The pilot first notices a decrease in the blue fluid quantity, and infers that there must be a leak: either in the blue reservoir, in the rudder primary servodyne, or in the aileron primary servodyne, or some combination of these, but not in the green reservoir (*Inference A*). The pilot then moves both control switches to the green position.

(*ii*) Next, the pilot observes the cessation of the blue leak, coupled with a decrease in the green fluid, and infers that there must be a leak in either the green reservoir, in the rudder secondary servodyne, or in the aileron secondary servodyne, or some combination of these, but not in the blue reservoir (*Inference B*). Combining this with (*Inference A*), she concludes that there must be a leak in one of the primary servodynes *and* a leak in one of the secondary servodynes and not in either the blue or green reservoir (*Inference C*).

(*iii*) The next step is to move the rudder switch to the blue position, whereupon the pilot notices a decrease of fluid in *both* systems. From this she infers that there must be a leak in either the blue reservoir or the rudder primary *and* one in either the green reservoir or the aileron secondary (*Inference D*). Combining this with (*Inference C*), it can be concluded there are leaks in the rudder primary and the aileron secondary and not in either the blue or green reservoirs (*Inference E*).

(*iv*) The final actions are to switch the rudder to green and the aileron to blue, resulting no leaks being observable. From this one can infer that there is no leak in either blue or green reservoirs, rudder secondary or aileron primary (*Inference F*). Combining this with (*Inference E*), yields the final conclusion that there are leaks in the rudder primary and the aileron secondary servodynes *only* (*Inference G*).

Of course, this isn't the shortest procedure that leads to the achievement of Goal 1 (curing the problem). For example, immediately switching the rudder to the green system cures the problem right away, but fails to satisfy Goal 2. More importantly, the scenario as described above is one that could plausibly occur as a result of a pilot following procedures (which, for very good reasons, indicate that, as a first step, both levers should be moved to green) or methodically aiming to solve the problems.

In order understand a bit more about what is involved in this process, we can represent the course of events a little more formally. The model we use contains the propositions explained in Table 1.

Actions taken by the pilot will be written as $R \rightarrow B$ (move the rudder switch to the blue position), $R, A \rightarrow G$ (move both rudder and aileron switches to the green position, etc.).

The course of events in the scenario, including actions taken, status information presented, and inferences made can be tabulated as in Table 2.

Representing the scenario like this immediately suggests three types of cognitive act in which the pilot engages:

− Making inferences based on the current indications and a knowledge of how the system works (recorded as inferences A, B, D, and F in the "Inf. No." column).

Table 1. Propositions used in the model of hydraulics reasoning

Controls settings		
RB	Rudder is on the blue system	$open(V_{R1})$ & $\neg open(V_{R2})$
RG	Rudder is on the green system	$open(V_{R2})$ & $\neg open(V_{R1})$
AB	Aileron is on the blue system	$open(V_{R1})$ & $\neg open(V_{A2})$
AG	Aileron is on the green system	$open(V_{A2})$ & $\neg open(V_{A1})$
Indications		
Bd	Decrease in blue reservoir fluid quantity	$\frac{dq_{Blue}}{dt} < 0$
Gd	Decrease in green reservoir fluid quantity	$\frac{dq_{Green}}{dt} < 0$
Internal state		
B	Leak in the blue reservoir	$leakyR(Blue) > 0$
G	Leak in the green reservoir	$leakyR(Green) > 0$
R1	Leak in the rudder primary servodyne	$leakyS(R1) > 0$
R2	Leak in the rudder secondary servodyne	$leakyS(R2) > 0$
A1	Leak in the aileron primary servodyne	$leakyS(A1) > 0$
A2	Leak in the aileron secondary servodyne	$leakyS(A2) > 0$

– Making inferences by integrating the current state of play and conclusions previously drawn (inferences marked C, E, and G).
– Selecting which switches to flip.

For the purposes of the remainder of this paper, the focus will principally be on inferences of the first type. However, it should be emphasised that it would be a mistake to treat the three elements above completely separately in a full analysis. Each of the aspects of the activity raise interesting questions about how the pilot makes use of the internal and external information resources at her disposal. In particular, what information is needed about the system? Where is it located — in the head of the pilot, or in the interface? What information is needed about leakiness in earlier states of the system, and where is that located? How can this information be employed as part of a strategy for deciding how to act?

3.1 Inferences about the system

In order to carry out the scenario, certain inferences need to be made about the possible causes of the observed behaviour. For example, the following two implications can account for the two conjuncts of the inference made in step (*i*) in Table 2.

$$\left. \begin{array}{l} RB \ \& \ AB \ \& \ Bd \Rightarrow B \vee R1 \vee A1 \\ \neg Gd \Rightarrow \neg G \end{array} \right\} \tag{2}$$

Note that this isn't an abductive process of hypothesis generation; it is purely deductive, and the inferences here can be derived from the formal model described in Section 2. The inferences used in the other steps of the interaction sequence are as follows:

$$\left. \begin{array}{l} RG \ \& \ AG \ \& \ Gd \Rightarrow G \vee R2 \vee A2 \\ \neg Bd \Rightarrow \neg B \end{array} \right\} \tag{3}$$

Table 2. Diagnostic inferences

Step	Control settings	Indications	Inferences	Inf. No.	Actions
(i)	Blue / Green — Rudder Aileron — RB, AB	Bd, $\neg Gd$	$(B \vee R1 \vee A1)$ & $\neg G$	(A)	$R, A \to G$
(ii)	Blue / Green — Rudder Aileron — RG, AG	$\neg Bd$, Gd	$(G \vee R2 \vee A2)$ & $\neg B$ $(R1 \vee A1)$ & $(R2 \vee A2)$ & $\neg B$ & $\neg G$	(B) $+A(C)$	$R \to B$
(iii)	Blue / Green — Rudder Aileron — RB, AG	Bd, Gd	$(B \vee R1)$ & $(G \vee A2)$ $R1$ & $A2$ & $\neg B$ & $\neg G$	(D) $+C(E)$	$R \to G$ $A \to B$
(iv)	Blue / Green — Rudder Aileron — RG, AB	$\neg Bd$, $\neg Gd$	$\neg B$ & $\neg G$ & $\neg R2$ & $\neg A1$ $R1$ & $A2$ & $\neg B$ & $\neg G$ & $\neg R2$ & $\neg A1$	(F) $+E(G)$	

$$RB \ \& \ AG \ \& \ Bd \Rightarrow B \vee R1 \ \Big\}$$
$$RB \ \& \ AG \ \& \ Gd \Rightarrow G \vee A2 \ \Big\} \qquad (4)$$

$$RG \ \& \ AB \ \& \ \neg Bd \Rightarrow \neg A1 \ \Big\}$$
$$RG \ \& \ AB \ \& \ \neg Gd \Rightarrow \neg R2 \ \Big\} \qquad (5)$$

4 Designing external representations

From a design perspective, one question for this paper is how do different representations of the problem lead to different support for the kinds of inferences that need to be made? Two subcomponents that we'll treat as different, though closely related, design problems are: making inferences about the current state indications, and making inferences based on the history of previous states.

50

4.1 Supporting inference about the current state

Design 1 The most simple means of displaying information is simply to present the basic sampled parameters in a way that allows the pilot observe changes in them. No particular attempt is made to aggregate data into more high-level information structures, nor to support particular inferences about the behaviour of the underlying system.

A direct presentation of the information in this example is simply to show the quantity of fluid in each of the hydraulics reservoirs. In the example display design below, based on a real aircraft, the shaded "piechart sector" representation of fluid quantity, allows detection of the changes in fluid quantity denoted by *Bd* and *Gd*. The display also shows the current hydraulic system selections as a table. Although a familiar and obvious way of representing the connection between hydraulic reservoirs and control surfaces, tables are not without problems from a usability point of view (Draper 1996). The state of the display below shows the starting state for this scenario (i.e., *Bd*, ¬*Gd*, *RB*, and *AB*).

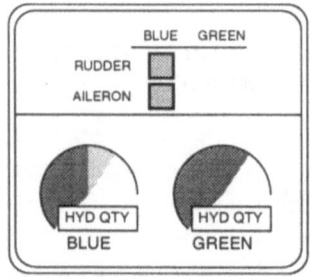

In order to make the inferences about the state of the system, one possible strategy will be for the pilot to read the display and interpret in order to determine propositions about the control settings (*RB*, *AG*, etc) and fluid quantity changes (*Bd*, *Gd*). The relevant knowledge about the inner workings of the system (expressed as inferences (2)-(5) above) must be deduced or recalled from memory and applied to draw a conclusion about the causes of the observed phenomena.

Design 2 One feature of the above design is that in order for the "flight deck system" (Hutchins 1995b) to correctly carry out its diagnostic activity, it is necessary for the pilot to possess a good deal if knowledge about the workings of the hydraulics system, and to be able to apply this knowledge in the right way. The second design suggestion aims to externalise some of this knowledge by representing it in the display. Furthermore, the representation aims to integrate more closely this external representation with the propositions to which it is to be applied, changing (and hopefully making easier) the co-ordination task the pilot must perform. In Section 5 we will see more clearly what it means to use and co-ordinate such an external representation. The design simply lists, below the quantity indicator for a hydraulics system the control surfaces currently connected to that system.

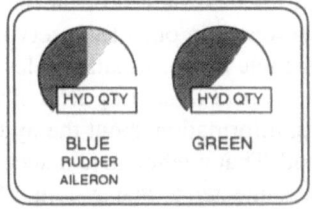

The display therefore contains an indicator from which a decline in fluid quantity may be observed, and a list of names of control surfaces connected to that reservoir. The inferential process a pilot must engage in is therefore simpler: *if a decline is observed in a quantity indicator, then there must be a leak in at least one of the systems/control surfaces listed below* it. If there is no decline in quantity, then *there is no leak in any of the listed control surfaces and systems*. Thus the structure of interface therefore suggests a strategy by which a user may reason from observed effects to hypothesised causes (see, for example (Tufte 1983) for more discussion), while still allowing the more complex lookup to be carried out.

5 Displays, representations and the implementation of inference

In this section of the paper we propose possible approaches to performing the diagnosis work. We do not claim that this is *the* description of how the human-machine system functions but rather that we can provide logically sound accounts for *possible* reasoning behaviour strategies. Informally at least, our accounts do not seem to be inconsistent with the reports of flight engineers who use the current system.

Considering only the blue system, in order to make the relevant part of inference (A), $B \vee R1 \vee A1$, the pilot must, among other things, observe the decline in the blue system hydraulic level indicator and assimilate this with the fact that the rudder and aileron servodynes are connected to the blue system and could therefore be a cause of the decline. This will tell the pilot about the relationship between B, $R1$ and $A1$.

In order to provide an explanation of reasoning leading to inference (A), we will establish, in three stages, a connection between the real-valued model described by Equation 1 and a sufficient procedure for arriving at inference (A). Firstly, since we are only considering the blue system and therefore are only interested in the primary servodynes, we can extract the following equation from Equation 1.

$$Bd \Leftrightarrow B \vee \left(\bigvee_{S \in \{A,R\}} SB \ \& \ S1 \right) \tag{6}$$

However, this seems very far from an account of how the pilot might coordinate information in the interface. Fortunately, a small calculation shows that the following statement is implied by the apparently obscure Equation 6.

$$Bd \Rightarrow B \vee \left(\bigvee_{S \in \{A,R\} \ \& \ SB} S1 \right)$$

This statement can be read as "if there is a drop in the blue system fluid level then there is a leak in the blue reservoir or in one of the servodynes currently connected to the blue system". Thus, to assemble the information relevant to diagnosis of fluid level drop from a hydraulic system, instead of starting from first principles each time, there is the possibility of embedding information about the hydraulics system "once and for all" in a straightforward method. That method is to detect that the level is dropping and find out which servodynes are connected to that system. The development above can be viewed as a soundness and completeness argument for this straightforward method.

Returning to our specific example, the pilot observes that the hydraulic fluid level in the blue system is dropping, Bd and finds out that the aileron and rudder are both connected to the blue system, respectively AB and RB. From this she can conclude that there is a leak in the blue system reservoir, or at the rudder servodyne, or at the aileron servodyne, $B \lor R1 \lor A1$. We will now investigate the support provided by the two different designs for this strategy.

Rather than attempting to make an opaque statement that design 2 is better than design 1, or the converse, we would like to be able to understand how the designs differ in terms of their ability to support the pilot in detecting which servodynes are connected to the leaky hydraulics system. In order to do this we need to understand certain key features of the two candidate displays. We wish to investigate the extent to which the proposed inference scheme is supported by the interface, and the primary variation between the design 1 and design 2 is in their physical layout. Rather than discussing this layout aspect of the designs entirely in words, we have sought an intermediate means of expressing our assumptions about the visual structure of the designs. A framework which allows us to do this is the structure diagram notation of (May, Scott, and Barnard 1997). We acknowledge that we are not using this notation in quite the sense for which it was intended but it seems more reasonable to borrow their notation, with which readers may be familiar, than to invent a new one.

In Figure 3, we have modelled design 1 as a structure diagram, showing that it is composed of two parts, an upper part with a table and a lower part with dials. The lower right panel has not been modelled since it is similar to the lower left panel and will not feature in our analysis. Its omission is indicated by the dashed line.

In order to perform the task of detecting a leak and finding the connected servodynes with design 1, the pilot can scan the dials to find that one is showing a drop in hydraulic fluid from the reservoir and observe which system this is. Then this information can be coordinated with information in the upper table to reveal which servodynes are connected. This coordination revolves around the labels "BLUE" which provide the link between the relatively distant, in terms of their external representations, dial information and the table information. Figure 4 shows, through highlighting, the elements of the display which are involved in this process of coordination, and shows, through enclosure, the subgroups involved in specific parts of the inference. Our highlighting shows the parts of the display involved in the inference and should not be confused with that used in (May, Scott, and Barnard 1997), where it is used to indicate that one element in a group "pops out".

The structure diagram for design 2, shown in Figure 5, shows that the display comprises a left and a right portion, each possessing a dial and some labels.

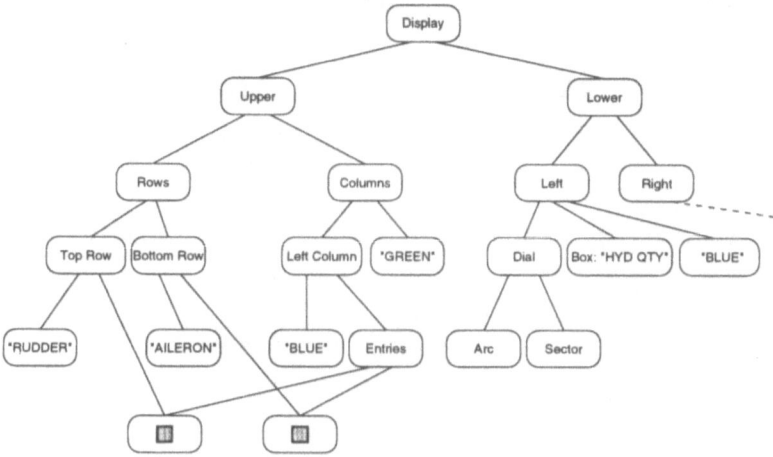

Fig. 3. Structure diagram for design 1

In order to perform the same task of detecting a leak and finding the connected servodynes with design 2, the pilot can scan the dials, observe which system has a problem and associate this with its connected servodynes. The pilot can coordinate the information that fluid level is dropping, represented in the dial display, with the information about which servodynes are connected to that system, represented in the list of labels under that dial. This time, the focus of coordination, the "BLUE" label for the dial and the "BLUE" label for the servodyne list, is unified in the external representation: there is just one "BLUE" label. Figure 6 shows the parts of the display involved in this coordination process and the subgroups associated with parts of the inference. It reveals how the dial display and the servodyne list share the same "BLUE" label.

This makes a case that design 2 will support the pilot's inference process better than design 1 but rather misses the point. The pilot using design 2 has the option of using an altogether different strategy, where there is not so much a coordination between distinct, separate representations but a direct exploitation of the grouping embodied in the external representation. The association of the connected servodynes with the falling hydraulic fluid display is made in the external representation and is *independent* of the pilot's use of the label "BLUE". The pilot can scan for the dial showing a leak and then just read off the connected servodynes from the list below it.

6 Conclusion

In this paper we have looked at the design of a highly critical device from the point of view of the way it functions as a representational artefact in the workplace of those who use it. We have modelled the problem solving domain in order to understand and document how information gathered in different system configurations can contribute to achieving work goals of the pilot. and used this model to show that a plausible interaction strategy combines information sufficient to make inferences about the state of

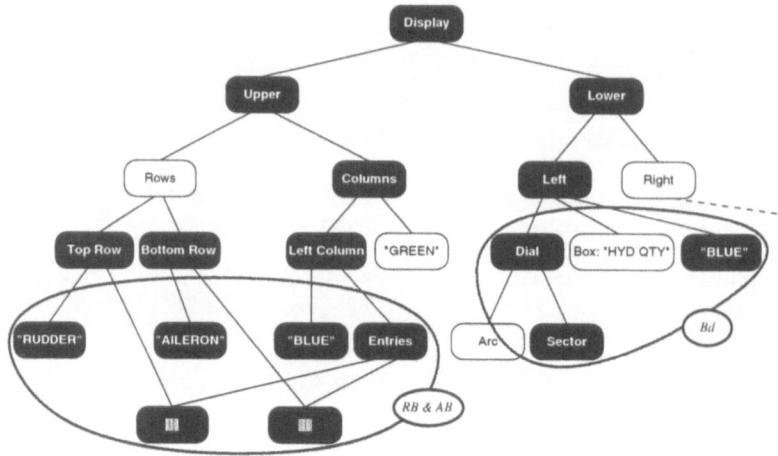

Fig. 4. Augmentation of Figure 3 with annotations to show parts used in inference

the system. We have also presented models of two candidate displays and used them to consider the extent of the displays' support for this interaction strategy.

The particular focus adopted here has been on representations and the way they are distributed around a system and co-ordinated to provide task-relevant resources. This goes some way beyond a number of design approaches in HCI (*e.g.* task analysis, or cognitive modeling), where it often seems to be the case that more attention is paid to the represented information rather than the representation of information.

Of course, work from the distributed cognition perspective does look in some detail at the role played by external representations, the way internal and external representations may be co-ordinated, and the effect that representational form has in transforming tasks (see for example, (Hutchins 1995b), (Zhang 1996), (Scaife and Rogers 1996)). This work, however, is not (and does not attempt to be) well integrated into a user interface development process. Some simple, but quite general design lessons can be abstracted from the work described here. For instance, it is often the case that an inferential process requires a connection to be established between two groups of information, such as between the fact that the blue quantity is declining, and the fact that both rudder and aileron are connected to the blue system. In such a situation, the connection can be established in the interface (see Figure 6) rather than solely in the head of the human (Figure 4).

Finally, we note that the present paper employs a number of models, each introduced for a specific purpose and integrated not at a semantic level but in a more informal, procedural manner. In this respect, the paper is an example of the multiple model approach argued for in (Fields, Merriam, and Dearden 1997). However, we observe that the models presented here do, in fact, combine and contribute to each other to a much closer degree than required by the multiple model approach. The real-valued model has provided the foundations of a simulator for interface prototyping. Furthermore it has

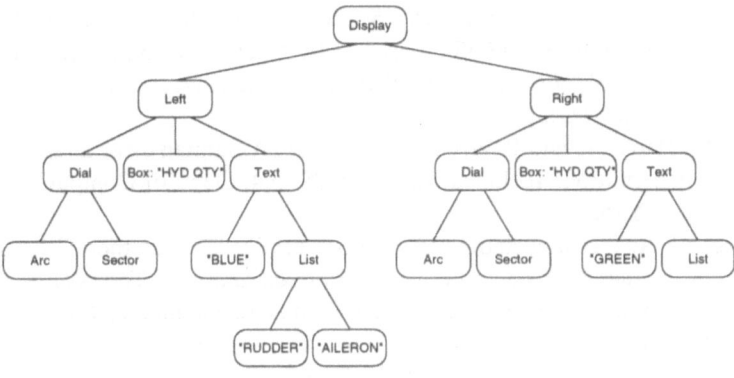

Fig. 5. Structure diagram for design 2

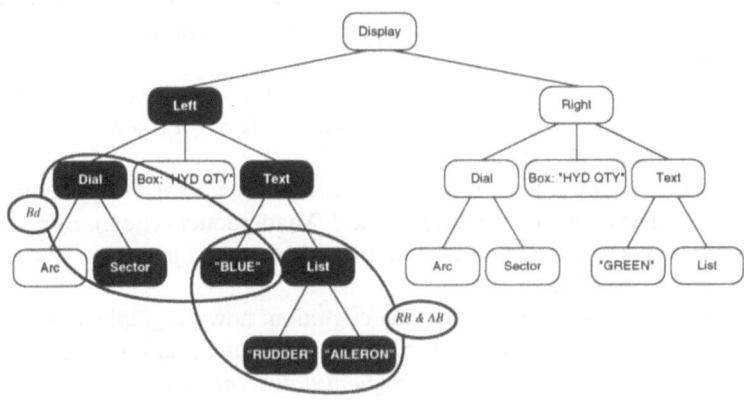

Fig. 6. Augmentation of Figure 5 with annotations to show parts used in inference

allowed extraction of a truth-valued propositional model of inferences in diagnosis and "repair". And the structure diagrams have allowed us to model displays in a way which, by recording groupings, provide a means to assess support for an interaction strategy, which in turn has been validated in the inference model.

References

Annett, J. and K. D. Duncan (1967). Task analysis and traning design. *Occupational Psychology 41*, 211–21.

Casner, S. M. (1991). A Task-Analytic Approach to the Automated Design of Graphic Presentations. *ACM Transactions on Graphics 10*(2), 111–151.

Draper, S. W. (1996, May). Visualisation by tables. Available online at http://www.psy.gla.ac.uk/ steve/Position96.html.

Elwert, T. and E. Schlungbaum (1995). Modelling and Genereation of Graphical User Interfaces in the TADEUS Approach. In P. Palanque and R. Bastide (Eds.), *Eurographics Workshop on Design, Specification and Verification of Interactive Systems*. Springer-Verlag.

Fields, B., M. Harrison, and P. Wright (1997). THEA: human error analysis for requirements definition. Technical Report YCS-294, Dept. of Computer Science, University of York.

Fields, R. E., N. A. Merriam, and A. M. Dearden (1997). Design, modelling and validation of interactive systems. In M. D. Harrison and J. C. Torres (Eds.), *Eurographics Workshop on Design, Specification and Verification of Interactive Systems*. Springer-Verlag.

Hutchins, E. (1995a). *Cognition in the Wild*. MIT Press.

Hutchins, E. (1995b). How a cockpit remembers its speeds. *Cognitive Science 19*, 265–288.

Kirwan, B. and L. K. Ainsworth (1992). *A Guide to Task Analysis*. Taylor & Francis.

Lindgaard, G. (1995). Human performance in diagnosis: can expert systems help. *Interacting with Computers 7*(3), 254–272.

May, J., S. Scott, and P. Barnard (1997). *Structuring Interfaces: A Psychological Guide* (Fourth ed.). ICS Project. Online at http://www.shef.ac.uk/ pc1jm/guide.html.

Palanque, P. (1996). Towards an integrated proposal for Interactive Systems design based on TLIM and ICO. In F. Bodart and J. Vanderdonckt (Eds.), *Eurographics Workshop on Design, Specification and Verification of Interactive Systems*, pp. 69–85. Springer-Verlag.

Scaife, M. and Y. Rogers (1996). External cognition: how do graphical representations work? *International Journal of Human-Computer Studies 45*, 185–213.

Tufte, E. R. (1983). *The Visual Display of Quantitative Information*. Graphics Press.

Zhang, J. (1996). A representational analysis of relational information displays. *International Journal of Human-Computer Studies 45*, 59–74.

An Ontology for Task World Models

Martijn van Welie, Gerrit C. van der Veer, Anton Eliëns

Vrije Universiteit, Department of Computer Science
De Boelelaan 1081a, 1081 HV Amsterdam, Holland
+31 20 4447788, {martijn,gerrit,eliens}@cs.vu.nl

Abstract. Many different task modeling methods exist. In this paper, we discuss 1) ingredients common to most task models, 2) how task modeling relates to the design of user interfaces, and 3) our proposed ontology for task analysis. We then show our task analysis tool that is based on the ontology. It is our belief that task models should be based on an ontology that describes the relevant concepts and the relationships between them, independently of any used graphical representations. Such an ontology helps to understand the different task modeling methods and it can also be operationalized for use in tools.

Keywords. Groupware Task Analysis (GTA), task models, task analysis, ontologies, user interface design (UID), CSCW.

1   Introduction

It has been generally accepted that task analysis may substantially contribute to the design of usable products because it focuses on the end user. Task analysis investigates users' characteristics and the task world of which they are a part. The information should be recorded in a task model that captures relevant aspects of the users and their task world. The resulting model should help designers in their process of designing a new product.

What is and is not relevant for the design process is determined by two factors: by what the analyst wants to record and by the task modeling method that is used. Each modeling method has certain defined concepts and relationships that are used to record information about the users and their task world. The concepts (e.g. tasks, roles, etc.) often come from the field of psychology and are clearly defined, but the relationships between concepts are usually only roughly sketched, leading to confusion when performing the actual task analysis.

Although specific task models differ, they have many things in common (e.g. task decomposition and task flow). Almost all task modeling methods also use graphical representations to show the information of the model. It is our belief that task models should be based on an ontology that describes the relevant concepts and the relationships between them, independently of any used graphical representations. An ontology can be defined as a view on a "world" that describes the nature and relations of it. In this case the task world of users is being described. In order to be useful in task analysis such an ontology should be rich enough to accommodate the extraction of the information needed to generate all the commonly used visual representations, e.g. task trees and flow diagrams. Different graphical representations would then show certain aspects of the ontology depending on the purpose of the view.

In this paper we explore the common ingredients of task models, and then introduce our ontology that makes all concepts and their relationships explicit. The ontology is the result of our attempt to clarify the concepts and relationships of our conceptual framework *Groupware Task Analysis* (GTA)[14]. We also provide an example of a tool based on this ontology. We believe that the use of this ontology could improve the results of task analysis firstly because it can be used as a reference model and secondly because it helps to structure the activity of task analysis when the used tools are based on the ontology.

2 Ingredients of task models

Task models are usually filled with several ingredients that are then related in some way. Some ingredients are less common than others, as the ideas about them have not yet stabilized; for instance, with the recent developments in CSCW systems and agent technology, modeling group processes has become important, although it is not yet clear how this should be done. This section will discuss common ingredients .

2.1 Task Decomposition

Task Decomposition is the most common ingredient of task models. It results in the classical task tree usually enhanced with constructors that indicate time relationships between tasks. This is probably the oldest ingredient and has a strong psychological basis; humans think in a structured way about their activities, which can be captured in a task decomposition[11].

Tasks and Goals. A common definition for a task is "an activity performed to reach a certain goal." However, in practice the relationship between tasks and goals is not always so clear. Some methods presume a 1-to-1 mapping between tasks and goals; for instance a *Task Knowledge Structure* (TKS[3,5]) contains a goal substructure (which would be called a task substructure by others' methods). Other models, such as GTA[14] and *Méthode Analytique de Description* (MAD[10]), allow a goal to be reached in several ways. In these models, the goal of a task is a specific state that is reached after successful execution of the task. In complex task trees based on real life situations, tasks near the leaves in a tree are usually connected with individual goals, and tasks represented by high level nodes are often closely tied with organizational goals[16]. When analyzing the tasks of an individual this is less apparent than when analyzing tasks on an organizational level. When modeling complex situations where the organization is of great relevance, it is important to be aware of the difference between individual and organizational goals and the ways they are related.

2.2 Task Flow Specification

Another common feature of most task models is Task Flow, which indicates the order in which tasks are executed. Two forms of flow models can be distinguished:

(1) workflow representations, with time on one axis, and

(2) task trees enhanced with the "classic" constructors that give a kind of time structure (although mixing time and task decomposition).

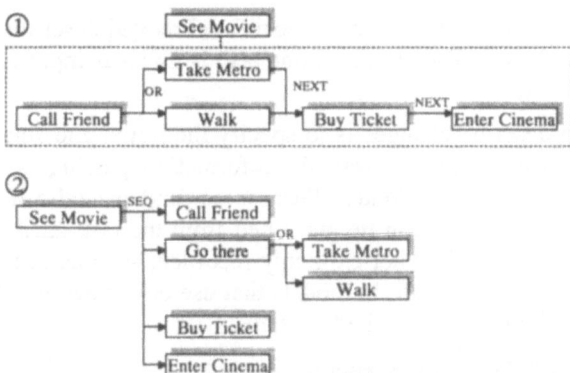

Fig. 1. Going to the cinema

Theoretically they are equally powerful to express any kind of task flow. However, the second type of flow model suffers from the fact that usually many constructors are needed and extra tasks need to be added. For example, in figure 1, two representations are used. The first one is a task flow representation with time on the x-axis. The second is a task decomposition with constructors that represents the same task flow as the first representation. Because constructors scope over all subtasks, the second representation needs an extra task "Go there" which *may* not be desired. In Paterno's "ConcurTaskTrees"[9] these types of tasks are called "abstract tasks." The important point here is that for both representations the specified task flow is basically the same but the visual representation does not always allow specification of the task structure as desired. Since both representations can be useful there is a need for an underlying model that allows both.

2.3 Object Modeling

Object Modeling is an addition to task analysis that comes close to the data structure modeling of the final design and implementation. The purpose is to say something about the objects, as they are physically present in the task world or mentally present in the user's mind. Not every object may be directly included in the new design but in the case of models for automated user interface (UI) generation there is usually a very strong link between objects and UI widgets, such as buttons or menus.

The question remains how much object modeling should be in task models. Extensive data modeling does not appear to directly help in improving the usability of the product. It also depends heavily on the purpose of the task model; models used as a basis for automatic UI generation have different requirements than models used for evaluation. For example, in GTA only the structure of the objects and the tasks they are used in are recorded. Other models such as ConcurTaskTrees[9] and TKS[3,5] also include actions that are performed on the object.

Information passing. The most important purpose of a task is that it "changes" something, otherwise the task has no reason for existence. By change we mean any sort of change, including adding information (changing an unknown to a known).

Some task analysis methods such as ConcurTaskTrees[9] describe this with task input and task output objects. The output of one task is given as input to the next task, thus passing information.

Another way to describe changes is to specify the initial and final states in terms of object attribute values. In this way the information passing is indirectly achieved through changes in object attributes. There is no fundamental difference since the list of input and output objects can be generated from the task attributes. However, it is possible that the changes are not explicitly recorded, such as in the mental processes involved in a human's decision. In models that use object actions, changes are usually defined in the actions instead of the task states.

2.4 Recording of Concept Characteristics

Another common part of most task analysis models is the recording of relevant characteristic attributes of the concepts. Often mentioned attributes of tasks are pre- and post conditions, state changes, duration, etc. However, what specifically is recorded can be very different depending on the level of detail or purpose of the model. While there is no standard for concept recording, there are guidelines like the ISO 9241-11 standard[1] that suggest what could be recorded for tasks, actors and parts of the task world.

2.5 Task World Modeling

Task World modeling is for investigating the users and the world in which they act. In the past most methods have focused on modeling one user and that users' tasks. However, in current applications, group aspects are becoming very important. Every major software supplier now develops its products for use in multi-user distributed environments. Classic task modeling methods lack the power to deal with these situations, modeling only the static part of the task world by identifying roles. This neglects other parts of the organization and dynamic aspects of the task world.

People and Organizations. Modeling the task world means modeling the people that are part of it and modeling its structure, which is often a part of the organizational structure. While it may add perspective to see a model of the "official" organizational structure, for task analysis, the structure of how tasks are *actually* being done is more relevant than how they officially *should be* done. Specifying roles in the organization and actors' characteristics gives relevant information that can be used in design. The roles then need to be attributed to actors. In TKS[3,5] a role is defined to be responsible for performing the tasks it encompasses; for example, a movie projectionist is responsible for starting a movie. However, in real organizations, task responsibilities frequently need to be handled more flexibly resulting in responsibilities being shifted by delegation or by mandate. The actor playing a role may therefore not perform the task he or she is responsible for; a movie projectionist could have someone from the snack bar push the button to start the movie.

Roles and Actors. In classic task analysis literature, as well as in ethnography, concepts such as *actors* and *roles* are commonly referred to regarding tasks and the task world. Although these terms are intuitively appealing, they can cause confusion when they need to be named during task analysis.

A role is defined by the tasks the role is responsible for. E.g. a projectionist is responsible for starting and stopping the movie projector as well as setting op the movie projector. Mayhew[7] defines an actor as a class of humans whereas others consider a particular person an actor. Usually there is no need to consider a particular person and provide a name for an actor (e.g. Chris, Pat) since we are only interested in describing relevant characteristics of the actor. Confusion arises when an actor is to be named and the only sensible name seems to be the role name. For instance the actor who has the projectionist role is most intuitively called the "projectionist" which is already his/her role name. Therefore it is usually better to name these actors arbitrarily (A,123, People having role X) and simply record characteristics such as language, typing skill, computer experience, knows how to use Word etc. The important part is their characteristics and their relationships with roles.

In other cases, where it does not matter *who* actually performed the task, it is sometimes more useful to specify that a task was performed by a role rather than by a particular actor. Sometimes even a computer system is the actor of a task (e.g an automated movie projector). Therefor in GTA the concept of actor was renamed *agent* to avoid any confusion.

Events. When designing it is useful to know what factors influence the actor when he is performing the task and what impact they have. *Events* model dynamic aspects of the task world: things that happen in the task world, over which the actor does not always have direct control (e.g. the film breaks, or the cinema has a power failure). Sometimes there may be no need to explicitly incorporate the event in the new design but in other cases incorporation is more important. For example, it may prove very useful to model the projectionist's reaction to the event of the film breaking.

3 Task modeling for user interface design

After looking at several aspects of task models, some questions remain unanswered. What distinguishes UI task models from other task models (such as multi agent models in the field of *Artificial Intelligence*)? More importantly, what exactly should a task model include in order for its use to improve the usability of systems in the task world? We will look at the last question more precisely.

Markopoulos and Gikas[8] take a formal approach in using task models in system design. They argue that although a designer has a task model, it is still unclear how it helps him in designing. A task model needs to be formalized in order to conform to the task world *and* be useful in UI generation system.

In general UI task models should be able to represent psychological, social, environmental and situational aspects of the actors and their tasks. Hierarchical structures such as task decompositions and object structures can give a hint to a good system structure but for other aspects, such as user characteristics or timing properties, the relationship with the design is less obvious. Task analysis literature shows that each task model is designed for a certain purpose. For example, there are task models that can be used to:

- **Validate.** Some models are only meant as informal validating tools. They validate if the designers know enough about the task world for which they are designing. Methods such as HTA[6] are in this category. These methods result in quite informal models and do not have a very strong direct relationship with the design.

- **Generate User Interfaces**. Models like HUMANOID[12] and ADEPT[4] are designed to automatically generate a prototype of a user interface. To make the generation possible they need to be very precise and do not really produce human readable specifications. They are, not surprisingly, focussed on specifying the user interface behavior in detail, which makes them much more formal than the previous category.

- **Aid Design**. A more advanced use of a task model as a validating tool is to use it as a design aid. Methods like GTA[14], TKS[3,5] or GOMS[2] give a designer some "handles" for the design. Extensive task modeling gives concrete information about which objects or structures should be reflected in the design. Modeling the roles and agents can give information about the need for user identification or adaptability of the user interface for users. These methods are more formal than methods such as HTA[6] but less formal than UI generation methods such as ADEPT.

In principle a task model should not be used for specifying the user interactions with the system. Notations like User Action Notation[17] or ETAG[13] allow user actions to be specified in detail. What is needed is a mechanism to link a task analysis model to a user interaction model. That way the structure and task flow of the interaction model can be constructed out of a task model. A prerequisite for this is a formalized task model. This is however still the missing link in user interface design. Task models are often too informal which makes them hard to connect with interaction models. A relatively new approach called model-based interface design can be seen as an attempt to connect task models and interface models in a more fluent way. In this approach the design process consists of refining several models that each represent a different aspect of the design. A formal definition language that is used in every model relates all models with each other. Currently the task models used in such approaches are rather basic which limits the power of this approach. In the next sections we will present an ontology that may fill in this gap in user interface design because it gives a formal definition of the concepts and relationships that can be used to describe a task world.

4 An ontology

So far we have discussed common ingredients of task models, and some ways task models are used in the design of user interfaces. Now we propose an ontology that incorporates the mentioned ingredients, each to a certain extent. Although the ontology is mostly based on GTA it can serve as a reference for comparing other models such as TKS and MAD as well.

It is called an ontology because it describes logical relationships between concepts, something only informally done (if at all) by the various task analysis models that are currently being used. The ontology does not imply any graphical representation because it is defined in concepts and relationships and it therefor makes an extra abstraction.

4.1 Concepts and Attributes

The *concepts* defined here are based on the conceptual framework of GTA and can be found in most other task models as well (with the exception of the *event* concept). This section will define the concepts and the next section will define their relationships in detail.

Object. An object refers to a physical or non-physical entity. A non-physical entity could be anything ranging from messages, passwords or addresses to gestures and stories. Objects have attributes consisting of attribute-name and value pairs. What can be done with an object is specified by actions, for instance *move, change, turn off* etc. Furthermore, objects may be in a type hierarchy and can also be contained in other objects, for example a form may contain an address field, and a cinema can contain a snack bar. Objects are typically used in tasks but they can also influence the task execution sequence when they cause events to occur.

Agent. An agent is an entity that is considered active. Usually agents are humans but groups of humans or software components may also be considered agents. Agents are not specific individuals (like Chris) but always indicate classes of individuals with certain characteristics. Attributes of the agent can include *skills, attitude* and other *miscellaneous*. Agents perform tasks and always play certain *roles* within the task world.

Role. A role is a meaningful collection of tasks performed by one or more agents. The role is meaningful when it has a clear goal or when it distinguishes between groups of agents. A role is consequently *responsible* for the tasks that it encompasses. Roles can be hierarchically composed and are assigned to an agent in a certain way. The role can be obtained by assignment, delegation, mandate or because of a situational context.

Task. A task is an activity performed by agents to reach a certain goal. A task typically changes something in the task world and requires some period of time to complete. Complex tasks can be decomposed into smaller subtasks. Tasks are executed in a certain order and the completion of one task can *trigger* the execution of one or more other tasks. A task could also be started because of an event that has occurred in the task world.

Important for the task concept is the distinction between unit tasks and basic tasks, where (ideally) a unit task should only be executed by performing one or more basic tasks. The relationship between the unit task and basic task is interesting because it can indicate the problems that an agent may have in reaching his goals.

A unit task is defined by Card, Moran and Newell[2] as the simplest task that a user really wants to perform. A basic task[13] is a task for which a system provides a single function. Usually basic tasks are further decomposed into user actions and system operations. A user action is an action done by the human users that is only meaningful in the context of its basic task (e.g. a key press). A system operation is an action done by a system; it is not a typical task because it, as such, serves no goal for the user. The *type* attribute captures the task type, which can be either *unit, basic* or *composite* (consisting of unit, basic and/or composite tasks). In case of a basic task the *user_actions* and *system_operations* attributes are valid.

Tasks are started because of the completion of other tasks or because of events. For successful execution of a task a number of start-conditions have to be fulfilled. The stop-condition specifies when the task has reached completion. The changes in the task world that have taken place because of this task are described by the difference in the initial and final state.

Event. An event is a change in the state of the task world at a point in time. The change may reflect changes of attribute values of internal concepts such as Object, Task, Agent or Role or could reflect changes of external concepts such as the weather or electricity supply. Events influence the task execution sequence by *triggering* tasks. This model does not specify how the event is created or by whom.

4.2 Relationships

The concepts defined in the previous section are related in specific ways. In this section we sketch the relationships that we are using now. For each relationship the first-order predicate definition is given and explained. Figure 2 shows all the concepts and relationships together in a diagram.

Uses. The uses(Task,Object,Action) relationship specifies which object is used in executing the task and how it is used. The Action specifies what is being done with the object. It typically changes the state of the object.

Triggers. The triggers(Task/Event, triggeredTask, triggerType) relationship is the basis for specifying task flow. It specifies that a task is triggered (started) by an event or a task and the type of the trigger. If the task is part of a choice the triggertype is OR. Other possible triggers are: AND for specifying parallel executed tasks, and NEXT for indicating linear succession of tasks. The triggers relationship is very similar to triggers used in workflow representations and allow for specifying concurrency in various ways. We will explain later how this relationship is used to generate a visual representation of a flow diagram.

Plays. Every agent should play one or more roles. The plays(Agent, Role, Appointment) relationship also indicates how this role was obtained. Currently, the Appointment parameter can be ASSIGNED, DELEGATED, MANDATED or SOCIAL. In the future, we want to look more closely at role appointing, so this relationship may undergo changes in subsequent versions of this ontology.

Performed_by. The relationship performed_by(Task, Agent/Role) specifies that a task is performed by an agent. This does not mean that agent is also the one who is responsible for the task because this depends on his role and the way it was obtained. When it is not relevant to specify the agent that performs the task, a *role* can also be specified as the performing entity.

Subtask. The subtask(Task, SubTask) relationship describes the task decomposition.

Subrole. The subrole(Role, SubRole) relationship brings roles into a hierarchical structure. The subrole relationship states that a role includes other roles including the responsibility for the task that encompass the role. When a role has subroles the task responsibilities are added up for the role. For example, the role of *snack bar worker* may have the subroles of *popcorn maker, snack bar cashier*, and *daytime janitor*.

Responsible. The responsible(Role, Task) relationship specifies a task for which the role is responsible. Continuing the example above, the snack bar worker role is *responsible* for all the tasks of the subroles popcorn maker, snack bar cashier, and daytime janitor.

Used_by. The used_by(Object, Agent/Role, Right) relationship indicates who used which object and what the agent or role can do with it. The agents' rights regarding objects can be of existential nature (CREATE and DESTROY), indicate ownership (OWNER), or indicate daily handling of objects (USE, CHANGE).

The relationships of this model form a minimal set of relationships that exist. However, when using this model there are also other relationships that can be of interest. Consider for instance a relationship *involved_role* that indicates which roles

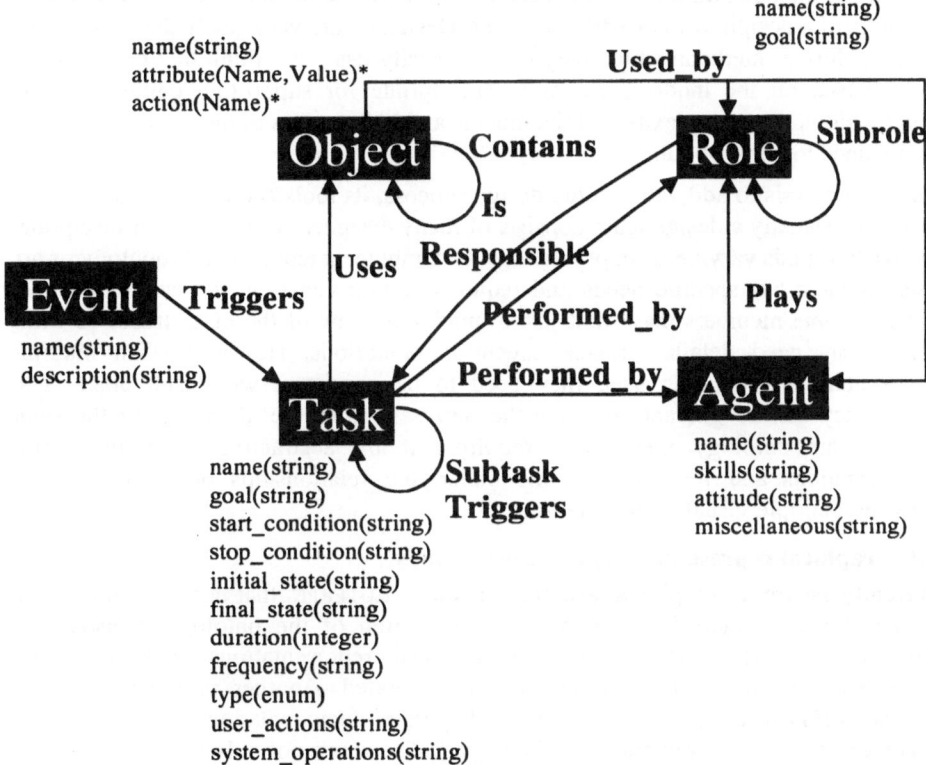

Fig. 2. The concepts and relations

are involved in a task. Such a relationship could be defined as the roles of the agents involved in the task and all the involved roles of the subtasks. The *involved_role* relationship is not part of the ontology because it can be defined using only the relationships of the ontology. The next section will show how all these relationships can be used in practice.

5 Supporting task analysis

Anyone who has ever done task analysis knows that even with the use of models it is still not an easy task. The biggest problem is often not in *applying* one technique[15], but in *communicating* results to a client or to other members of a design team. If the results of a task analysis are not communicated well their value for the design process rapidly diminishes. This section addresses this issue of how task analysis can be supported.

5.1 Formal models and tools

The ontology described in the previous section is not very formal and still leaves task details in the darkness. Many other task-modeling methods end up with quite formal models. Our experience with design situations, both in education and industry, shows that formal methods do **not** (by themselves) improve the communication between the members of a design team or with the client. Designers are very easily demotivated by pages of formal methods which they can not easily use. We think that task analysis tools (based on the models) are more appropriate for supporting communication, thereby hiding the complexities of the models and hiding parts of the models designers do not need to know about.

For task analysis to add value to the design process, its tools should be tailored to the designer. Usually a design team consists of many designers from different disciplines and backgrounds varying from psychology or computer science to anthropology or art. Each of them has specific needs and requires certain views on the task model. For instance some members may want just a quick overview of the task structures while others may need details on task execution conditions. However when multiple representations are being used they need to be consistent with each other. This consistency can be guaranteed when the representations are all based on the same model. Our ontology meets this requirement by abstracting from the visual representations and focussing on the underlying relationships between concepts, allowing multiple visual representations.

5.2 Graphical representations and the ontology

Currently we are developing a task analysis tool - EUTERPE- that uses the ontology as a basis for task analysis[1]. A Prolog representation of the ontology is used as a relational database from which several visual representations such as simple templates, lists, trees, or flow models are generated. Another possible view is a generated HTML document that serves as hypertext documentation of the task model which can only be viewed and not edited (yet). The views not only allow designers to inspect a task model but also allow modification and creation of new instances of tasks etc. which will automatically show up in other views as well. Figure 3 shows the basic structure of the tool.

One part of our research is to investigate which visual representations are useful to designers from different disciplines. One example of new visual representation is a

---

[1] The latest information about GTA and our tools can be found at: http://www.cs.vu.nl/~martijn/gta/index.html

kind of fish-eye view where you only see a part of all the information for instance about a certain task. Shifting the fish-eye to a related object shows all the information related to that object. By distinguishing between the underlying ontology and the graphical representations, views can be changed or added to without having to completely revise the underlying data or ontology. It is our goal to find views that are useful and to provide an environment in which these views are available to all members of the design team.

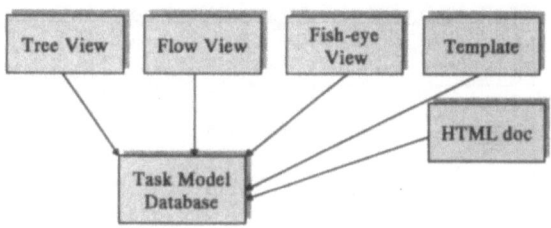

Fig. 3. Basic tool structure

5.3 Generating visual representations

Our tool EUTERPE uses the ontology directly to generate the visual representations. Consider a task tree. For editing and viewing the task tree we have program code that takes care of all the user interaction handling. To do this you need at least a tree datastructure that is created by querying the prolog engine. The algorithm looks like this:

procedure BuildTaskTree(startNode) {

    (1) ask the database for all subtasks of startNode (in Prolog: subtask(startNode,X))

    (2) add them as siblings of the startNode

    (3) call BuildTaskTree() for every sibling of startNode

}

This procedure recursively builds up a tree datastructure that is used in the tree drawing routines. In a similar way other views can be generated using the ontology. Consider the task flow representations of Figure 1. This task flow representation can be expressed using the triggering relationships as follows:

        triggers("Call friend","Take Metro",OR).

        triggers("Call friend","Walk",OR).

        triggers("Take Metro","Buy Ticket",NEXT).

        triggers("Walk","Buy Ticket",NEXT).

        triggers("Buy Ticket","Enter Cinema",NEXT)

A task flow viewer can generate visual representations by asking for the specified triggering relationships. The algorithm looks like this:

procedure BuildFlowGraph(startNode) {

    (1) ask the database for all tasks triggered by startNode (in Prolog: triggers(startNode,X,Y))

(2) add them as nodes and add edges between them and the startNode

(3) call BuildFlowGraph() for every node that has an edge starting in startNode

}

Note that even the extra task "Go There" can be automatically detected in case of a task tree with constructors; move tasks to the next level if the trigger type is not NEXT and tasks with NEXT triggers exist in that level.

For the templates similar techniques are being used, complemented by

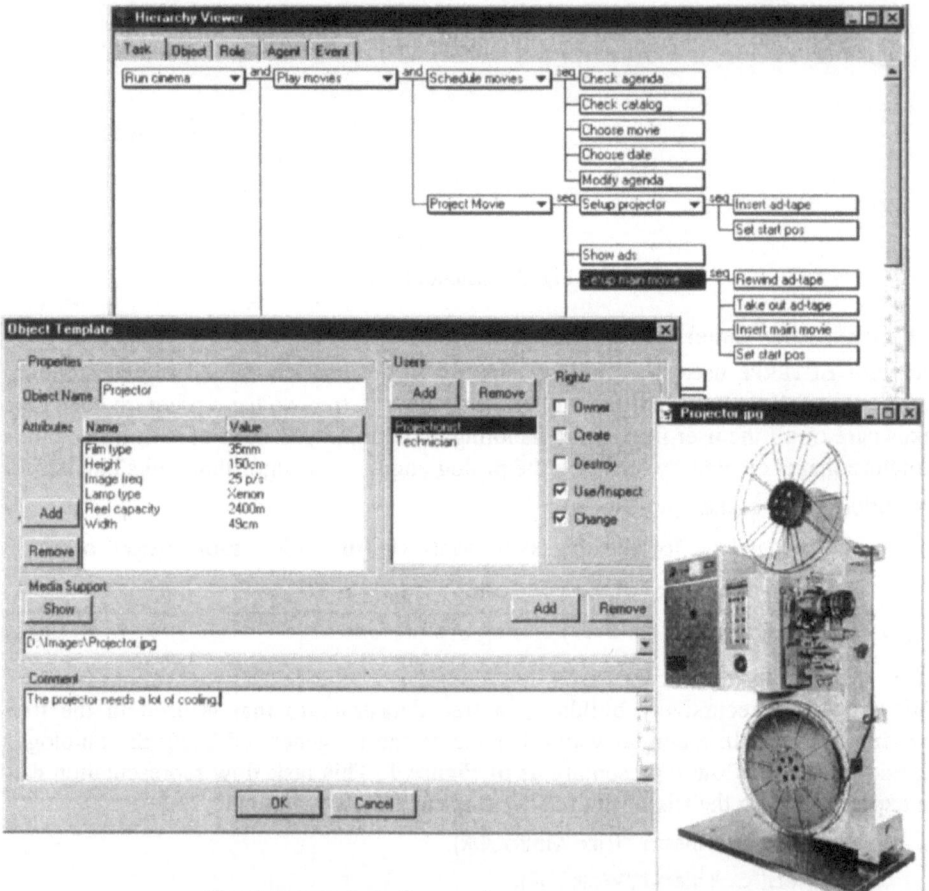

Fig. 4. Screenshot of some views

straightforward querying of attributes. Besides the relationships from the ontology Euterpe also uses derived relationships such as *involved_role* that was mentioned earlier.

6 Operationalizing the Ontology

Figure 4 shows some views that are generated based on the ontology. The user of the tool does not need to be completely aware of the underlying ontology. For the user it can be just a useful aid in a task analysis. However the ontology is the Structuring principle of the tool and the user is implicitly offered a structured approach to task analysis.

The operationalized ontology in the tool also contains an extra attribute *media_object* in every concept. It allows designers to attaches any kind of media such as movies, audio files or images to a concept. In this way results of ethnographic studies are also immediately available to the design team.

7 Conclusions

In this paper, we have covered:

1. Ingredients common to most task models, including task decomposition, task flow, and task world modeling.
2. How task modeling relates to the design of user interfaces.
3. Our proposed new ontology for task analysis, allowing multiple visual representations to be generated from the same data.
4. A task analysis tool showing how this ontology can be used to support the design of user interfaces.

We believe that task models should be based on a clear underlying ontology that captures all relevant aspects of the task world, and allows multiple visual representations to be generated from it. We hope that this will facilitate the process of using task models to aid the design of user interfaces.

Acknowledgements

We wish to thank Melissa G. Schofield and Steve P. Guest for their enthusiastic help and invaluable suggestions.

References

1. Bevan, N.: *Ergonomic requirements for office work with VDTs*. part 11, ISO DIS 9241-11
2. Card, S.K., Moran T.P., Newell, A.: *The Psychology of Human-Computer Interaction*. Hillsdale, NJ: Erlbaum
3. Johnson, P., Johnson, H.: *Task Knowledge Structures: Psychological basis and integration into system design*. Acta Psychologica 78, pp 3-26, 1991
4. Johnson, P., Wilson, S., Markopoulos, P., Pycock, J.: *Adept - Advanced Design Environment for Prototyping with Task Models*. Proceedings InterCHI'93, Demonstration Abstract, Addison-Wesley, April 1993.
5. Johnson, P., Johnson, H., Waddington, R., Shouls, A.: *Task-Related Knowledge Structures: Analysis, Modelling and Application*. People and Computers IV 1988, Proceedings 4th British Computer Society HCI group
6. Kirwan, B., Ainsworth, L.K.: *A Guide to Task Analysis*. Taylor & Francis Ltd 1992
7. Mayhew, D.J.: *Principles and Guidelines in Software User Interface Design*. ISBN 0-13-721929-6, Prentice Hall PTR, New Jersey, 1992.

8. Markopoulos, P., Gikas, S.: *Towards a Formal Model for Extant Task Knowledge Representation*. In C. Stary (ed.), First Interdisciplinary Workshop on Cognitive Modelling and User Interface Development, Vienna, December 1994.

9. Paterno, F., Mancini, C., Meniconi, S.: *ConcurTaskTrees: A Diagrammatic Notation for Specifying Task Models*. Proceedings of Interact 97, 14-18 July 1997

10. Scapin, D., Pierret-Golbreich, C.: *Towards a method for task description: MAD*. Work with display units 89, Elsevier, Amsterdam

11. Sebillotte, S.: *Hierarchical planning as method for task analysis: The example of office task analysis*. Behaviour and Information Technology *7(3)*, 275-293, 1988

12. Szekely, P., Luo, P., Neches, R.: *Beyond Interface Builders: Model-Based Interface Tools*. In Proceedings of INTERCHI '93 April, 1993, pp. 383-390

13. Tauber, M.J.: *ETAG: Extended Task Action Grammar - A language for the description of the user's task language*. In D. Diaper, D. Gilmore, G. Cockton and B. Shackel, Proceedings INTERACT '90, Amsterdam, Elsevier

14. van der Veer, G.C., Lenting, B.F., Bergevoet, B.A.J.: *GTA: Groupware Task Analysis - Modeling Complexity*. Acta Psychologica 91, 1996, pp. 297-322 Acta Paper

15. van der Veer, G.C., Mariani, M.: *Teaching Design of Complex Interactive Systems*. Learning by Interacting TeaDIS, Teaching Design of Interactive Systems, Schaerding, Austria, 20 - 23 May 1997

16. van der Veer, G.C., van Welie, M., Thorborg, D.: *Modeling Complex Processes in GTA*. Sixth European Conference on Cognitive Science Approaches to Process Control (CSAPC), pp. 87-91, Rome, Italy, 23-26 september 1997

17. Rex Hartson, H., Siochi, A.C., Hix, D.: *The UAN: a user-oriented representation for direct manipulation interface designs*. ACM Transactions on Information Systems Vol.8, No. 3 (July 1990), pp. 181-20

Formal Models for Cooperative Tasks: Concepts and an Application for En-Route Air Traffic Control

F. Paternò [(1)], C. Santoro [(1)], S. Tahmassebi [(2)]

[(1)] CNUCE-C.N.R., Pisa, Italy
[(2)] CENA, Toulouse, France

Abstract. This paper presents a proposal for specifying task models for cooperative applications that allow designers to describe the relationships between the activities performed by various users involved in cooperative environments. To this end we extend the ConcurTaskTree notation so that new information useful for describing complex cooperative applications can be clearly specified. An example of application to describe En-Route Air Traffic Control (ATC) is given to illustrate and clarify our approach.

1 Introduction

Formal methods are based on the use of notations with a precise semantics that allow designers to clarify many aspects, remove ambiguities in their specifications, and develop rigorous reasoning about the properties of these specifications. However, both learning and applying formal methods is time-consuming. We believe that these costs are motivated when designers consider applications where a bad design can generate heavy consequences.

Safety critical applications [6] are an interesting application area where the current user interfaces need to be improved, as demonstrated by several studies which show how most accidents are predominantly due to human errors and the need to improve their analysis [4]. It is thus important to develop a formal analysis of user interfaces for these applications [5] in order to have a full understanding of the possible effects of user interactions.

One of the most interesting results of the application of formal methods in the HCI field [9] is that precise descriptions of task models [7, 10, 13] can be given. Thus it is important to have a rich set of temporal operators and to define a precise semantics which can explain the behaviour described when these operators are composed in complex expressions.

In the European MEFISTO Project we aim to develop formal task models to improve the analysis and the design of safety critical interactive applications. We started by considering a case study consisting of an application for air traffic control during the en-route phase.

We soon realised that besides being a safety-critical application because an error caused by the controller can have serious consequences, it is also a highly cooperative application. In fact, for each sector there is one strategic controller and one executive controller, who communicate with each other and, in the application currently used, the executive controller communicates with the pilots, and the strategic controller communicates with the strategic controllers of the other neighbouring sectors.

This raises the need for an integrated analysis of usability, safety and cooperative aspects in the design of user interfaces for these applications. In fact, many of the possible safety and usability problems are related to how the various users cooperate with each other to reach common goals.

In the design of complex co-operative environments more and more attention is being paid to the horizontal mechanism of co-ordination between different roles. This calls for consequently more innovatiye tools and notations to describe these interactions. ConcurTaskTrees [11] is a notation that supplies a hierarchical graphical notation providing a precise semantics for describing concurrent task models of every role. However, in the previous version, it does not allow designers to specify explicitly how the cooperation among different users is performed, since each task model is related to only one user. When we developed the task model for the different types of users we thus realised that our notation provides good representations of task models of single users but it does not highlight sufficiently the co-operative aspects which are relevant for applications such as the ones considered in this report. This is a limitation for many approaches to task modelling, apart a few exceptions such as GTA [13].

We thus decided to develop an extension to our notation which allows designers to describe these co-operative aspects, yet still maintaining compatibility with the other parts of the ConcurTaskTrees specification that describe the task model associated with each user role. We aim to obtain a structured approach to the design of cooperative applications taking into account relevant aspects of this class of applications [1, 3]. More specifically the goals of the work presented in the paper are:

- *to describe a new proposal for specifying cooperative task models* based on the ConcurTaskTrees notation previously developed which has proved to be a powerful approach to describe task models but which was limited to address single users applications;
- *to show an application of the new proposal to a realistic case study,* this is important to understand the scalability of the approach which is a key element if it has to be used in analysing and designing real applications.

In this paper we first discuss the possible representations of temporal relationships between tasks performed by different users, and motivate our choice. Then we give the reader an overview of the main features of the case study considered. We describe the associated task model and indicate the relevant information that should be provided for describing the cooperative relationships. Finally, some concluding remarks and indications for future works are given.

2 How to specify cooperative task models

Task models for cooperative applications need to integrate different aspects. Designers can specify models describing the tasks from the viewpoint of different users, and then they have to indicate their relationships. This allows designers to analyse and develop task models from different angles and to check consistency and completeness. The viewpoints that we apply in the new version of ConcurTaskTrees are essentially of two types: the first one is the viewpoint of individual users, the second refers to the relationships among the tasks of various users in reaching global objectives. For example in the ATC application we consider below there are many *subjective* views (the strategic controller's view, the executive controller's view, the pilot's view), and only one *objective* view which gives an overall description of the working environment including communication between users.

We define a cooperative task as a task that requires activities from two or more users for its performance. After a user has performed a subtask belonging to a cooperative task, some reaction by one or more users is expected and necessary in order to complete the task. For example, the handling of the transfer of one flight to a new sector or the management of the conflict among two flights are two cooperative tasks since they require activities by more than one user. On the contrary, annotating one flight strip is not a cooperative task, according to our definition, because only one user performs it even though it might be a subtask of a cooperative task.

Note that in a cooperative environment, *all* the activities performed by the users obviously aim to eventually achieve the global goals. Nevertheless, we prefer to define «cooperative» only those tasks that strictly define the structure of cooperation, so that the roles users play with respect to the whole cooperative activity can be highlighted.

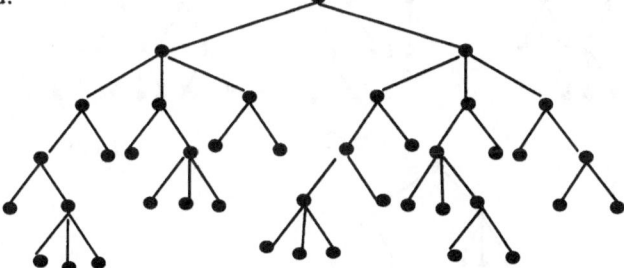

Fig. 1. The monolithic solution for cooperative task models

In order to extend the ConcurTaskTrees notation to explicitly providing representations of cooperative aspects there are at least three solutions:

- *A monolithic solution*, to develop directly one global task model including cooperative and single users tasks (see Figure 1). Note that in this picture (as in

74

the next two pictures) the parent-child relationship describes the hierarchical decomposition of the task in its sub-tasks;

- *A graph-oriented solution,* to join together the task tree of each role involved in a single structure in which any co-related actions or sub-tasks (performed by distinct users) are connected by lines or arcs with operators showing existing temporal relationships. For example, it should be possible to show a task of user1 activating a task of user2 by a line connecting the two tasks and the indication of the related temporal relationship associated with it (see Figure 2).

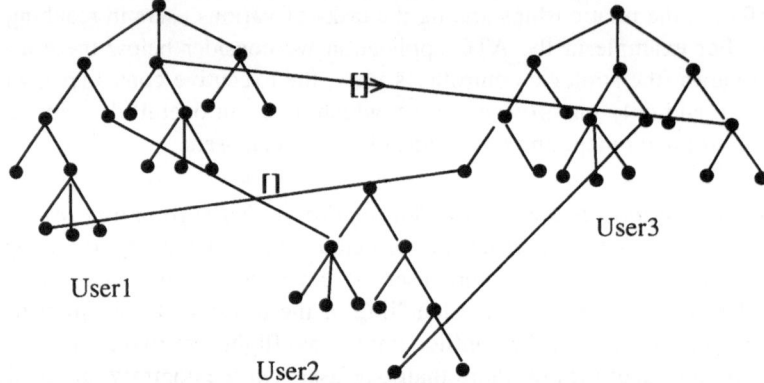

Fig. 2. A possible representation of temporal relationships between tasks of different users

- *An additional cooperative task solution,* to add another tree (the *Co-operative* tree) which shows the temporal relationship between tasks belonging to different users (see Figure 3). For each basic task the user who performs it is indicated. Then we still maintain for each role a tree indicating the related tasks.

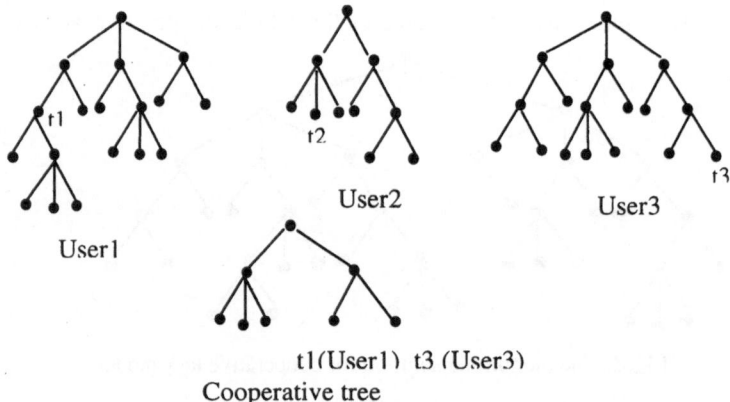

Fig. 3. Another possible representation of co-operative tasks

The first solution can easily generate task models that are too complex to interpret. Although the second solution is immediate, it does not seem to be the most effective especially when there is a high number of relations. In fact, as shown in Figure 2, the understanding of the overall behaviour might be difficult because the intersecting links could generate a complex graph.

We have decided to adopt the third solution (i.e. an additional cooperative task) because it enables designers to edit the cooperative part of the task model separately. This solution highlights the communicative aspects (information and/or activities) from the viewpoint of the tasks that involve cooperation among two or more users, their main features and their relationships.

3 Tool support for cooperative task models

In the specification of the co-operative aspects we still use a hierarchical representation with operators to describe temporal relationships among tasks at the same abstraction level. Thus we obtain an additional task tree whose main purpose is to define the relationships of the task trees associated with each type of user.

In this task tree we decompose the cooperative tasks until we obtain tasks performed by a single user. If such tasks can be further decomposed into subtasks performed by that user, the description of this decomposition is given in the task tree associated with the related user.

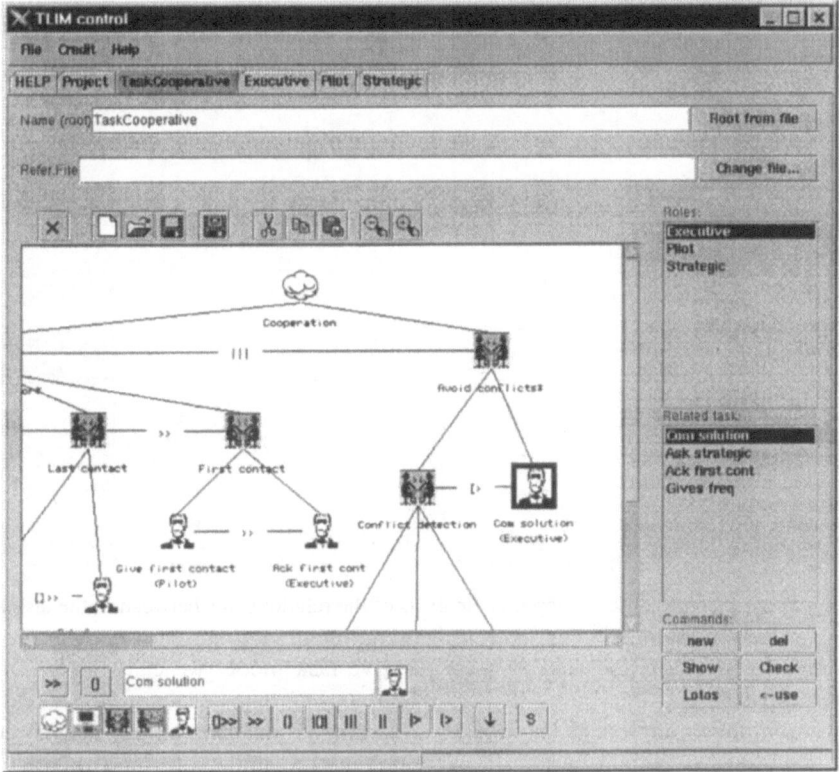

Fig. 4. The tool supporting analysis and editing of cooperative task models.

The leaves of the cooperative task tree can be either *basic* or *high level* tasks in the tree of the related user. In the first case, leaves in the cooperative tree remain leaves in the trees of the related users, whereas in the latter case the leaves in the cooperative tree will be further decomposed in the tree of the related user.

We are implementing a tool that supports the editing of cooperative task models in the third solution. When the user selects a basic task in the model of the cooperative part (see Figure 4, the *Com solution* task) this triggers another window (Figure 5). The new window shows the decomposition of the selected task in the task tree of the corresponding user, thus highlighting their relationships.

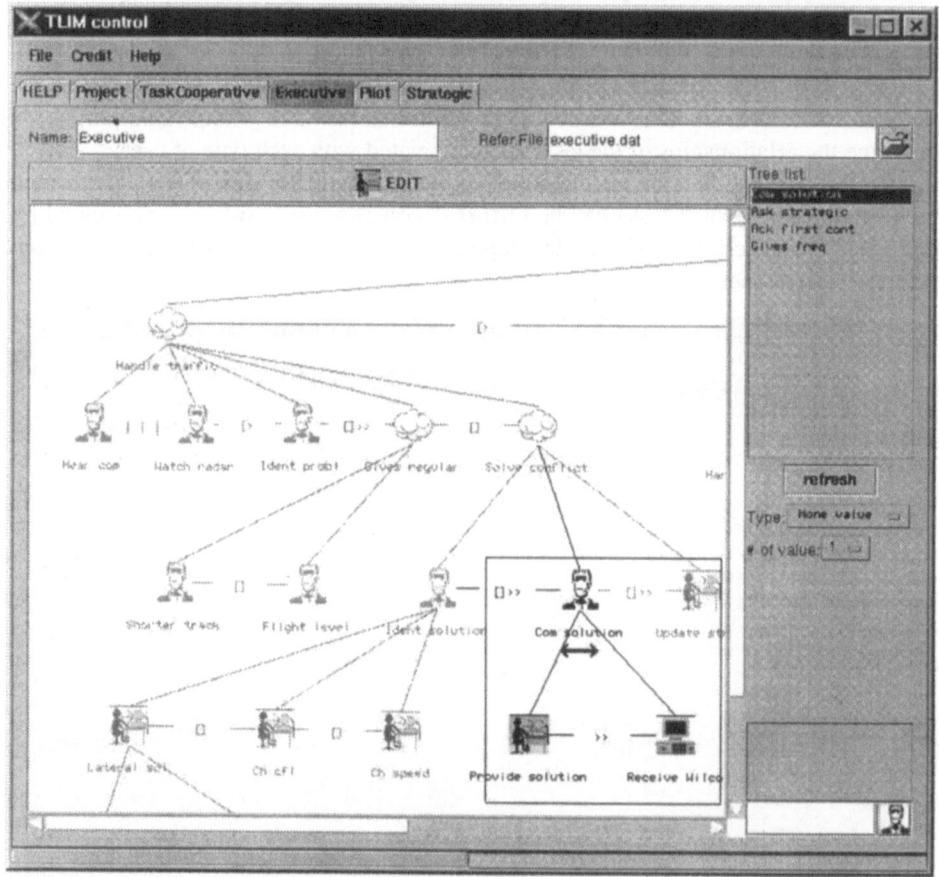

Fig. 5. An example of tool-supported analysis of the relationships between in the task model

In order to develop and analyse a cooperative task model we can follow two main approaches:

- a *top-down* approach, in which —starting from the overall activity of the system— we should derive the activities of the single roles and in what extent every role contributes to carry out the general activity

- a *bottom-up* approach, where the first analysis of every role's activity with the consequent initial task allocation helps to achieve a more modular comprehension of the overall behaviour in the cooperative application.

We preferred the second one in our case study because it allowed us a more structured and simpler way to achieve the specification of the task model for the cooperative application considered. Anyway it is worth to point out that the development of the specification was not a one-step process. It was an iterative process because once we had defined the specification of all the task trees (one tree for every role, and the cooperative tree) we had to check and modify it until the complete and correct specification was achieved. For example, if analysing whether all the activities had been described in the cooperative tree, we discovered that some were missing then we had to add them in the cooperative tree and then to analyse how every role takes part in them. Another point to note is that this approach forces the designer to check the possible inconsistencies or ambiguities inside the specification, so improving the correctness of the specification.

Designers need to specify other information apart from the roles that execute the subtask of the cooperative tasks. Thus, for each basic cooperative task (a cooperative task which is no longer decomposed into other cooperative tasks), we allow them to specify the following information:
1. task name,
2. roles of users involved,
3. names of the sub-tasks which have to be performed by each type of user,
4. the interaction media used to communicate,
5. type of communication protocol (for example, synchronous or asynchronous, point-to-point or broadcast), this aspect is often related to the media chosen,
6. the objects which are manipulated to perform the task,
7. roles cardinality (how many users for each role are involved in the cooperative task),
8. some additional informal comments that can be added to further describe the task or some of its main features.

4 The case study considered

We have considered an application for air traffic control during the en-route phase. The air space is divided into sectors. Two controllers control each sector: the executive and the strategic. They both perform surveillance and system updating tasks. Also, the executive controller is responsible above all for direct communication with pilots (by radio), the strategic controller for communication with the strategic controllers of other sectors.

Fig. 6. The contextual environment of a controller

The environment of a (French) controller (see Figure 6) includes radar screen, paper strips, and a touch input device which allows controllers to update in the ground system some flight data such as the time, level and track. The ground system generates and prints the paper strips, displays radar data, and manages flight plans. The paper strips are printed and delivered to a given control position about ten minutes before the flight enters the sector handled by that position. The main goal of this application is safety and regularity of flights (shorter time, less fuel consumption). In this context the main safety problem is to avoid flight conflicts, when two or more aircraft are in the same place at the same time.

5 The task model of the strategic controller

Below is an informal list of what a strategic controller typically does when only radio communication with pilots is supported:

- They receive information on paper strips about entering aircraft.
- They check possible conflicts with other aircraft in the air. If they detect any they inform the executive controller.
- When a flight is changing sector if problems are detected then they phone the strategic controller of the other sector and negotiate the optimal flight parameters to enter in the new sector (change parameters: level, track, etc.). When there is a change in sector the sender controller can change parameters and update the system, the receiver controller takes the strips, checks the colour and gives them to the executive.
- They can perform surveillance tasks: check conflicts and communicate with the executive for modifications.
- They can update the system at any time and not only when the aircraft is leaving a sector.

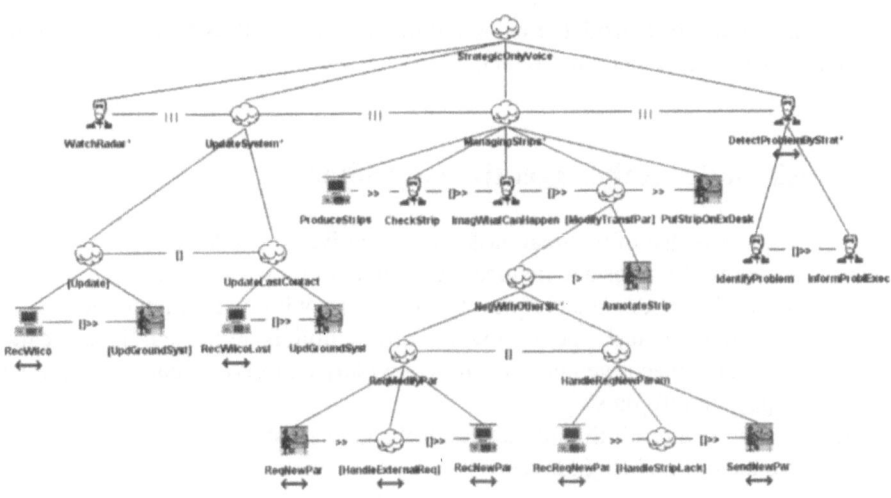

Fig. 7. The task model of the strategic controller

Figure 7 describes the activities of a strategic controller. There is a set of iterative activities (this is described by the iterative operator, *). At a high level of abstraction we can identify four main activities: watching the radar for surveillance purposes, updating the ground systems with the modifications of flight plans performed, managing strips, and detecting problems.

The concurrent activities (composed by the ||| operator) can be performed without any constraints on the number of times (thus these tasks are iterative). In the specification in Figure 7 we show only the first levels of the specification thus when an abstract task is on the bottom of the tree it means that it is further decomposed in the complete specification

Update system is decomposed into two cases: when the pilot communicates that the last contact will be performed then the system has always to be updated whereas in the other cases the updating of the system is optional (optional tasks are indicated with the name in squared brackets).

Managing strips means to check the paper strip which is generated by the system and contains information on a flight arriving into the sector. By considering the flight plan described in the paper strip the strategic controller has to imagine what can happen during the temporal evolution. Then there is an optional task. The option depends on whether there is the need to modify some flight parameter. If some parameters have to be modified this requires a negotiation with the strategic controller of the sector from where the flight is coming. In case of modification of parameters the strip is annotated. Finally the strip is located on the desk of the executive controller.

When a problem is detected the strategic controller informs the executive controller. The problem can be identified either watching the radar or because of the strips. The problem with the strips can be because the system failed to generate them either in the sector of the controller considered or in another sector (and thus there is a request of information from the related controller).

6 The task model of the executive controller

Below is an informal list of the main tasks for executive controllers:
- They receive flight strips and deduce the flight evolution;
- They receive the first contact request from the pilot with its flight parameters;
- In the first contact task the following information is indicated: identification, flight level. The executive checks if they are okay and gives clearance, otherwise s/he changes the info on strips;
- They give to the aircraft the frequency for the next sector;
- They give the optimal flight level;
- They control the aircraft and detect any possible conflicts (if conflicts are detected then they have to create a 3D separation whose parameters depend on the altitude).

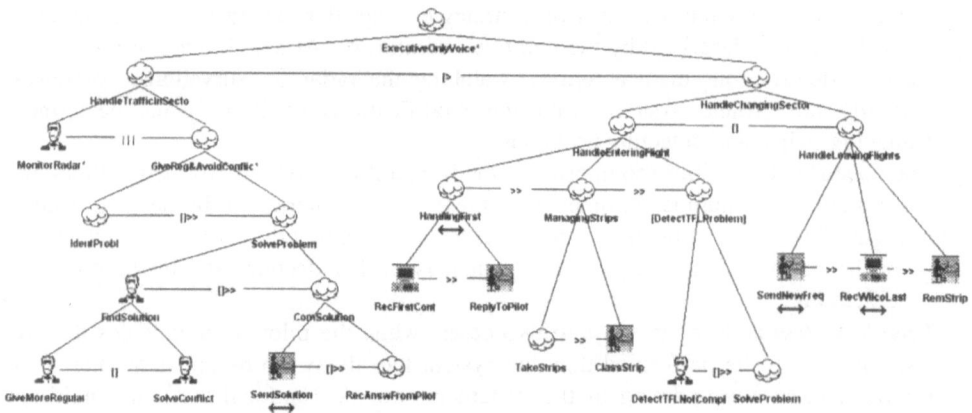

Fig. 8. The task model of the executive controller

The task model of the executive is first decomposed into two main activities: handling traffic inside the sector and handling change of sector of one flight. The first activity is decomposed in watching the radar for surveillance purposes and handling the air traffic (giving regularity to the flights and avoiding conflicts).

Once the executive controller identifies a problem which may require either giving more regularity to one flight (by giving a shorter track or changing a flight level) or solving a conflict then s/he has to identify a solution (that in the case of conflict can be a lateral solution, changing heading or beacon, or a vertical solution, changing flight level, or a longitudinal solution, changing speed) and finally to communicate it.

HandleChanging sector means either that a flight is leaving the sector or that a flight is entering into the sector.

In case of leaving flights, the executive controller gives the frequency of the next sector, receives the answer from the pilot and then removes the strip of the leaving flight. When there are entering flights the executive controller receives the first contact from the pilot, replies and then has to manage the related strip. Finally he can detect whether some flight parameters do not comply with the flight plan (optional task).

We recall that the priority order among operators is: choice > parallel composition > disabling > enabling, where choice is the "[]" operator, enabling is the ">>" operator and parallel composition can be either completely interleaving among tasks ("|||" operator), or interleaving with synchronisation on some actions.

7 The task model of the pilot

The task model of the pilot is very simplified and only considers those parts that are strictly connected to the tasks performed by the controllers. The pilot's normal behaviour can be interrupted by the *RequireExecOperation* or *Changing sector* tasks. In the ordinary course of events the pilot receives messages from the controllers, follows the flight plan and monitors the equipment.

RequireExecOperation means that the pilot sends a request to the executive controller for performing an operation. Then he waits for the answer and finally he sends either a command indicating the performance of the operation or the inability to perform it. When changing the sector the pilot first receives the frequency of the new sector from the controller of the old sector and then he provides the first contact to the controller of the new sector. In some cases after the first contact the executive can ask some information to the pilot.

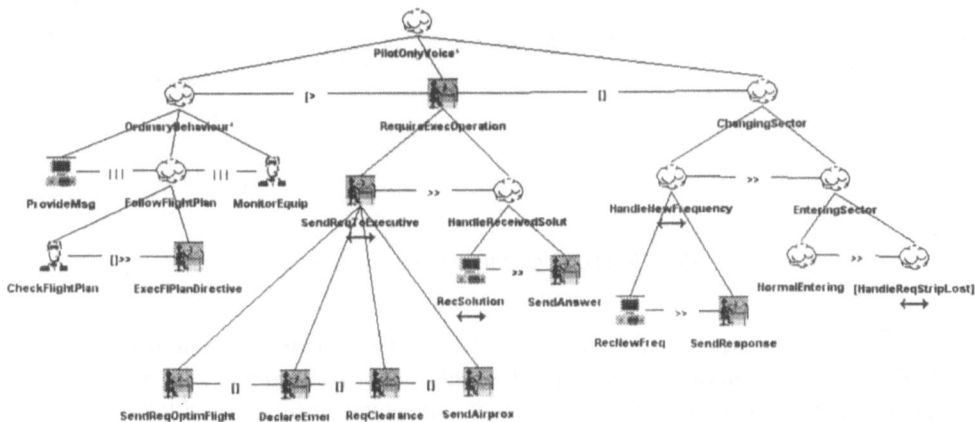

Fig. 9. The task model of the pilot

8 The specification of the cooperative tasks

We have defined above a *co-operative* task as a task which requires actions from two or more users for its performance. For example, the *Give Solution* task (see Figure 10) requires actions from the executive controller who sends the solution and the pilot who receives it.

In the specification in Figure 10 we can see that there are two main cooperative activities: one related to the change of sector of one flight and the other related to avoiding conflicts inside a sector.

The former can be subdivided into other cooperative tasks: handling last contact and first contact. After a first contact of one flight it is possible to activate the change of sector of another flight and the last contact of that flight concurrently.

The *HandleTrafficInSector* task can require cooperation among the executive controller, the strategic controller and the pilot or only between the two controllers. The cooperation can be motivated by the goal to optimise the flight (more regularity or less fuel consumption) or to solve a new problem.

The *ChangingSector* task can require also cooperation among strategic controllers associated with different sectors.

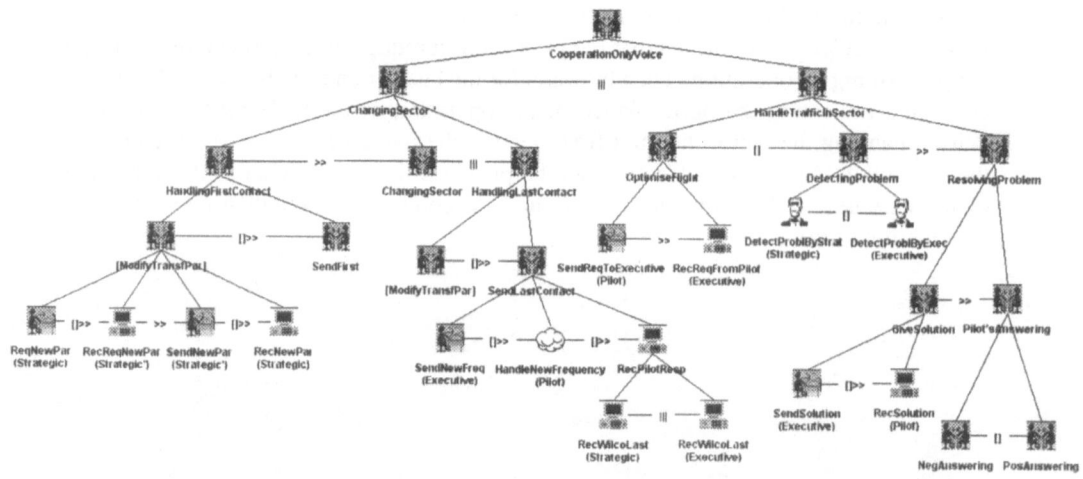

Fig. 10. The Cooperative tree of the example

The tasks that are performed to complete a cooperative task are indicated by the double arrow symbol in the related single user task model, whereas in the specification of the cooperative part there is one new type of icon (with two persons) which indicates cooperative tasks. In Figure 10 we show only the higher levels of the specification of the cooperations. When leaf in the tree is associated with a cooperative task it means that it will be further decomposed in the complete specification.

9 Templates for basic cooperative tasks

In addition, for each task in the cooperative part which cannot be further decomposed into other cooperative tasks we allow designers to specify the following information: task name, roles of users involved, names of the sub-tasks which have to be performed by each type of user, type of communication protocol (for example, synchronous, asynchronous and broadcast), roles cardinality, the media used to interact and communicate, the logical objects that the task needs to manipulate and some additional informal comments which can be added to further describe the task or some of its main features.

For example the *Send first* cooperative task which is part of the *Changing sector* co-operative task is described as:

task name: Send First; *roles involved*: pilot, executive controller; *subtasks performed by the users involved*: give first contact (pilot), acknowledge first contact (executive controller); *interaction media*: radiotelephony; *communication protocol*: asynchronous; role cardinality is one executive-many pilots with radiotelephony; *objects*: the conceptual objects used in this task are: frequency, sector and flight (see Table 4).

The *Send first* task involves two roles: the pilot and the executive controller. The pilot calls the executive controller of the entering sector. The controller replies with an acknowledgement message. They perform the *Give first contact* and *Ack first contact* subtasks respectively in order to complete the cooperative task. The communication flow is bidirectional, and it can be realised by radiotelephony. Because all the pilots crossing a sector share the same frequency the communication from the executive controller to the pilot is from *one* executive controller to *n* pilots in the radiotelephony case. We indicate an asynchronous communication protocol as we assume that after that the controller has given the frequency s/he can still perform other tasks before receiving an answer from the pilot.

We use a tabular representation to clearly indicate the information associated with a co-operative task as mentioned above. For example, the information concerning some of the cooperative tasks in the cooperative tree in Figure 10 are shown in the following tables.

T1	Task name = Send Last Contact
Roles and subtasks	*Executive*. SendNewFreq, RecWilcoLast *Pilot*: HandleNewFrequency *Strategic*: RecWilcoLast
Objects	Frequency, Sector, Flight
Interaction Media	RadioTelephony (VHF or HF)
Protocol	Asynchronous - Broadcast
Role Cardinality	Pilot : Executive : Strategic (N,1, 1)
[Comments]	The executive controller of the exiting sector gives the new frequency to the pilot who provides an answer to the controllers.

Table 1. The table for *Send Last Contact* task

T2	Task name = Optimise flight
Roles and subtasks	*Pilot*: SendReqToExecutive *Executive*: RecReqFromPilot
Objects	Flight level, Speed, Heading
Interaction Media	Telephone
Protocol	Asynchronous - Broadcast
Role Cardinality	Pilot : Executive (N,1)
[Comments]	The pilot asks for some optimisation of the route of the flight

Table 2. The table for *Optimise flight* task

T3	Task name = ModifyTransPar
Roles and subtasks	$Strategic_i$, ReqNewPar, RecNewPar $Strategic_{i+1}$, RecReqNewPar, SendNewPar
Objects	Frequency, Sector, Flight
Interaction Media	Telephone
Protocol	Synchronous - Point to Point
Role Cardinality	$Strategic_i \leftrightarrow Strategic_{i+1}$ (1,1)
[Comments]	The strategic controller of one sector interacts with the strategic controller of a neighbouring sector in order to negotiate the parameters of one flight which is changing sector

Table 3. The table for *ModifyTransPar* task

10 Conclusions

In this work we have presented a new approach to modelling tasks in cooperative applications and we have shown its application to a case study in the air traffic control field. We have identified various benefits of the use of formal task models:

- An understanding of how the activities in the current work context of the application considered are carried out;
- The possibility of analysing a cooperative activity from different viewpoints (the *subjective* points of view of each role involved in the cooperation and the *objective* point of view of the overall activity);
- A useful aid to the identification of what the "shared" (in some sense "critical") objects involved in the cooperation are.

Future work will be dedicated to consider the following aspects:

- The use of task models for analysing and evaluating the different organisation of activities determined in the application considered by the introduction of new technologies or by different design choices. For example, the introduction of a data link communication between controllers and pilots;
- In order to consider more safety-critical applications we plan to integrate the approach presented with Hazop-like techniques. The goal is to combine the advantages of the first one (to clearly specify the cooperations occurring in an application) with those of the second one (to support identification of possible deviations with respect to the design intent, during the cooperations, which can generate hazardous situations).

Acknowledgements

This work is supported by the MEFISTO (http://giove.cnuce.cnr.it/mefisto.html) European Esprit Reactive Long Term Research Project (N.24963).

References

1. Calvary, G., Coutaz, J., Nigay, L.: From Single-User Architectural Design to PAC*: a Generic Software Architecture Model for CSCW, pp. 242-249, ACM Press, Proceedings CHI'97.

2. Druart, J., Novales, L.: En route Control Standards. Mefisto Report WP1-4, November 1997.

3. Dix, A.: In: Beale R. (eds.): Remote Cooperation, Springer Verlag 1996.

4. Field, R., Wright, P., Harrison, M.: A task centred approach to analysing human error tolerance requirements. IEEE Press, Proceedings RE'95, York.

5. Johnson C.W.: The Formal Analysis of Human-Computer Interaction During Accident Investigations. In: Cockton, G., Draper, S., Weir,G. (eds.): People and Computers, IX, pp. 285-300, Cambridge Uni. Press, 1994.

6. Levenson, N.: Safeware, System Safety and Computers. Addison Wesley Publishing Company, 1995.

7. Markopoulos, P., Johnson, P., Rowson, J.: Formal Aspects of Task-based Design., pp. 209-224. Springer Verlag, Proceedings DSV-IS'97.

8. Palanque, P., Bastide, R., Paternò, F.: Formal Specification as a Tool for Objective Assessment of Safety Critical Systems, pp. 323-330. Chapman&Hall, Proceedings Interact'97.

9. Palanque, P., Paternò, F. (eds.): Formal Methods in Human-Computer Interaction. Springer Verlag , FACIT Series, ISBN 3-540-76158-6, 1997.

10. Paternò, F.: Understanding Task Model and User Interface Architecture Relationships, CNUCE Internal Report, December 1997.

11. Paternò F., Mancini C., Meniconi, S.: ConcurTaskTrees: A Diagrammatic Notation for Specifying Task Models, pp. 362-369, Proceedings Interact'97.

12. Tahmassebi, S.: Controller Pilot Data Link Communication (CPDLC) description, Mefisto Report WP1-1, November 1997.

13. Van der Veer, G., Lenting, B., Bergevoet, B.: GTA: Groupware task analysis - Modelling complexity, pp. 297-322. Acta Psychologica, 91, 1996.

The role of formal proof in modelling interactive behaviour

Richard Butterworth[1], Ann Blandford[1] and David Duke[2]

[1] School of Computing Science, Middlesex University, London, N11 2NQ. UK.
[2] Department of Computer Science, University of York, York, YO1 5DD. UK.

Abstract. When proving properties of formally described interactive systems, trade-offs have to be made between the simplicity of the model — which relates to the ease of performing proofs — and the real-world validity of the model. This issue is particularly important when the proof incorporates properties of user behaviour as well as the device specification. This paper discusses these trade-offs, using a simple model of a web-browsing system as an example. The property we focus on relates to usability: showing whether or not the things a user wants to do are easy to do.

As well as adding detail to move from a point where the modelled system is simple but does not satisfy a stated usability property, through a model that satisfies the property but is 'unreasonable', to one that is both reasonable and usable, we also move from a 'safety'-based proof to a 'liveness'-based proof, arguing that although liveness proofs are generally more difficult to execute, they correspond better to our intuitive understanding of what it means for a system to be usable, and are therefore more valuable.

1   Introduction

A formal design process involves the iteration through a proposal, evaluation and refinement of system models until the models are so refined that they can be implemented as actual systems. Formal cognitive modelling allows usability decisions to be made early in the interactive system design life-cycle rather than in a *post hoc* manner as is more prevalent in current design practice. (We define 'system' as the closed composition of all the entities that we are interested in during an analysis, not just the automated part of the system, which we refer as the 'device'. Hence when we refer to a system we include the user population.)

Methodologies and techniques for describing and refining device models formally are well researched and documented (*e.g.* [2, 15, 9] *etc.*) and there is now a considerable literature (*e.g.* [11, 12, 14] *etc.*) describing how formal techniques can be applied to the design of highly interactive systems. However, these techniques do not, in general, incorporate explicit assumptions about user behaviour within the system about which properties are proved.

We draw on the work of the PUMA (Programmable User Modelling Applications) project to incorporate a more user-centred perspective, by capturing cognitive models used in PUM (Programmable User Models) [17, 4, 5] in a rigorous, formal manner and showing how they can be integrated into a more formal development cycle. This paper reports on work done of formalising the cognitive models. This has been done in a very abstract way that focuses on user behaviour, rather than user cognition. Our long term aim is propose a corpus of cognitive models expressed at varying levels of abstraction and complexity. Furthermore we wish to show the interrelations between these models and be explicit about what properties we believe the models to be good at demonstrating.

1.1 Usability properties and formal proof

A property is a general statement about system behaviour that (typically) we would like a system to fulfill. Much previous work (*e.g.* [16, 10]) has catalogued usability properties (and accompanying device and user models), but in many cases it has not been demonstrated how one would go about actually proving that a given model fulfills a given property. Proof is often seen as a costly business; it is time consuming and highly skilled. Reasoned argument and simulation often come to the same conclusions (a conclusion being a statement of whether a model will be usable or not) as a full proof without the effort involved. In this paper we exemplify some proofs performed on very simple models of interactive systems and discuss issues such as perceived cost of proof and the insights gained by performing proofs.

Previously [3] we have formalised a PUM-like cognitive architecture and shown how we can simulate behaviour with it. This model was rather operational in nature and it is doubtful whether it could be used to formally prove arbitrary usability properties. In this paper we have pared the cognitive assumptions to a bare minimum to give a model which we can prove properties for. Having done so we can discuss whether such models are expressive enough to capture properties with real world validity.

1.2 User models in a design process

A cognitively valid model of a user allows device models to be analysed in terms of usability. The analytic approach we demonstrate here concerns the proposal and description of a device model, cognitive assumptions and a usability property (of the type 'the user finds it easy to do what she wants to do'). We then show how we can test whether the composition of the device model and cognitive assumptions fulfill the usability property, and then how we change the cognitive assumptions such that the property is satisfied. This process allows the analyst to gauge whether the assumptions made about the user's knowledge and actions for that user to successfully interact are plausible or reasonable. If they are not then this would suggest the need for the redesign of the device model.

Putting this a little more formally: both system models and usability properties can be expressed as temporal logic formulae. Given a user model *user* and a device model *device* the system is the conjunction of the two; $user \land device$.

Furthermore, given a usability property *prop* then showing that the property is fulfilled by the system is a case of showing that...

$$device \land user \Rightarrow prop$$

(In other words, if the system model is 'true' then the property must hold true also.) Now assume that we show that the system does not fulfill the property ($device \land user \not\Rightarrow prop$) so we propose a further constraint *implausible* and show that the addition of this constraint fulfills the property...

$$device \land (user \land implausible) \Rightarrow prop$$

Now we decide that *implausible* is an unreasonable demand to place on the user; assuming we cannot devise another constraint which, added to the system, fulfills the property then this suggests that the device needs redesigning.

This is a sketch of one way that user models can fit into a formal design process; the common theme with all such approaches is that they force us to make assumptions explicit and inspectable. These assumptions can then be discussed and validated (or not) by workers who need not be software engineers or formalists. In the case above we would want to ask a human factors expert whether or not *implausible* is a reasonable assumption to make.

The formal language used in this paper is Lamport's TLA (Temporal Logic of Actions) [13] which allows the expression of system models and properties as temporal logic formulae, and has proof techniques defined for it.

1.3 Safety and liveness

Alpern and Schneider [1] showed that any system can be described as a conjunction of 'safety' and 'liveness' properties. A safety property is one which states that 'bad' things never happen within a system whereas liveness states that something 'good' eventually happens within a system.

We propose two formal descriptions of interactive systems which we call the safe model and the live model. We prove very similar properties with them. The difference between the two is that the safety property states that the user *can never* get into a 'bad' situation, whereas the liveness property states that user *always does* something 'good'.

The safety proof is rather simpler than the corresponding liveness proof yet we believe that the liveness properties tend to be a more intuitive representation of the properties we are trying to describe. We illustrate their relative strengths in the example presented below, then discuss the issues raised in conducting these proofs.

2 The 'safe' model of web browsing behaviour

As our example in this paper, we present a model of web browsing behaviour. We first model the state space of the system, followed by the actions both the device and the user can perform, and then bring all this together into a system specification.

2.1 The state space

The web A web is modelled as a graph of linked nodes. Each node is a page and a link is a pair of pages, directionally linking the first page in the pair to the second.

$$Page \mathrel{\hat{=}} \ldots \tag{1}$$

$$pages \,:\, \mathcal{P}(Page) \tag{2}$$

$$links \,:\, \mathcal{P}(pages \times pages) \tag{3}$$

pages and *links* are treated as 'fixed variables' ('constants' in traditional programming terms) — their value does not change over the behaviour of the system. Hence this model does not capture a dynamic web exemplified by search engines *etc.*

The web browsing device The device consists of two variables which represent the 'history list' of a web browser.

$$history : Page^* \tag{4}$$

$$index : \mathbb{N} \tag{5}$$

history is a list of the pages visited, maintained by the device, and *index* points to one of those pages as the current page. (Note that *index* must always have a value between 1 and the length of *history*.) The device state is the composition of these two variables. For readability reasons the variable *dev* denotes all the variables in the device.

$$dev \mathrel{\hat{=}} (history, index) \tag{6}$$

The user There is a set of pages that the user would consider to be interesting and would wish to visit.

$$interesting : \mathcal{P}(Page) \tag{7}$$

Again this is treated as a fixed variable — we do not consider cases where the user modifies her ideas about what is and is not interesting mid-interaction. Derived from this and the model of the web is the relationship *goodLinks*, which holds if a page is linked to an *interesting* page.

$$goodLinks \mathrel{\hat{=}} \{(p,q) \mid p \, links \, q \wedge q \in interesting\} \tag{8}$$

An obvious and useful fact to which we shall refer is that *goodLinks* is a sub-set of *links*.

$$goodLinks \subseteq links \tag{9}$$

The user maintains a variable *mustVisit*, which is a collection of pages they find *interesting* and that they have seen links to during their interaction.

$$mustVisit : \mathcal{P}(Page) \tag{10}$$

Note that *mustVisit* should always be a sub-set of *interesting*. The variable *cog* denotes all the cognitive variables (although in this model it seems fairly vacuous — there being only one).

$$cog \,\hat{=}\, (mustVisit) \tag{11}$$

2.2 System actions

The user The user performs one action on her cognitive state, namely to look at the links exposed on the current page and add appropriately to her *mustVisit* set.

$$View \,\hat{=}\, mustVisit' = mustVisit \cup \{p \mid history'(index')\, goodLinks\, p\} \tag{12}$$

View is an action; it describes a change in state. Unprimed variables denote the value of that variable at the beginning of the action and primed variables denote their value at the completion of the action. $x' = x + 1$ is the action of incrementing x for example. (Note that *history* and *index* are primed because we shall assert that *View* occurs in parallel with device actions and we want *mustVisit* to be updated with the new links exposed as a result of the device action completing.)

The device The device allows the user to invoke two actions — *Go*ing to a page in the history list and *Jump*ing to a page linked to the current page.

$$\begin{aligned} Go(n:\mathbb{N}) \,\hat{=}\,\ &1 \le n \le |history| \,\wedge \\ &history' = history \,\wedge \\ &index' = n \end{aligned} \tag{13}$$

$$\begin{aligned} Jump(p:Page) \,\hat{=}\,\ &history(index)\, links\, p \,\wedge \\ &history' = history(1\mathinner{\ldotp\ldotp}index)^\frown\langle p\rangle \,\wedge \\ &index' = index + 1 \end{aligned} \tag{14}$$

Note that if a jump is performed when the index is not at the end of the history list then the end of the list is 'pruned'. (This model is based on the Netscape stack with pointer model as described in [8].)

2.3 System behaviour

Now we can discuss the behaviour of the system. Initially the system starts with a single page in the history list and the user has decided that she *mustVisit* all the interesting pages linked to it.

$$init \,\hat{=}\, dev = (\langle p\rangle, 1) \wedge cog = (\{q \mid p\, goodLinks\, q\}) \tag{15}$$

The user performs a *View* action every time there is a device action. Overall, therefore, the next state action of the system $\mathcal{A}$ is the disjunction of each device action conjoined with *View*.

$$\mathcal{A} \,\hat{=}\, (View \wedge Go(n)) \vee (View \wedge Jump(p)) \tag{16}$$

The system specification is the initial condition and the stuttering repetition of this action.

$$\Phi \,\hat{=}\, init \wedge \Box[\mathcal{A}]_{(dev,cog)} \tag{17}$$

This formula describes any behaviour which starts in a state described by *init* and henceforth[1] each subsequent state change is either the null state change[2] or is described by the action $\mathcal{A}$. We do not deal with fairness in this model, a point that we shall return to later.

2.4   Proving properties

Now we have a formula Φ that represents the interactive system. We can also express properties of this system as a temporal logic formula P. Showing that the system fulfills property P is a case of showing that the theorem $\Phi \Rightarrow P$ holds.

A usability property One of the problems with web browsing is that the user is offered many choices about where to go next in their interaction and more than one of these choices may be of interest to the user. Therefore the user will navigate down branches that are interesting, then should be able to back up the branch to other interesting pages and navigate on from there. One usability problem, as anyone who has used the web knows, is that getting lost becomes very easy and a huge amount of frustration arises from having seen a page that looks interesting, but not being able to get back to it.

More formally we propose a usability property whereby all the pages the user has seen that are interesting (*i.e.* the set *mustVisit*) can be easily visited. We define *easyVisit* as the set of all pages that it is easy for the user to visit. *i.e.* all those pages on the history list or at most one jump away from a page on the history list.

$$easyVisit \triangleq \{p \mid history(i) \; links \; p \land 1 \leq i \leq |history|\} \cup \mathbf{ran} \; history \quad (18)$$

Therefore our usability property requires that every page in *mustVisit* is also in *easyVisit*.

$$usable \triangleq mustVisit \subseteq easyVisit \quad (19)$$

To show that the specification of the browsing system fulfills this property we need to show that...

$$\Phi \Rightarrow \Box(usable) \quad (20)$$

An attempt to prove the usability property Here we sketch an attempt to prove theorem 20. The proof fails and it would be easy to show this by a simple counter example. However we follow the steps of the proof through here because most of the proof is reused in the next section.

---

[1] The temporal operator $\Box$ denotes 'henceforth' or 'always'.

[2] Square brackets around an action denote the action itself or the null state change (*i.e.* no change to the variables sub-scripted to the action). $[\mathcal{Q}]_x \triangleq \mathcal{Q} \lor x = x'$

The proof of formula 20 decomposes into the following two theorems according to the rule INV1 from the TLA proof rules [13, Fig 5, pg 888]...

$$init \Rightarrow usable \tag{21}$$

$$usable \wedge [\mathcal{A}]_{(cog,dev)} \Rightarrow usable' \tag{22}$$

(Note that $usable'$ denotes a formula such that all the free variables in $usable$ are primed; $mustVisit' \subseteq easyVisit'$.) Informally the rationale behind this is quite simple — $usable$ must hold in the initial state and if $usable$ holds before the action $\mathcal{A}$ it must hold after too. Hence $usable$ must hold at all times during the behaviour of the system.

Formula 21 is simple to demonstrate; by substituting the definitions of $init$, $easyVisit$ and $usable$ we get the equivalent formula...

$$mustVisit = \{q \mid p\,goodLinks\,q\} \wedge easyVisit = \{q \mid p\,links\,q\} \cup \{p\}$$
$$\Rightarrow \tag{23}$$
$$mustVisit \subseteq easyVisit$$

... which can be seen to be true, based on the fact that $goodLinks$ is a sub-set of $links$ (formula 9).

The proof of formula 22 decomposes into the stuttering case and the disjoined actions as follows...

$$usable \wedge ((dev, cog) = (dev, cog)') \Rightarrow usable' \tag{24}$$

$$usable \wedge (View \wedge Go(n)) \Rightarrow usable' \tag{25}$$

$$usable \wedge (View \wedge Jump(p)) \Rightarrow usable' \tag{26}$$

Formula 24 is easy to show; $easyVisit$ is derived from the device state dev and $mustVisit$ is the cognitive state cog. If $mustVisit \subseteq easyVisit$ before the stuttering action and neither the device or cognitive state change then neither do $mustVisit$ and $easyVisit$ and $mustVisit \subseteq easyVisit$ must hold after the stuttering action.

To prove formula 25 we attempt to show that what is added to the set $mustVisit$ is a sub-set of $easyVisit$. Note that the action Go does not alter $history$ and therefore does not alter $easyVisit$ either, which is derived from it. So in this context $easyVisit$ and $easyVisit'$ are interchangeable. The set theoretic axiom we appeal to is...

$$A \subseteq X \wedge B \subseteq X \Rightarrow (A \cup B) \subseteq X \tag{27}$$

We substitute $easyVisit'$ for X, $mustVisit$ for A and what is added to $mustVisit$ by the action $View$ for B. Therefore $mustVisit'$ is $A \cup B$.

By substituting in the definitions appropriately we arrive at the following formula...

$$\{p \mid history'(index')\,goodLinks\,p\}$$
$$\subseteq \tag{28}$$
$$\{p \mid history'(i)\,links\,p \wedge 1 \leq i \leq |history'|\} \cup \mathbf{ran}\,history'$$

As we know that $goodLinks$ is a sub-set of $links$ and that $index'$ is always between 1 and $|history'|$ then we argue that the above formula must hold and

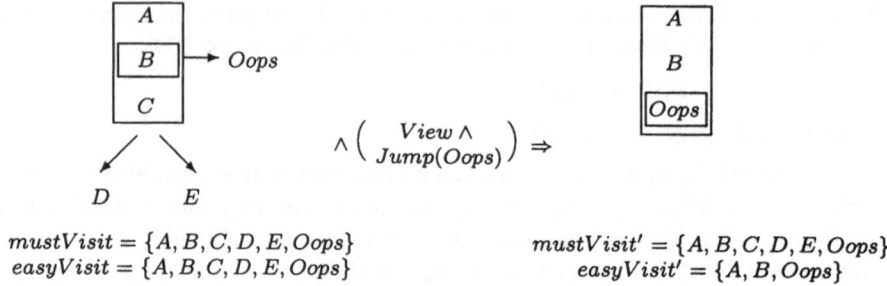

$$mustVisit = \{A, B, C, D, E, Oops\}$$
$$easyVisit = \{A, B, C, D, E, Oops\}$$

$$mustVisit' = \{A, B, C, D, E, Oops\}$$
$$easyVisit' = \{A, B, Oops\}$$

Fig. 1. A counter example to formula 26

therefore formula 25 also holds.

Formula 26 does not hold and we show this by counter example. Figure 1 represents this counter example. The history list contains three pages A, B and C and the current page is B (*i.e. index = 2*). There are *goodLinks* to pages D and E from C and there is a *goodLink* to *Oops* from B. Therefore *mustVisit* = *easyVisit* = $\{A, B, C, D, E, Oops\}$, so trivially *mustVisit* ⊆ *easyVisit*.

Now assume the action *View* ∧ *Jump(Oops)* takes place. C is pruned from the history list and therefore D and E can no longer be *easyVisited*. They remain in *mustVisit* however, therefore *mustVisit'* ⊄ *easyVisit'*.

Because formula 26 does not hold, the rest of the proof fails. Hence we conclude that $\Phi \not\Rightarrow \Box(usable)$.

2.5 The more constrained model

So we have shown that there is a usability problem with a system that fulfills the simple specification given here. In a sense this is obvious (and certainly obvious to anyone who has used a web browser and found that a great chunk of their history list has mysteriously and irretrievably vanished) because the history mechanism implemented by the device is 'lossy'; if the user *Jumps* when not at the end of the history list then some of the list is lost.

If we think of ourselves as users we can argue that we can overcome this problem by only *Jumping* when at the end of the history list. Hence none of the history list is lost and we will always be able to easily visit any *interesting* pages we have seen links to. This is simply formalised by adding a further precondition to the *Jump(p)* ∧ *View* action. This gives a new action $\mathcal{A}_c$ (where the subscripted c stands for 'constrained') and a new specification Φ_c.

$$\mathcal{A}_c \hat{=} (View \wedge Go(n)) \vee (View \wedge Jump(p) \wedge index = |history|) \tag{29}$$

$$\Phi_c \hat{=} init \wedge \Box[\mathcal{A}_c]_{(dev,cog)} \tag{30}$$

Now we propose that this constrained specification fulfills the usability property.

$$\Phi_c \Rightarrow \Box(usable) \tag{31}$$

We have already performed the majority of this proof in the previous section. All we need to prove here is that. . .

$$usable \wedge (View \wedge Jump(p) \wedge index = |history|) \Rightarrow usable' \qquad (32)$$

We start by rewriting the *Jump* action to take account of the new precondition. . .

$$\begin{pmatrix} Jump(p) \wedge \\ index = |history| \end{pmatrix} \Leftrightarrow \begin{pmatrix} history(index) \; links \; p \; \wedge \\ history' = history^\frown \langle p \rangle \; \wedge \\ index' = index + 1 \end{pmatrix} \qquad (33)$$

Now we can substitute in the various definitions based on this new action to get the following to statement. . .

$$(Jump(p) \wedge View \wedge index = |history|) \Rightarrow \qquad (34)$$
$$mustVisit' = mustVisit \cup \{q \mid p \; goodLinks \; q\} \wedge$$
$$easyVisit' = easyVisit \cup \{q \mid p \; links \; q\} \cup \{p\}$$

The important part here is to see that *easyVisit* expands by all the pages *link*ed to p; it cannot contract because it is derived from *history* which is no longer lossy. *mustVisit* expands by the *interesting* sub-set of those added to *easyVisit* and we can conclude therefore that *mustVisit'* is a sub-set of *easyVisit'*.

Hence we have a proof of formula 32 and combining this with formulae 25, 24, 21 and 22 allows us to conclude that formula 31 holds. QED.

3   A critique of the safe model

Let us take a step back and see what we have done here. We have specified a system Φ and shown that it does not fulfill a simple usability property. We then added a constraint to the specification giving Φ_c and showed that this specification did fulfill the property. There are a number of points raised here.

Firstly what exactly does this constraint represent? A constraint by its nature reduces the possible behaviours of a system. We may consider Φ to be a 'shorthand' for the set of behaviours where anything can happen within the bounds of legality for the device; from the user's point of view Φ represents the set of all possible web search strategies, even very bad ones. Φ_c represents a sub-set of Φ, constraining the strategies to a set we consider to be 'good'.

How then would this constraint be implemented on the actual system? It cannot be implemented by the device, because it exists to prevent the user from throwing away (links to) pages that the user *mustVisit*. *mustVisit* is a cognitive variable and therefore not apparent to the device. Furthermore, browsers are very *laissez faire* when it comes to how they allow users to browse. Therefore the constraint lies with the user — in order not to have problems getting to pages that have been seen but not yet visited, a user must only use the browser in a very constrained manner. It is not difficult to argue that this constraint is too heavy — indeed it prevents much behaviour that could be considered to be good.

Imagine a situation where the user has been browsing and has been loyally only performing *Jumps* when at the end of the history list. Now she comes to a page where there are no interesting links to follow, but there are unexplored interesting links from pages up the history list. She *Goes* to one of these pages but now cannot actually *Jump* to it because this action has been constrained out of the behaviour. Paradoxically we have ensured that the user never loses the *potential* of easily visiting an interesting page whilst denying her the *ability* to do so! With these arguments we could claim that the constraint modelled here is fundamentally flawed.

An answer to this problem is to never allow *Jumps* from the history list when doing so would lose pages with unvisited *interesting* links from them; we assume that once the user has visited a page then she does not mind not visiting it again.

On a different level however there are peculiarities with the model itself; notably the system is not 'live' — a sequence consisting of no state changes is legal according to this specification and what is more peculiar, such a 'null' sequence would satisfy our usability property. The problem (if it is a problem) is that we have modelled what a user *can do* as opposed to what they *actually do*. What we have demonstrated is that a 'safety property' holds for the system. A safety property is one that states that nothing bad ever happens; in this case we have shown that no pages the user wants to visit are difficult to visit. What we have *not* shown is that the user actually *will* visit the pages they want to — this would be a 'liveness property' (where liveness expresses that something good eventually happens). So the constrained model does not actually say that the system *does not* act in an un*usable* way, it says that the system *cannot* act in an un*usable* way. The two are subtly different.

We would argue however, that as long as the modeller is explicit about what the model represents then there should be no problem. Indeed taking what primarily appears to be a liveness problem and converting it to a safety problem has the distinct advantage that safety proofs are simpler and better supported by automated tools.

4   A live model of web browsing behaviour

In order to address the problems discussed above we now reformulate the model. We will attempt to show a property asserting that if the user decides to visit a page then she will eventually do so.

The device side of the model remains unaltered; *pages, links, history, index, dev, Go* and *Jump* all retain their previous definitions.

On the user side there is still the fixed variable *interesting* and the flexible variable *mustVisit*. However we now introduce a new flexible variable which represents all the pages so far visited...

$$hasVisited : \mathcal{P}(Page) \tag{35}$$

cog needs to be redefined in order to denote the fact that the cognitive state consists of two flexible variables.

$$cog \; \hat{=} \; (hasVisited, mustVisit) \tag{36}$$

Also the derived relation *goodLinks* is changed to capture the fact that we do not want our users to visit pages that have already been visited.

$$goodLinks \; \hat{=} \; \{(p, q) \mid p \; links \; q \wedge q \in (interesting \setminus hasVisited)\} \tag{37}$$

Note that *goodLinks* is no longer fixed because it is derived from the flexible variable *hasVisited*. It is still the case that $goodLinks \subseteq links$ however.

Initially the browser has one page in the history list; the user has visited it and decided on the pages she would like to visit that are linked to it. For reasons that will become apparent later we define a specific fixed home page to start from.

$$home \; : \; Page \tag{38}$$

$$init \; \hat{=} \; dev = (\langle home \rangle, 1) \wedge \tag{39}$$
$$cog = (\{home\}, \{q \mid home \; goodLinks \; q\})$$

Now we define two user actions to capture the fact that the user only really does anything when they come across a new page, *i.e.* when they jump to a page; using the *Go* command can only get the user to previously visited pages. So when visiting a new page the user adds it to *hasVisited* and adds all the interesting unvisited pages to *mustVisit*. There is also the enabling condition which states that the user only wants to look at new pages if they are interesting and have not already been visited.

$$viewNew(p : Page) \; \hat{=} \; p \in (interesting \setminus hasVisited) \wedge \tag{40}$$
$$hasVisited' = hasVisited \cup \{p\} \wedge$$
$$mustVisit' = mustVisit \cup \{q \mid p \; goodLinks \; q\}$$

$$viewOld(n : \mathbb{N}) \; \hat{=} \; cog' = cog \tag{41}$$

So we now combine the actions to produce a next-step relation $\mathcal{B}$ and put all this into a specification Ψ.

$$\mathcal{B} \; \hat{=} \; (Go(n) \wedge viewOld(n)) \vee (Jump(p) \wedge viewNew(p)) \tag{42}$$

$$\Psi \; \hat{=} \; init \wedge \Box[\mathcal{B}]_{(cog,dev)} \wedge \mathrm{WF}_{(cog,dev)}(Go(n) \wedge viewOld(n)) \wedge \tag{43}$$
$$\mathrm{WF}_{(cog,dev)}(Jump(p) \wedge viewNew(p))$$

This specification now asserts that the actions are weakly fair. This means that they cannot be indefinitely enabled without occurring, or, to put it another way, if there is something to be done then it will eventually get done. Consider a system which starts with a (not null) set of pages in *mustVisit*. ($Jump(p) \wedge viewNew(p)$) is enabled because there are pages to jump to and weak fairness asserts that this action must *eventually* occur. A major difference between this model and the safe model is that assuming the device starts off on a page with interesting pages linked to it then the system *will* actually do something. Weak fairness rules out systems that do nothing indefinitely whilst there are actions enabled.

So what can we say about this model? It suffers from exactly the same problem as Φ, namely that the history list is 'lossy' and there is nothing to prevent the user from pruning out part of the history list which still has interesting pages linked to it, hence there may be pages in *mustVisit* which become inaccessible.

Adopting the same strategy as before we attempt to add constraints so that this sort of behaviour becomes illegal. We argue that if we make *Go* impossible while it is possible to jump to new interesting pages and we make it only possible to *Go* to the highest page on the history list such that a subsequent *Jump* does not lose interesting links then we get a depth first search.

We formalise this as follows...

$$viewOld_c(n : \mathbb{N}) \;\hat{=}\; \neg Enabled\langle Jump(p) \wedge viewNew(p)\rangle_{(cog,dev)} \wedge \qquad (44)$$
$$\{p \mid history(n)\ goodLinks\ p\} \neq \emptyset \wedge$$
$$\{p \mid history(i)\ goodLinks\ p \wedge n < i \leq |history|\} = \emptyset \wedge$$
$$cog' = cog$$

Again the cognitive state is not altered by this action, but the crucial part is the enabling condition. The first line asserts that the user only wants to look at old pages when there are no new pages to *Jump* to. The second line asserts that the page that the user *Goes* to has *goodLinks* from it and the third line asserts that all the pages above the nth in the history list have no *goodLinks* from them.

Now we define the system behaviour using this new constraint.

$$\mathcal{B}_c \;\hat{=}\; (Go(n) \wedge viewOld_c(n)) \vee (Jump(p) \wedge viewNew(p)) \qquad (45)$$

$$\Psi_c \;\hat{=}\; init \wedge \Box[\mathcal{B}_c]_{(cog,dev)} \wedge \mathrm{WF}_{(cog,dev)}(Go(n) \wedge viewOld_c(n)) \wedge \qquad (46)$$
$$\mathrm{WF}_{(cog,dev)}(Jump(p) \wedge viewNew(p))$$

4.1 Proving a usability property for the live model

We can now outline a proof of a usability property for the specification Ψ_c. As we hinted at the beginning of this section we shall show that once a user has decided that she must visit a page then eventually she will have visited it. Formally...

$$liveUsable \;\hat{=}\; p \in mustVisit \rightsquigarrow p \in hasVisited \qquad (47)$$

(The formula $P \rightsquigarrow Q$, pronounced 'P leads to Q', is a syntactic shorthand for $\Box(P \Rightarrow \Diamond Q)$ — 'it is always the case that if P is true then eventually Q is true.'). The theorem we need to show is...

$$\Phi_c \Rightarrow liveUsable \qquad (48)$$

In order to prove this property we first restate it in a manner easier to prove. For any web there is a sub-set of pages that are linked via *interesting* pages to the *home* page. We call this set *willVisit* and define it inductively as follows...

$$willVisit : \mathcal{P}(Page) \qquad (49)$$

Base case $\{p \mid home\ links\ p \wedge p \in interesting\} \subseteq willVisit$

Induction case $\{q \mid p\ links\ q \wedge p \in willVisit \wedge q \in interesting\} \subseteq willVisit$

Extremal case No other pages are in *willVisit*

(Note that *willVisit* is fixed; it is determined only by *links* and *interesting*.)

Now we argue that if we show that if *hasVisited* is eventually as large as *willVisit* then this is sufficient to show formula 48.

$$\Diamond hasVisited = willVisit \tag{50}$$

Our reasoning is as follows; in order for a page to be visited the user must first have placed it in *mustVisit*. Furthermore *mustVisit* is always a subset of *willVisit*, so for any arbitrary page to be in *mustVisit* it must be in *willVisit* and once *hasVisited* = *willVisit* then that arbitrary page must be in *hasVisited*.

However to make these arguments we must rely on the fact that *willVisit* is finite.[3] If *willVisit* is infinite then we cannot argue that *hasVisited* will be as large as *willVisit* in a finite number of steps (*i.e.* eventually) because we can only add (at most) one page at a time to *hasVisited*.

Now we know that *hasVisited* is always a sub-set of *willVisit* and we have assumed that *willVisit* is finite. From this we argue that the assertion that *hasVisited* always increases in size whilst it is smaller that *willVisit* is sufficient to show that they are eventually equal (formula 50).

$$\left(\begin{array}{c} hasVisited = P \wedge \\ P \subset willVisit \end{array} \right) \rightsquigarrow \left(\begin{array}{c} hasVisited = P \cup \{p\} \wedge \\ P \cup \{p\} \subseteq willVisit \end{array} \right) \tag{51}$$

To show that this formula is entailed by Φ_c we need to show the following three hypotheses (rule WF1 in [13, Fig 5, pg 888])...

1. a $\mathcal{B}_c$ step never decreases the size of *hasVisited*
2. there is a fair action in $\mathcal{B}_c$ that increases the size of *hasVisited*; and
3. $\mathcal{B}_c$ is never disabled whilst *hasVisited* is a proper sub-set of *willVisit*.

The first two hypotheses here can be shown simply by substitution of definitions and set theory. The action $(Go(n) \wedge viewOld(n))$ has no effect on *hasVisited* and $(Jump(p) \wedge viewNew(p))$ adds to *hasVisited*, so the first hypothesis holds. Similarly because $(Jump(p) \wedge viewNew(p))$ increases the size of *hasVisited* and is fair, the second holds.

The third hypothesis is the critical point. It is easy to show by counter example that it does not hold with the unconstrained action $\mathcal{B}$ because we can throw away parts of the history list that are unvisited and *interesting* and so at some point $\mathcal{B}$ may become disabled whilst *hasVisited* is a proper sub-set of *willVisit*.

We argue that the constrained precondition of $\mathcal{B}_c$ forces the user into a depth first search. Because no links to *interesting* and unvisited pages are thrown away, $\mathcal{B}_c$ remains enabled while *hasVisited* $\subset$ *willVisit*. QED.

5   Conclusions

The models presented here confirm our view of interactive systems (expressed in [6]) that an interactive device determines a set of possible behaviours and the addition of user concerns constrains this set.

---

[3] Note that asserting that *pages*, *links* or *interesting* are finite is sufficient to show that *willVisit* is finite.

The principal source of constraints here is the definition of preconditions[4] in the actions. We have described device preconditions (for example we cannot *Go* to the *n*th page in the history list if n is greater than the length of the history list) which delimit the device behaviour. The addition of preconditions to the user actions (such as only *Go*ing to pages when we do not want to or cannot *Jump* anywhere) define 'most contexts' in the previous sentence and the usability property defines what we mean by 'undesirable'. In this respect our work differs from the early PIE [7] models and properties which dealt with devices only.

We have shown one of the strengths of proof in this paper, namely that it promotes a better understanding of what is going on in the model and can therefore help considerably in redesign. While we could have shown that the simple specification Φ did not fulfill the usability condition by using a model checker this would not get us too far forward, because although we would know that the model fails we would not particularly understand *why* or, for that matter, have any understanding of how the problem could be circumvented.

In the sketch proofs for both the live and safe models we have not only shown that the usability property holds or otherwise; the failed proofs have also pointed to where the problem lies. Furthermore in proving that the constrained model Φ_c fulfills the property we reused most of the proof from the failed attempt. Proof does have a high learning and effort curve, but here we have demonstrated that typically small changes in models and properties need only small changes in the associated proof.

The question of liveness versus safety is interesting and warrants much more investigation. Both the safe and live models presented here have been used to show approximately the same thing. The safety proof was easier but the model it is based on could easily be misconstrued as describing something it does not (*i.e.* that the user does do something with the device rather than that they can). The (slightly) more detailed live model allowed us to describe the constraint needed to avoid unusable behaviour in more detail than was the case with the safe model. The constraint described in the live model has better real-world validity; the constraint in the safe model is overly strong.

This paper has shown a separation of concerns between user assumptions and device specifications. We integrated the two together to describe system behaviour and showed sketch proofs of properties that we believe have usability relevance. We contend that proof based evaluation aids the analyst's understanding of the system and is therefore useful should redesign be necessary. We have also shown the basis of an incremental approach to evaluating interactive system models — starting with a high degree of abstraction that allows for tractable evaluation, then detail is added to move towards real world validity. The step from safety to liveness is an example of this addition of detail and increase in real world validity.

---

[4] A precondition in a TLA action is typically a sub-formula that contains no decorated terms. We have applied the syntactic convention in this paper that preconditions are expressed on the first lines of the action definition.

Acknowledgements

The authors are grateful for enlightening discussions with John Cooke, Richard Young and Jason Good and for the comments of the anonymous reviewers. This work is funded by EPSRC grant GR/L00301. See the world-wide web site at http://www.cs.mdx.ac.uk/puma/ for further details.

References

1. B. Alpern and F. Schneider. Defining liveness. *Information Processing Letters*, 21:181–185, 1985.
2. D. Andrews and D. Ince. *Practical formal methods with VDM*. Series in software engineering. McGraw-Hill, 1991.
3. A. Blandford, R. Butterworth, and J. Good. Users as rational interacting agents: formalising assumptions about cognition and interaction. In Harrison and Torres [12], pages 43–60.
4. A. Blandford and R. Young. Specifying user knowledge for the design of interactive systems. *Software Engineering Journal*, pages 323–333, 1996.
5. R. Butterworth and A. Blandford. Programmable user models: the story so far. Technical report, Middlesex University, 1997. PUMA working paper WP8. Available from http://www.mdx.ac.uk/puma/.
6. R. Butterworth and D. J. Cooke. On biasing behaviour to the optimal. In Harrison and Torres [12], pages 291–306.
7. A. Dix. *Formal Methods for Interactive Systems*. Computers and People Series. Academic Press, 1991.
8. A. Dix and R. Mancini. Specifying history and back tracking mechanisms. In *Formal methods in human-computer interaction*, Formal approaches to computing and information technology, chapter 1, pages 1–23. Springer, 1998.
9. A. Hall. Seven myths of formal methods. *IEEE Software*, pages 11–19, September 1990.
10. M. Harrison and D. Duke. A review of formalisms for describing interactive behaviour. In R. Taylor and C. Coutaz, editors, *Software engineering and human-computer interaction (Lecture notes in computer science vol. 896)*, pages 49–75. Springer Verlag, 1995.
11. M. Harrison and H. Thimbleby, editors. *Formal Methods in Human-Computer Interaction*. Cambridge series on HCI. Cambridge University Press, 1990.
12. M. Harrison and J. Torres, editors. *Design, specification and verification of interactive systems '97*. Eurographics, Springer, 1997.
13. L. Lamport. The temporal logic of actions. *ACM Transactions on Programming Languages and Systems*, 16(3):872–923, 1994.
14. C. Roast and J. Siddiqi, editors. *Proceedings of the BCS-FACS Workshop on Formal Aspects of the Human Computer Interface*. Springer Verlag, 1996. Proceedings published electronically at http://www.springer.co.uk/ewic/workshops/FAHCI/.
15. J. Spivey. *The Z Notation: A Reference Manual*. Series in Computer Science. Prentice Hall International, 1989.
16. B. Sufrin and J. He. Specification, analysis and refinement of interactive processes. In Harrison and Thimbleby [11], pages 153–199.
17. R. Young, T. Green, and T. Simon. Programmable user models for predictive evaluation of interface design. In K. Bice and C. Lewis, editors, *Proceedings of CHI '89: Human Factors in Computing Systems*, pages 15–19. Association of computing machinery, 1989.

Validating semi-formal specifications of interactors as design representations

P. Markopoulos, G. Papatzanis, P. Johnson and J. Rowson

Department of Computer Science
Queen Mary and Westfield College, University of London
Mile End Road, London E1 4NS, UK

Abstract. This paper discusses the nature of research in specifying and verifying interactive systems; it argues that researchers must assess the relevance of the models they propose to the concerns of user interface designers. The paper outlines a semi-formal representation of user interface software and reports a case study which assesses the relevance of the representation to the designer who is interested in the usability of a system. The paper discusses this case study and its findings, and discusses some methodological concerns about the validation of design representations of interactive systems.

1 Introduction

The application of formal methods to the design of interactive systems is an active research area, but also one which has not had a significant impact on interactive software development practice [16]. This is an instance of a wider phenomenon for software engineering [3], which is examined here within the narrower scope of interactive systems design. A plausible explanation relates to the type of research that has been pursued. Contributions to previous events of the DSV-IS series [2, 14, 24, 27] share an emphasis on the development of novel formalisms rather than on their practical application. Researchers introduce and advocate formal models, arguing on the ability of their models and their notations to specify and, less frequently, to verify some aspects of a user interface design. There appears to be a mismatch between the type of research pursued and the type of research required to apply and disseminate modelling techniques. This mismatch is typified by two issues arising regularly in working-group discussions in the DSV-IS series of workshops. One issue can be characterised as the constant search for the 'killer question' and the other as the need for a 'formal methods shopping list'. (Both these terms have come up in working-group discussions in previous DSV-IS events).

The 'killer question' reflects the expert's view of formal models. Confronted with a new model or notation, the expert researcher tries to identify which aspects of interactive system design are not captured sufficiently by the model. In other words, a formal model can be characterised by the range of properties it models successfully and those it does not; new models are introduced to rectify limitations of earlier models. For example, abstract interaction models were found inadequate for constructive use prompting the development of Agent models [1]. Grammatical specifications of interaction dialogue were found inadequate for modelling multithreaded dialogue, prompting the development of event based models [11]. This type of scrutiny provides a deeper understanding of the requirements for the formal models studied, resulting in lucid accounts of the strengths and weaknesses of the various formal models, e.g., [7]. An unfortunate side-effect is a proliferation of models and formalisms, without due emphasis on their practical application. Further, formal models tend to become all-encompassing, extending their scope to multiple facets of interaction, e.g., tasks, application semantics, user interface appearance, user cognitive processes, etc.

A recent survey of modelling techniques for the design of interactive systems [9] has identified this trend and has recommended a shift of focus towards partial representations that serve an analytical purpose rather than as the focal point of all design activities. [9] also recommended the combined use of multiple modelling techniques which will be recruited as and when they are needed. Such a use of modelling techniques requires support for the recruitment and application of the models by their potential users. This observation pertains to the formal methods 'shopping list' discussed below and the need to validate the proposed representations.

The formal methods 'shopping list' is a common request from prospective users of the modelling techniques proposed by researchers. These perspective users may be experienced software developers, interface designers, etc., who are generally not experts in formal methods and who weigh the advantages, the limitations and the afforded uses of the proposed modelling techniques. Unfortunately, the awareness of the 'killer questions' for each model is not easily available to them. [16] discusses how researchers are naturally reluctant to document the weaknesses and flaws of the modelling techniques they use. To encourage the potential users of formal models, the latter should be described in terms of how they will be used, which interface design issues they model and which not. This suggests the need for an empirical comparison of what can be expressed and verified using formal models against what the designer needs to specify. To address the general concerns raised here it is necessary to establish:

- Whether design decisions are adequately modelled using the proposed representations.

- Whether modelling facilitates the development user interface software.

- The relevance of formally specified/verified properties to user interface development.

These questions are significant research issues and this paper is an initial attempt to address the first of them with respect to the Abstraction-Display-Controller (ADC) interactor model. The ADC model, introduced in [19, 20], was specified formally in the LOTOS [18] specification language and was developed with the primary concern of affording a range of analytical uses and supporting a standardised specification style to help reading, writing and verifying formal specifications of user interface software.

Section 2 discusses the distinction between models and their representations, in order to clarify the relationship between the representation of ADC interactors used in this paper and earlier formal representations of the same model. Section 3 introduces a *semi-formal* representation of ADC interactors which provides a flexible scheme for the specification of user interface software. The characterisation 'semi-formal' indicates that the specification follows some notational conventions but does not comply to a formal syntax and semantics. It was found necessary to develop such a scheme in order to allow the concepts captured by the model to be tested without the costs and limitations of the formal representation, i.e. without training the interaction design expert in the LOTOS specification language. A case study, described in sections 4 and 5, gauges the relevance of the model to interactive system design concerns. Also, it compares the semi-formal representation of ADC interactors to the User-Action-Notation (UAN) of [13], by measuring the extent to which each representation captures design issues which are shown to be important by a usability evaluation. The findings of the study, its limitations and directions for future research are discussed in section 6.

2   Interactor models and their representations

The discussion which follows distinguishes between the notions of a *model* and of a *representation*. A model has an underlying conceptual semantics which dictates what is described and how the model can be used. Examples of models of interactive systems are the PIE model [6] or software architectures like the PAC model [4, 5]. Models can have a variety of representations which capture some aspects and uses of the model while they omit others. For example, the PIE model can be represented functionally or as a state-based specification [6]. Similarly, the PAC model was introduced independently of its implementation and can be instantiated in different programming languages.

The present research assumes that software system designers and implementers will benefit from models which take into account the internal organisation of the software which supports the externally observable interaction. Software architectures are design abstractions (models in the terms used here) which aim to assist developers to identify software components, organise their interconnections, reason about them and maintain them [5]. Interactors are primitive architectural abstractions which model interactive systems and their components, modelling their state, the way this state is perceived by users and the way these components interact with their environment.

Formal representations of interactors have been proposed in action based formalisms, e.g., [9, 27, 20], or state based descriptions, e.g., [8]. Object-based architectures of user interface software can be seen as prescriptive interpretations of this general concept. While they did not use the term 'interactor', the MVC [17] and the ALV [15] architectures support the notion of an interactor as an implementation construct. The PAC architecture [4] supports this notion at a conceptual level. These are object-based software architectures which prescribe interactive objects as compositions of elementary components, prescribing their content, their role and how these objects can

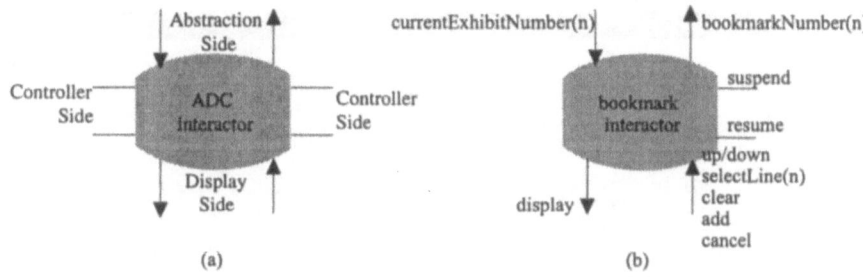

Fig. 1. Diagrammatic representation of an interactor and an example description of a bookmark list interactor

be composed to build a user interface system. These are the essential features of an architectural model, which are common to formal and informal models [8], and it is along these dimensions that the ADC interactor is described below.

3   The Semi-Formal Specification of ADC interactors

An ADC interactor is defined as an interactive entity which encapsulates two state components: the *Abstraction* and the *Display*. The Display models the appearance of an interactor on the screen. The Abstraction holds state information resulting from the interpretation of data already received by the interactor. This distinction between the two state components is a common feature of the models mentioned above. The Abstraction information may be interpreted by the interactor to provide input to the application or to other interactors it is connected to. The environment of an interactor can be the user, the functional core or other interactors. The ADC interactor can model the user interface as a single monolithic ADC interactor which mediates between an application and a user. Alternatively, the ADC interactor can model a small scale interactive component. In such a case, the user interface can be thought of as a graph, whose nodes are the interactors and whose edges correspond to connections between them, with the application or with the user. Connections describe dependencies of the dynamic behaviour of interactors or even data flows between each other. (In the formal model [20] connections correspond to LOTOS process algebraic operators used to combine interactor specifications into more complex behaviour expressions). The architecture and the dynamic behaviour of the composed user interface are described partly in the individual interactors and partly in the way they are composed together.

The specification of a user interface needs to describe:

- The Display and Abstraction data and how they are used to interpret input and to produce output.

- The dialogue specification, which describes the temporal ordering of interactions.

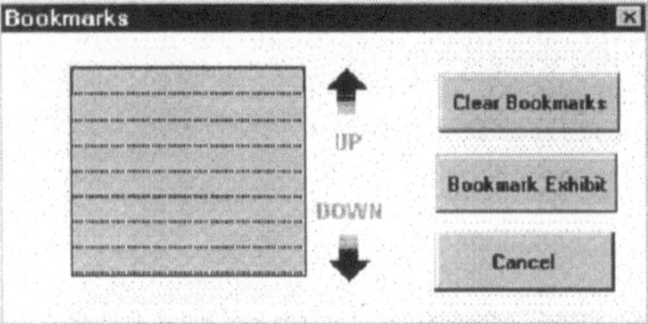

Fig. 2. The display of the bookmark interactor.

- The architectural configuration. The interactor is primarily an architectural entity: its architectural configuration pertains to the concept of a 'public interface' through which its state is accessed and through which the interactor interacts with its environment. Further, the architecture describes the composition of interactors to describe more complex entities.

Figure 1(a) illustrates an ADC interactor as a barrel shaped node. This node illustrates the architecture of a single interactor. Arrows and lines indicate *gates* of the interactor. Gates are an architectural concept used to localise interactions with the same purpose. Each gate has a *role* which determines how interactions on the gate affect the subsequent behaviour of the interactor: e.g., by modifying its state parameters, by reading their values, as part of the dialogue supported by the interactor, etc. The role of the gate can be one of the following: graphical input, graphical output, abstract (non graphical) input, abstract (non graphical) output, control.

Graphical input and output gates are denoted by the arrows on the bottom side of the interactor, which is called its *display side*. Non graphical input and output gates are drawn as arrows attached to top side of the interactor, which is called the *abstraction side*. For example, speech input would be an input on the abstraction side as long as the (particular) interactor does not interpret this input with respect to the contents of its display. Finally, control gates are drawn as simple lines attached to the vertical (the controller) sides of the interactor. Control interactions do not affect the abstraction and display states and do not convey data to or from an interactor, but they are used for the specification of the interaction dialogue.

Figure 1(b) describes the architecture of an interactor called 'bookmark'. The type of data communicated with interactions is written next to the gate names. These data types are not specified formally; the informality, it is hoped, will help the user organise the specification in units that correspond to ADC interactors while avoiding the cost of the formalisation. The naming of gates and the allocation of gates to 'sides' constitutes the architectural specification of an interactor.

The Abstraction of the interactor corresponds to the usual computer science notion of an abstract data type, so types like list, collection, bounded value, string, etc., are typical examples. The Display concerns graphical representations, e.g., a palette, a

Table 1. Tabular specification of the bookmark interactor.

Graphical Input Gates	
up/down	press on the up/down buttons
selectLine(n)	select a bookmark from the list
clear	clear the list of bookmarks
add	add the current page to the list of bookmarks
cancel	user presses on cancel button
Graphical Output Gates	
display	display of bookmark interactor
Abstraction Input Gates	
currentExhibitNumber(n)	number of currently shown exhibit
Abstraction Output Gates	
bookmarkNumber(n)	exhibit selected from the list
Control Gates	
suspend	suspend the 'bookmarks' interactor
resume	resume the 'bookmarks' interactor
Abstraction Status	
List	A list of bookmarks
currentSelection	Exhibit selected from the 'bookmarks list'
currentExhibit,	The exhibit currently viewed in the 'stage' interactor
Display Status (see figure 2)	
ListSegment	The part of the list of bookmarks which will be displayed in the list box
Up/Down	Up/Down buttons are greyd-out depending on the number of entries in the list
Controller	
(choice x in [up, down, clear, add] x; display) lll cancel; display; suspend; resume lll selectLine(n); display; bookmarkNumber	

push button, a menu, an icon, etc. For an informal description, it can be more appropriate to sketch the display of an interactor rather than describe its Display data type in text. This suits best graphical aspects of the user interface. The Display may be sketched on a drawing tool, it can be hand drawn or it can even be a screen-shot, so figure 2 can be the display-specification of the interactor 'bookmark'. Drawing tools or paper and pencil sketching are mentioned to suggest the flexibility of semi-formal representations. Rather than the consistency and completeness of the specification, what matters is to achieve a clear conceptualisation of the user interface design.

Operations on the data components are invoked by interactions on the gates. Rather than specifying these operations explicitly, each interaction is associated with a textual explanation in a tabular specification of the interactor, as in table 1. The final component of the interactor specification is dialogue specification which describes the temporal ordering of interactions. Here, the LOTOS prefix operator ';' denotes

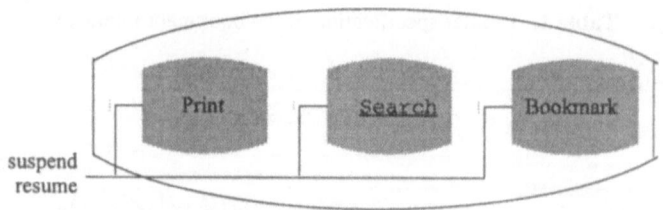

Fig. 3. The composition of the bookmark and other interactors, forming a group of interactors.

sequence of actions and the interleave operator 'III' denotes independent dialogue constraints. These operators are a notational convenience but no attempt has been made to specify dialogue formally using LOTOS, as in [20]. Pseudo-LOTOS describes the sequencing constraints but the controller specification is not syntactically correct LOTOS. During the case study corresponding operators of UAN were used for the controller description and, there also, no formal syntax was adhered to. In summary, the tabular specification of an individual interactor describes the gates of the interactor distinguished by their roles, the state components and the controller (local dialogue) specification. Where appropriate textual descriptions are associated with interactions and pictorial representations with the display description.

An interface is defined as a composition of interactors. In the formal representation of ADC interactors the range of compositions was dictated by the LOTOS syntax and semantics (see [20, chapter 6]). Here, connections are specified diagrammatically as, e.g., the interactors in figure 3. In this case interactors synchronise on interactions which cause them to suspend or resume their behaviours. The three interactors are enclosed in a barrel to illustrate that they form a group.

4   The Museum-Assistant Guide and its Specification

The case study concerned the design specification of a prototype of an interactive application using the semi-formal specification scheme outlined in section 3. This application was designed and implemented by a group of four graduate students. A specification of the prototype using the semi-formal representation of the ADC interactor was reverse engineered. A thorough usability evaluation produced a set of design recommendations. These recommendations were assumed to indicate design issues which are significant from an interface designers' perspective -at least they are significant with respect to the usability of the interactive system. Subsequently, it was attempted to specify the design recommendations as modifications of the specification. The extent to which these design recommendations could be described as changes in the specifications was taken to indicate the relevance of the specification to the concerns of the user interface designer.

To obtain some measure of comparison, this exercise was performed in parallel using the User Action Notation (UAN) of [13]. UAN was chosen because it also is a semi-formal specification, in that it adopts some syntactical conventions: a tabular

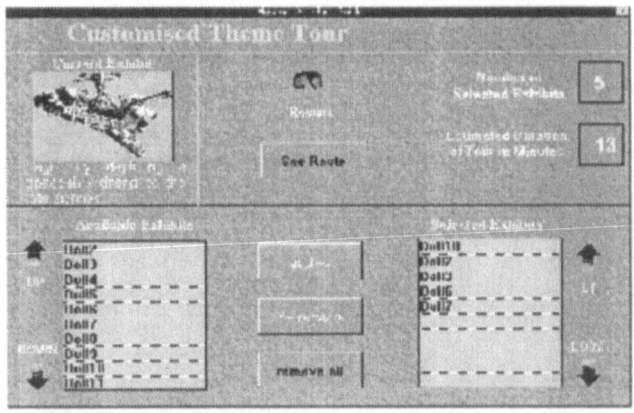

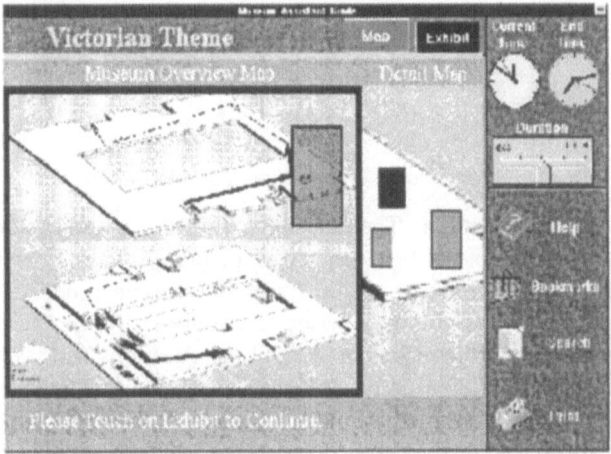

Fig. 4. The Customise and Map screens, where the user constructs a tour as a list of exhibits to see and can view a route around the museum.

presentation which is read left to right and top-down and an extensible set of symbols. UAN and ADC have a similar scope: they both specify the interface to an application rather than the interactive system as a whole. However, they are very different, in that UAN is task-centred while ADC is architectural. UAN considers the interface as a single monolithic entity, without considering its structure, but models the structure of the tasks performed with it. ADC models the architectural structure of the user interface but does not describe the structure of the tasks performed with it. Note, that the exercise is not a comparative assessment of how useful or usable the two notations are. Such a comparison would have to cover different and wider issues than those addressed here, such how easy the notations are to learn and comprehend, their cost-effectiveness, how they combine with other representations used in design, etc. Further, it is not suggested that the two representations are mutually exclusive.

The system specified was a prototype of a hand held device for use as an educational museum guide assistant (referred to as the Assistant below), for the Bethnal Green

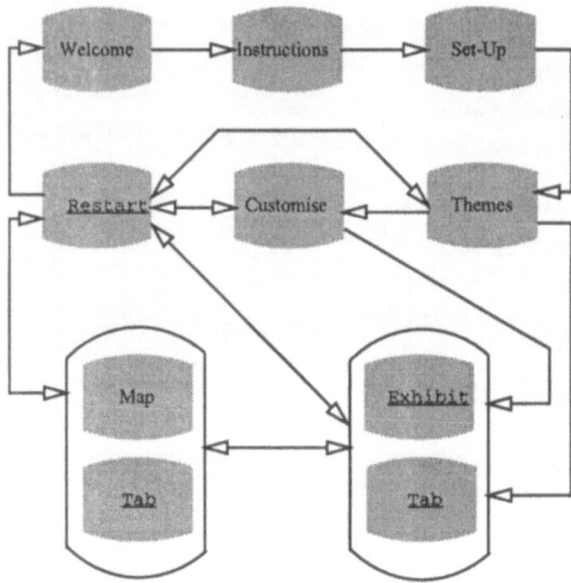

Fig. 5. The interface as a composition of ADC interactors.

Museum of Childhood in London. The museum exhibits toys and has displays tracing the history of childhood from the 17th century to the present day. Educational visitors are the main users of the museum. The Assistant was designed to be used with minimal training by teachers guiding classes of children through the museum. The Assistant should provide information about exhibits, questions and tasks for the class to complete, and manage an interactive itinerary of the visit. The system exhibits a range of functionalities and media types which are common to contemporary interactive applications. A detailed task analysis was performed which produced a set of design requirements. A task model was defined and modified as a high level design of the system, before building a prototype of the system. The prototype for the device was programmed using Asymetrix Toolbook™. The prototype is not fully functional, so only parts of the information about exhibits were included. The envisaged system would be a hand held device, roughly the size of an A4 pad of paper, equipped with a touch screen and a system for positioning the system in the museum. The prototype offered interaction with the mouse on a desktop computer.

The teacher is presented with some introductory screens and can then move on to browse and to select themes to be shown to the class. An introductory set-up screen lets the teacher input the age of the group of pupils, the duration of tour, whether wheel chair access is needed and to make choices as to the type of material that is relevant to the curriculum. The Assistant comes up with a list of themes which the teacher can choose from, with associated pictures and brief textual descriptions. Selecting a theme will take the user to further screens where the exhibits relevant to the theme are chosen. A tour through the museum is constructed as a selection of exhibits and a route to follow is displayed on a map (see screen-shots on figure 4). The bookmark interactor shown in figure 2 is invoked to help the teacher mark and return to exhibits of interest. The idea is that the system should monitor the progress of the visitors through the planned tour, provide the relevant information as text or video and suggest how the tour should proceed. The user interface, which was specified in UAN and ADC, mediates between a user and a functional core which retrieves information about exhibits and supports functionality such as printing requests of the user, monitoring progress, offering suggestions for tasks for the class, etc. The UAN specification is not described here, as it followed the standard conventions for the notation [13]. The ADC specification consisted of 21 interactors. Its structure is described below in brief.

The ADC specification addressed a high level of abstraction, where an interactor can be a dialogue box containing several buttons and list-boxes, or a whole screen containing various buttons, images and lists. Sometimes a screen was defined as a group of interactors resulting in a hierarchical decomposition of the specification. Figure 5 shows the overall structure of the specification. Arrows illustrate the navigation between interactors modelling different screens modelled as pairs of suspend/resume interactions for the interactors connected. Grouped interactors are enclosed in a barrel, or where the decomposition is not shown the interactor name is underlined. The initial screens are modelled by elementary interactors. The Tab interactors can be seen on the right of the map on the 'Map' screen of figure 4. The decomposition of the Tab interactor has already been shown in figure 3 and one of its components is the 'BookMark' interactor which was specified in section 3.

5 Assessing the content of the semi-formal specification with respect to usability concerns.

The prototype was evaluated in order to derive a set of design recommendations. A combination of three evaluation methods was employed in an attempt to extract a wide range of design recommendations to enable the generalisation of the case-study conclusions.

The first method used was scenario-based *heuristic evaluation* [23]. Evaluators, selected among postgraduate students, evaluated the interface with respect to a set of design heuristics. They used a set of scenarios aiming to address problems from the task level through to the screen-layout level. The set of heuristics was produced after an adaptation of the original list of heuristics by Nielsen and Molich [23].

The second evaluation method used was *Cognitive Walkthrough*, which is an evaluation methodology which focuses on the user's cognitive activities, the goals and knowledge of a user while performing a task. It is particularly appropriate for the evaluation of 'Walk Up and Use' interfaces which like the Assistant should be used with no training. The simple step-by-step guide of Newman and Lamming [22] was used for this evaluation. The user is assumed to start with a rough plan of what they want to achieve. The evaluator 'walks' through the interaction, asking the following questions at each step:

• Will the correct action be made sufficiently evident to the user?

- Will the user connect the correct action's action description with what they are trying to do?

- Will the user interpret the system's response to the chosen action correctly, i.e. will the user know if they have made the right or the wrong choice of action?

Finally, *Cooperative Evaluation* [21] was used, which is particularly suitable for partly implemented systems, such as the Assistant. A user is given the prototype and is encouraged to criticise the system, while at the same time the evaluator is given the chance to clarify points of confusion and maximise the effectiveness of the method. Audio tape and paper notes were used to record problems experienced by the users.

There are several factors which constrained the evaluation. Assistant only existed as a prototype and many of its functions were not implemented. The evaluation could not take place in the intended context of use (the museum), as only a simulation of the hand-held system on a desktop computer was available. Also, it was difficult to find teachers experienced in museum tours who would help with this evaluation. This problem was partly addressed by the use of scenarios. Even though these are serious limitations for the utility of an evaluation exercise, the combined use of the three evaluation techniques provides a wealth of design recommendations and gives a good impression of the type of issues that concern the overall usability of the system, to the extent that it is assessed by the three evaluation techniques mentioned.

The combined evaluation results were recorded on a screen-by-screen basis and corresponding design recommendations (59) were produced. The specifications of the system in UAN and ADC were revisited and an attempt was made to specify these recommendations as changes to the specifications. For the purposes of presenting the results of the evaluation coherently, design recommendations were classified as in table 2 after the re-specification of the interface. The table also indicates the success in capturing the design recommendations using UAN and ADC.

The results of table 2 show that whole category of design issues, which can be described as 'display aesthetics', were not captured by any of the two representations. This however was anticipated since they correspond to issues that were intentionally abstracted away from. 'Layout' design recommendations were described successfully in ADC, although it is clear that its formal counterpart is not appropriate for such a specification. 'Labelling' concerns appear, at a first glance, to be a very low level issue, which should not concern the abstract representations discussed. Both UAN and ADC were successful at specifying labelling changes where some identifier of the representation was involved. However, both representations missed crucial information on labels that were non interactive but were crucially informative to the user. Both ADC and UAN seem to neglect important aspects of UI design, which concern static (non-interactive) information, which helps users determine how to carry out tasks. This displayed information prompts user actions without itself being the feedback of any user action, e.g., static text, the presence or absence of icon-labels, etc. The difference between the two was explained by the fact that explanatory labels were sometimes part of the display-status specification in ADC, while UAN only described what the user can act upon and what the response of the system is to the user

Table 2. Design recommendations classification and case study results.

Category	Explanation	Number of rec/dations	UAN	ADC
Layout	Layout of interactors within each screen	5		5
Display	Aesthetics, colour, size of interactors	5		
Labelling	Naming of interactors - or absence of labels	17	8	12
Functionality	New features suggested/functionality missing	20	15	20
Task structure	Issues relating to the dialogue of the interface such as enabling of buttons, defaults, etc.	5	2	4
Miscellaneous	None of the above	7	2	5
	Total	59	27	46

actions. However, the ADC specification was exceptionally accurate in this respect as it was reverse engineered from the prototype so it was annotated with screen shots. In a forward engineering context more abstract design representations should result which would not specify displays in this level of detail. Most recommendations in the 'functionality' category were captured by both notations; it is not wise to draw general inferences from the different scores in this category. The category 'Miscellaneous' included dialogue design issues, e.g., provide a *restart* button, a 'back' button, etc., providing directions to the user, removing the end time clock to simplify the display. A couple of such design recommendations concerned a level of description that was too low to be related to the specifications. This is not considered detrimental for the representation techniques.

6   Discussion

The semi-formal scheme introduced above for the specification of user interfaces uses a range of representation forms, with varying degrees of formality, textual or graphical. These diverse representations are integrated by the common conceptual framework of the ADC interactor. The ADC interactor suggests orthogonal dimensions for the description of user interface software which define the scope of each representation technique and the relationships between them. These are the abstraction and display states, the architectural configuration of an interactor, its dialogue and the composition of interactors to form more complex specifications. An important motivation for developing the semi-formal representation scheme is to reduce the cost of formulating a design. The reduction in the formality of the approach means that the range of design representations are not necessarily consistent and that some parts of the specification may be incomplete. If the informal specification is used as the starting point of a formal specification or an implementation, then this will be remedied. However, if it is used on its own as a communication tool it may incur problems to the design team. The benefits of using such an informal specification in practical design have to be weighed against the cost of increasing the formality.

The case study was prompted by the need to validate the formal ADC interactor model with respect to the designer's need for descriptive and analytical power. It was recognised that formality itself presented an obstacle for the application of the model, so a semi-formal scheme was developed which is addressed at 'HCI designers' rather than 'formalists'. The semi-formal representation is much richer and more flexible than its formal interpretation in LOTOS, but lacks its analytical power. However, the semi-formal representation is seen as more than a step towards formalisation. It can help articulate and communicate initial and 'sketchy' design ideas. Further, it is not restricted by the expressive power of any formal framework, so it gives a representation which is more faithful to the abstract concept of an interactor.

It was not the intention of this case study to assess the usability of the ADC and UAN as notations. It was noted though that in both cases it was inconvenient not to have a 'library' of pre-defined specification components available. However, the representation scheme described for ADC interactors cannot be put forward a practical tool for designers. Such a venture should take into account the type of representations they use currently and would require the development of appropriate tool support.

Related work for the validation of the ADC interactor as an architectural abstraction has applied the model as an implementation architecture [10]. ADC interactors were implemented as a JAVA class, with significant advantages for the modularity of the code. Thus, the ADC interactor model integrates at a conceptual level an implementation architecture, a formal specification and a semi-formal specification intended to facilitate the articulation and modification of design ideas.

This paper has argued that formal methods research needs to validate and document the representation schemes proposed. The case study reported has had a very modest target. It provided corroborative evidence that an architectural model of an interactive system describes design issues which are salient with regard to the usability of the system. Compared to the wealth of the formalisms that exist few attempts have been made to assess their relevance to designers interested in the usability of a system. By demonstrating the relevance of the semi-formal specifications of interaface designs we have, to an extent, validated our conception of the interactor abstraction. We have not though provided any positive evidence for the utility of supporting an event based abstraction, or indeed some other formal interpretation of the interactor model.

Further research, needs to assess the utility and the validity of the predictions made by such formal specifications of user interfaces. Unfortunately, the experience of designing and evaluating the Assistant is not very encouraging for the action based formal specification of ADC in LOTOS. Design issues raised by the evaluation did not concern properties which can be modelled, predicted and verified with the action based specification in LOTOS. This is attributed to the type of application discussed, which was selected as an interesting and typical design problem, rather than for how well it matches the ADC model. Future work should extend the scope of the case study to different application domains, e.g., safety critical applications, computer mediated communication, etc., where the requirements from the representation scheme and the results of the usability evaluations might be dramatically different. A methodological caveat must be flagged here: a single design issue might justify the use of a different formalism regardless of how well this formalism captures general usability concerns as measured above. Further, the significance of design issues varies with the type of design problem addressed. Constructing a suite of 'benchmark' interactive system design problems (to use the term of [16]), each associated with a different set of design concerns, can help validate and assess the utility of ADC, or other representations for interactive systems design.

7   Acknowledgements

This research is funded by EPSRC, grant number GR/K79796.

8   References

[1]   Abowd, G.D. (1992) Formal Aspects of Human Computer Interaction, PhD thesis, University of Oxford, Technical Report YCS 161, University of York.

[2]   Bodart, F. & Vanderdonckt, J. (Eds.) Design, Specification and Verification of Interactive Systems '96, Springer(Wien), 1996.

[3]   Bowen, J.P. & Hinchey, M.G. (1995) Seven more myths of formal methods. IEEE Software, Vol. 12, No. 4, pp. 34-41.

[4]   Coutaz, J. (1987) PAC, an Object Oriented Model for Dialog Design. Proceedings INTERACT-'87, North-Holland: Elsevier, 431-436.

[5]   Coutaz, J., Nigay, L. & Salber, D. (1995). Agent based modelling for interactive systems. AMODEUS project report, System Modelling, WP53, ftp://ftp.mrc-apu.cam.ac.uk/pub/amodeus, 1995.

[6]   Dix, A. (1991) Formal Methods for Interactive Systems, Cambridge University Press, 1991.

[7]   Dix, A. & Abowd, G. (1996) Modelling status and event behaviour of interactive systems. Software Engineering Journal, Vol. 11, No 6, pp 334-346.

[8]   Duke, D., Faconti, F., Harrison, M.D. & Paternó, F. (1994) Unifying Views of Interactors. In Proceedings of the Workshop on Advanced Visual Interfaces '94, Bari, ACM Press, pp. 143-152.

[9]   Fields, B., Merriam, N., & Dearden., A. (1997) DMVIS: Design, Modelling and Validation of Interactive Systems. In [14].

[10] Graham, M. (1997) Validation of the ADC model as an implementation architecture for user interface software. MSc Project Report, Dpt. of Computer Science, Queen Mary and Westfield College, University of London.

[11] Green, M. (1986) A Survey of Three Dialogue Models. ACM Transactions on Graphics, Vol. 5, No. 3, pp. 244-275.

[12] Hall, A. (1997) Do interactive systems need specifications? In [14]

[13] Hartson R.H., Siochi, A.C. & Hix, D. (1990) The UAN: A user oriented representation for direct manipulation systems. ACM Transactions on Information Systems, Vol. 8, 181-203.

[14] Harrison, M.D. & Torres, J-C. (Eds.) Design, Specification and Verification of Interactive Systems '97, Springer (Wien), 1997.

[15] Hill, R.D., Brinck, T., Rohall, S.L., Patterson, J.F. & Wilner, W. (1994) The Rendezvous architecture and language for constructing multiuser applications, ACM Transactions on Computer Human Interaction, Vol. 1, No. 2, pp. 81-125.

[16] Johnson, C. (1996) The Namur Principles: Criteria for the evaluation of user interface notations. Report on working-group discussion, DSV-IS'96, http://www.info.fundp.ac.be/~jvd/dsvis/ table96.html.

[17] Krasner, G.E., & Pope, S.T. (1988) A Cookbook For Using the Model-View-Controller User Interface Paradigm in The Smalltalk-80 System. Journal of Object Oriented Programming, 1, 3, 26-49.

[18] ISO (1989) Information Processing Systems-Open Systems Interconnection-LOTOS-A Formal Description Technique based on the Temporal Ordering of Observational Behaviour, ISO/IEC 8807, International Organisation for Standardisation, Geneva.

[19] Markopoulos, P, (1995) On the Expression of Interaction Properties within an Interactor Model. In [24].

[20] Markopoulos, P. (1997) A formal compositional model for the specification of user interfaces. PhD Thesis, Queen Mary and Westfield College, University of London, June 1997.

[21] Monk, A., Wright, P., Haber, J. & Davenport, L. (1993). Improving your Human-Computer Interface, BCS Practitioners Series, Prentice-Hall.

[22] Newman, W.M. & Lamming, M.G. (1995) Interactive Systems Design, Addison-Wesley.

[23] Nielsen, J. & Molich, R. (1990) Heuristic evaluation of user interfaces, Proceedings CHI'90, ACM Press.

[24] Palanque, P. & Bastide, R. (Eds.) Design, Specification and Verification of Interactive Systems '95, Springer (Wien), 1995.

[25] Papatzanis, G. (1997) Validation of Semi-Formal Representations for User-Interface Specification. MSc Project Report, Department of Computer Science, Queen Mary and Westfield College, University of London.

[26] Paternó, F. & Faconti, G. (1992) On the use of LOTOS to describe graphical interaction. In Monk, A., Diaper, D. & Harrison, M.D. (Eds.) People and Computers VII, Proc. HCI'92, Cambridge University Press, pp. 155-173.

[27] Paternó, F. (Ed.) Interactive Systems: Design, Specification and Verification, Springer, 1994.

The role of informal representations in early design

Sara Jones and John Sapsford

S.Jones, J.Sapsford-Francis@herts.ac.uk
Department of Computer Science, University of Hertfordshire,
College Lane, Hatfield, Herts, AL10 9AB, UK

Abstract. Early design activities are of critical importance to the success of a system, yet are fraught with difficulty. This paper presents the results of two small-scale studies which investigated the role of informal and semi-formal graphical representations in the early design of interactive systems. We argue that informal graphical representations may have an important role to play in early design in enabling designers to think creatively about possible design solutions. However, we demonstrate that reliance on informal diagrams as the primary means of communicating and recording design decisions is associated with a number of difficulties. We also identify a number of challenges in relation to the post hoc recording of design decisions using semi-formal notations. We end by discussing the way in which both informal and semi-formal notations may be used to maximum benefit.

1 Introduction

Early design activities are of critical importance to the success of a system, yet are fraught with difficulty. Decisions made in the design stage have far reaching, and sometimes devastating effects on subsequent development work. The design phase is particularly challenging in the development of systems employing new and fast-developing technologies such as multimedia and virtual reality where boundaries are constantly being pushed forwards and a wide range of expertise is required from different members of the development team [3]. In this paper, we focus on situations such as these where:

- novel or state-of-the-art systems are being developed and designers are required to think creatively about different possible approaches to solving a problem;
- design teams are made up of individuals from different backgrounds and with varying expertise so that developing an understanding of the system to be built which is shared by all members of the team is particularly challenging;
- there are no fixed roles within the design team and membership may vary over time so it is important that there should be unambiguous records of design decisions which can be understood by those joining the team later in the project.

We look, in particular, at design activities carried out during the course of the SPIRE project [1], whose aim was to develop a multimedia system that would provide information for staff and students about the integration of students with disability into the Higher Education environment. Development of the SPIRE system was begun in 1994 when the application of multimedia technology was much less common than it is today. The team were unaware of any systems similar to what was thought to be needed, and creativity was therefore required in considering what system should be built.

Five designers were involved during the early stages of the project, each with different levels experience of the application domain, of the chosen development platform, and of the development of information systems in general. Three of the designers had worked together on projects in the past, but two were new to the team and did not share this experience. Finally, different designers attended different meetings so membership of the design team effectively varied over time.

In design meetings for the SPIRE project, and in other design meetings associated with ongoing projects in our own department at the University of Hertfordshire (UH), we have observed that members of design teams often use graphical representations of various forms to communicate their ideas and form a basis for discussion. We believe that much can be learned from experience in these areas, about the process of design, about the role of graphical representations within it, and about what aspects of the process - and the corresponding use of graphical representations - may be improved.

This paper presents the results of two small-scale studies which investigated the role of informal and semi-formal graphical representations in the development of interactive systems. These studies were designed to help us gain insight into what various forms of graphical representation are used for, and what difficulties may be caused by the use of such representations. The following two sections describe each of the studies in turn. The results are discussed in section 4.

2 Study 1: Use of informal representations

2.1 Introduction

A range of different activities are involved at different stages of the design process. Early on in design, there is often a need to search for creative solutions. For example, in the SPIRE project, much effort was expended on trying to devise innovative yet appropriate ways of providing access to useful information about supporting students with disabilities.

If creativity is an important part of design, the tools and techniques used in design should, at very least, allow it to take place. One widely adopted means of encouraging creativity is brainstorming [7]. Although there is some doubt about the efficacy of brainstorming in groups, it is widely accepted as an effective approach for the generation of a large number of ideas [6]. Brainstorming involves generating many ideas whilst avoiding the premature evaluation of those ideas. Thus creativity appears to flourish through the fluent generation of ideas and a postponement of evaluative judgement. This suggestion is supported by a study of creativity in artists carried out by Getzels and Csikszentmihalyi [4]. These authors identified 'problem finding' as an important pattern of behaviour in successful artists. This behaviour is typified by:

- spending time exploring alternative approaches to work before settling on one in particular
- remaining ready to change directions when new approaches suggest themselves
- not viewing a work as fixed even when it is finished

Thus we may suggest that to enable creative thinking, representations used in early design should not only maximise fluency and discourage premature evaluation, but also encourage explorations and allow changes in direction.

In novel problem solving situations it may also be desirable to be able to introduce novel concepts. Furthermore, such concepts should be at an appropriate level for the task. One example of difficulties caused by working at an inappropriate level of abstraction is the problem of 'functional fixedness' which occurs when problem solvers have, perhaps unconsciously, introduced too many constraints. Looking for alternative ways of representing problems can help here. Glucksberg & Danks [5], for example, found that labelling of objects when solving problems does not always help, sometimes it hinders. Labelling an object as a screwdriver prevents us seeing it as a potential circuit connector. Using nonsense names apparently makes it significantly easier to see new uses for objects.

All of these arguments suggest that informal graphical representations or diagrams (doodles!) with no fixed semantics may have an important role to play in early design in enabling designers to think creatively about possible solutions to the design problems they are posed. However, from our earlier consideration of the context within which design often takes place (where there are inter-disciplinary design teams with changing membership), we can see that the representations used in design meetings may also need to fulfil other requirements: they may need to act as a medium for communication between different members of the design team, or even as a record of decisions made during design meetings.

The diagrams commonly used in meetings by designers at UH to help them to reason about particular system designs are often unstructured and do not use any one set of drawing conventions. The level of detail often varies in different parts of a diagram, depending on the difficulty (to the designers) of describing the corresponding parts of the system. Designers also introduce new diagrammatic conventions to describe problems encountered for the first time in new domains or with novel system architectures. In a close-knit design team, this fluidity of diagram semantics may not cause a problem, with the designers communicating effectively, even through changing and informal specifications. However, in larger design teams whose members have various levels of experience, misunderstandings may more easily arise. Backtracking from formal specifications or prototypes developed by individual members of the design team on the basis of such mistaken understandings is at best time-wasting, and can have more serious implications if customers have also been misled by the informal descriptions.

The study described in this section looks at the extent to which informal representations of a kind typically used in design meetings at UH may be expected to fulfil roles other than simply supporting creativity. It will focus on:

- the effectiveness with which they may be said to support an understanding of the system to be developed which is shared by the whole design team, and
- the extent to which they can be relied upon as accurate records of decisions made at particular design meetings.

2.2 Procedure

This study was based around a fairly difficult meeting of the SPIRE project design team at which 4 members of the team (J, S, M and F) were present. During the meeting the designers were trying to deal with a number of important but intangible design decisions to do with the conceptual design of the system. A number of diagrams were drawn.

After the meeting the diagrams were collected and the participants were interviewed later the same day. They answered questions about each of the diagrams. The diagrams shown were photocopied, although the originals were available to be viewed if necessary. Each participant was asked to:

1. Say who drew each diagram
2. Put the diagrams in order of their creation
3. Say what issue surrounded the creation of each diagram ("Why was this diagram drawn? What main issue does it relate to?")
4. Identify the parts of each diagram which were labelled on the photocopy ("What did this part of the diagram mean?")

Four diagrams had been produced during the original design meeting. These are referred to here as the 'layer' diagram, the 'local' diagram, the 'triangle' diagram, and the 'classes' diagram. Results relating to two of the diagrams (the 'layer' and the 'local' diagram - see fig.s 1a and 1b) will be discussed in detail.

Fig. 1a. The Layer Diagram (Showing labels 1 - 9)

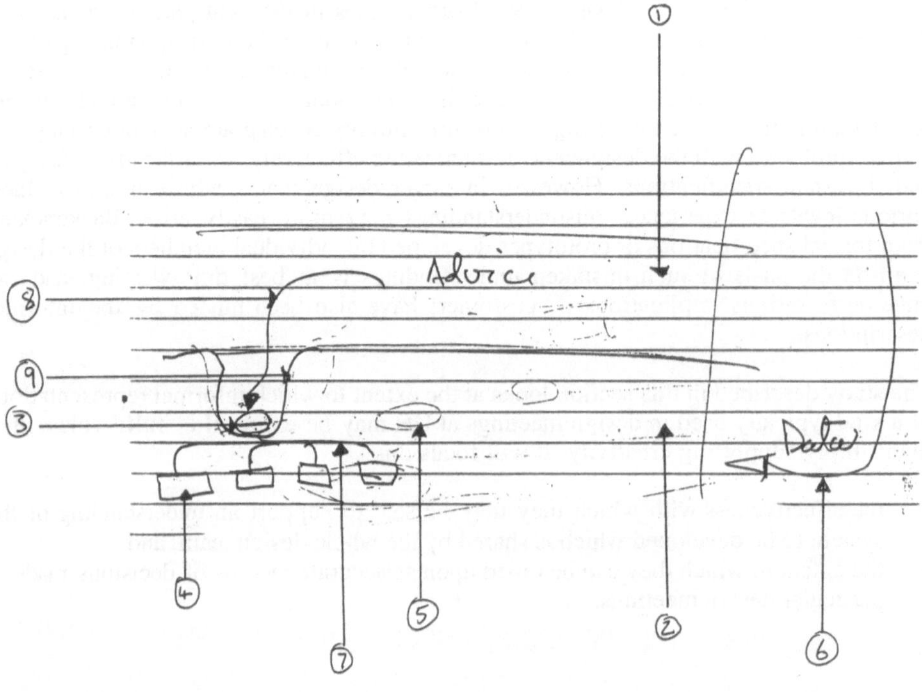

Fig. 1b. The Local Diagram (Showing labels 1 and 2)

2.3 Results

There was broad agreement about who drew each of the diagrams and the order in which they were produced. A large number of statements were collected about the issues that surrounded the creation of the diagrams. For some of the diagrams there was considerable agreement amongst designers (including the creators of the diagram) about the issues they related to, but for other diagrams there was much less agreement.

The 'layer' diagram. All four designers said that the layer diagram (see fig. 1a) was constructed to help decide where class descriptions of data objects should be presented to the user: whether they should be placed in the advice layer -essentially a hypermedium - or in the data layer -a structured database that the user can search or browse. The designers' responses to question 3 (about the purpose of the diagram and the issues surrounding its creation) are given below:

J: "We were discussing whether class descriptions should be part of advice or part of the database"

S: "Having problems to do with what is going in advice layer and data layer. Particularly where class descriptions should go"

M: "Talking about class descriptions and where they fit into our three level hierarchy. There was some argument about whether it went in the bottom layer or the middle. User's and designer's models: F said does it matter form the user's point of view? J argued for the bottom layer, F argued for the middle layer"

F: "I drew this after the other triangular diagram. Its about the three layer model. Whether classes of data should be in the advice layer or the data layer. We decided this confused user and designer views"

This agreement between designers over the issues surrounding the layer diagram suggests that informal diagrams can be an effective aid to communication (and hence to the development of a shared understanding) in contexts such as those of interest in this paper.

Broad agreement was also shown in the identification task (step 4 of the procedure above) carried out in relation to the layer diagram as shown in the table below, although some designers (J and S) had a more detailed memory of the meaning of various diagram components than others.

Table 1 Features of the 'layer' diagram identified by each subject
('•' means the relevant component of the diagram was correctly identified)

	J	S	M	F
1 Advice Layer	•	•	•	
2 Data Layer	•	•	•	
3 Class Description	•	•	•	•
4 Entities / Data Organisation	•	•	•	•
5 Other Class	•			
6 User Access	•	•	•	•
7 Data / Class Link		•		
8 Advice Class Link		•		•
9 Advice Layer Boundary	•	•		

The 'local' diagram. The observations described above contrast with those relating to the local diagram (see fig. 1b). Here it was harder to identify any one shared view about the purpose of the diagram. The designers' statements about the issues to which the local diagram related are given below:

J: "J describing contents list like a help system. Subtopics for local information. We discarded this...or did we?"

S: "J responding to F's prompting about class description "local". She was proposing that people should access the data via a hierarchical contents list."

M: "To do with things having lots of parents. Instances relating to multiple class descriptors. Something to do with an implementation issue to do with whether we should keep lists of classes attached to objects."

F: "J drew this to show that we could just have a list of local equipment rather than links. I felt we were assuming that data was just equipment at this point."

Identification of the features labelled in the 'local' diagram was also somewhat inconsistent as shown below:

Table 2 Names given by each subject to features labelled in the 'local' diagram

	Feature 1	Feature 2
J	topic heading	sub topics
S	class description (?)	class descriptions; indentations show 'is a subclass' relationships
M	local class	lot of local objects/equipment
F		class members

2.4 Conclusions

From what we know about creativity and the conditions under which it thrives, we have surmised that informal graphical representations may have an important role to play in early design in enabling designers to think creatively about possible solutions to the design problems they are posed. However, this study has demonstrated that reliance on informal diagrams as the primary means of communicating and recording design decisions is likely to lead us into difficulties. The lack of agreement between designers about either the significance (in terms of related issues) or meaning of some of the diagrams (for example, the local diagram) suggests that informal representations such as those discussed here may not be a reliable means of developing a shared understanding of the system to be developed, and are not suitable for use as permanent records of decisions made.

One solution to problems such as these which is proposed by the software engineering community is to translate decisions made into more formal (or at least semi-formal) notations such as data flow diagrams or entity relationship models. It is often assumed that this translation would be carried out by a requirements engineer who would be present at design meetings and would then record what was decided outside of the meetings.

The aim of the second study reported in this paper was to investigate whether this was likely to be a useful and reliable way of supporting the design process.

3 Study 2: Use of semi-formal representations

3.1 Introduction

This study takes up the question described above; whether semi-formal representations generated by a requirements engineer, who has been present at a design meeting, may be used as a reliable record of design decisions made during the meeting. The aim of the study was to investigate the use of three different kinds of 'semi-formal' graphical representations in recording decisions about high level dialogue design. We wished to investigate whether each designer's memory for the design decision reached was the same as that of the others by comparing the way in which decisions were recorded in each of the notations (see step 3). We were also interested in whether agreement between designers would apparently be greater when decisions were recorded using one notation rather than another.

3.2 Procedure

This study was done following a further SPIRE project meeting at which a high level design for part of the SPIRE system dialogue was discussed. Four designers were present at the meeting (S, M, P and J). Note that S, M and J had been part of the previous study, but that F was replaced by P in this meeting. At the end of the meeting, each of the designers' own graphical representations of the dialogue agreed upon were collected. These had been drawn during and after discussions in the meeting which related to a fifth drawing on the white board.

In this study, each participant was approached on the day after the meeting and was asked to:

1. Describe in general terms what his/her own diagram was about.
2. Label all important parts of his/her own diagram.
3. Draw a representation of what was decided upon in the meeting using:

   • a Flowchart
   • a State Transition Network (STN)
   • a Jackson Structure Diagram (JSD)

   using the prompt sheets provided to find out what symbols to use for each notation, and what those symbols should mean. Drawings could be done in any order.

4. After each drawing, describe any problems with using the notation ("Was there anything you wanted to represent but couldn't using this notation?" "Did you have any difficulties with understanding how to use the notation?").

5. Note any further comments e.g. about how the notations compare.

(Note that the purpose of steps 1 and 2 was mainly to remind participants of what had been discussed in the meeting in preparation for attempting step 3.)

3.3 Results

No consistent patterns were observable in the orders in which designers chose to tackle drawing diagrams using the three notations requested, or in the times they took to produce those diagrams.

The characteristics of diagrams drawn using each of the notations were as follows.

Flowcharts. An analysis of the diagrams in terms of the occurrence of symbols given to the participants on the prompt sheets shows that they were used in the following way.

Table 3 Numbers of flowchart processes, conditions and arrows drawn by each designer

	Total Processes	Total Conditions	Total Arrows
S	7	2	13
M	7	6	18
P	7	5	15
J	8	2	10

Some processes (such as an initial Start or Enter process, and database and advice browsing processes) were identified by all designers. Others (such as Quit, Set Profile, and Browse Tasks) were only identified by some. The setting of user profiles was treated differently by different designers: for example, one (P) broke this down into three separate processes, while others treated profile setting as a single process; also two designers (P and M) indicated that the user could return to setting the profile from other points in the dialogue, whereas two (S and J) showed the setting of the user profile as a one-off activity at the beginning of the dialogue.

Table 4 Flowchart processes drawn by each designer
('•' means the process indicated was included in the relevant subject's flowchart)

	S	M	P	J
Start / Enter	•	•	•	•
Quit	•	•	•	
View Subject Index	•			
Access / Browse Database	•	•	•	•
Browse / Read Advice	•	•	•	•
Set Profile	•	•		•
Select User Type, Disability and Division				•
Set User Type			•	
Set Disability			•	
Set Division			•	
Set Default Profile	•	•		•
Browse Tasks		•		•
Refined View of Database				•

The comments recorded by the designers after producing flowcharts were as follows:

- Couldn't show details of 'setting profile' procedure. (S)
- Couldn't show that advice given depends on profile. (S)
- Ended up filling in bits of design I didn't feel were decided on in the meeting. (S)
- Not sure if I'm using flowchart syntax properly (horizontal arrows). (S)
- Hard to fit ideas into this sort of framework. (M)
- OK for this decision as it lent itself to simple Y/N questions, but I wouldn't use it for preference. (J)
- The flowchart was OK but suffers from the same drawbacks as JSD [see below] as well as being too procedural. (M)

State Transition Networks (STNs). An analysis of the STNs produced by the four designers reveals that the numbers of states specified by all designers was the same (though what these states varied considerably - see below), but that differing numbers of transitions were recorded.

Table 5 Numbers of STN states and transitions drawn by each designer

	Total States	Total Transitions
S	7	9
M	7	1 4
P	7	1 2
J	7	8

Again, some states (such as an initial Start or Enter state, and database and advice browsing states) were identified by all designers. Others (such as Quit, Access Mode Choice, Viewing the Subject Index, and Viewing Task Hierarchy) were only identified by some. The setting of user profiles was also treated differently by different designers: some gave a more detailed description of the states involved in this process than others.

Table 6 STN states drawn by each designer

	S	M	P	J
Start / Enter	•	•	•	•
Quit			•	
Access Mode Choice	•			
Viewing Subject Index	•			
Database Access / Browsing	•	•	•	•
Advice Browsing	•	•	•	•
Viewing Task Hierarchy	•	•		•
Profile Setting	•	•		•
User Profile Setting		•		•
Default Profile Setting		•		•
Set Student			•	
Set Disability			•	
Set Division			•	

The comments recorded by the designers after producing their STNs were as follows:

- Assume can quit system at any point. (S)
- States are always linked with what's on the screen. (S)
- Could put some information about transitions on arrows but not enough e.g. couldn't describe that advice displayed depends on profile set and task chosen very easily. (S)
- Filled in some bits not decided in meeting. (S)

- Not sure whether the bits circled in red are valid system states/transitions - possibly this is just one transition? (M)
- I keep wanting to put more interface detail in re: where do you go after Select Task or DB Access. This was not discussed at meeting and could be misleading if added. (J)
- Of the three notations, the STN was the most expressive for the ideas I wanted to capture. (M)

Fig. 2. STN produced by designer P for study 2

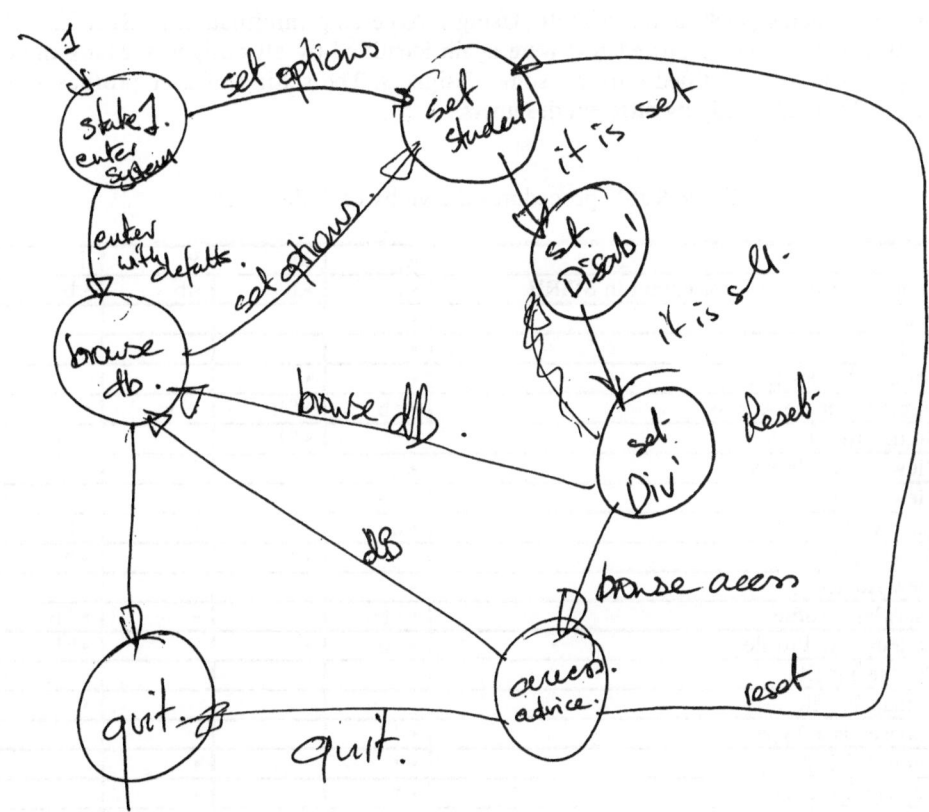

Jackson Structure Diagrams (JSDs). The following numbers of procedures were used:

Table 7 Numbers of JSD procedures drawn by each designer

	Total Procedures
S	19
M	12
P	9
J	10

Some procedures (such as the overall Using / Accessing Information in SPIRE, and Direct Database Access procedures) were again identified by all designers. Many more components were identified only by some designers. The setting of user profiles was again tackled differently by different designers.

Table 8 JSD procedures drawn by each designer

	S	M	P	J
Using / Accessing Information in SPIRE	• b	• b	• b	• b
Start	•			
Quit	• *			
Choose Access Route	•	•		
Direct Database Access	• ° b	• ° b	• ° •	• °
Guided Information	• ° b	• ° b		• ° b
View Subject Index	•			
View Database	• * • *	•• °		
Set Profile	• b	• * b	• b	• b
Select Task		• °		• *
View Advice	• *	• °		• *
User Sets Profile	• ° b	• °	•	• ° b
System Sets Profile	• ° b	• °	•	• ° b
Choose Profile				•
Default Profile				•
Choose User Type	• *		•	
Choose Disability	• *		•	
Choose Division	• *		•	
Set User = Student	•			
Set Disability = All	•			
Set Division = All	•			
Browse Data		•		

•• : procedure occurs twice in the diagram
b : procedure is broken down further
°   : procedure is defined as optional
* : procedure is defined as iterative

The comments recorded by the designers after producing their JSDs were as follows:

- Can't show relation between two 'view info from db' boxes. (S)
- Can't show swapping between advice and data layer or subject index and data layer (but not sure this decided in the meeting anyway). (S)
- Can't show that advice given depends on profile. (S)
- Good to be able to break down functions. (S)
- Diagram got unwieldy. (S)
- Not sure if this is the right way to represent choices. (S)
- Doesn't seem very suitable for designing flexible dialogues. (S)
- In general I found it harder to do this than the other two methods. I think this was because in the meeting we talked about conceptual design rather than implementation and I have always seen JSD as more biased towards implementation issues. (M)
- Found this harder than flow chart. (J)
- I don't think it makes the selection decisions very obvious. (J)
- Wasn't sure where to put the detail of profile selection. (J)
- Numbering looks cumbersome. (J)
- How do I show select one or the other? (J)
- I found the JSD too low level for high level design ideas and too restrictive. (M)

3.4 Conclusions

A number of challenges were identified in relation to the post hoc recording of design decisions using semi-formal notations.

The same designer may record design decisions differently using different notations.

One example of this is the specification of a quit option. The possibility of quitting from the program under design was not actually discussed during the meeting, and no explicit decisions regarding quitting had been made in any previous meeting. Thus, the fact that J never specified how a user would quit from the program may reflect the fact that she was faithfully following the instructions of the study to specify only what she felt had been decided in the meeting. However, the other designers decided to incorporate a quit into their graphical specifications. Interestingly, each incorporated it (explicitly) in only some of their diagrams. While S included it explicitly in both the flowchart and JSD representations, she did not include it in the STN, but noted that she was assuming it would be possible to quit at any point. M included quit only in his flowchart representation, and P only in the flowchart and STN.

Table 9 Occurrences of the 'Quit' option in each designer's representations

	Flowchart	STN	JSD
S	•	Assumed from anywhere	•
M	•		
P	•	•	
J			

Another example of this problem is that in her flowchart representation, J specified that users should be able to move from one part of the system (where they were viewing advice) to another (where they would be able to see a refined view of the database). In her STN, she did not specify that this should be possible.

It is too early to say what features of the notation are significant here, though we might speculate that the sequential view of interactions which flowcharts and JSD force on the designer are more likely to lead to the specification of a quit option as the final procedure in a chain of interactions. Specifying the fact that the user should be able to quit from the system at any time is never easy in a graphical notation and quickly leads to diagrams becoming too complex to be helpful.

Different designers may use the same semi-formal notations in different ways.

With flowcharts, some designers used a condition to denote a point where the system asks the user for input and then acts according to the input received (e.g. J's condition: 'Do you want to?'). Others used a condition to describe something which the system does internally without the user being aware of it (e.g. S's condition: 'Profile set?').

In the State Transition Networks, there were differences in emphasis about what different designers thought should be represented as states. S's states corresponded to what might be on the screen at a particular point in the interaction. M's and J's were more task-related. Furthermore, some people put in states what others put in transitions. For example, S used a state to represent the point where users could choose between the two available access modes, whereas other designers simply specified two possible transitions from the previous state. Some people gave more detailed descriptions of transitions than others. An example from S's diagram is: 'Profile set: use user type to choose task hierarchy'. Examples from J's diagram are: 'Yes', 'No', 'Select DB', 'Select Guided Information'.

Three of the designers used the JSD notation in much the same way. The diagram produced by the fourth was much sketchier.

Designers who are not experienced or trained in the use of a semi-formal notation may use it incorrectly.

One of the participants in the study was confused over whether they had used the flowchart notation correctly, some designers did not label all transitions in the State Transition Networks, and three of the designers used the JSD notation incorrectly, despite having access to a prompt sheet which gave a general description of how to use it.

Some differences in designers' views and recollections of design decisions remain constant when decisions are recorded in different notations.

Sometimes, designers included in their diagrams things which were not discussed at the meeting but were assumed to follow from previous meetings. Not all designers agree on these issues. For example, S recorded the fact that users should access one part of the system (the database) in a particular way (via a subject index), but no other designer mentioned this. The use of a subject index to access the database had been discussed at a previous meeting but not explicitly decided upon. As a result of that meeting, S apparently assumed that it was to be used in the way specified, but other designers did not.

As another example, P had recorded a different and more detailed view of a particular part of the interaction (that in which a user's 'profile' is set) than other designers in each of his diagrams. It is interesting to note that the diagram drawn by P during the meeting was the only one to have been drawn 'as a discussion tool' rather than as a record of the design decision reached, so that his memory for what was decided might not have been so precise as that of other designers who recorded the decision in the meeting.

If diagrams using particular notations become too complex, designers may forget to put some things in.

For example, S recorded the fact that users would see a particular part of the system (the task hierarchy) in her flowchart and STN diagrams, but not in the JSD (which was drawn third). Her JSD representation had already become quite complex by the time she came to specifying the relevant part of the system - it practically filled the page already - and she may have forgotten to specify the use of the task hierarchy because of the size and apparent complexity of the diagram.

4 Discussion

The results of study 2 suggest that caution should be exercised in assigning the job of recording design decisions, or specifying design solutions, after design meetings to a single individual. For each of the semi-formal notations investigated, the decisions recorded by different designers after the meeting were different. Some of the differences in view were common across notations - these differences between the designers' memories for decisions reached were constant no matter what notation was used to record them. Other differences in view were apparent only when certain notations were used.

Each of the semi-formal notations used in the study appeared to have its own drawbacks. Comments about the difficulties experienced in using the three notations can be broadly categorised into three main areas:

- difficulties in expressing particular design decisions (different notations make different things difficult)
- use of semi-formal representations encouraging specification of more detailed design than was decided
- concern over diagram complexity

It seems likely that restrictions imposed by the notations used (and possibly also by the designers' lack of familiarity with the notations) could have lead designers to adapt and accommodate their memories of the design decisions made to the constraints of the notations, thereby tending to increase the differences between the decisions recorded by different designers.

The use of informal representations such as those considered in study 1 has the advantage that it does not impose any conceptual constraints on those drawing them. This is very useful, particularly during the early stages of a project where creative thinking is required. Such diagrams are commonly used in design meetings when new ideas are being discussed, and designers creating and viewing such representations can develop a reasonable degree of shared understanding, particularly in relation to informal representations which are relatively well-developed (such as the 'layer' diagram). However, understanding in relation to sketchier representations (such as the 'local' diagram) is less reliable. While the sense of agreement generated by the discussion of common artefacts during a meeting may be useful in terms of strengthening the team, it can have undesirable effects if it is, in fact, not based on proper understanding. It is worth noting here that the members of the design team who are likely to mis-understand each other most are those who do not share a great deal of experience - for example new comers to the design team (who will often be the programmers responsible for fine tuning the design!) are likely to mis-understand something which is agreed between senior members of the team on the basis of shared experience from previous projects.

One solution to the problems of relying on informal representations which is proposed by the software engineering community is to have requirements engineers translate decisions made into semi-formal notations outside of the meetings. This solution has its own problems. If no real agreement between designers has been generated during a meeting, then the view recorded by an individual requirements engineer may easily not be representative of all designers' views. The constraints imposed by the use of a semi-formal notation are likely to lead to further deviation from the views of those present in the initial meeting.

We suggest that designers should be encouraged to continue sketching out informal representations during design meetings held early in a project, and also during the early stages of later meetings, both for general discussion and for their own personal use. We have already discussed the way in which using informal representations in general discussion enables creativity and the development of a feeling of shared understanding. We also note that in study 2, where three of the designers (S, M and J) drew their own (informal) representations of what was being agreed during the course of the meeting whereas the fourth (P) did not, the semi-formal representations drawn by P after the meeting showed consistent differences from those drawn by S, M and J. Thus drawing even informal representations of decisions during a meeting appears to assist designers in appreciating and accurately remembering what is discussed.

In addition to using such informal representations, we suggest that as the project progresses, it is worthwhile to focus discussions by attempting to generate semi-formal representations during the later stages of a meeting with all designers present. This facilitates the development of a more detailed, but still shared, understanding of the design solutions proposed, and means that the representations produced serve as a reliable record of what was actually agreed during the meeting. Semi-formal representations can be used as a basis for discussion, negotiation, and specification of agreement during the meeting - effectively playing the role of a joint contract agreed by all designers present. Diagrams drawn using semi-formal notations can be composed by one or more of the designers present in a public way and taking account of the views of all designers present - conflicts being publicly resolved as necessary. We suggest that this might be done using shared physical or computer-based (CASE) tools which support the creation of appropriate diagrams - for example allowing designers to easily manipulate symbols used in notations appropriate for describing the relevant design decisions. We aim to continue our research in this area in order to investigate the feasibility of this approach.

References

1. Bearne, M., Hewitt, J., Jones, S. and Sapsford-Francis, J. "Providing public access to information in complex and weakly structured domains: a 3-layered model for hypermedia information systems", *New Review of Hypermedia and Multimedia, Applications and Research*, vol 2 (1996).

2. Bransford, J.D, Sherwood, R.D., and Sturdevant, T. "Teaching Thinking and Problem Solving" in Baron J.B. and Sternberg R.J. (Ed.s) *Teaching Thinking Skills: Theory and Practice.* Freeman (1987).

3. Britton, C. Jones, S. Myers, M. and Sharif, M. "A survey of current practice in the development of multimedia systems", *Information and Software Technology*, vol 39, 695-705 (1997).

4. Getzels J. and Csikszentmihalyi M. *The creative vision: A longitudinal study of problem finding in art.* New York, Wiley (1976).

5. Glucksberg, S. and Danks "Effects of discriminative labels and of nonsense labels upon availability of novel function" *Journal of Verbal Learning and Verbal Behaviour*, vol 7, 72-6 (1968).

6. Meadow, A., Parnes, SJ. and Reese, H. "Influence of brainstorming instruction and problem sequence on a creative problem solving test" *Journal of Applied Psychology* , vol 43, 413-416 (1959).

7. Osborn A.F. *Applied Imagination.* New York, Scribner (1953).

Pragmatic Formal Design:
A Case Study in Integrating Formal Methods into the
HCI Development Cycle

Meurig Sage and Chris Johnson,
GIST,
Department of Computing Science,
University of Glasgow, Glasgow,
Scotland United Kingdom, G12 8QQ.
E-mail: {meurig,johnson}@dcs.gla.ac.uk

Abstract Formal modelling, in interactive system design, has received considerably less real use than might have been hoped. Formal methods can be expensive to use, with poor coverage of the design life cycle. In this paper, we suggest a pragmatic approach to formal design. We rely on a range of models that can help at different stages of development. We use as a case study, the design of a multi-user, design rationale editor. In the early stages of our design, we use a range of semi-formal notations, to perform a task analysis. We then develop a prototype in Clock, a high level functional language. From this, we derive a LOTOS specification, which we use to verify that our system satisfies important design requirements. The task analysis helps here, in highlighting these requirements. Throughout we rely on tool support to simplify the process, and so make it cost effective.

1 Introduction

Formal specifications, of interactive systems, have been proposed as a means of improving design [19, 30]. Unfortunately, they have experienced less real use than might have been hoped. Fields et al [12] argue that they can be overly cumbersome for use in initial design stages. Developers often do not wish to expend the considerable amount of effort necessary in producing detailed formal specifications, if they may need to reconsider the whole design and alter significant portions of the model. It can be difficult to get a good idea of what a system will look like without an initial prototype. Certainly designers may be unwilling to carry out complex proofs until they are reasonably happy with the initial design. Instead, Fields et al [11] argue that lightweight, simple models may be useful to help focus in on specific design problems. Only later might a more detailed specification be useful to help guarantee properties about a system, and only then if it could be produced in a cost efficient way.

1.1 A Pragmatic Design Approach

This paper presents an approach to design that deals with some of these problems. We take a pragmatic approach that aims to:
- re-use existing techniques;

- make good use of tool support to assist design stages;
- provide good coverage for all stages of development.

A summary of our approach can be seen in Fig. 1. We use a set of lightweight models at the initial stages of the design, including high-level task designs, paper prototypes and more detailed interaction models to focus on parts of the design. These allow us to quickly focus on early design issues. We develop a prototype in Clock, a constraint based language [14]. This allows us to program at a very high level of abstraction, and enables us to quickly produce a well structured prototype. We then derive a LOTOS specification from this prototype. This allows us to develop a full specification of the system with a minimum of cost and effort. We can then attempt to guarantee properties about the system using LOTOS simulation [31, 27] and model checking [13, 30] technology. We rely here on the earlier task analysis to direct the formal model checking. We make use of design rationale methods [26], to attempt to justify design decisions throughout, and to link parts of the design together. The whole design method is iterative; each stage can feed back into earlier stages. We do not formalise each and every step, but we do maximise our use of well developed HCI techniques such as task analysis [24], design rationale and iterative development. This pragmatic approach is adopted because of the costs associated with full formal refinement.

The paper is organised as follows. In Section 2 we introduce our example, showing why it is appropriate. We then introduce each stage of our design method in Section 3. In Section 4 we then discuss the actual design, highlighting some important development decisions that were made, and how each stage helped us to consider these decisions. Finally, in Section 5 we present some conclusions about the effectiveness of our approach.

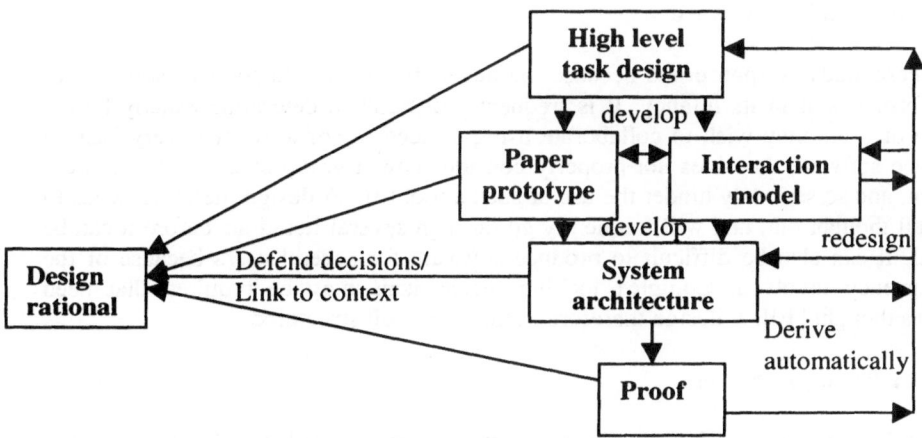

Fig. 1 - The Design Approach

2 Case Study: A Multi-user Design rationale Editor

2.1 The Case Study

We use, for our example, the design of a multiple user, design rationale editor. This provides for a fairly complex case study, where significant design decisions are needed and where concurrency is required. This concurrency adds an extra level of complexity that makes formal specification and proof helpful. For instance, in ensuring liveness and safety requirements are satisfied for multiple users of a shared workspace. However, this work still represents only an initial feasibility study with our approach.

2.2 Design rationale

Design rationale has received a lot of attention [28]. A number of semi-formal notations have been developed that attempt to document clearly why design decisions were made. The Questions, Options and Criteria (QOC) notation is one such notation developed at Rank Xerox [33]. It is a graphical notation that highlights key questions in a design, and links them with possible options and criteria that support those options. Several studies [eg 34] have highlighted the need for tool support for this notation. A variety of tools have been developed, frequently based on hypertext systems. However, current tool support is frequently inadequate for designers needs [35]. In particular, tools often provide little support for multi-user activities. Buckingham Shum [35] argues that design rationale itself is still in its infancy. This makes it difficult to be sure exactly how designers will wish to use these tools. Iterative development is therefore required to explore different ways of satisfying the needs of designers.

2.3 Collaborative Software

This case study is appropriate because the development of collaborative software of this form is still in its infancy. It is frequently difficult to determine exactly how a group of users may wish to collaborate using a piece of software. It is very easy to produce software that does not properly consider how a group of users may share a design, and so seriously hinder the use of such a tool [3]. A design therefore needs to be well thought out, and will frequently go through several iterations before it can be useful. It can also be difficult to produce software for several users because of the concurrency involved. Complex locking mechanisms may be required that need serious thought [10]. A design therefore needs to be well structured.

2.4 Our Prototype System

Figure 2 shows the interface for the prototype system we produced. It allows several users to build a QOC rationale. Users can create nodes (Questions, Options or Criteria) and connect them together. They can edit the design at any time. When one user is modifying a node, other users are prevented from manipulating it. Users can also note their actions, and any extra textual information using a shared log. Finally, each user can hide or view certain nodes to make browsing easier. Using the view menu, they can filter their view of nodes to show only Questions and Decisions; Questions, Decisions and Criteria; Questions and all Options; Questions, all Options and Criteria. They can also hide all nodes following a particular node, as has been done with "Q:24" in Figure 2. The problems in our initial interface design will be removed through the process of iterative prototyping and evaluation.

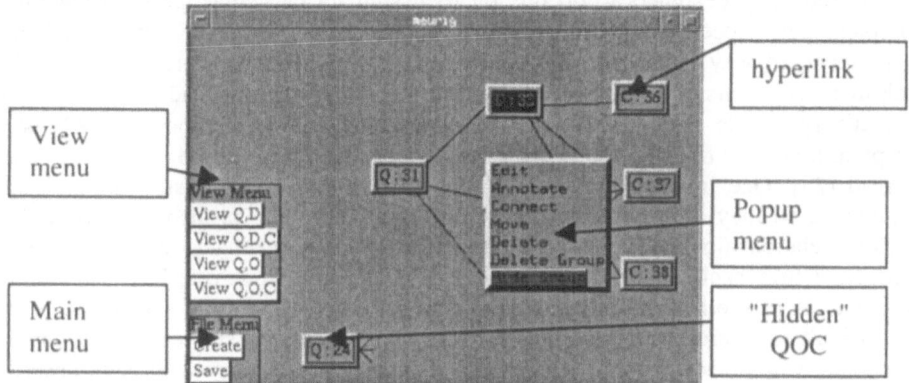

Fig. 2 - The QOC editor

3 The design approach

We will now discuss our design method, and how each design phase helped in the development of this system.

3.1 Requirements Elicitation

As discussed earlier (Fig. 1), we use an iterative development method with several stages. The very first stage in the development process is requirements elicitation. We need to gain contextual knowledge, from activities such as observational studies and questionnaires. For our example, we rely on the results of observational studies of design rationale use by Buckingham Shum and Maclean [34, 35, 26]. We concentrate on the design approach that follows these initial requirements gathering exercises.

3.2 Task analysis & Paper Prototyping

We use a high-level task design is to summarise the results of a contextual analysis, and structure the design. This is accompanied by initial paper prototyping to aid in focussing the design. More detailed specifications and prototyping can follow. Design decisions at each of these stages are linked back to the contextual information that has been gathered, through the use of design rationale. This process is, however, very iterative. For instance, a basic amount of prototyping was required to gain a deep enough understanding for a good high-level task specification.

3.3 Semi-Formal Interaction Design

When developing complex concurrent systems, interaction becomes more complex. This means that designers should be able to consider and discuss the details of multi-user interaction. Scenario design can help in describing how users may interact with the system and each other [7]. Semi-formal notations such as the User Action Notation (UAN) [20] help designers to do this by focussing on particular tasks. Producing a complete UAN specification for a design can be costly. However, when used in a more focussed way it can be helpful, for instance, when considering the complex locking mechanisms in a collaborative system. UAN has the major advantage that it is a relatively simple notation to learn. A study by Johnson, comparing UAN with temporal logic and transition networks, showed that designers found it relatively easy to read [23]. One important use of UAN here can simply be documenting design arguments, so they are visible to others. Informal reasoning is also supported. The obvious relationship between user actions and interface feedback makes it easy to consider issues such as the predictability of a design. However, UAN has some problems. As a semi-formal notation it has no fully defined formal semantics. It can be difficult to express complex actions that require choice. However, this can be overcome, where necessary, by using LOTOS temporal operators with it, to describe the more complex activities. XUAN [16], an extension to UAN, made use of LOTOS like operators. As we show in Section 4.5, the focus provided by UAN can be used as a basis for testing the system design later on.

3.4 Prototyping

The next important stage in the design is prototyping. Recent tools for rapid prototyping, such as Visual Basic, have made developing software easier. A simple prototype can be developed very quickly. However, such tools tend to sacrifice structure for flexibility [14]. It may be easy to produce a piece of software, but if it becomes unmanageably complex it may hinder iterative development. This becomes a more significant problem when dealing with multi-user systems. The development of such systems requires concurrency. Some data may be shared between a group of users; other data may only be accessible to one user. A well structured design is needed to make it clear to a programmer how data is shared, and what effect several users acting on the same data will have. This complexity stretches many first generation HCI prototyping tools such as Alexander's "me too" [2]. A high-level, constraint based programming language, such as Clock [14] is, however, suitable for this sort of development. In Clock, architectures are built visually, in a component-based way, allowing for a good understanding of the structure of a system. We will discuss Clock in more detail in section 4.3. Graham et al [15] suggest a method for developing UAN specifications into Clock architectures. Development can therefore take place in a structured way, and we can develop prototypes rapidly.

3.5 Formal specification and Proof

When building a complex concurrent system it can be difficult to guarantee its behaviour. Though structured design and semi-formal models are helpful, formal specifications and proof can be very important. For example, though UAN supports informal reasoning, it does not support interaction proofs. Recent work on formal system modelling can help here. However, designers may be put off if the effort required to develop a specification, and prove it correct, is too great. To make this stage as simple as possible, we derive a LOTOS interactor network from our Clock prototype. When we are satisfied with the initial design, the Clock architecture can be transformed into a LOTOS specification (See Section 4.4). We can then perform some proofs with this specification (See Section 4.5). We can also demonstrate task conformance between the LOTOS behaviour of the UAN specification, and the LOTOS system specification [27].

4 The QOC Editor Design

4.1 High level task specification

The first stage in the design was the development of a high-level task specification. For this we made use of ConcurTaskTrees [4]. This notation provides a graphical representation, in a tree structure. Tasks can be related by a set of operators, based on those provided with LOTOS. The notation separates tasks into four different categories, user tasks, application tasks, interaction tasks and abstract tasks. User tasks are those carried out only by the user or between groups of users; application tasks are those carried out completely by the system; interaction tasks involve the use and the application, while abstract tasks relate to higher level goals in the system.

The LOTOS operators that we use, in this example, to compose tasks together are:
- interleaving (|||) - the actions of two tasks are mixed and carried out in any order
- sequencing (>>) - two tasks are carried out one after another
- choice ([]) - either of two tasks can be performed

The task specification for our design is shown in Fig. 3. It says that the tasks involved in use of the QOC editor consists of creating and redesigning QOCs. Creating a QOC consists of adding questions, options and criteria (*Create Nodes*) and noting down any more detailed information about these nodes (*Support Rationale*). These nodes can be connected together (*Connect Nodes*). For instance, supporting criteria will be linked to objects. The QOC will undergo discussion and redesign (*Redesign*). When dealing with a large design, users will probably wish to focus in on particular QOCs (*Focus*). Users can modify their design. They may add new criteria, or delete old ones that are considered irrelevant. Particular nodes (Questions, Options or Criteria) may, for instance, be renamed (*Change Label*). Certain criteria may also be changed into options, or questions may be decomposed further (*Change Node Type*). These different activities have been noted in empirical and observational investigations into use of design rationale [35]. Users will also want to move objects around as a design continues to make the QOC more visually appealing (*Beautify QOC*).

The activity of focussing in on a design (*Focus*) may require different forms of support. Users may wish to follow a design through a set of questions and decisions, ignoring discarded options. They may also wish to see how different criteria relate to each other, or how the design has progressed over time [34].

Some tasks may simply be performed by individual users. However, there is a core of individual tasks that are dedicated to multiple user activity. The discussion activities (surrounded by a box in Fig. 3) will involve the activities of multiple users. As the development continues users may also wish to work together to modify and create new design rationales.

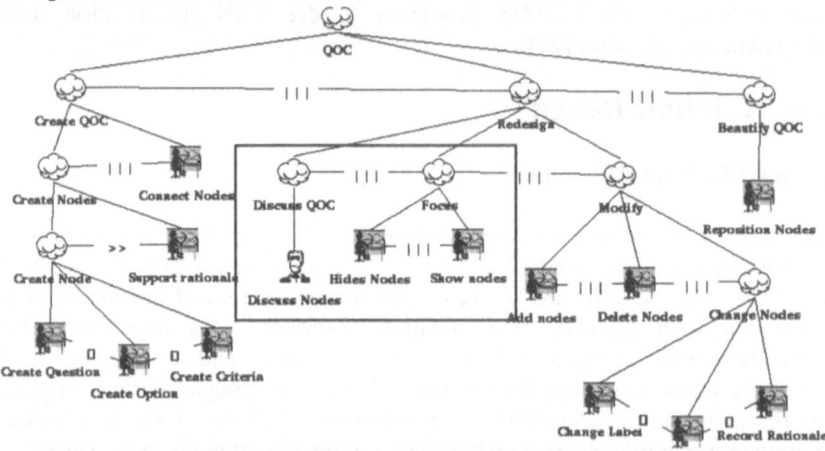

Fig. 3 - ConcurTaskTree Specification

The use of a ConcurTaskTree specification provides a visually appealing, clear description of the basic aims of the design. The use of LOTOS operators gives a clear definition to the task design , and helps to maintain consistency across our design approach. Again, it also satisfies one of our prime objectives: to integrate existing HCI techniques to support formal methods in the development cycle.

4.2 Detailed Interaction Design

The Approach. The next stage in the development was to produce a more detailed system design. To do this we used a mixture of paper prototyping, UAN specifications and design space analysis. For the design space analysis, we bootstrap the design of the QOC editor using QOCs themselves. The use of QOCs here helped relate possible designs back to the contextual requirements. It also helped link information gained from UAN analysis to design decisions. This process was therefore one of literate specification [22], where different elements of a design are linked together, to make understanding it easier. For this stage, we could have made use of other design rationale languages, such as gIBIS [8]. This use of QOCs again relates back to our pragmatic criteria as the notation is well known, simple and easy to read.

The paper prototyping was used initially to feed back into the task design. The key design feature needed was flexibility: designers should be able to put QOCs together in any order. Design tools have often faced problems because they restricted the way a designer could work. In our system nodes can be created and moved, connected or deleted in almost any order. Their text can be annotated, both the label and the type of the node (eg is it a Question , Option or Criteria). Users can also filter their view of the whole QOC. The resulting interaction is fairly complex, but becomes more so when several users are involved. We will consider the basic locking mechanism, and an example of users deleting parts of a QOC, as examples of how semi-formal notations helped our design.

Interaction Design Example I - Locking mechanisms. Users have to be able to design QOCs together. Though users may face no problems when working on different QOCs, when they come to discuss the design of one particular QOC in more detail they may face problems. At this stage, one user may attempt to edit a question, while another attempts to delete that question. Collaborative working can then become difficult.

There are several solutions that can be taken to this problem. The first is simply ignore it, and let users develop their own social protocols [1]. In this case, it is simply up to the users to agree a strategy that prevents them from modifying the same data simultaneously.

Alternatively, we could implement a locking mechanism that prevents more than one user altering the system at a time. Locking mechanisms can be implemented at various different grains [1]. For instance, we could force only one user to make any modifications to the QOC design at a time, thereby using a *coarse* grained locking mechanism. This would usually be too severe. A more sensible approach would be to prevent more than one user from modifying any node at a time. This results in a more *finely* grained locking mechanism.

Once we have decided on this general mechanism, we need to consider exactly how the locking mechanism should be implemented for a particular interface. For instance, we should consider when exactly should locks be enabled: should the locking mechanism be implicit or explicit.

The QOC in Fig. 4 can be used to summarise the argument. Implicit locks require less effort on the part of the user and are therefore to be preferred. The possible race conditions mentioned in the QOC criteria can be understood by looking at the UAN specification in Table 1. Two users both attempt to alter a node. Both have accessed the menu, but user two clicks faster than user one. User one may therefore be confused that they have attempted to modify a node but have failed part way through. Another possibility would be to lock the node immediately after the menu was selected. This would prevent this sort of race condition. However, it would also prevent one user accessing the node's log while another user was editing it.

The scenario above assumes a "non-optimistic" locking policy, where a user is forced to wait for a lock before they can proceed [18]. More "optimistic" forms of locking policy are possible, where a user interface allows changes to be made while waiting for a lock. If a lock is not then granted all changes will be automatically undone. In this case our scenario would be more complex, and our interface design would require greater sophistication to prevent confusion.

UAN helps highlight this sort of scenario in an easy to read way. It helps us consider this kind of interaction and guarantee that we provide appropriate feedback in cases of mutual interaction. It makes it easier to share these considerations and decisions with other designers. This would be very much more difficult with the ConcurTaskTree (Fig. 3) representation because of its higher level of abstraction.

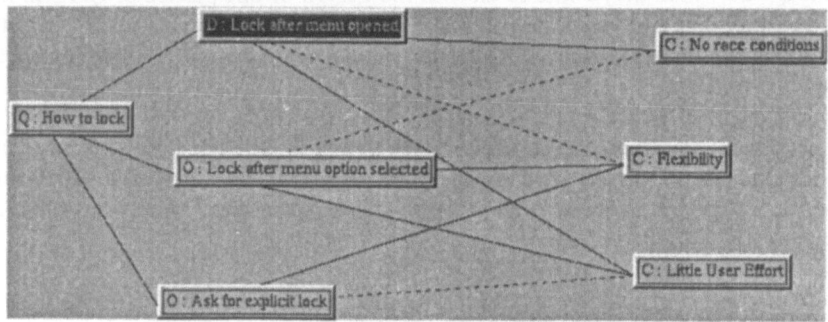

Fig. 4 - QOC for basic locking mechanism

Table 1 - UAN Specification - Lock after menu selection

User 1			User 2		
User Action	Feedback	Interface State	User Action	Feedback	Interface State
Select menu	Menu appears				
			Select menu	Menu appears	
		Node appears locked on user's screen	Select edit	Unlocked => Enter edit mode	Unlocked => Lock, Begin Editing
Select delete	Locked => Error message	Do nothing			

Interaction Design Example II - Hiding and deleting nodes. A potentially serious problem can be discovered when we look at filtered views of a QOC design. This problem emerged as a result of our UAN analysis, and so provides a good example of why the notation is useful.

Users need to be able to hide part of a QOC design when it becomes large enough, so as to prevent too much clutter on the screen. In our editor, we provide a number of hiding strategies. One of the above is the ability to hide part of a QOC. For instance, consider the situation in Table 2. There are two QOCs in existence, but only one of them is fully viewable. This ability to hide QOCs has an effect on the ability to treat them as groups, particularly the ability to delete. We might wish, for example, to be able to delete a group of QOC nodes. Several possible choices are shown in Fig. 5.

We can choose not to allow deleting of objects when they are filtered. Alternatively, we can choose to reshow the whole group and then delete that node. The most flexible alternative is to provide a "Delete Group" operation. This flexibility is important as it relates to what Green [17] calls viscosity. Without it, making changes to the QOC editor would be far more cumbersome. However, when adding this flexibility, we have to seriously consider whether it will be safe, in relation to multi-user interaction.

We can demonstrate a possible problem and solution using UAN (Table 2). If user one attempts to delete a whole QOC, while user two is altering part of that QOC, there will be a problem. This will require some form of feedback. Again UAN can be used to consider the scenario and attempt to provide a safe route through it.

At an early design stage, a number of problems will be faced. Designers need to be able to consider such activities without resorting to time consuming, heavy weight formal models. They are, in fact, unlikely to want to do so. A variety of modelling approaches can instead be used [11]. More task centred, light weight models are easier for considering the initial interaction design. Because of their simplicity, they allow designers to rapidly consider possible scenarios. Though UAN is a semi-formal modelling language, with many restrictions [19], it can still be used to successfully consider early design problems.

Table 2 -UAN specification for delete group design

User 1			User 2		
User Action	Feedback	Interface State	User Action	Feedback	Interface State
			Select menu for Question Q	Menu appears	
			Select Hide Group after Q	All nodes after Q vanish (including criterion C)	
Select menu for criterion C	Menu appears				
Select edit	Unlocked => Enter edit mode	Unlocked => Lock criterion C			Criterion C locked
			Select menu for Question Q	Menu appears	
			Select Delete Group	Not all unlocked => error message *	Not all unlocked => do nothing

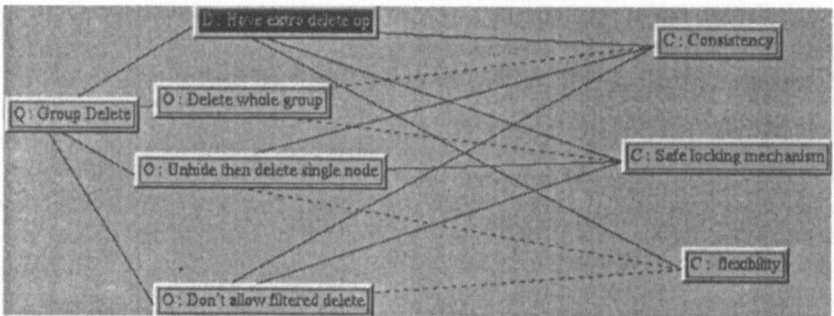

Fig. 5 - QOC to discuss deleting

4.3 Developing a prototype

Possible Approaches. While we can use design notations to consider the interaction in a system, to get a real idea of what a system will look like we need to use a prototype. To do this, we need a high-level, rapid prototyping environment. This should minimise the translation between prototype and formal specification [2]. There are a number of possible languages that could be used at this stage [eg 29, 32]. We make use of Clock a constraint based functional language [14].

The Clock Development Language. Clock is a graphical architecture language that can be used to describe how systems fit together and a textual language to describe the behaviour of each component. It is based on the MVC [25] model. A system is described by decomposing a design from the root view into a number of component sub-views. Components can communicate via constraints, and update events. In a similar way to the PAC architecture model [9], a system therefore appears as a hierarchy of components.

Components contain an *event handler*, which takes user inputs and sends updates. This *event handler* is similar to the *controller* part of the MVC model. Components also contain abstract data types (*ADTs*) which represent the MVC *model* and can receive inputs and accept requests. A component has a view, which is defined as a relation of the model. This is therefore similar to Hill's ALV model [21].

Clock architectures are produced interactively using a visual tool called *ClockWorks* [14]. This allows programmers to design and modify their architectures easily. It provides easy access to a library of components. Fast iterative design is therefore possible.

Clock also supports groupware applications [14]. View functions are provided to allow windows to be opened up on different users' screens. A distributed version has also been developed. Programmers can specify that some data should exist on the user's side and other data should exist on the client's side. This aids the easy development of groupware applications.

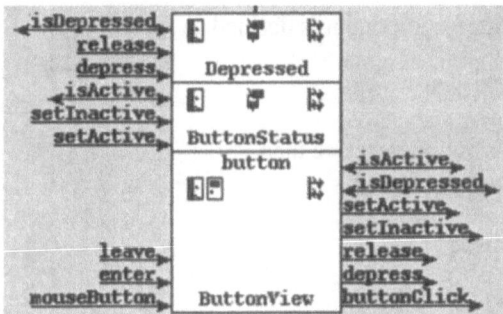

Fig. 6 - A Clock Button

An Example with Clock. As an example of a simple Clock application, consider the definition of a button. When the user presses it, it appears pressed; when the button is released it performs an action. The Clock architecture for this object can be seen in Fig. 6. It is made of three objects, named *Depressed*, *ButtonStatus* and *ButtonView*.

The *Depressed* object is an ADT. It has three methods: *release*, *depress* and *isDepressed*. The first two are updates that set the state of the ADT, the last is a request method that returns the state. The *ButtonStatus* ADT is similar.

The *button* object is of class *ButtonView*. It accepts mouse actions (*mouseButton*, *enter* and *leave*). It can uses the methods provided by *Depressed* and *ButtonStatus*. It can also send a *buttonClick* event.

The controller part of the button component is defined as follows:

mouseButton "Down" =
  if **isActive** then **depress**
  else **noUpdate**
  end if.

  mouseButton "Up" =
  if **isActive** then all [**release, buttonClick** myId]
  else **release**
  end if.

  enter = **setActive**.
  leave = **setInactive**.

When the mouse enters the button, the button becomes active; when the mouse leaves the button it becomes inactive. If the mouse button is pressed when the mouse is over the button it becomes depressed, if it is released over the button then a button click has occurred.

The view part of the button component is defined as follows:

```
view = let
          setRelief v =
          if isDepressed and isActive then
            Relief "sunken" v
          else
            Relief "raised" v
          end if,

          buttonView = Text myId
      in
          setRelief buttonView
      end let.
```

The button has a label, which is its name. When the button is both depressed and active, it appears in the sunken state. The view is therefore a constraint of the model, and simply specifies a relation between the model and the user interface appearance.

The complete code for the *Depressed* ADT is:

```
 type State = Bool.
 initially = save False.

 depress = save True.
 release = save False.

 isDepressed = this.
```

The predefined function *save*, sets the new state of the ADT. The predefined function *this* returns the current state of the ADT. Therefore the *depress* and *release* methods simply set the state of the ADT to True and False, respectively. The predefined function *initially* says what to do when an instance of the ADT is created.

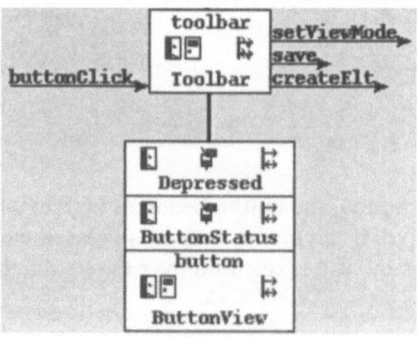

Fig. 7 - Clock architecture for counter

There is a strict set of rules defined to explain how these updates can be used. Updates can only travel up the tree hierarchy. They are therefore guaranteed to terminate at or before the root. Infinite constraint loops are therefore impossible. Requests can also only travel up the tree, so a component can only use constraints based on values in its parent components' ADTs. A component can use 0 or more instances of each of its subcomponents. These are created through the subview relationship. An instance of a subcomponent will be created when a subview is used to create that components view. For instance, we could create the toolbar of buttons, used in our editor (see Fig. 2) as shown in Fig. 7.

The toolbar view would be defined as:

view = above (map button labels).

labels = ["View Q,D","View Q,D,C","View Q,O",
          "View Q,O,C","Create","Save"].

In this case six instances of the button sub-component would be created. These appear stacked vertically on the screen.

The Clock architecture language therefore provides good support for iterative design [14]. Requests and updates from a component are routed automatically by Clock. Programmers do not explicitly say how components are to be connected. The only explicitly defined relationship is the subview. Requests and updates are simply routed up the tree to the first component that can deal with that type of action. This means that it is easy to move objects around in the tree, as no explicit connections will be broken. For instance, if we wished an abstract data object (ADT) that had been used by one component, to be shared by several, we could just move it up the tree. This would not cause any problems.

The Clock Design of the QOC Editor. The Clock architecture for this example is shown in Fig. 8. The architecture structure relates closely to the visual appearance of the system. Each user has an editor view (*Editor*) which consists of the workspace and the tool bar (which has the save, create and view buttons.) The workspace consists of a set of nodes (Questions, Options and Criteria) along with connecting edges and possibly a rubber band line (if two nodes are being connected.) A node has a label, a local editor (*Annotations*) for the user and a view of the shared log for that object (*SavedAnnotation*). An edge will also have a log, a view and possibly a label. The system is built from a set of relations. Some data is local to individual users, some is global to all users. For instance, at the root level are ADTs that hold information about all the nodes, edges, positions and the shared log. At the editor level the list of nodes will be filtered, to consist of those that are visible because of the current view. The workspace component displays a node for every node visible provided by the editor.

148

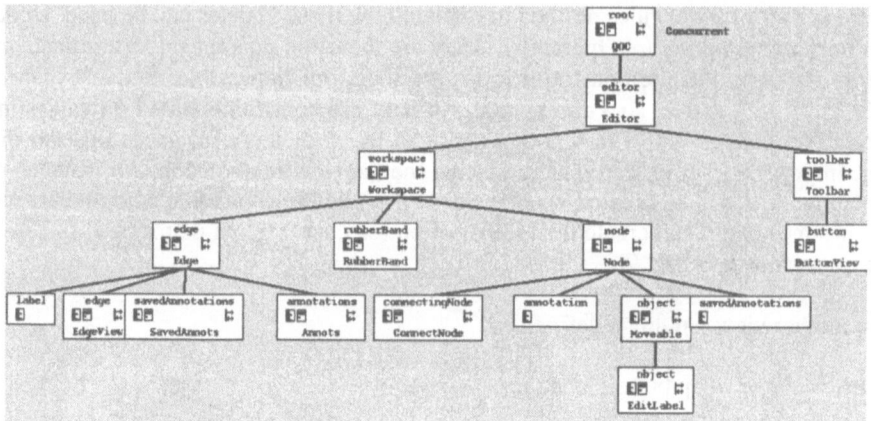

Fig. 8 - Clock Architecture for QOC Editor Example

The structure of the Clock architecture makes it easy to design and iteratively build complex systems. As an example of the ease with which modification can be made, we were able to add the different view filters (Questions and Decisions, Questions Decisions and Criteria etc) to the original design in under 20 minutes, in only a few simple lines of code.

4.4 Developing a formal specification

The final stage in the development is to attempt to prove certain properties about our design. To perform interaction proofs, we could exploit an important relationship between Clock architectures and interactor networks. We can consider each Clock component to be equivalent to a LOTOS interactor [30]. It accepts updates from the user side, and receives values from the application side via requests.

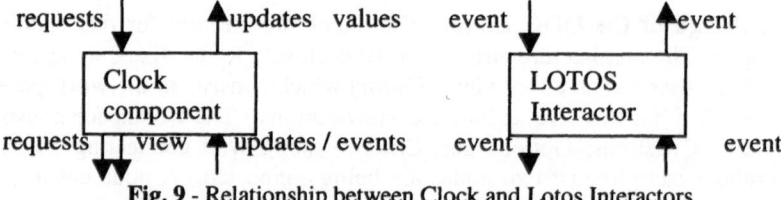

Fig. 9 - Relationship between Clock and Lotos Interactors

We can translate a Clock hierarchy into an interactor network in three stages.
- Turn each Clock component into an interactor
- For each subview relationship a parent component can send disable and enable events to its children.
- Link requests and updates between components.

The significant difference is that Clock implicitly updates values through requests. Programmers must explicitly send updates up the tree (towards the application). Clock then sends request values back down the tree (towards the user), after evaluating constraints.

For any Clock implementation we can derive a LOTOS interactor network. We can specify the behaviour of these interactors in equivalent LOTOS. We are currently developing tool support to make this translation automatic. The developer must still, however, translate functional data types into the algebraic Act One language. Better language support for specifying data types is therefore necessary.

The Clock approach also has much in common with the York interactor model and state based system modelling [19]. Clock abstract data types (ADTs) can be seen as similar to the internal state of a York interactor, the view function is like the York rendering relation, and the event handler is similar to a set of behavioural equations. The use of constraints to relate components is significant here. We can specify complex systems in terms of these constraints and so easily guarantee such properties as state-display conformance. The Clock architecture design makes it easy to consider such concepts as the visibility of a system, as we can define in the relation exactly what is visible.

We could have made use of this relationship to transform our Clock prototype into a York style interactor model. Though ongoing research is looking at automated proof with York interactors[6], currently the tool support available for verifying LOTOS specifications appears to be more powerful. The combination of a state-based architecture and event-based model also aid in providing alternative views onto our design.

4.5 Proof

Once we have a LOTOS specification we can attempt to verify properties about our specification. This can help us to guarantee critical properties about our design. However, to be pragmatic we must focus this verification effort. In this section, we show how we used proof to guarantee important properties about our system design that were shown to be important in our earlier UAN task analysis (see sections 4.2.2, 4.2.3).

We could perform this verification in one of two ways, using LOTOS simulation or model checking technology. Markopoulos [27] has shown how the LOLA simulation tool can be used to demonstrate task conformance between a LOTOS task specification and system specification.

We have made use of model checking technology to verify properties about our design. Model checking provides a powerful approach to formal verification. Given some specification (that can be translated into a Finite State Automata), and some temporal logic formula, a model checker can perform a fully automated proof of whether the specification satisfies the formula. This makes it easy to perform complex proofs in the context of iterative design. If the specification is altered, performing the proof again requires only that the temporal formula be checked automatically against the new specification. This form of rechecking can be as automatic as using regression tests in software design. This is in contrast to Theorem Proving, where a whole series of lemmas may be required, before a formula can be completely proven. However, model-checking environments also tend to have some disadvantages. In general, they can only perform proofs across finite systems, using finite types. We therefore need to transform our LOTOS specification into a finite instance. For instance, with our QOC editor specification we prove properties about an instance where there are only a finite, and given number, of users, nodes and edges in existence. Tool support can again help here in producing such a finite specification.

We have made use of the Caesar/Aldebaran toolkit (CADP) [13] which makes use of the mu calculus [13] to perform verifications. For instance, with it we can verify that our system implementation supports the locking properties that were highlighted in our task analysis:

- No two users can alter the same node at the same time;
- If one user has locked a node it cannot be deleted by another user, even with delete group.

The first statement can be expressed in temporal logic as follows:
ALL (
   ["SelectNode !1 !1"]
   SU (["SelectNode !1 !2"]F) (<"ReleaseNode !1">T)
)

This statement says that , in all states, if user one selects a node no other user can select that node, until user 1 releases that node. The statement ["X"]F means that in the current state it is impossible to perform "X"; the statement <"X">T means that in the current state it is possible to perform an "X". The mu calculus allows us to express proofs over events with specific data. It does not, however, allow us to express statements over an event with any data. We must therefore verify our specification over a restricted, but sufficient set of users and nodes.

We can do something similar for our second requirement:

ALL (
  ["SelectNode !1 !1"]
  SU (["DeleteGroup !(SET 1) !2"]F)
    (<"ReleaseNode !1">T)
)

This statement says that, in all states, if one user has selected a node, then another user cannot delete a group containing that node, until the node has been released.

Though this formal verification still cannot guarantee that our design is perfect, it can enable us to have more faith in the correctness of our design. The use of tool support in deriving a LOTOS specification and performing model checking makes this activity easier and more cost effective. The strong link between the task analysis and system proof is also important. We have not tried to perform exhaustive proofs about our design, instead we have focussed upon usability requirements highlighted in the earlier task analysis.

6 Conclusion

In conclusion, the development of interactive systems requires a variety of modelling approaches. The DSVIS'97 workshop proceedings stressed this point, suggesting that some of the more formal methods described in previous DSVIS proceedings, are unsuitable for early stages of a design and analysis [12]. Instead we require a variety of lightweight models that can be used to give multiple views on a system [11]. In this paper, we have shown how some lightweight models can be used in a design. To do this properly, we need tool support to link these multiple views together, to enable designers to see how they relate to each other and the design at large [7]. Brown et al [5] have taken a step towards solving this problem by providing tool support to help link UAN specifications to Clock prototypes. This makes it easier to see where changes in one model must result in changes in another.

High-level prototyping languages, such as Clock, can help in this development process. They provide a means to produce rapid and well structured prototypes. The use of constraint based programming allows a level of abstraction closer to that provided by state based modelling approaches [19], but also allows immediate user testing.

The ability to derive LOTOS specifications, from a Clock prototype, and then reason about the specification, all in a tool supported manner makes the use of formal specifications more cost effective. The development of a full LOTOS specification requires considerable time and knowledge; tool support can help to simplify this process.

Now that we have demonstrated the initial feasibility of our approach, there are some remaining issues that need to be addressed.
- Coverage - we have a good but incomplete coverage of the design life cycle. We now intend to look at how other modelling approaches could fit in with this approach, particular user modelling which may help in performing error analysis on an initial design.
- Training & Cost - we need to demonstrate that our method is really usable by others. We have made use of a variety of pre-existing techniques. This may help here. However, the range of techniques used may still make the approach too costly in terms of time and training.
- Iterations - we need further consideration about how the different design stages link together. We also intend to perform user testing upon the artefact we have produced to investigate how usability evaluations fit into the design cycle.
- Team work - since design is a group activity, we need to properly investigate how easy it is for groups of designers to work together using our approach.

References

1. G Abowd and A Dix (1992), Giving undo attention. *Interacting with Computers*, 4(3):317-342.

2. Heather Alexander (1990), Structuring dialogues using CSP, in MD Harrison and H Thimbleby, *Formal methods in Human computer interaction*, Cambridge University Press.

3. R Bentley (1994) *Supporting multi-user interface development for cooperative systems*, PhD thesis, Lancaster University.

4. I.M. Breedvelt-Schouten, F Paterno, C Severijns (1997) Reusable structures in task models, in MD Harrison, JC Torres (eds), *Design, Specification and Verification of Interactive Systems '97*, Springer Computer Science, pp 225-241.

5. Judy Brown, T.C. Nicholas Graham and Timothy Wright (1998). The Vista Environment for the Coevolutionary Design of User Interfaces. *In Proceedings of Human Factors in Computing Systems (CHI'98)*, ACM Press, Los Angeles, USA, April 1998 (to appear).

6. JC Campos, MD Harrison (1997), Formally verifying interactive systems: A review, in MD Harrison, JC Torres (eds), *Design, Specification and Verification of Interactive Systems '97*, Springer Computer Science, pp 109-125.

7. Steven Clark (1997), *Literate Development*, PhD thesis, University of Glasgow.

8. J Conklin and ML Begeman (1989) gIBIS a tool for all reasons, in *J. Amer. Soc. Info. Sci* 200-213.

9. Joelle Coutaz (1997) PAC-ing the Architecture of Your Interface, in MD Harrison, JC Torres (eds), *Design, Specification and Verification of Interactive Systems '97*, Springer Computer Science, pp 13-29.

10. A. Dix and G. Abowd (1996) Modelling status and event behaviour of interactive systems, in *Software Engineering Journal*, 11(6) pp. 334-346.

11. R Fields, N Merriam, A Dearden (1997) DMVIS: Design, modelling and validation of interactive systems, in MD Harrison, JC Torres (eds), *Design, Specification and Verification of Interactive Systems '97*, Springer Computer Science, pp 29-45.

12. R Fields, N Merriam (1997) Modelling in Action. Reports from the DSVIS'97 working groups, in MD Harrison, JC Torres (eds), *Design, Specification and Verification of Interactive Systems '97*, Springer Computer Science, pp307-320

13. Hubert Garavel (1996), An Overview of the Eucalyptus Toolbox. In Z Brezocnik and T Kapus, eds, *Proceedings of the COST 247 Interanational Workshop on Applied Formal Methods in System Design* (Maribar, Slovenia), pages 76-88. University of Maribor, Slovenia, June 1996.

14. T.C. Nicholas Graham and Tore Urnes (1996). Linguistic Support for the Evolutionary Design of Software Architectures. In *Proceedings of the Eighteenth International Conference on Software Engineering.* IEEE Computer Society Press, Berlin, Germany, pp. 418-427, March 1996.

15. T.C. Nicholas Graham, Herbert Damker, Catherine A. Morton, Eric Telford and Tore Urnes (1996). The Clock Methodology: Bridging the Gap Between User Interface Design and Implementation. York University Technical Report CS-96-04. York University, August 1996.

16. Phil Gray, David England and Steve McGowan (1994), XUAN: Enhancing the UAN to capture Temporal Relations among Actions, Technical Report IS-94-02, Department of Computing Science, University of Glasgow.

17. Thomas R Green (1989) Cognitive dimensions of notations. In A Sutcliffe and L Macaulay, eds, *People and Computers IV*, pages 443-460. Cambridge University Press, Cambridge, United Kingdom.

18. Saul Greenberg and David Marwood (1994), Real Time Groupware as a Distributed System: Concurrency Control and its Effect on the Interface, *ACM 1994 Conference on Computer Supported Cooperative Work (CSCW'94)*, ACM SIGCHI & SIGOIS.

19. Michael D. Harrison and David J. Duke (1994), A review of formalisms for describing interactive behaviour, lecture notes in computer science 896, *Software Engineering and Human-Computer Interaction*, (ICSE'94 Workshop on SE-HCI).

20. H.R. Hartson, A.C. Siochi and D Hix (1990), The UAN: A User-Oriented Representation for Direct Manipulation Interface Designs. *ACM Transactions on Information Systems*, 8 (3) :pp191-203.

21. Ralph Hill. (1992) The abstraction-link-view paradigm: Using constraints to connect user interfaces to applications. In *ACM SIGCHI 1992*, pages 335-342, April 1992.

22. CW Johnson (1996). Literate specifications, in *Software Engineering Journal*, July 1996, pp 225-237

23. CW Johnson (1997) Utility of User interface notations, submitted to the *Journal of Human Computer Interaction*, 1997.

24. P Johnson, S Wilson, P Markopoulos & J Pycock (1993) - ADEPT - Advanced design environment for prototyping with task models, Demonstration abstract. In Aschlund S et al (eds), *Bridges Between Worlds- INTERCHI'93*, Addison-Wesley, pp 56.

25. Glen E Krasner and Stephen T Pope (1988), A cookbook for using the Model-View-Controller interface paradigm. *Journal of Object-Oriented Programming*, 1 (3):26-49.

26. A Maclean, R Young, V Bellotti, and T Moran (1996), Questions, Options and Criteria: Elements of Design Space Analysis, in Moran (1996).

27. Panos Markopoulos (1997), *A compositional model for the formal specification of user interface software*, PhD Thesis, QMW College, University of London.

28. TP Moran , JM Carroll (1996) (eds) *Design Rationale: Concepts, techniques and use*, Hillsdale, Lawrence Erlbaum Asoociates.

29. Brad A Myers, Dario A Giuse, Roger B Dannenberg, Brad Vander Zanden, David S Kosbie, Edward Pervin, Andrew Mickish and Philippe Marchal (1990), Garnet: Comprehensive Support for Graphical, Highly Interactive User Interfaces. In *IEEE Computing*, pages 71-85, Novermber 1990.

30. F Paterno and M Mezzanotte (1995), Formal verification of undesired behaviours in the CERD case study, in *Proceedings of EHCI'95*, Chapman & Hall Publisher.

31. S Pavon & D Larrabeiti (1993) LOLA (LOtos LAboratory) User Manual v3.4, http://www.dcs.upm.es/~lotos

32. M Sage and CW Johnson (1997) Interactors and Haggis: Executable specifications for interactive systems, in MD Harrison, JC Torres (eds), *Design, Specification and Verification of Interactive Systems '97*, Springer Computer Science, pp 93-109.

33. S Shum (1991) Cognitive dimensions of design rationale. In D Diaper and N Hammond, eds, *People and Computers VI: Proceedings of HCI'91*. Cambridge University Press, Cambridge, United Kingdom.

34. S Shum (1993) QOC Design Rationale Retrieval: A Cognitive Task Analysis & Design Implications, Rank Xerox EuroPARC, Technical Report EPC-93-105

35. S Buckingham Shum (1996) Analyzing the Usability of a Design Rationale Notation, in Moran (1996).

The role of verification in interactive systems design

José C. Campos and Michael D. Harrison

Human-Computer Interaction Group
Department of Computer Science, University of York
Heslington, York YO10 5DD, U.K.
e-mail: {Jose.Campos,Michael.Harrison}@cs.york.ac.uk

Abstract. In this paper we argue that using verification in interactive systems development is more than just checking whether the specification of the system has all the required properties; and that changing the focus from a global specification into partial, property oriented, specifications can provide a number of advantages and make verification act as an aid to decision making. We also present a compiler that allows for the verification of interactor specifications to be done in SMV, as well as a simple case study where verification is used to inform a design decision.

1 Introduction

The introduction of automation in safety critical environments raises the question of system correctness. When an automated system is responsible for the control of a sensitive process, even a *small* failure might have unacceptable outcomes. This problem is particularly relevant in reactive systems, as it becomes hard to comprehend and predict all the different interactions the system might have with its environment.

The use of formal mathematical models during development can impact system design at two levels [21]:

- the use of rigorous mathematical concepts and notations can help in the organization and communication of ideas;
- mathematical models can allow us to reason rigorously about properties of the system being designed.

The latter, although sometimes seen just as a side effect of formal specification, is particularly relevant when we think of guaranteeing the correctness of a system, and has long been an object of study [16].

Formal reasoning, however, tends to be a delicate, detailed, and time consuming process. This has led to the study of mechanical reasoning techniques as a way to (at least partially) automate the analysis. Two main categories of methods can be identified:

- algorithmic methods (i.e. model checking – see [5]): these are fully automated and, given a suitable system description and property, are capable of determining if the property is valid in the system;
- deductive methods (i.e. theorem proving): these are semi-automated methods where a more traditional mathematical proof is performed by a tool under user guidance (examples of theorem provers are PVS [6] and the Larch system [13]).

Interactive systems are special cases of reactive systems, and have growing application in safety critical environments (aeroplanes and nuclear power plants being two of the most commonly cited examples). These systems have raised interest in the application of verification techniques to their development. In the last four years a number of approaches to verification have been proposed. For example, Abowd et al. [1] use Action Simulator [19] to represent very abstract, action level, descriptions of interactive systems. These descriptions can then be translated into the SMV model checker for verification. Paternó [20] also uses a model checker, but the specification is more detailed. He uses Lotos interactors, to derive a specification of the system from its task description. Bumbulis et al. [3] and d'Ausbourg et al. [7], on the other hand, use specifications built at a lower level of abstraction: buttons, mouse clicks, etc. While the first authors use the HOL theorem prover, the second use a model checking related technique. For a review of these approaches see [4].

In the remainder of this paper we will identify some of the problems that arise when trying to apply these approaches and propose a means of integrating verification into the development process of interactive systems. In section 2 we will argue that a shift in focus is needed when thinking of the verification of interactive systems, and in section 3 we will present some work that is being done in this context. In section 4 we illustrate the previous discussion with an example. And finally, in section 5 we draw some conclusions, and propose some further work.

2 Changing the focus

Whatever the level of abstraction and tool used, all the approaches mentioned above tend to see verification as a final step in validating a specification against a set of desirable properties (see figure 1). Some authors have proposed templates for interesting

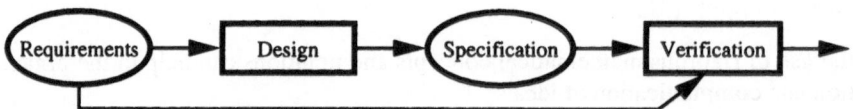

Fig. 1. Verification as a final step in development

properties that can be verified with their approaches (see [1] and [20]). So in Abowd et al., templates deal mainly with what user interface states can be reached. On the other hand, in Paternó, templates deal mainly with what user interface actions can be executed. Whether states or actions are used, an attempt is made in both approaches to map these states/actions to significant concepts at the user interface level: tasks, modes, visibility, etc.

On the whole, these sets of templates tend to explore what the model checking will allow (what meaning can be attributed to checkable properties), rather than being driven by the requirements needs.

On the role of models All the above cited approaches are based around the notion of a single specification. However, given the complex and semantically rich nature of interactive systems, it becomes impossible to make sure that we have tied down all relevant details of a system in a specification at the outset.

In fact, given the diversity of perspectives we can take on an interactive system, it has been argued, by Fields et al. [12], that no available single specification notation is powerful enough to capture all relevant details of a given system. Instead the authors argue that, if we are to be able to validate a system design against an heterogeneous set of requirements, then a number of specialised models will be needed. Each model taking an appropriate viewpoint on the system, vis-à-vis the requirements being considered.

We can start to identify a trend towards a type of approach to verification in which we are not restricted to a particular verification tool or technique.

On the role of properties By defining a set of property templates for a given class of systems, we try to pinpoint what properties are relevant and/or impact the quality of those systems. Regarding interactive systems, a number of factors complicate this purpose.

First of all, we do not yet have a global theory of interaction to act as a guide in design and as a global measure of quality. The lack of such global measures, means that *every system is a theory* and it is hard to make generalisations. So, the interesting properties will be dependent on the system being developed and it becomes hard to define a set of templates that are generically useful and applicable.

Additionally, given the complexity of interactive systems, and the number of different perspectives that we can have on them, it becomes difficult to make design decisions based on prescriptive theories alone. The ability to check the impact of possible choices in different aspects of the system could be very helpful in this. The validation process could be used as a guide to the process of choice as it provides insight into the problem that is being tackled.

A further problem with defining a set of templates is that the properties of interest will depend on the particular specification being used. Consider, for instance, a template stating that it should be possible to execute a task from every state in the context of a hypothetical teller machine specification. The applicability of the template changes drastically with the level at which the specification is done. If we choose to consider only individual interactions between the machine and its user, then the template should not be used: in each interaction, we want the user to be able to perform only one task. However, if we take a broader look at the system, and choose to consider the successive interactions of different users, then the property is relevant as we want the user to be able to insert the card again to perform a new task.

Thus, the role that properties play is dependent, not only on the system under consideration, but also on the particular specification that is used. We can conclude that we must exercise care when looking for what properties we should prove of specifications.

On what exactly is being proved Seeing the verification step as a final step in the development process, and trying to use *off the shelf* properties, might lead us to end up looking for properties of the specification instead of the system. Although this is not, in itself, negative (we might want to make sure that the specification is consistent and has no mistakes) care must be taken not to confuse the two types of properties.

Consider again the property that every task is possible from every state. If the specification is done with finite state machines, and tasks are defined as some target state, this tells us those target states are always reachable. How much does it tell us about the system? It is quite different if we need ten actions or one hundred actions to achieve task completion. No information about this is obtained from verifying the property though.

On the applicability of the techniques The number of different perspectives that we might have on interaction means that if we aim to have a global unified specification encompassing all the relevant information, we will get a very complex model. This is specially problematic as we still lack tools comprehensive enough to enable the verification of systems as rich as interactive systems. As has been pointed out in [21], model checkers can be used to reason about control, but lack more generic expressive power, while theorem provers are good at dealing with rich data but lack the ability to reason easily about control. While some attempts have been made to combine both techniques, further work is needed in the area.

Even if a powerful enough tool were available, it turns out that it is still hard to derive and prove the relevant properties from the system specification. On the one hand, general purpose specifications might not have all the information required for a specific property. On the other hand, a general purpose specification might have too much unnecessary detail (so far as a specific property is concerned) making the proof more difficult, if not impossible.

At a different level, it is also true that the style of specification drastically influences what and how analysis can be done. Consider for instance model checking. If our specification is not reducible to a finite state machine, we simply cannot use model checking on it[1]. If we do use a finite state machine, however, then theorem proving becomes of little use. Generally, model checkers are better at analysing finite state machines.

In the case of theorem provers, the situation can become even more complex. The fact that we can use a theorem prover to verify a specification, does not mean necessarily that it will be easy to do so. In fact, different styles of specification can have a drastic impact on how easy (feasible) it is to prove one thing or another, and different properties can ask for different styles of reasoning.

All this means that the specification should be written with the type of proof that we intend to perform in mind.

On changing how verification is applied It is now clear that a shift in focus is needed. Instead of focusing verification on the specification, we must focus on the system itself and its properties. This way, specification and validation become part of the same development process, where validation is used to inform design decisions. This can be achieved by using, not a monolithic specification of the system which tries to encompass all of the system (at its level of abstraction), but a set of specifications (or models – cf. [12]) each taking a particular viewpoint on the system.

This way, we can achieve a number of benefits:

- by focusing on properties, we use verification to validate the choices that are made in relation to what is important of the system, not its specification;
- by using a number of models, instead of a single specification, we are able to apply the most appropriate verification technique to each property;

---

[1] To help obviate this problem, some work has been done on model checking non-finite state machines. For an example of the application of this type of technique to HCI see [18].

– conversely, by using a number of models, we can develop each model in the most suitable formalism, regarding the tool that will be used;
– using models that focus on properties also means the models will be simpler and easier to manage and verify, so we will be able to verify properties that otherwise would be too difficult to check;
– another possibility raised by this approach is the reuse of properties and their proofs: because we focus on properties, we might be able to reuse the proofs when thinking of related properties of different systems.

As pointed out in [12], the use of a number of models to represent different aspects of the same reality does raise some problems. In particular, problems with consistency between models, and with the veracity of the models towards the system being modelled. We tend to agree with the authors in that these issues are not necessarily disadvantages or even specific to the approach, and that, in the end, these concerns have to do more with the designer than with the tool.

Nevertheless, it is also the case that an appropriate tool should support the designer in dealing with these concerns. Although we do not address the issue in the present paper, it does deserves further consideration.

3 An Interactors to SMV compiler

From what has been said so far, it can be seen that we will need a toolbox of different verification strategies tailored to work with our specifications. We have been experimenting with different techniques and tools, and, in this context, we are developing a compiler to allow the verification of interactor based specifications with SMV.

The notion of Interactor [20,9] is basically that of an object capable of making its state perceivable to its users. York interactors do not prescribe a specific specification notation to describe the interactor's state and behaviour. Instead, they act as a mechanism for structuring the use of standard specification techniques.

In SMV [17] the state of the system is defined by a set of variables (boolean or enumerated). The behaviour is defined as a transition relation on states. This is done, either by a set of logic expressions asserting which transitions of the state are valid, or by a set of firing rules.

In [1] Abowd et al. presented an application of SMV to the verification of interactive systems specifications. Their approach, however, is based on a simple propositional production system based description of the interactive system written in Action Simulator. This means only very simple abstract specifications can be checked, and, in fact, the authors propose the approach to be used at a very high level of abstraction in early interactive system design.

With interactors, however, specifications are built compositionally. The system is broken down into a number of meaningful components, and each component is specified by an interactor. These interactors communicate between themselves and/or with the user as appropriate.

It seems clear that this style of specification is potentially more expressive than a PPS, and will not, in most cases, be adequately translatable into a single PPS. We need then investigate how to express such specifications in SMV.

Specifying one interactor Several different formalisms have been used to specify interactors, including Z [9], modal action logic (MAL) [10], and VDM [14].

The fact that we want to be able to model our interactor specifications in SMV, influences the choice of notation to describe interactors. When defining exactly what kind of interactor to use, we have to decide on:

- how the state of the interactor is defined;
- how the behaviour of the interactor is specified;
- how communication between interactors is modelled.

In order for the interactor specification to be reducible to a finite state machine, SMV deals only with boolean and enumerated type variables. This restriction will be carried forward to our interactor notation. Although this is a major restriction, we feel the approach will still be useful because we are interested in building partial, property oriented, models. And, in fact, this is a restriction common to all approaches using model checking techniques.

As to the modelling of interactor behaviour, of the different approaches to modelling with interactors, the use of MAL seems to be a good candidate for modelling interactor behaviour. MAL augments propositional logic with the notion of action and three operators:

- OBL — $OBL(ac)$ means action ac must happen next;
- PER — $PER(ac)$ means action ac can happen next;
- [ ] — $[ac]prop$ means after action ac proposition $prop$ holds.

The operators OBL and PER correspond to some form of quantification over the actions that may be initiated by the user in a given state:

- $OBL(ac) \equiv \forall_{ac_1} \bullet [ac_1]true \Rightarrow ac = ac_1$
- $PER(ac) \equiv \exists_{ac_1} \bullet ac = ac_1 \wedge [ac_1]true$

where $[ac_1]true$ means "it is possible to perform action ac_1 in the current state" (i.e. there is, at least, one trace from the current state that starts with action ac_1). Although we do not use these two operators in this paper, the potential for asking questions about obligation and permission are of interest to us.

The formula

$$[]prop$$

indicates that $prop$ holds before any action is taken (i.e. $prop$ holds in the initial state of the system). Formula

$$prop_1 \Rightarrow [ac]prop_2$$

means that when proposition $prop_1$ holds, performing action ac makes proposition $prop_2$ true.

If we interpret propositions $prop_1$ and $prop_2$ above as pre- and post-conditions of action ac, we can use this type of formula to define a production system in a similar way to Action Simulator. The difference is that each interactor defines its own finite state machine, while with Action Simulator we have only one global finite state machine.

We follow loosely Dearden and Harrison's syntax in [8]. As an example consider the following which represents a window defining whether it is mapped on the screen or not:

interactor *window*
attributes
   mapped : *boolean*
visible
   mapped
actions
   map, *unmap*
axioms
1. $[]\neg mapped$
2. $\neg mapped \Rightarrow [map]\text{next}(mapped)$
3. $mapped \Rightarrow [unmap]\neg\text{next}(mapped)$

The state of the interactor is defined by a set of attributes. These attributes can then be associated with modalities to specify how they should be rendered in the presentation. In the present case, the only information in the state is whether the interactor is mapped on the screen or not, and this information must be visible in the presentation of the interactor (cf. **visible** clause).

The behaviour of the interactor is defined by a set of axioms on the available actions. These axioms define all possible behaviours of the interactor. In the present case we have two actions (to toggle the state on or off), and three axioms. Axiom 1 states that the initial state of the interactor is unmapped. Axioms 2 and 3 define when the actions are available and their effect on the state. Axiom 2, for instance, states that if the interactor is not mapped then action *map* can take place and gives rise to a new state where the interactor is mapped. As we assume the axioms to define all possible behaviours, if the interactor is not mapped, only the *map* actions can occur. Note that next(*mapped*) means the value of *mapped* in the next state.

The algorithm to translate one interactor into the SMV input language is very similar to that presented in [1]. The major difference being that we include in each state, not the next action to be executed, but the last action that was executed (the action that led into the present state instead of the action that leads out of the present state). This avoids the *explosion* of the initial states (simplifying the composition of interactors) but makes the detection of deadlocks more difficult.

The algorithm has been implemented in a prototype compiler. If we run the example above through the compiler we get the following SMV module (where POSTnil represents the post-condition of the stuttering step):

```
MODULE window
VAR
mapped: boolean;
action: {nil, map, unmap};
DEFINE
POSTnil := (next(mapped)=mapped);
INIT
!mapped & action=nil
TRANS
   (mapped & next(action)=unmap & !next(mapped))
 | (!mapped & next(action)=map & next(mapped))
 | (next(action)=nil & POSTnil)
```

```
FAIRNESS
!action=nil
```

The structure of the module is similar to that of the interactor. The state is defined by a set of variables. The variable `action` was introduced to hold the value of the action that led into the present state. Because this variable is an enumerated type, we cannot have parametrised actions. To overcome this limitation we can *explode* parametrised actions into a set of actions, one per parameter value.

`INIT` defines the initial state of the module and was generated from axiom 1 in the interactor. `TRANS` defines the behaviour of the module and is generated from the axioms of the interactor, excepting those defining the initial state. Axioms of type

$$pre \Rightarrow [ac]post$$

are translated into

```
pre & next(action)=ac & next(post)
```

and *ored* together with the stuttering formula:

```
next(action)=nil & POSTnil
```

Note that the intuitive translation would be:

```
(pre & next(action)=ac) -> next(post)
```

However, this would allow `next(post)` to hold even if the pre-condition and action did not. Because we are assuming that axioms specify all possible behaviours, we use the first translation instead.

The fairness condition shown is a default condition and can be overridden in the interactor definition (see below).

Note that the modality (**visible**) has not been included in the module. At this stage the modalities are not directly represented in the SMV code and have to be taken into account informally during the verification process.

Besides the clauses shown in the example, our interactor notation allows for three additional clauses:

- **importing** — allows one interactor to reuse the state and behaviour of another interactor, in SMV this is done by simply repeating the code in the new module;
- **fairness** — this clause allows the definition of a fairness expression to be used by SMV;
- **define** — enable us to give names to expressions as can be done in SMV, the names can then be used instead of the corresponding expressions.

Multiple interactors So far, we have only considered the one interactor situation. Now we will see how to compose interactors and how to model their communication.

Interactors are organised in a hierarchy, where one interactor (the parent) can have other interactors (the children) as part of its state.

Parents can access the state of children using the notation:

child.attribute

By convention, a parent should only access attributes that have an appropriate modality.

Parents can also *send* actions to their children, either explicitly:

$$child.\text{action} = ac$$

or implicitly, by imposing conditions on the next state of the child. Consider the following excerpt:

interactor *main*
attributes
  mail : *window*

  ...

axioms
  $\mathcal{P}rop \Rightarrow \text{next}(mail.mapped)$

  ...

The axiom effectively implies that, if $\mathcal{P}rop$ is true and the window *mail* is not mapped, then an action to map it must be performed.

In order to translate these hierarchies of interactors into SMV, we use the notion of module. So each interactor will be a module in SMV, and we demand that an interactor named main exists.

In SMV, if a module is declared a process, then it progresses independently from other modules in the system. This would allow for the different interactors in the systems to progress independently of each other (modulo their interactions). For this to work, however, the modules must be completely independent. In our case, because parents can influence the behaviour of their children, there is no guarantee that the modules will be independent (in fact its very unlikely that they will) so declaring modules as processes has no effect. That is the reason why explicit stuttering had to be introduced through the use of the nil action.

Finally, in order to test properties of the specification a new clause was introduced: **test**. It can only be declared in the main interactor, and it is used to specify a CTL formula whose validity is to be verified by SMV.

4   An example

In this section we will show how the ideas presented above can be applied in practice. We will use as example an e-mail client. The basic requirements of the client are that:

– it should be able to receive mail messages;
– it should announce new mail to the user;
– it should allow the user to compose and send mail messages;
– it should work within a windowing environment.

For the purpose of this discussion, we will focus on whether or not the user is made aware of new mail. Following the ideas put forward in section 2, we will take a fish-eyed view of the system, and we will build models that concentrate on what is relevant for the issues at hand. Although the example will be kept very simple, we feel that it is still representative at two levels.

- it shows how, by focusing on a specific view of the system, we can build models that are simple but nevertheless relate to features of the overall design;
- it also shows how SMV, in conjunction with the interactors compiler, can be used to analyse multiple interactor specifications, and discuss the relative merits of alternative design options[2].

As we consider that the e-mail client is to be used in a windowing environment, a way is needed to represent the windows on the screen. Because we are only concerned with visibility issues, we will build our models of windows around the following information:

- whether the window is *mapped* on the screen — when a window is mapped it becomes present on the screen until it is unmapped;
- whether the window is *visible* on the screen — a window might be mapped but hidden by another window;
- if the window has *new information* being displayed — a window is considered to have new information from the moment that it is *updated* until the information is *seen* by the user.

Were we to be interested in a different aspect of the system, the set of attributes to include in the specification would be different. In the context of our interest, the interactors representing windows have the following attributes:

attributes
> *mapped : boolean*
> *visible : boolean*
> *newinfo : boolean*

For each of these attributes, actions to set and unset them are introduced:

actions
> *map, unmap, hide, show, update, seen*

The complete definition of the `window` interactor can be seen in appendix A.

Two mechanisms for announcing new mail were considered. We will now describe the specification and analysis performed for each of them.

Using a simple mail agent window The first possibility considered was to put information regarding the new message(s) in the mail client window. This can be done in a number of different ways. For the analysis that we want to perform, however, we do not need to know exactly how it is done, so we will use the simple window interactor described above (see also appendix A).

In order to represent the interplay between the e-mail window and other windows on the screen, the specification considers two windows:

- *mail* — the e-mail client window;

---

[2] Note that we are not saying we will be able to perform all types of analysis this way. The possibility of using different formalisms and different verification tools, as appropriate, is one of the advantages of building specialised models.

– *others* — represents all other possible windows in the screen.

The only axiom that is needed states that, unless both windows are mapped, visibility can only change explicitly (see appendix B). Once the specification is complete, we can start to explore it. The first test is done just to increase our confidence in the soundness of the specification:

$$EF(mail.mapped \ \& \ others.mapped)$$

it simply verifies if we can have both windows mapped (thus verifying that the finite state machine is not empty - note that initially both windows are unmapped). Next we try to see if after a new message arrives that information is available to the user:

$$AG(mail.\text{action} = update \rightarrow mail.visible)$$

The answer to this test is no and we get the following counter example[3]:

```
state 1.1:                      state 1.2:
others.mapped = 0               mail.newinfo = 1
mail.newinfo = 0                mail.action = update
mail.visible = 0
mail.mapped = 0
```

What this shows is that if the e-mail window is not visible when the new message arrives, then the user has no way of knowing about this new message.

This prompts us to think about the next mechanism we will consider: using a pop up window to announce new mail. But first, we do another test: what happens when the e-mail window is visible and a new message arrives? Will the window still be visible?

$$AG(mail.visible \rightarrow AX(mail.\text{action} = update \rightarrow mail.visible))$$

The answer here is that it is possible that the user might not be able to notice the new message, as some other window might hide the e-mail window.

Using a pop-up window Having identified a problem with the previous approach, we now try to devise a new design that might solve it. We will consider introducing a pop up window to warn about new mail.

A pop up window is defined as a window which is mapped every time it is updated. Thus, the behaviour of the *update* event is redefined (at present, redefining the behaviour of an event is still done is a rather clumsy manner, future versions of the compiler are expected to allow for a better syntax):

interactor *popup*
importing
  window[*dummy*/*update*]
actions
  update
axioms
  !action = *dummy*
  [*update*]next(*mapped*)&next(*newinfo*)&next(*visible*)

---

[3] Note that only attributes of the state that change are shown. Also, we stripped the counter-example of irrelevant attributes.

The main specification now includes three windows:

- *mail* — the e-mail main window;
- *alert* — the pop up window;
- *others* — all other possible windows in the system.

Whenever a message is received, *mail* and *alert* alike must be updated. This is expressed by the following axiom:

$$mail.\text{action} = update \leftrightarrow alert.\text{action} = update$$

Additionally, if the user resets the e-mail client, the alert window must be reset:

$$mail.\text{action} = seen \rightarrow !alert.newinfo$$

The complete specification is presented in appendix C. Once the specification is complete, we can repeat the same tests as previously. First we check the three windows can be mapped:

$$\text{EF}(mail.mapped \ \& \ others.mapped \ \& \ alert.mapped)$$

Once again this serves only to enhance our confidence in the specification itself.

The first real test is whether the pop up window becomes visible when a new message arrives:

$$\text{AG}(mail.\text{action} = update \rightarrow alert.visible)$$

In this case the answer is yes.

This step accomplished, we can increase our demands upon the system. One thing is the alert window to become visible, another is for the user to see it. To test that the window will always be visible until the user sees it, we test that it can only disappear by direct action of the user (that is, the user has to *see it* before it goes away):

$$\text{AG}(mail.\text{action} = update \rightarrow$$
$$\text{A}[(alert.visible \ \& \ alert.newinfo) \ \text{U} \ (alert.\text{action in} \ \{seen, unmap\})])$$

Unfortunately in this case the answer is no, and the counter example shows us that some other window might hide the alert window before the user gets a chance to see it.

From this analysis we can conclude that this approach, although better than the previous one, still does not guarantee that the arrival of new messages will be noticed by the user. A similar analysis could now be carried out for the case where an icon showing the state of the mail box is always present in the desktop, or for the case where the pop up window cannot be hidden by another window.

Discussion In terms of the example, from the previous discussion we can conclude that, if we want to maximize user awareness regarding the arrival of new mail, we must use some kind of permanent window displaying the status of the mail box. This is not a terribly ground breaking or surprising result. In fact, we could easily reach the same conclusion by simply *thinking* about the problem in some sort of informal way. The hope is that the same kind of analysis applied to more interesting (non trivial) examples, might allow us to reach conclusions about the systems that are not so obvious.

The example, however, does not illustrate all the aspects of the matter. In this case, we are only using model checking. The properties we are interested in regard reachability questions, so model checking is the appropriate tool. Were we, for instance, to consider how the list of messages is kept sorted by date, model checking would probably not be the right tool. In that case we would have to use a theorem prover. That, however, does not have any implications in the analysis performed above, as the specifications used in each case would be independent.

Another aspect to consider when choosing what type of mechanism to use in order to announce new main, is whether a permanent icon will produce screen clutter. This analysis is outside the scope of the present specification (probably of the technique). Nevertheless, if some (probably) psychological study regarding desktop clutter can be carried out, we may then combine its results with the results of the present analysis to make a choice.

5 Conclusions

We have argued that using verification in (interactive) systems development is more than just checking whether the specification of the system has all the required properties. Global specifications tend to be too complex for verification, and different types of properties ask for different proof styles/techniques (hence, different specification styles). In this context, we propose that a number of partial models/specifications of the system should be built, allowing for the most appropriate verification technique to be used in each case.

Changing the focus from a global specification into partial, property oriented, specifications can also give a number of additional advantages: we can have greater confidence in that we are checking properties which are relevant to the system (not only of its specification); the specifications to verify become simpler; we can think of reusing proofs on systems with similar requirements.

Furthermore, the properties we want of the system must be considered during design. The development and verification of partial models can then be used as an aid to decision making. In the paper, we present a simple case study where verification is used to inform a design decision.

In order for this type of approach to be feasible, we will need an ensemble of verification tools tailored to work with our specifications. We present an interactor compiler which is being developed as part of a wider study on the applicability of different techniques to the verification of interactor specifications. The compiler allows for specific type of interactors to be checked by SMV and is used in the example.

Although we think that the use of verification as an aid to development helps in making verification more usable and useful, a number of problems remain open.

The interactor notation accepted by the compiler has a number of restrictions. We need to apply it to *real life* systems in order to access its potential. Although the sheer size of a system might not be a problem (the use of interactors should allow the specifications to scale up well), the restrictions on the variables and on the specification of behaviour limit the expressiveness of the approach. Another point to consider is whether it is possible to include the modality annotations in the SMV generated code. At the moment they have to be taken into account *informally*.

The use of theorem provers has not been addressed in this paper, but suitable representations of interactor specifications have to be developed that can be verified with that type of tool.

At the methodological level, the use of multiple models raises the questions of consistency and veracity. In [12] it is argued that consistency can be exploited in benefit of the development process, and that, regarding veracity, this problem is not exclusive of a multiple models approach to development.

Finally, in the example we looked at a very simple system property. In more realistic applications, what should guide the use of verification? In what areas should we apply it, and what are the roles of notions like tasks, mode of interaction, or modality of interaction? We envisage that some form of task model, or scenario driven design (cf. [11]) might be useful here.

Acknowledgements

We wish to thank the anonymous reviewers for their comments. José Campos is supported by Fundação para a Ciência e a Tecnologia (FCT, Portugal) under grant PRAXIS XXI/BD/9562/96.

References

1. Gregory D. Abowd, Hung-Ming Wang, and Andrew F. Monk. A formal technique for automated dialogue development. In *Proceedings of the First Symposium of Designing Interactive Systems - DIS'95*, pages 219–226. ACM Press, August 1995.

2. F. Bodart and J. Vanderdonckt, editors. *Design, Specification and Verification of Interactive Systems '96*, Springer Computer Science. Springer-Verlag/Vien, June 1996.

3. Peter Bumbulis, P. S. C. Alencar, D. D. Cowan, and C. J. P. Lucena. Validating properties of component-based graphical user interfaces. In Bodart and Vanderdonckt [2], pages 347–365.

4. José C. Campos and Michael D. Harrison. Formal verification of interactive systems: A review. In Harrison and Torres [15], pages 109–124.

5. E. M. Clarke, E. A. Emerson, and A. P. Sistla. Automatic verification of finite-state concurrent systems using temporal logic specifications. *ACM Transactions on Programming Languages and Systems*, 8(2):244–263, April 1986.

6. Judy Crow, Sam Owre, John Rushby, Natarajan Shankar, and Mandayam Srivas. A tutorial introduction to PVS. Presented at WIFT'95: Workshop on Industrial-Strength Formal Specification Techniques, April 1995. http://www.csl.sri.com/sri-csl-fm.html.

7. Bruno d'Ausbourg, Guy Durrieu, and Pierre Roche. Deriving a formal model of an interactive system from its UIL description in order to verify and to test its behaviour. In Bodart and Vanderdonckt [2], pages 105–122.

8. A. M. Dearden and M. D. Harrison. Risk analysis, impact and interaction modelling. In Bodart and Vanderdonckt [2], pages 229–247.

9. David J. Duke and Michael D. Harrison. Abstract interaction objects. *Computer Graphics Forum*, 12(3):25–36, 1993.

10. D.J. Duke, P.J. Barnard, J. May, and D.A. Duce. Systematic development of the human interface. In *Asia Pacific Software Engineering Conference*, pages 313–321. IEEE Computer Society Press, December 1995.

11. Bob Fields, Michael D. Harrison, and Peter Wright. THEA: Human error analysis for requirements definition. Technical Report YCS 249, Department of Computer Science, University of York, Heslington, York, YO1 5DD, England, 1997.

12. Bob Fields, Nick Merriam, and Andy Dearden. DMVIS: Design, modelling and validation of interactive systems. In Harrison and Torres [15], pages 29–44.

13. John V. Guttag, James J. Horning, et al. *Larch: Languages and Tools for Formal Specification*. Texts and Monographs in Computer Science. Springer-Verlag, 1993.

14. M. Harrison, R. Fields, and P. C. Wright. The user context and formal specification in interactive system design (invited paper). In C. R. Roast and J. I. Siddiqi, editors, *BCS-FACS Workshop on Formal Aspects of the Human Computer Interface*, electronic Workshops in Computing. Springer, September 1996. http://www.springer.co.uk/ewic/workshops/FAHCI/.

15. M. D. Harrison and J. C. Torres, editors. *Design, Specification and Verification of Interactive Systems '97*, Springer Computer Science. Springer-Verlag/Vien, June 1997.

16. C. B. Jones. The search for tractable ways of reasoning about programs. Technical Report UMCS-92-4-4, Department of Computer Science, University of Manchester, June 1992.

17. K. L. McMillan. *The SMV system*. Carnegie-Mellon University, draft edition, February 1992.

18. M. Mezzanotte and F. Paternó. Verification of properties of human-computer dialogues with an infinite number of states. In C. R. Roast and J. I. Siddiqi, editors, *BCS-FACS Workshop on Formal Aspects of the Human Computer Interface*, electronic Workshops in Computing. Springer, September 1996. http://www.springer.co.uk/ewic/workshops/FAHCI/.

19. Andrew F. Monk and Martin B. Curry. Discount dialogue modelling with Action Simulator. In G. Cockton, S. W. Draper, and G. R. S. Weir, editors, *People and Computer IX - Proceedings of HCI'94*, pages 327–338. Cambridge University Press, 1994.

20. Fabio Paternó. *A Method for Formal Specification and Verification of Interactive Systems*. PhD thesis, Department of Computer Science, University of York, 1995.

21. John Rushby. Model checking and other ways of automating formal methods. Position paper for panel on Model Checking for Concurrent Programs, Software Quality Week, San Francisco, May/June 1995.

A A Window Interactor specification

interactor *window*
attributes
    mapped : *boolean*
    visible : *boolean*
    newinfo : *boolean*
visible
    mapped visible newinfo
actions
    map, *unmap*, *hide*, *show*, *update*, *seen*
axioms
    $[]!mapped$ & $!visible$ & $!newinfo$
    $!mapped \Rightarrow [map]\text{next}(mapped)$ & $\text{next}(visible)$ & $\text{next}(newinfo)=newinfo$
    $mapped \Rightarrow [unmap]!\text{next}(mapped)$ & $!\text{next}(visible)$ & $\text{next}(newinfo)=newinfo$
    $mapped$ & $visible \Rightarrow [hide]\text{next}(mapped)$ & $!\text{next}(visible)$
                       & $\text{next}(newinfo)=newinfo$
    $mapped$ & $!visible \Rightarrow [show]\text{next}(mapped)$ & $\text{next}(visible)$
                         & $\text{next}(newinfo)=newinfo$
    $[update]\text{next}(mapped)=mapped$ & $\text{next}(newinfo)$
    $newinfo \Rightarrow [seen]\text{next}(mapped)=mapped$ & $!\text{next}(newinfo)$

B Specification of the simple mechanism

interactor *main*
attributes
   mail : *window*
   others : *window*
define
   mail_changevis := next(*mail*.action) in {*map, unmap, show*}
   others_changevis := next(*others*.action) in {*map, unmap, show*}
axioms
♯ How visibility might change...
   !(*mail.mapped* & *others.mapped*)
   → ((next(*mail.visible*)=*mail.visible* & next(*others.visible*)=*others.visible*
) | *mail_changevis* | *others_changevis*)

C Specification of the pop up window

interactor *popup*
importing
   window[*dummy*/*update*]
actions
   update
axioms
   !action=*dummy*
   [*update*]next(*mapped*) & next(*newinfo*) & next(*visible*)

interactor *main*
attributes
   mail : *window*
   others : *window*
   alert : *popup*
define
   mail_changevis := next(*mail*.action) in {*map, unmap, show*}
   others_changevis := next(*others*.action) in {*map, unmap, show*}
   alert_changevis := next(*alert*.action) in {*map, unmap, show*}
axioms
   mail.action=*update* ↔ *alert*.action=*update*
   mail.action=*view* ⇒!*alert.newinfo*
   !((*mail.mapped* & *others.mapped*) | (*mail.mapped* & *alert.mapped*)
    | (*others.mapped* & *alert.mapped*))
   →((next(*mail.visible*)=*mail.visible* & next(*others.visible*)=*others.visible*
     & next(*alert.visible*)=*alert.visible*
) | *mail_changevis* | *others_changevis* | *alert_changevis*)

Integrating rendering specifications into a formalism for the design of interactive systems

Rémi Bastide, Philippe Palanque, Duc-Hoa Le, Jaime Muñoz

LIS - FROGIS

Université Toulouse I, Place Anatole France, 31042 Toulouse cedex, France
{bastide, palanque, leduchoa, munoz} @univ-tlse1.fr

Abstract

In interactive systems, the term rendering applies to any form of communication directed from the application towards the users. The present paper deals with the specification of rendering, and its relationship with the formal specification of the dialogue between application and user. We first present a taxonomy of rendering according to its function in the application. We briefly recall the basics of the ICO formalism, which is used for the formal specification of the application. We then present a case study illustrating how various categories of rendering are taken into account in the ICO formalism. Lastly, we show how mathematical analysis can be performed on the ICO models to verify predictability properties of the interactive system.

1. Introduction

Although a lot of work has recently been devoted to the formal specification of interactive systems, the presentation component has received much less consideration than the dialogue component. However, as stated in [10], "arguments about the properties of an interactive system cannot be relied upon without placing requirements on the presentation mapping". This statement holds at the stage of requirements engineering, and holds even more when reaching the stage of detailed system specifications.

Indeed, since the early work of [9] a lot of research has been devoted to the enumeration and the classification of presentation-related properties such as observability, insistence, honesty, and predictability [14]. These properties, expressed in an abstract and generic way, allow the categorisation of interactive systems, but are not meant to help in the specification of a system to be designed.

In the detailed specification phase, it is quite difficult to talk about the presentation of an interactive system without being immediately stuck into implementation details that heavily depend on the underlying graphic toolkit. Most of the research papers dealing with the executable specification of interactive systems either face the need to give the detail of the presentation code in terms of the graphical toolkit used [23, 3] or choose to remain at a more general level and lose the ability to reason about the presentation [12].

The Arch model makes apparent this strong coupling between the specification of presentation and the physical interaction component (PIC).

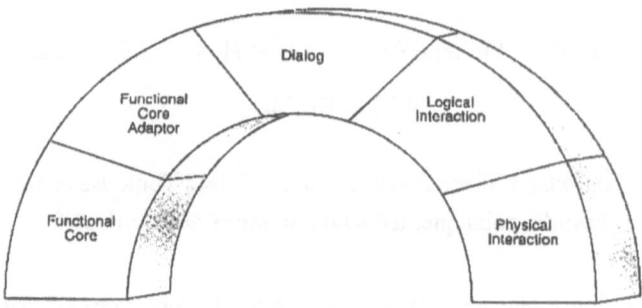

Fig 1. The Arch model from [14].

On the contrary, the dialogue component, which stands at the top of the arch, is loosely coupled to implementation constraints and can be dealt with in a more abstract manner, as several attempts have demonstrated [20, 1, 12].

The presentation component deals with input (communication user -> system) and output (communication system -> user). These two communication channels, that we call respectively activation and rendering, are fundamentally different, as activation is event-based while rendering is state-based [4]. Moreover, in modern window systems, activation is centralised in the main event loop, while rendering is distributed throughout the code of the event handlers. This difference is at the origin of the current weakness of output specification techniques.

The present paper deals with the specification of rendering, and its relationship with the formal specification of the dialogue. We first present a taxonomy of rendering according to its function in the application. We briefly recall the basics of the ICO formalism, which is used for the formal specification of the application. We then present a case study illustrating how various categories of rendering are taken into account in the ICO formalism. Lastly, we show how mathematical analysis can be performed on the ICO models to verify predictability properties of the interactive system.

2. Taxonomy of Rendering

We use the generic term "rendering" for qualifying any form of communication from the application towards the user. The taxonomy presented here does not attempt to classify the different categories of rendering according to their form or medium, but according to their semantic in the application. In the following, we do not preclude any possible form or medium of rendering: communication may be performed in "static" form (e.g. by presenting a string of text) or in dynamic form (e.g. via sound, synthesised voice or animation).

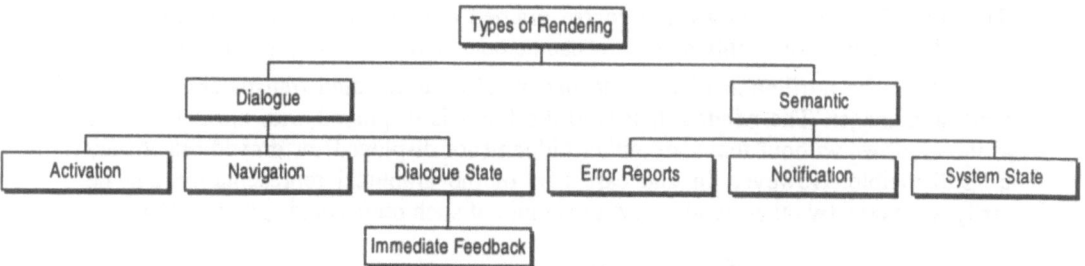

Fig 2. Hierarchical taxonomy for rendering.

2.1 Dialogue rendering

We put in the category of *Dialogue rendering* any form of rendering that aims at keeping the user informed of the evolution of the interaction that is going on with the system. This category can be further refined into *activation rendering* (the rendering of legal actions), *navigation rendering* (dealing with the navigation among the screens or windows of the application) and *dialogue state rendering* (displaying values that belong to the dialogue).

2.1.1 Activation. Actions that are allowed by the system at any given moment. As the user-system dialogue proceeds, the set of legal actions offered to the user changes dynamically. We call the set of legal actions offered by the system at a given moment the *interaction space* of the user.

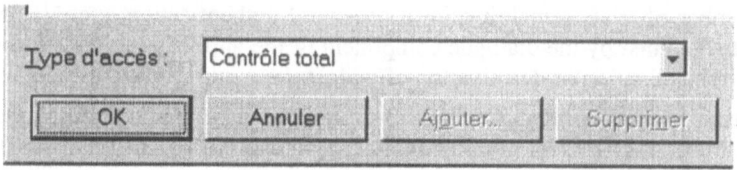

Fig 3. Rendering the interaction space.

The interaction space needs to be made apparent to the user, and this is usually done by greying out any widget or menu item that might be used in the interface to trigger a currently illegal action.

Using this technique for rendering the interaction space is quite common, but presents the drawback of providing very little information on the reasons why a particular action is currently disabled, and gives even less clues on the possible ways to make it available. Other forms of interaction space rendering that does not suffer these drawbacks can be devised [17].

2.1.2 Navigation. Any complex application faces the need to partition its presentation into several screens or windows in order to prevent screen cluttering or to group information into logical units. This induces the need to offer the user some means to navigate the application's screens, and of course to render this navigation.

Navigation between windows is a coarse grained dialogue between application and user, while interaction within a window can be considered as fine grained dialogue.

Most often, the attribution of focus to one window is handled transparently by the window manager. The window that hold the focus is displayed with normal colours while windows without focus are either hidden (not displayed) or greyed out if they are still visible. However, in that case part of the graphical representation can be partly recovered by other windows. An example of such rendering is given in Fig 4.

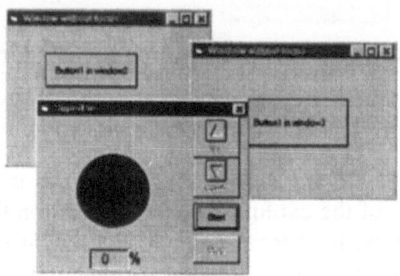

Fig 4. An example of navigation rendering: the focus window.

2.1.3 Dialogue state and immediate feedback Other kinds of information that belong to the state of the dialogue may be of interest to the user. It is sometimes necessary to show the user that he/she is in a given state of interaction (e.g. by changing the form of the mouse cursor). Other examples of dialogue state rendering might be to show the number of times the user has accessed any particular function, or the number of trials remaining for a password authentication, etc. Values of this kind are maintained by the dialogue component of the application, but are not directly related to the activation or deactivation of widgets.

Modern user interfaces increasingly adopt a direct-manipulation style of interaction, giving the user the illusion of directly acting on the objects of interest rather than indirectly accessing them through command buttons and data-entry widgets. Direct manipulation requires immediate feedback of very low-level user actions such as mouse moves or drags. The handling of these low-level actions calls for a much finer grained dialogue modelling than is required for conventional indirect manipulation interfaces. For example, when dragging of an object on top of another there is a need to visually notify whether a given area is a legal target for a drop.

2.2 Semantic rendering

The ultimate goal of an interface is to provide means for a user to interact with semantic objects that belong to the functional core of the system. The user actions may trigger the creation or deletion of objects, obtain information on the objects' state, or change its state.

2.2.1 System State. Any interactive application has to display part or all of the system's state. In an object-based world, the application may wish to display any public attribute of objects belonging to the functional core, or the result of any method call performed on these objects or any functional combination thereof.

2.2.2 Notification. The state of objects that belong to the functional core may change due to causes independent from the user interface (e.g. when a software monitors some kind of physical system). This change of state is spontaneous in the user's point of view, because it is not triggered by a user action. This kind of changes needs also to be made apparent to the user.

2.2.3 Error Reports. A user-initiated action may trigger a call to the functional core that fails to complete properly, and the call will usually return some form or error status or exception. These error reports must be notified in some way to the user, providing as much information as possible on the nature of the error, its potential cause and possible cures.

3. The ICO Formalism

This section recalls the main features of the ICO formalism, that we use in §4 to model the case study.

3.1 Introduction

The ICO formalism uses concepts borrowed from the object-oriented approach (dynamic instantiation, classification, encapsulation, inheritance, client/server relationship) to describe the structural or static aspects of systems, and uses high-level Petri nets to describe their dynamic or behavioural aspects.

ICOs where originally devised for the modelling and implementation of event-driven interfaces. An ICO model of a system is made up of several communicating objects, where both behaviour of objects and communication protocol between objects are described by Petri nets. When two objects communicate, one is in the position of a "client", requesting the execution of a service and waiting for a result, while the other is in the position a "server" whose role is to execute the service. In the ICO formalism, an object is an entity featuring four components: behaviour, services, state and presentation.

3.2 Behaviour

The behaviour of an ICO states how the object reacts to external stimuli according to its inner state. This behaviour is described by a high-level Petri net called the Object Control Structure (ObCS) of the object. A Petri net is a directed bipartite graph whose nodes are either *places* (depicted as circles) or *transitions* (depicted as rectangles). Places and transitions are connected by arcs. Each place may contain any number of *tokens*. In high-level Petri nets, tokens may carry values. In our formalism, tokens may hold conventional values (integer, string, etc.) or references to other objects in the application.

A transition may feature a *precondition* that is a Boolean expression that may involve the variables labelling the input arcs of the transition.

A transition *is fireable* (may occur) if and only if:

(i)   each of its input places carries at least one token

(ii)   if the transition features a precondition; it exists tokens in the input places for which the precondition holds

When a transition is fired, it removes one token from each of its input places, and sets one token in each of its output places. A transition features an *action* part, which may request services from the tokens involved in the occurrence of the transition, or perform arbitrary algorithms manipulating the values of tokens.

3.3 Services

An ICO offers a set of services that define the interface (in the programming language meaning) offered by the object to its environment. In the case of user-driven application, this environment may be either the user or other objects of the application. Each service is related to at least one transition in the ObCS, and a service is only available when at least one of its related transitions is fireable. This relationship between transitions (T) and services [13] is defined by the *availability function*:

$$Avail: \quad Services \quad \rightarrow \quad P(T) \quad \text{where P(T) is the power set of T:}$$

- $\forall s \in Services, Avail(s) \neq \emptyset$

- $\forall s, s' \in Services / s \neq s', Avail(s) \cap Avail(s') = \emptyset$

Using the ICO formalism, we distinguish between two kinds of services:

- services offered to the user, called *user services*, are represented in the ObCS by *user transitions*, and that directly relates to the presentation part of the ICO. Their graphical representation is a transition with a broken arrow and a greyed circle

- services offered to other objects that are graphically represented by a transition with an incoming broken arrow

3.4 State

The state of an ICO is the distribution and the value of the tokens (called the *marking*) in the places of the ObCS. As services are related to transitions, this allows defining how the current state influences the availability of services, and conversely how the performance of a service influences the state of the object.

3.5 Presentation

The Presentation of an object states its external look. This Presentation is a structured set of *widgets* organised in a set of windows.

The user → system interaction will only take place through those widgets. Each user action on a widget may trigger one of the ICO's user services. The relation between user services and widgets is fully stated by the *activation function* that associates to each couple (widget, user action) the service to be triggered.

More precisely the activation function is defined as follows:

$$Act: \quad (W \times Event) \quad \rightarrow \quad Services$$

The system → user interaction is fully specified by the *rendering function* that relates to each node (places or transitions) of the ObCS a set of Widgets that can be used by the node to render information to the user.

$$Rend: \quad P \cup T \quad \rightarrow \quad W$$

3.6 Architectural considerations

The ObCS plays the role of the *Dialogue* component in the Seeheim model. The *Application interface* and *Application kernel* are modelled by the classes of the tokens flowing in the net. The *Presentation* component is made of a set of interactors (widgets) that may display and edit data (for example text entry fields or radio buttons), or trigger events of interest to the application (for example menu items or buttons).

The communication between the *Dialogue* component and the *Application kernel* is thus described both by the flow of tokens in the net and by the call of tokens methods in the transitions' actions.

The communication between the *Dialogue* component and the *Presentation* component is more complex to describe, since several aspects are to be taken into consideration:

- The *Presentation* component influences the dialogue through the occurrence of events. This occurrence is modelled in the ObCS by special places called event places. The *Presentation* component is able to deposit tokens in those event places after the occurrence of an event. A transition in the ObCS net may have at most one input event place. A transition with an input event place is called an event transition. The very notion of interface place is made necessary by the fact that a given incoming event may trigger different actions in the system, according to the system's inner state. This is modelled by two or more event transitions in the ObCS sharing a common event place. Those transitions are therefore in structural conflict, and this indeterminism has to be relieved by the structure of the ObCS.

- Conversely, the state of the *Dialogue* component (i.e. the marking of the ObCS net) influences the *Presentation* component: according to this state, several events may be disabled, and their associated interactor greyed out. This is described by associating event transitions to one or several interactors in the presentation: when a transition is not fireable, all of its associated interactors are greyed out or disabled.

Lastly, the state of the ObCS net must be displayed by the presentation. This is done by associating a rendering action to each place of the ObCS. Such actions may call methods of the tokens held in the place in order to display whatever information is appropriate.

4. Case study

In order to exemplify the various kinds of rendering that have been presented in section 2 we will use the SuperPiechart case study. Although this case study is very simple, it features a complex enough behaviour in order to represent most of the elements of the rendering taxonomy.

4.1 Presentation of the case study

This simple application allows users to enter a percentage using several input elements and to have an immediate feedback of the percentage on different output elements. Fig 5 gives the presentation part of this application.

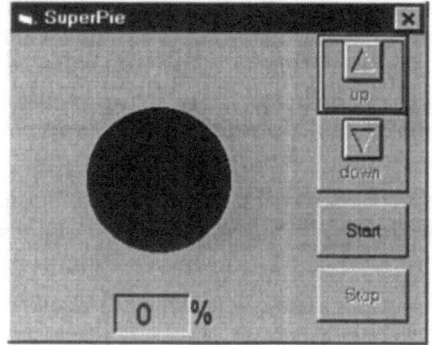

Fig 5. A snapshot of the presentation part   **Fig 6.** A snapshot of the presentation part
at start time.   at runtime.

The input elements are:

- A button "Up" that increments the value of percentage by one point. Up is not available to the user if the value of percentage equals 100.
- A button "down" that decrements the value of percentage by one point. Down is not available to the user if the value of percentage equals 0.

The input/output elements are:

- A text widget where the user can type out a new percentage
- A Piechart widget that can be directly manipulated by the user. Using a mouse, the percentage can be modified, first by pressing the left button of the mouse then by dragging the mouse to the desired value.

An important feature of the application is that the abstraction (corresponding to the value of the variable percentage) is always consistent with its various graphical representations. Thus, the value in the text zone and the graphical value of the Piechart always correspond to the same value and each user action on the widgets modifies both the graphical representations and the abstraction. A static representation of the application with consistent presentations is shown on Fig 6.

At the beginning, the application is stopped and the user can only start it by pressing the Start button. Then all the interactions described above are available until the user presses the Stop button that stops the application and puts it back into the initial state. This initial state is represented in Fig 5.

4.2 ICO-based specification of the case study

Using object-oriented modelling the SuperPiechart application can be modelled using a single class with only one instance.

Using the ICO formalism, this class is defined in Fig 7 as follows:

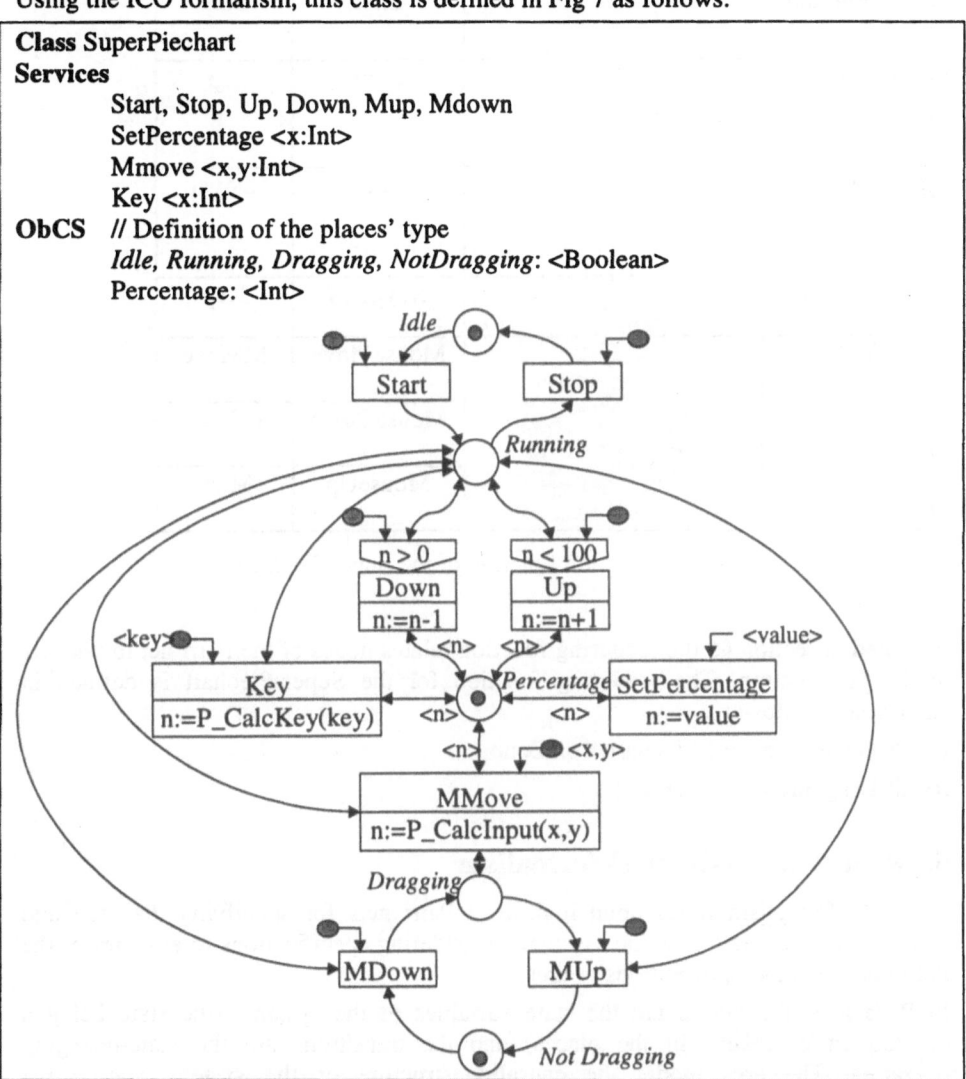

Fig 7. Dialogue specification of the Super-Piechart.

As stated in section §5 the activation function relates user events to the ObCS of the ICOs. Fig 8 corresponds to the activation function of the ICO class presented in Fig 7. The presentation part of this class is given on Fig 6 and the first two columns of the activation function relate to this presentation.

Widgets	Graphical representation	Events	Service
ButtonStart	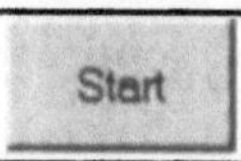 Start	Click	Start
ButtonStop	 Stop	Click	Stop
ButtonUp	 up	Click	Up
ButtonDown	 down	Click	Down
TextZone	 34	Keypress	Key
PieChart	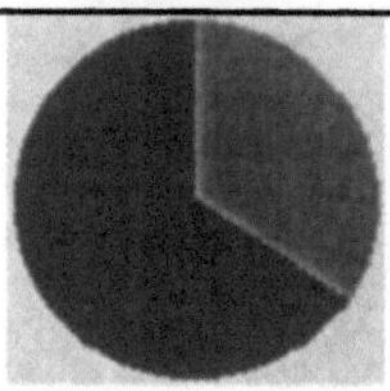	MouseMove	MMove
		MouseDown	MDown
		MouseUp	MUp

Fig 8. Activation function of the Super-Piechart.

As stated in section §5 the rendering function relates nodes of the Petri net to widgets in the presentation. The rendering function for the Super-Piechart is defined in extension as follows:

Rend(Percentage) = { Piechart, TextZone }

Rend(Dragging)= { Piechart }

5. Rendering in the ICO formalism

The ICO formalism relies upon high-level Petri nets for specifying dialogue and interaction. One could imagine associating rendering specifications to any part of the Petri nets, i.e. places, transitions or arcs.

In Petri nets, the places are the state variables of the systems (the state being a distribution of tokens in the places) and the transitions are the state-changing operators. The arcs model the causality structure of the system, stating the preconditions of state changes, and their effect on the system's state.

We consider that rendering deals with state: the very purpose of rendering is to make the inner state of the application visible to the user. It is therefore logical to associate rendering specification with the places of the Petri net.

However, a closer examination of the various types of rendering reveals the need to associate rendering specification to the transition of the net also: in the ICO formalism, the transitions model the atomic (non-interruptible) actions of the system. The transitions will often feature function calls to the non-interactive kernel of the application, and these function calls may take an arbitrary time to complete. It will often be necessary to inform the user that a lengthy operation is going on (e.g. by changing the form of the mouse cursor) or to show the progression of the operation (e.g. by displaying a progress bar). We could imagine going to a finer grained model of dialogue, and associate various sub-states (modelled as places) to the performance of the operation but this would lose the non-interruptible nature of the operation. The non-interruptibility could be restored only by a much more complex structure of the ObCS net. This reason led us to allow associating rendering specifications to the transitions as well as to the places of the ObCS.

5.1 Rendering in places

Any place in an ObCS may be associated with up to three rendering methods:

- A *token_entered* method, that will be triggered each time a token is added to the place by the occurrence of a transition,

- A *token_removed* method, triggered each time a token is removed from the place,

- A *token_reset* method, triggered each time a token stored in the place is accessed or changed by a transition connected to the place by a bi-directional arc.

The rendering methods are associated to the places of the net, and may access all the tokens contained in the place. The rendering methods receive as parameters the place itself, the token involved in the rendering and the set of widgets associated to the place by the rendering function (cf. §3.5).

The typical signature of a rendering method is:

```
void token_entered(Place aPlace, Token aToken, SetOfWidgets theWidgets);
```

5.2 Rendering in transitions

Any transition in an ObCS may be associated with an action, expressed as a function taking as input (resp. output) parameters the variables on the input (resp. output) arcs of the transition. This action is allowed to perform any kind of rendering on the widgets associated to the transition by the rendering function. Most often, a rendering will be performed when the action starts executing (e.g. changing the cursor shape), at several stages of the execution (e.g. updating a progress bar), and when the action completes (e.g. reverting the cursor to its original shape).

5.3 Taxonomy of rendering in the ICO

We will now present in more detail how rendering may be specified in the ICO formalism, according to the taxonomy presented in §2.

5.3.1 Activation. As stated in §2.1.1, *activation rendering* aims at displaying the *interaction space* of the user. In an ICO-based specification, the interaction space may be deduced from the current marking of the ObCS nets according to the set of enabled transitions. To this end, our specification exploits the availability function (relating services to transitions) and the activation function (relating widgets to services).

Let $T_e \subset T$ the set of enabled transitions.

The availability function *Avail* relates a service to a set of transitions. The set $S_a \subset Services$ of available services is thus:

$$S_a = \text{Avail}^{-1}(T_e)$$

And the set of available user services is:

$$S_{ua} = S_a \cap S_u$$

The activation function *Act* relates a couple (Widget, Action) to a user service. At any moment, the set of activated widgets is therefore defined as:

$$\text{Proj}_W(\text{Act}^{-1}(S_{ua}))$$

It is thus possible to compute, according to the current marking of an ObCS net, the set of enabled (and disabled) widgets at any moment in the interaction. It is important to note that no specific rendering information needs to be added to the ObCS nets to perform activation rendering because the net structure itself, along with the activation function, are sufficient to perform activation rendering automatically. We have already presented two alternative implementations techniques, based respectively on interpretation and compilation of the ObCS nets, that preserve sufficient information in the runtime system to enable automatic activation rendering [2].

In the case study presented in §4.1, activation rendering handles the active or inactive state of the various widgets in the interface. It is deduced from the availability and activation functions described in the ICO specification (§4.2).

5.3.2 Navigation. The ObCS nets may be used to model dialogue at various levels of details: an ObCS can describe the dialogue structure within a window, but can describe just as well the navigation between the various windows of an application. In this case, an ICO class is used to model the navigation structure of the application. The tokens flowing in this ICO's ObCS net will be references to other ICO objects modelling the various windows of the application. The navigation rendering will be performed by the rendering methods associated to the places. The entrance of a token in a place may trigger the display of a window on the screen, while the removal of such token might trigger the closing of the window.

This form of navigation specification is quite close to the one proposed in [12].

5.3.3 Dialogue state.

As the dialogue is modelled by a Petri net, the state of the dialogue is completely described by the marking of the ObCS nets. The marking is a distribution of tokens in the ObCS places, and the tokens can hold any kind of data that is relevant to the dialogue. *Dialogue state rendering* is therefore performed by the rendering methods associated to the places of the net, in the same way as navigation rendering.

Different forms of rendering (according to out taxonomy) are thus performed in the same way in our formalism, which may be an indication that it is difficult to distinguish between dialogue, navigation and application state, purely on formal terms.

In the case study, some form of dialogue state rendering is performed by changing the cursor shape while the user is dragging the super-pie. This is specified by two rendering method (token_entered and token_removed) associated to the place *Dragging*, expressed in pseudo-code follows:

```
Token_entered(Place aPlace, Token aToken, SetOfWidgets theWidgets) {
// The rendering function associates only the
// PieChart widget to the place Dragging.
// The aPlace and aToken parameters are unused
        for all w in theWidgets
                w.Setcursor(Cross_Cursor);
}


Token_Removed(Place aPlace, Token aToken,
        SetOfWidgets theWidgets) {
        for all w in theWidgets
                w.Setcursor(Normal_Cursor);
}
```

5.3.4 System State.

In the ICO formalism, the tokens flowing in the ObCS nets may hold references to objects that belong to the functional core. *System state rendering* is therefore specified in ICO in the same way as dialogue state rendering (§5.3.3), through the use of rendering methods. The rendering methods dealing with value rendering will perform arbitrarily complex algorithms that may access attributes or methods of the token objects, to compute the information that needs to be displayed.

In the case study, the system state is modelled as a single token that holds the percentage value. The rendering of this value is performed using a single rendering function associated to the place Percentage, and triggered each time a token is reset in this place:

```
Token_reset(Place aPlace, Token aToken,SetOfWidgets theWidgets) {
// The rendering function associates the
// PieChart and TextZone widgets to the place Percentage.
        for all w in theWidgets
                w.SetValue(aToken.Value);
}
```

It must be noted that the above code assumes that any widget may respond to the method SetValue, which will certainly not be the case in every possible interface toolkit. This points out the need to build a virtual toolkit abstraction that will isolate the idiosyncrasies of a particular toolkit, and provide each widget with the set of methods required by the dialogue.

5.3.5 Notification. The ICO formalism is object-oriented, and, as such, each ICO specification is presented as a class, featuring a set of services. As stated in §3.3, some of the services are meant to be triggered by the user through some input mechanism, and are therefore part of the activation function. Other services are simple methods in the usual object-oriented sense of the term, and are meant to be called by other objects in the application. Through this means, it is possible for objects in the functional core of the application to notify an ICO of the occurrence of some event of interest, by calling a service defined in the ICO class. The availability function relates the services to transitions and the invocation of a service will result in the firing of a transition in the ICO's ObCS.

Notification rendering will be specified either using the rendering functions associated to the net's places, or by the action of the service's transitions.

5.3.6 Error reports. The functions of the application core are called by the actions of the net's transitions. These actions have the opportunity to display the errors that may be generated by the function calls using any widget associated to the transition.

5.4 Rendering specification for the case study

ObCS element			Rendering
Places	Idle	All arcs	No rendering
	Running	All arcs	No rendering
	Percentage	Token entered	N/A (No incoming arc)
		Token removed	N/A (No outgoing arc)
		Token reset	**System state rendering** Display percentage in the *TextZone* and *PieChart* widgets
	Dragging	Token entered	**Dialogue rendering** Set mouse cursor to cross
		Token removed	**Dialogue rendering** Set mouse cursor to normal
		Token reset	No rendering
	NotDragging	All arcs	No rendering

Fig 9. Rendering function of the Super-Piechart

Fig 9 summarises the rendering specifications that need to be added to the ICO model of the super-piechart to completely define the rendering.

In this case study, no further rendering specification needs to be added to the ObCS transitions.

6. Formal verification

Formal verification aims at checking properties over a formal specification of a system. Some generic properties are of great interest for system specification and Petri nets theory offers predefined techniques for checking them. Such properties are liveness, boundedness and reinitialisability.

- A *system is live*, if for every state of the system, there exists a sequence of action that can trigger any given action of the system. That is to say that there is no dead branch in the system.

- A *system is bounded* if there is no production or consumption of resources during the activity of the system. This is an important property as it guaranties the fact that the system does not wear, i.e. its actual use does not jeopardise its future use [21].

- A *system is reinitialisable* if for any state the system can be in, it is always possible to find a sequence of actions that will set the system back in its initial state. This property relates to the previous although they are orthogonal [16], i.e. a system can be reinitialisable and not bounded and reciprocally.

6.1.1 Algebraic verification. In order to check the liveness property, we could apply Commoner's theorem [8]:

A free choice Petri net is live if and only if all siphons include an initially marked trap.

In order to apply this theorem we need first to check whether or not the Petri net in Fig 7 is free choice that heavily relates to the notion of structural conflict. Two transitions t1 and t2 are in structural conflict if they have at least one input place in common.

A Petri net is free choice [7], if and only if, for all the transitions in structural conflict with a place P, P is the only input place of the transitions (the two-way arcs are ignored). Fig 10, 11 and 12 give examples of free choice and not free choice Petri nets.

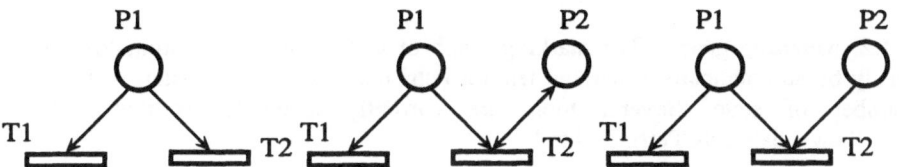

Fig 10. Free choice net.   **Fig 11.** Free choice net.   **Fig 12.** Not free choice net.

As there is no conflict, the system is free choice and thus Commoner's theorem applies.

The siphon (respectively trap) is a set of places such as its set of input (respectively output) transitions is included in the in its set of output (respectively input) transitions. By this definition, we can calculate the sets of siphons and traps. These sets contains the same elements:

{[P₃]; [P₁P₂]; [P₄, P₅]; [P₁, P₂, P₃]; [P₃, P₄, P₅]; [P₁, P₂, P₄, P₅] and [P₁, P₂, P₃, P₄, P₅]}

where $P_1:=Idle; P_2:=Running; P_3:= Percentage; P_4:=Dragging; P_5:=Not Dragging$.

As each of these elements holds at least one token in the initial state, all the traps are marked in the initial state. In this net, each trap is marked and each trap is also a siphon; therefore each siphon of this net contains a marked trap. Applying the Commoner's theorem, **the Petri net in Fig 7 is live**.

By definition, a system modelled by Petri nets is bounded if for every place P, there exists a natural number b such that $M(P) \leq b$ for every reachable marking M.

This notion is linked to P-invariant notion. A P-invariant is an integer positive solution of the linear system: $C^T . \vec{x} = \vec{0}$ where C^T is the transposed incidence matrix [16]. The boundedness theorem [18] states that a system modelled by Petri nets is bounded if there is a covering of P-invariant [18] (i.e. if each place appears at least once in a P-invariant [18].

The incidence matrix of the Petri net given in Fig 7

$$C = \begin{bmatrix} -1 & 1 & 0 & 0 & 0 & 0 & 0 & 0 & 0 \\ 1 & -1 & 0 & 0 & 0 & 0 & 0 & 0 & 0 \\ 0 & 0 & 0 & 0 & 0 & 0 & 0 & 0 & 0 \\ 0 & 0 & 0 & 0 & 0 & 0 & 0 & 1 & -1 \\ 0 & 0 & 0 & 0 & 0 & 0 & 0 & -1 & 1 \end{bmatrix}$$

Among the infinite number of integer positive solutions of the system $C^T . \vec{x} = \vec{0}$ one is $\vec{x} = (1,1,0,0,0)^T$ $\vec{x} = (0,0,0,1,1)^T$ and $\vec{x} = (0,01,0,0)^T$. As each place belongs at least to one P_invariant **the Petri net in Fig 7 is bounded**.

6.1.2 Marking graph. The marking graph of a Petri net is an automaton and can easily be automatically generated from a Petri net modelling a system with a finite number of state. Several tools are currently available to this end (see http://www.daimi.dk/Petrinets.html).

Most of the properties that one might be interested to check over a Petri net model, can be checked on the marking graph of this Petri net. However, when large-scale applications are concerned, the construction of the marking graph can be rather difficult[1]. This is not the case for the Super-Piechart application and the marking graph corresponding to the Petri net of Fig 7 is represented on Fig 13.

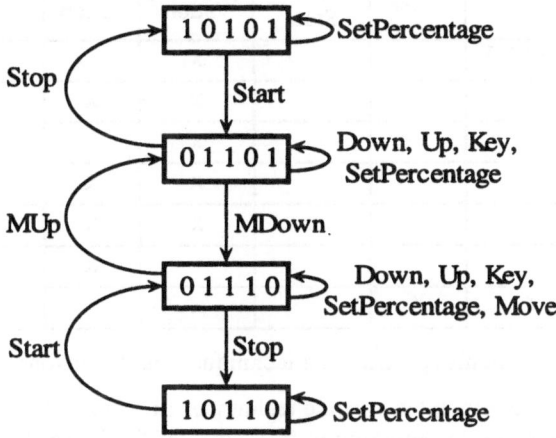

Fig 13. The marking graph corresponding to the Petri net of **Fig 7**.

As the marking graph is finite, the related Petri net model is bounded. It can be easily seen that the Petri net is live as every action can be reached from any state of the marking graph. The same reasoning can be applied in order to prove that the Petri net is reinitialisable.

6.1.3 Rendering-based properties. Various presentation-related properties (observability, insistence, honesty, and predictability) can be formally specified using declarative formal languages such as temporal logics. The aim is not here to present yet another specification of such properties but to show how such properties can be discussed with a detailed formal specification done using the ICO formalisms.

A property such as honesty (the dialogue structure ensures that users correctly interpret perceived information) cannot be proven without a clear representation of user model and without a precise description of cognitive user behaviour. This is beyond the work presented in this paper.

7. Related work

Any approach to the specification and design of interactive systems needs to provide some form of rendering specification. Fig 14 summarises how alternative approaches relate to our taxonomy of rendering.

---

[1] It is possible to cope with infinite marking graphs using symbolic marking graphs. This is usually mandatory when high-level Petri nets are concerned, i.e. when tokens can hold values [15]

	Dialogue			Semantic		
	Navigation	Dialogue State	Activation	Notification	Application State	Error report
Template Abstraction [22]			X	X	X	
Pie [9]			X	X		
York [11]			X	X	X	
CNUCE [19]			X	X		
IOG [5]		X	X	X	X	X
PAC [6]				X	X	
Tadeus [12]	X		X			X

Fig 14. Interactive systems specification techniques and the taxonomy of rendering.

Fig 15 summarises the principles of some techniques in terms of the mapping function used (how widgets relate to input/output behaviour of the interactive system), of the formalism used to model the dialogue, and of the possibilities offered for formal validation.

Aspects/ Approaches	Mapping Function	Dialogue Model	Properties Validation Language
Template Abstraction [22]	Results and Display Templates	Structuring Interaction	Output correctness Structural consistency
Pie [9]	Mathematical relationships		Z
York [11]	Mathematical relationships	Interactor	VDM, Z or MAL
CNUCE [19]	Interactor's function	Lotos language and Interactor	ACTL
IOG[5]	View Port	Interactive Object Graph	
PAC [6]	Control Module	PAC Agent	
Tadeus [12]	Interaction Table	Dialogue Graph	
ICO [1]	Activation and Rendering functions	High-level Petri nets	Analysis of Petri nets properties.

Fig 15. A comparison chart for interactive systems specification techniques.

8. Conclusion

The purpose of this paper was to show the introduction of rendering specification in the ICO formalism. Some of the new constructs have been exemplified on a simple but meaningful case study.

10. Doherty, Gavin; Harrison, Michael. A representational approach to the specification of presentations. in: Harrison, Michael; Torres, Juan C., Editors. 4th Eurographics workshop on Design, Specification and Verification of Interactive System (DSV-IS'97) Jun 4-6 1997; Granada, Spain. Springer-Verlag; 1997. pp. 273-290.

11. Duke, David J.; Harrison, Michael. Abstract interaction objects EUROGRAPHICS'93; 1993. pp. 25-36.

12. Elwert, Thomas; Schlungbaum, Egbert. Modelling and generation of graphical user interface in the TADEUS approach. in: Palanque, Philippe; Bastide, Rémi, Editors. 2nd Eurographics workshop on Design Specification and Verification of Interactive System (DSV-IS'95) Jun 7-9 1995; Toulouse, France. Springer-Verlag; 1995. pp. 193-208.

13. Fekete, Jean D. Les trois services du noyau sémantique indispensables à l'IHM. 8èmes journées sur l'ingénierie des l'Interaction Homme-Machine (IHM'96) Sep 16-18 1996; Grenoble, France. Toulouse, France: Cépaduès-Editions; 1996. pp. 45-50.

14. Gram, Christian; Cockton, Gilbert, Editors. Design principles for interactive software. Chapman et Hall ed.1995.

15. Jensen, Kurt. Coloured Petri nets: Analysis methods and practical use. 2nd edition Springer-Verlag; 1995.

16. Murata T. Petri nets: properties, analysis and applications. Proceeding of the IEEE 1989;77 (4).

17. Palanque, Philippe; Bastide, Rémi; Dourte, Louis. Contextual help for free with formal dialogue design5th international conference on human-computer interaction, HCI International'93 Aug 8-15 1993; Orlando Florida. North-Holland; 1993. pp. 615-620.

18. Paludetto, Mario. Sur la commande de procédés industriels: Une méthodologie basée objets et réseaux de Petri [Ph.D. thesis]. Toulouse: Université Paul Sabatier; 1991.

19. Paternò, Fabio. A methodology to design interactive systems based on interactors theory of user-interaction objects [CNUCE internal report]. 1993 Dec.

20. Paternò, Fabio; Faconti, Giorgio. On the LOTOS use to describe graphical interaction. HCI'92. BCS Conference Series; 1992. pp. 155-174.

21. Rees R. What is wear and wearout. IEEE Transactions on Reliability 1997;46(2).

22. Roast, Chris. Modelling interaction using templates abstractionsHCI'94, People and Computer IX: Cambridge University Press; 1994. pp. 273-284.

23. Sage, Meurig; Johnson, Chris. Interactors and Haggis: Executable specifications for interactive systems. in: Harrison, Michael; Torres, Juan C., Editors. 4th Eurographics workshop on Design, Specification and Verification of Interactive System (DSV-IS'97) Jun 4-6 1997; Granada, Spain. Springer Verlag; 1997. pp. 93-108.

Although the analysis techniques presented above cannot prove a property such as observability (the system makes all relevant information potentially available to the user), they may prove that a system fails to comply with it. For example, if the set of currently available actions is not rendered to the user the system cannot be said to be observable. The same holds for the predictability property (users can predict future states and response time from the current and prior observable states). The coupling of rendering specification techniques in the ICO with the analysis possibilities of Petri nets represents a promising direction for the proof presentation-related properties.

9. Acknowledgements

The authors are very grateful to the anonymous DSV-IS referees for their useful comments, and for the pertinent observations they provided in their reviews.

References

1. Bastide, Rémi; Palanque, Philippe. Petri Net based design of user-driven interfaces using the Interactive Cooperative Objects formalism. in: Paternò, Fabio, Volume editor. Interactive systems: design, specification, and verification (DSV-IS'94). Springer-Verlag; 1994. pp. 383-400.

2. Bastide, Rémi; Palanque, Philippe. Implementation techniques for Petri net based specifications of human computer dialogues. in: Vanderdonkt, Jean, Editor. 2nd workshop on Computer Aided Design of User Interfaces, CADUI'96; Université Notre-Dame de la Paix, Namur (Belgium). Presses Universitaires de Namur; 1996. pp. 285-302.

3. Bumbulis, Peter; Alencar, P.; Cowan, D.; Lucena, C. Combining formal techniques in user interface construction and verification. in: Palanque, Philippe; Bastide, Rémi, Editors. 2nd Eurographics workshop on Design Specification and Verification of Interactive System (DSV-IS'95) Jun 7-9 1995; Toulouse, France. Springer-Verlag; 1995. pp. 174-192.

4. Campos, José C.; Harrison, Michael. Formally verifying interactive systems: A review. in: Harrison, Michael; Torres, Juan C., Editors. 4th Eurographics workshop on Design, Specification and Verification of Interactive System (DSV-IS'97) Jun 4-6 1997; Granada, Spain. Springer-Verlag; 1997. pp. 109-124.

5. Carr, David. Interaction Object Graphs: an executable graphical notation for specifying user interfaces. in: Palanque, Philippe; Paternò, Fabio, Editors. Formal methods in Human-Computer Interaction. Springer-Verlag; 1997. pp. 141-155.

6. Coutaz, Joëlle; Nigay, Laurence; Salber, Daniel. Conceptual software architecture models for interactive system. ESPRIT BRA 7040 Amodeus-2; 1993 Mar. Report No.: WP11.

7. David, René; Alla, Hassane. Du Grafcet aux réseaux de Petri. Paris: Hermès; 1992.

8. Desel, Jörg; Esparza, Javier. Free choice Petri nets. Cambridge University Press; 1995. (Cambridge tracts on computer science; 40).

9. Dix, Alan J. Formal methods for interactive systems. Academic Press; 1991.

Practical Dialogue Refinement

R. E. Kurt Stirewalt

Department of Computer Science, Michigan State University
East Lansing, Michigan 48824, U. S. A

Gregory D. Abowd

GVU Center & College of Computing, Georgia Institute of Technology
Atlanta, Georgia 30332-0280, U. S. A

Abstract: Researchers have suggested viewing interactive system design as the refinement of an abstract user-task model into an object-oriented interaction model[1, 17]. Inherent in this view is a shift in the nature of the behavior being modeled. We explore the manifestations of such a shift by critically analyzing properties of the forms used to represent task and interaction models. The analysis enabled us to uncover four obstacles to dialogue refinement. We believe that if designers cannot systematically address these obstacles, then the task-model refinement process of development will not be practical on any large scale. We then suggest a refinement framework that systematically deals with these obstacles and demonstrate it on a small, but significant example.

Keywords: Dialogue modeling, refinement, LOTOS

1   Introduction

Dialogue refers to the two-way user-computer conversation of an interactive system[3]. Engineers require design methodologies to guide them in implementing this conversation in software. To answer this need, researchers have proposed interactive system life-cycle models, some of which[1, 17] characterize design as a process of refining dialogue from an abstract action-oriented form into a concrete object-oriented form. Inherent in these approaches is a design shift in the nature of behavior being modeled from one expression of the dialogue to its refinement. It is not clear that such a shift may be carried out systematically by practicing engineers. This shift potentially makes dialogue refinement impractical as a means for developing interactive systems. In this paper, we explore the manifestations of this shift in order to assess the practicality of this process model.

Both Bass and Coutaz[1] and Paternò[17] suggest viewing interactive system design as the refinement of an abstract *user-task* model into an object-oriented *interaction model*. Task models specify the temporal decomposition of tasks, and they generally represent the first specification of dialogue. Interaction models specify input device level operations and their orderings. These two artifacts—task models and interaction models—represent dialogue before and after refinement.

We feel that, to be useful to practicing engineers, refinement must be a systematic fleshing out of detail, which does not compromise the structure of the model being refined. Any refinement technique that relies on designer transformation and changes in notation can fail to be practical under our definition. We seek to discover a technique for systematically refining action-oriented task specifications into object-oriented inter-action specifications without forcing designers to re-implement the task specification in a new notation.

Such a technique is complicated by the fact that task and interaction models are most naturally expressed in different notations. Task models, for example, are easily expressed in a temporal action language like LOTOS[2]. Interaction models, on the other hand, are easily expressed in an object-oriented language like the OMT[7] dynamic modeling notation. With models expressed in different notations, it is difficult to rigorously define refinement. This makes it is more difficult to assess whether or not the process is systematic and, therefore, practical.

We address the systematic refinement of dialogue models by critically analyzing properties of task and interaction model representations. We use a running example to motivate our analysis (Sections 3 and 4). The analysis enabled us to identify four obstacles to systematic refinement (Section 5). We then propose a framework for sys-tematically refining LOTOS task models into OMT interaction models (Section 6). Our initial experience indicates that this framework makes dialogue refinement practical over the life-cycle of an interactive system.

2 Background and methods

2.1 Interaction models

Designers refine a task model into an interaction model, which specifies dialogue down to the level of input device behavior. The global user-computer conversation is cast into a carefully selected collection of *interaction techniques*, which blend presenta-tion graphics and device behavior. Interaction techniques are difficult to design and implement[6], and so they tend to be collected into toolkits and reused. We use the term *interactor* to define a customizable specification of an interaction technique. Inter-action models are collections of interactors customized to a particular application and connected together to implement user tasks.

Interactors in our framework encapsulate a complete gesture between the user and an input device like the mouse or keyboard. We represent these gestures using state diagrams much like those used in the Amulet environment[4]. Paternò[16] defines an *interactor* as a software component with a fixed set of incoming and outgoing data-flow paths. These paths support the transfer of control, data, and presentation and may be connected to paths of the opposite polarity in other interactors. Markopoulos[15] uses a similar definition of interactor, but his are structured according to a different user-interface architecture.

Markopoulos and Paternò define interactors formally as LOTOS processes. This is useful for reasoning about task refinement since task models can also be expressed in LOTOS. Paternò defines a development methodology called TLIM for analyzing and transforming task models into system models[17]. The obstacles to dialogue refine-ment, which we present in Section 5, occur in these other interactor frameworks.

2.2 Multiple models and interactive system design

The use of multiple models in the design of interactive systems is not new. The model-based approach to design bases system analysis, design, and implementation on a common repository of models. Developers using this approach build models that describe the desired system, rather than writing a program that exhibits the behavior[9].

The TRIDENT environment[20] supports the generation of systems from data models (based on entity-relationship diagrams) and a behavior notation an activity chaining graph (ACG). Though TRIDENT does not contain an explicit task model, its representations are derived from a TKS[14] specified hierarchical task model. Bodart et al.[5] demonstrate how TKS models suggest entities and relationships, from which the data model can be derived, and temporal ordering cues from which the Activity Chaining Graph can be derived. Such techniques are critical to support systematic refinement.

Other model-based approaches view task models as evolving entities within the life cycle of an interactive system. In MASTERMIND [10, 9, 12], task models are one of three models used to generate user-interface code. In ADEPT[8, 11], task models are refined into implementation models for which there is a code generator. The TADEUS[18] environment uses a visual representation called the *Dialogue Graph* to support automatic generation of interactive systems in a task-oriented development methodology.

2.3 Refinement through composition

To refine a task model, designers must incorporate device interaction idioms and presentation structure into the user-computer conversation. For the task sequencing to be preserved, this addition of information cannot violate the model's meaning. We view this as a classic multi-paradigm specification problem[22]. The task model is a partial specification of system functionality expressed in a notation that conveniently encodes complex sequencing behavior. Interactors, the building blocks of interaction models, are partial specifications of system functionality expressed in a notation that conveniently encodes input device behavior. In Section 6, we outline a strategy for systematically managing task refinement by treating task and interactor specifications as *constraints* that compose by conjunction[21]. Composition by conjunction allows partial specifications to influence each other directly through a shared vocabulary. Ideally, the model can be enriched all the way down to an implementation.

2.4 Methods

To analyze the restructuring of dialogue during refinement, we employ formal methods to express task and interaction models for a non-trivial example. The formality offered by these methods allows us to isolate and precisely articulate model semantics which must be preserved by restructuring. Moreover, we can use this formal understanding to critique automated refinement frameworks.

The subject application is an interactive checkers program taken from the Amulet[4] source distribution. We chose this application because the rules of the game are described at a level of abstraction that resembles the structure of an hierarchical task model. The strict sequencing in these rules combined with the direct-manipulation style make the interaction model difficult to generate automatically and hence interesting to study. Moreover, with an existing application that we did not write, we will be able to make objective comparisons between analysis and design (future work).

We propose a task model in which the rules of the game are represented in the LOTOS[2] notation. We express the interaction model using Harel-style state diagram notation[13] as used in the Object Modeling Technique (OMT) of Rumbaugh et-al.[7]. OMT allows us to clearly and compactly express object-oriented designs in a visual, programming language independent form.

3 Task model

The task model for this example identifies actors (the two players), actions (moves and jumps), and how these actions are related in time. The checkers task model has three parts. First is a task called *TakeTurn* that defines the actions involved in using a checker to take a turn in the game. Second is the definition of tasks *Red* and *Black* that define the tasks to be performed by the two players in the game. Third is an ordering called *EnforceTurns* that synchronizes the *Red* and *Black* tasks to ensure the rules of the game are not violated.

The task *TakeTurn* is defined as the following LOTOS process:

process *TakeTurn*[*move*, *jump*](p : **int**) :=
    move!p ; *TakeTurn*[*move*, *jump*](p)
  □ *jump*!p!q ; *TakeTurn*[*move*, *jump*](p)
endproc

This process names two gates *move* and *jump* and an integer parameter p. The gates represent the user actions of moving a checker and jumping a checker over another respectively. The parameter p identifies which checker is being used to perform this task. The task will be instantiated with either $\langle m_{red}, j_{red} \rangle$ or $\langle m_{black}, j_{black} \rangle$ and a value for the parameter p out of the integer set $[1 \ldots 32]$. The variable q is also an integer in the set $[1 \ldots 32]$ and identifies the checker being jumped over. For brevity, we do not elaborate on how the variable q takes on a value in this specification.

Player tasks are built up by interleaving *TakeTurn* tasks for each checker and providing for *TakeTurn* tasks to expire when their associated checker has been jumped by the opponent. The process *Expire*, defined:

process *Expire*[*jumped*](p : **int**) :=
    jumped?p ; **exit**
endproc

exits when it synchronizes with a *jumped* action that offers the same value as its parameter. This process can be used to disable *TakeTurn* processes when their pieces have been jumped over by the opponent. Let *RedSet* (respectively *BlackSet*) be a set of integers that uniquely identifies red (black) checkers. Then:

process *Red* :=
    $|||_{\alpha \in RedSet}$ (*TakeTurn*[m_{red}, j_{red}](α) $[>$ *Expire*(α))
endproc

A similar process description defines *Black* in terms of the set *BlackSet*. Note that the player tasks decompose into turns by interleaving. This allows for the correct subtask to be enacted based on the value offer of the checker being used.

With two player tasks in hand, we now define the sequencing of turns according to the rules of the game. Figure 1 describes these rules based on the gates and value offers of the *Red* and *Black* player tasks. The process is noteworthy for how it prescribes the correct behavior of *multi-jumping*. If, for example, the red player "jumps" one of the black checkers and ends in a position in which another jump is possible, the red player may use that same piece in another jump. With this process in place, the task model for the whole game can be expressed:

process $Turns[m_{red}, m_{black}, j_{red}, j_{black}] :=$
    $Turn[m_{red}, j_{red}, m_{black}, j_{black}] \;\square\; Turn[m_{black}, j_{black}, m_{red}, j_{red}]$
where
  process $Turn[m_x, j_x, m_y, j_y] :=$
      $Move[m_x, j_x, m_y, j_y] \;\square\; Jump[m_x, j_x, m_y, j_y]$
  where
    process $Move[m_x, j_x, m_y, j_y] :=$
      $m_x?p : \mathbf{int}; \; \text{\textfemininea} \; Turn[m_y, j_y, m_x, j_x]$
    endproc

    process $Jump[m_x, j_x, m_y, j_y] :=$
      $j_x?p : \mathbf{int}; \; ?q : \mathbf{int}; \; \text{\textfemininea} \, jumped!q \, \text{\textfemininea} \; (Turn[m_y, j_y, m_x, j_x]$
                              $\square\; JumpAgain[m_x, j_x, m_y, j_y](p))$
    where
      process $JumpAgain[m_x, j_x, m_y, j_y](p : pid) :=$
        $j_x?p : \mathbf{int}; \; ?q : \mathbf{int}; \; \text{\textfemininea} \, jumped!q \, \text{\textfemininea} \; (Turn[m_y, j_y, m_x, j_x]$
                                $\square\; JumpAgain[m_x, j_x, m_y, j_y](p))$
      endproc
    endproc
  endproc
endproc

Fig. 1. Dialogue constraints on turns.

process $Checkers :=$
  $Turns \;\|\; (Red \;\|\|\; Black)$
endproc

The *Red* and *Black* tasks are interleaved with each other, but both are made to synchronize with the *Turns* task. Note that when a jump is made by either *Red* or *Black*, *Turns* issues a *jumped* action which causes the *TakeTurn* task of the jumped checker to expire. The *Checkers* task model does not capture all of the rules of checkers, but it is rich enough for the purposes of this paper.

    This task model, defined in LOTOS, has a definite structure imposed by the ordering operators. The model is hierarchical, defining tasks in terms of subtasks, and it clearly describes the rule-level dialogue of the game. It does not, however, express interaction details such as the device events which cause a move or a jump.

4 Interaction model

The interaction model describes the dialogue in terms of customized interactors. To specify the model, the designer first constructs a *presentation* view of the checker board and checker pieces. She then customizes a reusable interactor specification with actions and conditions on attributes of these presentations. A customized interactor gives a detailed device input/visual output protocol for manipulating the checkers.

196

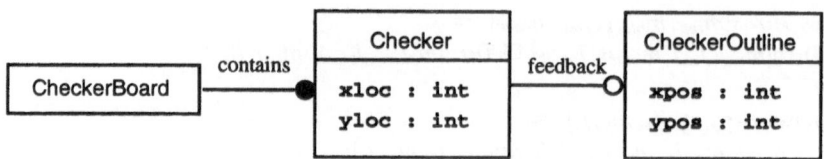

Fig. 2. Object view of the interaction model.

4.1 More detail

This application supports direct manipulation of checker graphics. Checkers are manipulated by clicking down on a piece, dragging an outline of this piece to a new location on the board, and releasing the mouse. During the drag, the outline assumes different appearances to indicate the legality of a drop. If the drop occurs over a legal square, an animation, which moves this piece from its initial position to the new location, is invoked. Otherwise, the outline disappears and no further system action is taken.

Figure 2 illustrates the object view of the interaction model using the OMT notation. The **CheckerBoard** object contains zero or more **Checker** objects. When the game begins there are thirty two checkers, but this number decreases during a game. The diagram indicates that a checker object may be associated with a **CheckerOutline** object to provide the visual feedback during a dragging operation. Objects of class **Checker** have attributes `xloc` and `yloc` which are grid coordinates over the checker board.

4.2 Checker interactor

The behavior of the interaction model is dominated by the behavior of the **Checker** objects. These are the interactors from which the interaction model is synthesized. Figure 3 illustrates the behavior of a checker interactor. When in the super-state Interim, we assume that a **CheckerOutline** object has been allocated and is following the mouse. The condition C captures the data dependencies which decide on the legality of a drop. The details of C are not important for our purposes.

4.3 Full interaction model

The interaction model in Figure 3 models device level interaction well, but it says nothing about how the turn-taking rules are implemented. Presumably, this interactor will need to be greyed-out at various points according to the turn-taking rules. Figure 4 shows an extension of the interaction model to incorporate the influence of these rules. Rule control is localized into an *orthogonal* state diagram that communicates with checker interactors by synchronizing on commonly named events. Transitions in this diagram are concurrent transitions of the components separated by the dashed line. For brevity, Figure 4 only demonstrates control of one interactor instance, RED CHECKER # 3, but other instances are easily included by orthogonal state diagram composition (See Rumbaugh[7, pg. 99] for more details). This extension intrudes on the specification of interactors only minimally, but it does intrude. Specifically, transition conditions have been added to enable and disable the interactor, and the interactor must at some point issue an event which coerces the controller into a new state. Examples of these coercions are the issuing of events $J_{red}(3, q)$ and M_{red} in Figure 4.

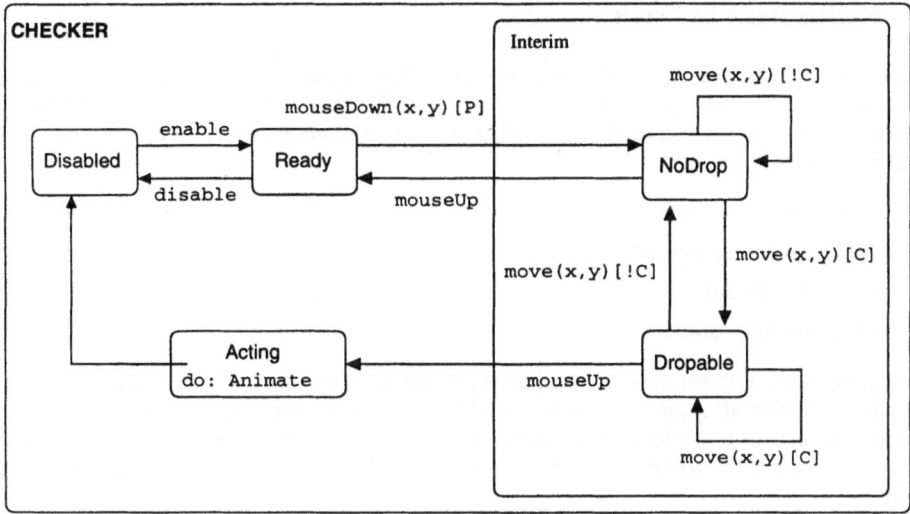

Fig. 3. Behavior of checker interactor.

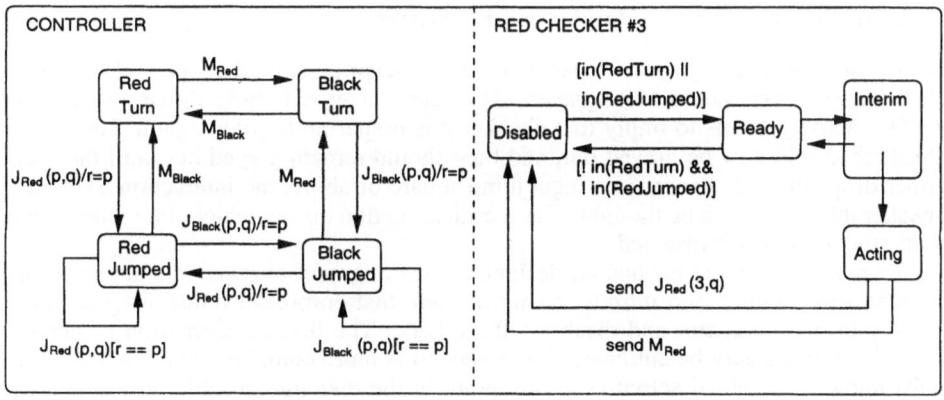

Fig. 4. Dynamic model of checker board interaction technique.

5 Refinement obstacles

Now that we have developed a task and interaction model for the checkers example, we discuss how ordering constraints, which are explicit in the task model, are hard to uncover in the interaction model. This structural incoherence gives rise to the following refinement obstacles:

- loss of mutual exclusion
- temporal residuation
- activity sharing
- redundant interaction

Designers must address these obstacles when refining task models into interaction models. These issues all relate to an inherent difference in LOTOS task models and object-oriented interaction models. Specifically, task actions expressed in LOTOS are atomic, but when the actions are implemented by direct-manipulation interactors, this atomicity is lost.

5.1 Loss of mutual exclusion

Since actions are atomic and direct-manipulation activities are non-atomic, behavior which is mutually exclusive in the task model might not be mutually exclusive in the interaction model. Consider, for example, that point in the task model in which action $j_{red}!p!q$ has just been observed. At this point, the following actions may be observed:

1. $j_{red}!p!q'$ for some $q' \in BlackSet$,
2. $m_{black}!r$ for some $r \in BlackSet$, or
3. $j_{black}!r!s$ for some $r \in BlackSet$ and $s \in RedSet$.

At this state in the dialogue, all red checkers (except p) should be greyed out, and all black checkers should be ungreyed. Now say player red clicks down on checker p. This activity seems to imply that checker p is preparing to jump again. The black checkers should now be greyed out, and they should remain greyed out until the user either drops the red checker in a legal jump square or aborts the interaction. The red checker interaction can be thought of as a critical section during which time interaction with other checkers is disabled.

To maintain mutual exclusion, designers must augment checker interactors to be enabled and disabled and introduce control logic that enforces exclusion by sensing activity in one interactor and disabling the others. The first augmentation is stereotypical and can easily be automated. The second is more complex. The control logic must know the enabled activities at any point in the dialogue, disable all but one of them on activity, and re-enable all of them if that activity is aborted. With a constantly changing number of checkers, the control logic can become complex.

5.2 Temporal residuation

A subtle consequence of implementing task actions by interactors is the *residuation* of sequencing information. When a task action is transformed into an interactor like that shown in Figure 3, the designer must also transform the temporal relationship between that interactor and other interactors. This temporal information exists in the task model as an action sequencing invariant. When interactors are introduced to implement actions, part of the task model is transformed, but a residue of temporal sequencing information remains. This residual information must be examined and encoded into the interaction model. We call this process *temporal residuation*.

Residual invariants encapsulate global sequencing information that cannot be specified in a single interactor. Figure 4 demonstrates what often must be done to accommodate residual sequencing information. What was a process in the task model (*Turns*) is implemented as an object whose behavior is described by a state diagram. To do this, designers must create states and transitions and hope they carry the same meaning as the original LOTOS process. Temporal residuation is yet another activity a designer must perform when refining task models into interaction models.

We should note that if the temporal relationship is simple and there are a static number of interactors, designers can combine the behavior of interactors using the composition mechanisms of state diagrams. This amounts to a homomorphic mapping between the LOTOS process into an aggregate interaction model. Homomorphic mappings can usually be derived automatically. If, however, the sequencing involves LOTOS operators other than those with strict analogues in the state transition notation, then automatic derivation is much more complex. We revisit the automatic derivation idea in Section 6.

5.3 Activity sharing

It is not always the case that task actions map to interactors one-to-one. The *Checker* interactor of Figure 4, for example, controls the actions m_{red} and j_{red}. We call this situation *activity sharing* because multiple activities share the same interactor. Activity sharing introduces dialogue subtleties that do not occur when interactors are bound one-to-one to task actions. These subtleties usually involve the legal ordering of actions, and they often result in a splintering of special cases in the interactor specification.

As an example, consider that point in the dialogue in which RED CHECKER # 3 has just jumped a black checker, and ends on a square in which another jump could be performed. In the task model, this situation is defined formally as:

$$Turn[m_{black}, j_{black}, m_{red}, j_{red}]$$
$$\Box \ JumpAgain[m_{red}, j_{red}, m_{black}, j_{black}]$$

At this point, RED CHECKER # 3 must be enabled so that it can implement the j_{red} action. Note, however, that the m_{red} action is illegal here. To function properly, the interactor requires some switching logic to prevent a move from being offered when it is not legal. Typically, designers use a global state variable to retain the jump/move status and then decorate the interactor transitions with conditions over this variable. This solution is dangerous, however, as it duplicates information in the task model and then requires careful maintenance to keep the variable consistent over time.

Activity sharing complicates the specification of an interactor by forcing the designer to distinguish between different task ordering contexts. Inevitably, this distinction winds up as redundant sequencing information in the interactor specification.

5.4 Redundant interaction

In activity sharing, we saw an example in which multiple task actions were refined into a single interactor. The multiplicity can go the other way. In some applications, the same logical task action may be performed by multiple (redundant) interaction techniques.

Fig. 5. Object structure.

Though a good example of this does not appear in the checkers application, it is very familiar in command-based interfaces. In modeling an Internet-browser, Browne et al.[12] note a redundancy in which multiple interaction techniques (ButtonSelect and MenuSelect) are used to implement the same action (GoBackOnePage).

6 Practical refinement

The issues in Section 5 result from the refinement of task actions into interaction activities. In each case, task ordering information was cast onto a representation which muddies its structure. A practical means of refinement would not involve this change of gestalt. We now propose a model of refinement that retains the natural separation between task ordering information and interactor information. Our representation of task information takes advantage of this knowledge and allows refinement without violating the ordering structure of task models.

The state of an interactor is a function of the *offering potential* of one or more task actions. Any task action, like $j_{red}!p!q$, may be offered at some points in time and not offered at others. An interactor that implements this action must align its state with the potential for the action to be offered. That is, if the action can be offered, the interactor should be enabled. Conversely, if the action cannot be offered, the interactor should be disabled. If we had objects that represented the different states of action offering potential, and if we could assume these objects are kept consistent by an omniscient task model agent, then we could easily connect interactors to actions irrespective of the temporal context of the actions in the task model.

Our approach codifies this observation by encapsulating a task model T into an object in the interaction model. This object is called a *TaskController*, and it hides all action ordering detail from the interactor specifier, presenting instead a collection of seemingly independent *Action* objects. *Action* objects, as the name suggests, correspond one-to-one with LOTOS actions. The state of these objects captures the offering potential of said actions. This state is governed by the *TaskController* object, and it can be observed and influenced by interactor objects. Figure 5 shows how *Action* objects act as an insulator to prevent action ordering information from entering interactor specifications.

Refinement now involves associating *Interactor* objects with *Action* objects. We now present the details of this association and argue that it supports powerful refinements without suffering the faults outlined in Section 5.

6.1 The action layer

Figure 5 shows how *Action* objects separate *TaskController* and *Interactor* objects. *Action* objects represent all of the information that affects the enabling, disabling, and communication with interactors. It is thus feasible for designers to refine task models by associating *Interactor*s with *Action*s irrespective of the temporal context of these actions.

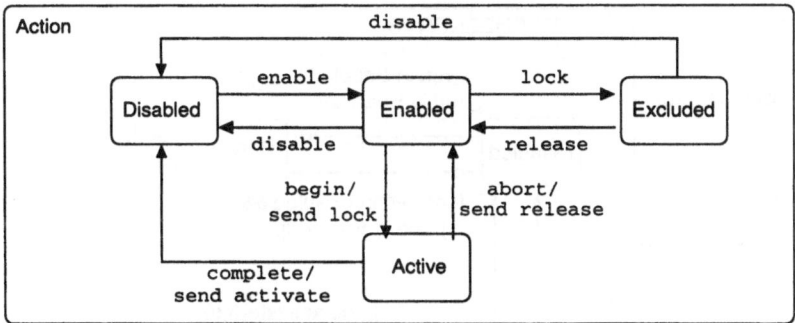

Fig. 6. Action behavior.

Action objects represent four distinguishable states (Figure 6). Two of these states—Disabled and Enabled—are purely a function of the state of the *TaskController* object. When in the Disabled state, the action has been precluded by the *TaskController* object. Conversely, in the Enabled state, action has been permitted by the *TaskController* object. When in the Excluded state, the action may be offered according to the task model, but the interactor associated with performing the action has been locked out by another (mutually exclusive) interactor. Finally, when in the Active state, interaction is in progress, and the action may be offered at any time.

Interactors interpret these states as follows. When Disabled, the interactor should be greyed out, and when Enabled, the interactor should be ungreyed. When the interactor begins servicing device input, the *Action* object goes into the Active state. An *Action* becomes Excluded when some other *Action*'s interactor begins activity. This is how mutual activity exclusion is implemented.

Action objects switch states in response to control events from *TaskController* and an *Interactor*. Specifically, the *TaskController* issues the events `enable`, `disable`, `lock`, and `release`; whereas an *Interactor* object issues the events `begin`, `abort`, and `complete`. Furthermore, the *Action* object occasionally sends control events to the *TaskController*. These events are `lock`, `release`, and `activate`.

Action objects capture all of the information needed to refine an interactor to one or more task actions. In some sense, all of the temporal ordering constraints of the task model have been interpreted and boiled down to the level of *Action* objects. This simplifies refinement because it removes a concern (temporal context) from the designer, and it prevents the designer from muddying the temporal ordering structure of the system by scattering it over his interactor specifications.

6.2 Example: checker refinement

To see how *Action* objects simplify refinement and preserve task structure, consider again the dynamic model of the interactor for checker number three. When the designer implemented this interactor (Figure 4), she actually had to do two things. First, she designed a state diagram (called CONTROLLER in the Figure) to represent the sequencing of task actions. Second, she decorated interactor transitions in the diagram with conditions from the new state diagram. Using *Action* objects, this process is greatly simplified.

Figure 7 shows the same checker interactor composed with *Action* objects. The designer needs to know nothing about the temporal ordering of m_{red} and j_{red} because

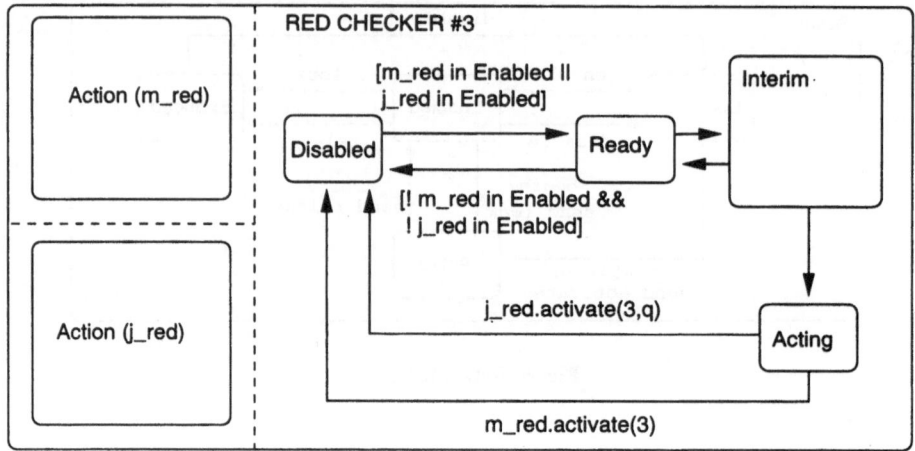

Fig. 7. Checker interaction model using Action objects.

it is managed by the *TaskController* object that is synthesized automatically. Rather, she only needs to know that there exists an object for actions m_{red} and j_{red} and that she can guard interactor transitions with conditions on the states of these *Action* objects. Moreover, since *Action* objects have idiomatic structure, there is no need to elaborate their substates in the diagram. This simplifies the model visually, and it insulates the interactor specification from incorporating task ordering information.

Note that though we don't see the internal structure of the Interim and Acting states, they could contain feedback states which distinguish the legality of a move or a jump and change dynamically in response to changes in the offering potential of the actions. Clearly, the use of *Action* objects helps modularize this interactor, and it does so without corrupting task model structure.

6.3 Assumptions

This research makes two fundamental assumptions. First, interactors have generic device-oriented behavior. Second, it is feasible to generate *TaskController* from a LO-TOS task model. We believe both assumptions are reasonable.

We assume that direct-manipulation interactors have the state topology of Figure 8. To preserve mutual exclusion and enforce temporal orderings through *Action* objects, interactors must distinguish a Disabled state from a Ready state. To distinguish the user's intent to commit an action from his committal of that action, the interactor must distinguish Interim and Active states. The distinction is required so that the mutual exclusion can be insured even when the user aborts an interaction. This topology generalizes to other interaction techniques like selection and text-entry. In the former, the Interim state represents mousing over potential selections. In the latter, the Interim state represents any time in which the text entry interactor has keyboard focus, and the transition from Interim to Action is initiated by hitting the tab or return key. This generic topology is consistent with that used in the Amulet interactors[4].

As discussed in Section 5.2, action sequencing information must be preserved in the translation to interactors. Stirewalt [19] has demonstrated the feasibility of auto-matically generating this temporal information from a LOTOS specification. Task-level

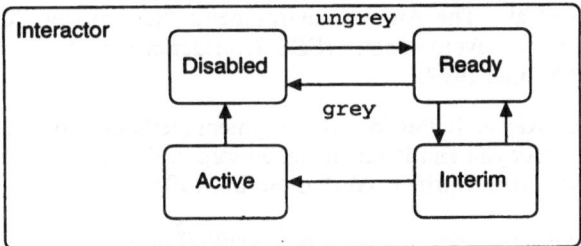

Fig. 8. Generic interactor behavior.

dialogue is specified as the sequencing and temporal dependence of actions. Code generators automatically synthesize *TaskController* objects from LOTOS expressions using a toolkit of reusable operator implementations.

7 Conclusions

We have identified a problem confronting the refinement of a high-level dialogue or task model to an executable interaction model. The genesis of this problem is a structural mismatch between the models resulting from atomic task actions being represented as non-atomic interaction activities. The structural mismatch requires a designer to do extra work in defining an interaction model because properties that were explicit in the task model do not automatically map into the interaction model. While a cautious designer can certainly reproduce the semantics of the task model in the refined interaction model, a practical refinement method would not require such tedious and error-prone activity.

We presented a framework for dialogue refinement that removes the necessity for encoding task-level sequencing behaviors in a lower-level interaction model. We have shown that when the task model is formally specified (in LOTOS it is possible to automatically generate a layer of sequencing behavior that effectively isolates the interactors in the interaction model from the sequencing behavior. The practicality of this dialogue refinement comes from the development of reusable translators from specification languages, such as LOTOS, to executable entities that embody critical features of the high-level task model.

It makes sense to extend the work in this paper from analysis through design and onto implementation. This will improve maintenance and lower time to market. We are also interested in incorporating the results of this research into a Graphical Refinement Assistant (GRA) which allows the editing of task models, the customization of interactors, and refinement by connection.

References

[1] L. Bass and J. Coutaz. *Developing Software for the User Interface*. SEI Series in Software Engineering. Addison-Wesley, 1991.

[2] T. Bolognesi and E. Brinksma. Introduction to the ISO specification language LOTOS. *Computer Network ISDN Systems*, 14(1), 1987.

[3] A. J. Dix et al. *Human-Computer Interaction*. Prentice Hall, 1993.

[4] B. A. Myers et al. The Amulet environment: New models for effective user interface software development. *IEEE Transactions on Software Engineering*, 23(6):347–365, June 1997.

[5] F. Bodart et al. Key activities for a development methodology of interactive applications. In D. Benyon and P. Palanque, editors, *Critical Issues in User Interface Systems Engineering*. Springer-Verlag, Berlin, 1995.

[6] J. D. Foley et al. *Computer Graphics: Principles and Practice*. Addison Wesley, Reading, Massachusetts, 1997.

[7] J. Rumbaugh et al. *Object-Oriented Modeling and Design*. Prentice-Hall, 1991.

[8] P. Johnson et al. ADEPT - advanced design environment for prototyping with task models. In *Bridges Between Worlds: Human Factors in Computing Systems: INTERCHI'93*, 1993.

[9] P. Szekely et al. Declarative interface models for user interface construction tools : The mastermind approach. In L. Bass and C. Unger, editors, *Engineering for Human-Computer Interaction*. Chapman & Hall, 1996.

[10] R. Neches et al. Knowledgeable development environments using shared design models. In *Intelligent Interfaces Workshop*, pages 63–70, 1993.

[11] S. Wilson et al. Beyond hacking: A model based approach to user interface design. In J. L. Alty, D. Diaper, and S. Guest, editors, *People and Computers VIII, Proceedings of the HCI '93 Conference*, 1993.

[12] T. P. Browne et al. Using declarative descriptions to model user interfaces with MASTERMIND. In F. Paternò and P. Palanque, editors, *Formal Methods in Human Computer Interaction*. Springer-Verlag, 1997.

[13] D. Harel. Statecharts: a visual formalism for complex systems. *Science of Computer Programming*, 8, 1987.

[14] P. Johnson. *Human-Computer Interaction, Psychology, Task analysis, and Software Engineering*. McGraw-Hill, London, 1991.

[15] P. Markopoulos. On the expression of interaction properties within an interactor model. In *Design Specification and Verification of Interactive Systems (DSV-IS'95)*, 1995.

[16] F. Paternò. A theory of user-interaction objects. *Journal of Visual Languages and Computing*, 5:227–249, 1994.

[17] F. Paternò and S. Meniconi. TLIM: a systematic method for the design of interactive systems. In F. Paternò and P. Palanque, editors, *Formal Methods in Human Computer Interaction*. Springer-Verlag, 1997.

[18] E. Schlungbaum and T. Elwert. Dialogue graphs: A formal and visual specification technique for dialogue modelling. In *Formal Aspects of the Human Computer Interface, BCS-FACS Workshop*, 1996.

[19] R. E. K. Stirewalt. *Automatic Generation of Interactive Systems from Declarative Models*. PhD thesis, Georgia Institute of Technology, 1997.

[20] J. M. Vanderdonckt and F. Bodart. Encapsulating knowledge for intelligent automatic interaction objects selection. In *Bridges Between Worlds: Human Factors in Computing Systems: INTERCHI'93*, 1993.

[21] P. Zave and M. Jackson. Conjunction as composition. *ACM Transactions on Software Engineering and Methodology*, 2(4):371–411, 1993.

[22] P. Zave and M. Jackson. Where do operations come from? a multiparadigm specification technique. *IEEE Transactions on Software Engineering*, 22(7):508–528, July 1996.

Which widgets?
Deriving implementations from
formal user-interface specifications

Andrew Hussey and David Carrington

Software Verification Research Centre
School of Information Technology
The University of Queensland
Brisbane, Qld, 4072, Australia
{ahussey,davec}@it.uq.edu.au

Abstract. We consider the process of transforming a formal user-interface specification, expressed using an interactor-based notation, to a form expressed in terms of "widgets" (common interactors). A set of patterns is provided for transforming user-interface specifications. By defining a user-interface design using widgets, determining the user-interface's presentation is simplified. Such transformation corresponds to redefinition of abstract user tasks at a more concrete level. We illustrate the process by reference to a simple file browser user-interface.

1 Introduction

A specification of a user-interface indicates those functional aspects of an interactive system (data and operations) that are perceivable by the user and the logical organisation of information provided by the interface. User-interfaces can be specified as a collection of interacting agents using an agent-based language [1]. Agents have state, operations upon that state, and may respond to and initiate events. An agent and its presentation together define an *interactor*. Defining the presentation aspects of interactors constitutes user-interface design.

Interactors are user-interface components that are used to structure user-interface specifications and designs. Each such component defines a portion of the behaviour and appearance of the user-interface. Composing the interactors for a user-interface produces the behaviour and appearance of the user-interface as a whole. Construction of user-interface specifications is informed by task analysis [13]. Tasks are defined by sequences of operations on interactors [2]. Object-Z [3], an object-oriented extension of Z [11], is used to illustrate interactor-based specification in this paper.

We describe a method for producing user-interface designs, expressed in terms of existing "widgets" (common interactors), from abstract interactor-based specifications. The method provides rules for restructuring user-interface specifications so that user tasks are defined in terms of operations on widgets. A specification that is expressed in terms of widgets can be used to readily derive a corresponding user-interface design.

The transformation process is depicted in Figure 1 [2]. Transforming a user-interface specification to a form expressed in terms of widgets guides a designer toward useful presentations of information and operations (input and output behaviour of a system). Identifying widgets simplifies designing a user-interface's presentation because the presentation of widgets is usually well defined. Our method provides assurance that a user-interface satisfies the abstract functional requirements for the system; assuming the system is deterministic, users must be able to reach the same goal states using either the transformed or the original system. By expressing a specification in terms of widgets, user tasks are

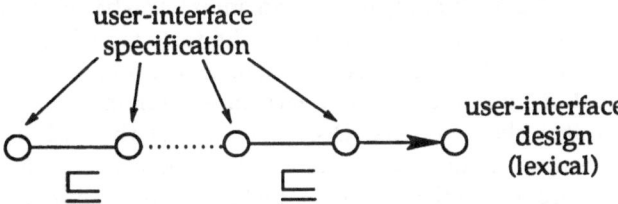

Fig. 1. Refinement relationship between specifications

defined in a form that more closely describes the actual activities that the user will perform. Redefinition of user tasks using widgets corresponds to task decomposition. Operations of the abstract specification are redefined in terms of concrete operations on widgets.

In Section 2, we review model-based design and consider how this work fits with previous research in the area. Section 3 specifies the user-interface for a simple file browser. In Section 4, we describe patterns for transforming user-interface specifications, using the file browser specification to illustrate. Section 5 discusses the benefits and implications of the research.

2 Model-based Development

In model-based design, designers create a model (specification) of an interactive system from which an implementation is derived. Many model-based methods, and tools to support them, have been developed; two of the more recent are Mobi-D [10], and Adept [16]. Existing model-based tools have not been widely accepted due to their inadequate support for customisation and for expression of complex relationships between widgets [12]. Further, existing tools do not assist developing implementations from an abstract user-interface specification. Rather, the specification of the user-interface that the designer provides is at a low level of abstraction. Some existing tools (such as Adept) provide automatic selection of widgets corresponding to a specification but this prevents choice between design alternatives according to the context.

Losavio and Matteo [5] have developed a method for user-interface development that is similar to ours. In their method, use-cases for abstract interactors are progressively redefined in terms of widgets. The most important difference between their method and ours is that our formal approach aids checking of compatibility between the original and transformed specifications. Likewise, the Adept environment [15] enables a designer to produce an "abstract interaction model" of a system by task decomposition, but again, there is no formal requirement of equivalence between the expression of tasks in the original and transformed specification.

Paterno and Mezzanotte [9] provide a set of general heuristics for the parallel decomposition of a task-analysis and an interactor-based specification of an interactive system. Each decomposition of the task model corresponds to a modification of the equivalent interactor model. Paterno et al.'s work is based on a process model of interactor syntax; each interactor in an abstract specification defines a single abstract task. Decomposition of the task corresponding to an interactor results in substitution of a new interactor for the original interactor. Rules are provided for associating tasks with interactors, decomposing tasks with corresponding increase of interactor detail (granularity of actions), decomposing tasks to produce an associated decomposition of interactors, and decomposing tasks with corresponding recomposition of existing interactors to capture temporal ordering of actions. Paterno and Mezzanotte provide an algorithm for applying the heuristics to the construction of interactive systems.

We give a method for performing task decomposition using state-based object-oriented notations. We apply a compatibility relation between interactors, such that one interactor is the result of a task decomposition with respect to another. System A is compatible with system B if system A can be used to perform all the tasks that are guaranteed as achievable with system B (i.e., the goal states that can be achieved using system B can also be achieved using system A). Because we use Object-Z to model systems, we define elementary tasks as operations on a system class; "constructed" tasks are defined by sequences of operations. Compatibility is achieved if the operations of system B can be expressed as sequences of operations of system A. The compatibility relation is similar to refinement (e.g., [6]), but we also allow transformation of operation interfaces (input and output attributes as denoted by ? and !). We make the assumption that, for a human user, provided the same core information is communicated, the *form* of that information is not important. For example, in our file browser case study below, there is an input for the operation *SelectFile* that is chosen from a set of files; during development, this input is replaced by an index into a list of files.

We give rules for transforming user-interface specifications to a form expressed in terms of widgets from a specification library. We give rules for modifying interactor-based specifications that are "equivalent" to Paterno's rules in the sense that they also enable the structure of an interactor-based specification to be modified by factoring interactors and the result is a decomposition of tasks. However, we consolidate and extend Paterno's rules, providing several additional useful transformations. Our method also differs from Paterno's because its focus is on redefinition of the specification in terms of components from interactor libraries. Our method enables a designer to derive both the presentation and an architecture for an interactive system from an abstract specification.

There are three primary advantages to performing transformations using interactor-based specifications:

- the presentation and partial architecture are derived synchronously as the level of abstraction of the specification is reduced;
- the method ensures that tasks are developed initially, and presentation only later, reducing wasted user-interface design effort;
- using a formal notation to describe interactors (and hence tasks) enables us to check the validity of task transformations.

3 A File Browser User-Interface Specification

Our file browser provides the user with facilities to display the file names (both directories and non-directory files) contained within a directory, to select a file and to view the contents of non-directory files. The user can browse only one directory at a time and the current directory can be altered. Altering the current directory results in the displayed set of file names becoming the contents of the new directory and makes the current file selection empty.

We declare types for file names and file contents: [*FileName, FileContents*].

In an Object-Z description, a class is defined by a named box encapsulating state and, optionally, initialisation and operations. The state schema in the class is un-named and contains attribute declarations and a constraining invariant. For example, a file is a named entity in the file system. A non-directory file is defined by its contents.

$$
\begin{array}{|l}
\hline
\textit{File} \\
\hline
\textit{name} : \textit{FileName} \\
\hline
\end{array}
\qquad
\begin{array}{|l}
\hline
\textit{NonDirectoryFile} \\
\hline
\textit{File} \\
\hline
\textit{contents} : \textit{FileContents} \\
\hline
\end{array}
$$

A directory is a file containing a sequence of files (some of which may be directories).

$$
\begin{array}{|l}
\hline
\textit{Directory} \\
\hline
\textit{File} \\
\hline
\textit{files} : \textit{iseq} \!\downarrow\! \textit{File} \\
\hline
\end{array}
$$

A class may be instantiated. For example, the declaration *files : iseq↓File* defines a non-duplicated sequence of *File* objects. The polymorphic operator (↓)

defines the type of each object in *files* as either the specified base class *File* or any class that inherits from it. Operations applied to such an attribute must be polymorphic, i.e., regardless of the actual class of the object, the operation must be defined.

A file selector interactor encapsulates the current directory that is being examined, the set of files for the current directory and the currently selected file. A file selector is an *interactor* because it describes a part of the data and operations that the user-interface presents to its users; the interactor's presentation provides a representation of its state. In this case, because the system is small, it is the only interactor needed to define the user-interface. We regard *File*, *NonDirectoryFile* and *Directory* as describing agent classes, so there is no attempt to define their presentation.

Some attributes of a class may be dependent on other attributes (i.e., their value is always derivable from those other attributes). In Object-Z, such dependencies are denoted by a Δ on a separate line preceding the dependent attributes (e.g., *files*). The nature of this dependency is captured by the class invariant. The initialisation schema is labelled *INIT* and defines the initial state of instances of the class.

$$\mid \quad InitialDirectory : Directory$$

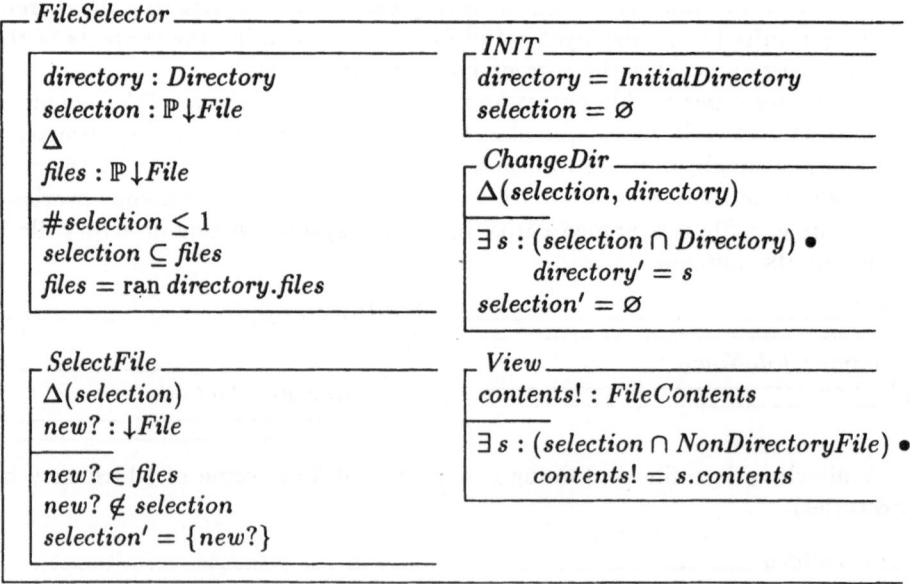

An operation schema is divided into two parts. The upper part defines the context of the operation including inputs and outputs. The Δ-list defines those state attributes that are altered by an operation. State variables not listed in the Δ-list are unchanged by that operation. The lower part defines a predicate relating the initial and final states of the operation.

Selecting a file is modelled by the operation *SelectFile* and changing directory is modelled by the operation *ChangeDir*. The selected file can be viewed by invoking the operation *View*, provided it is not a directory.

4 Specification Patterns

We use patterns to guide the re-structuring of interactor-based specifications. Our approach is based on the design patterns described by Gamma et al. [4] but we are more precise in defining the required state of the system for which each pattern may be applied. A pattern is a rule that states a problem to be solved and a solution to that problem. Each pattern is a "(description of) a recurring structural or behavioural solution" [14]. Patterns are most commonly used to assist in structuring object-oriented programs. They also generate a possible interactor-based architecture. Interactor frameworks such as VisualWorks' Model-View-Controller [8] can be readily used to construct implementations corresponding to user-interface specifications that are expressed in terms of widgets. However, this is not the primary purpose of applying the patterns; rather their purpose is to help a designer express a specification in terms of widgets so that designing the user-interface's presentation is simplified.

We describe three patterns that assist in transforming a user-interface specification so that it is defined in terms of interactors from a widget library: Flatten, Factor and Interface-Adapter. In each case, we illustrate the pattern by reference to the file browser example given in Section 3. We summarise the intent, motivation, applicability and form for each pattern. In the case of the Flatten and Factor patterns, there is no change to the system level operations and hence task decomposition is trivially satisfied. In the case of the Interface-Adapter pattern, the designer needs to show that the transformation results in a task decomposition.

4.1 Flatten

Intent The Flatten pattern incorporates elements of a sub-interactor[1] (its state, predicates and operations) into the enclosing interactor.

Motivation Composite interactors consist of several sub-interactors. The sub-interactors are attributes of the composite. To simplify matching specification interactors with library interactors, it may be necessary to replace one or more interactor attributes with its constituent state, predicates and operations.

Applicability The Flatten pattern is commonly applied to create an interactor that has the same state and operations (with suitable renaming) as one or more library interactors, so that the original interactor can be defined using library interactor(s).

---

[1] The patterns are expressed in terms of interactors but are also applicable to agents.

Form We commence with interactor classes *InteractorA* and *InteractorB*, such that an instance of *InteractorB* is a component of *InteractorA* (we assume a given type, *Type*).

```
┌─ InteractorA ──────────────────       ┌─ InteractorB ──────────────────
│                                       │
│  ┌──────────────────────────────┐     │  ┌──────────────────────────────┐
│  │ b : InteractorB              │     │  │ attribute_of_b : Type        │
│  │ ...                          │     │  └──────────────────────────────┘
│  └──────────────────────────────┘     │  ┌─ Op_on_B ────────────────────
│  ┌─ LocalOp ─────────────────────     │  │ ...
│  │ ...                                │  └──────────────────────────────
│  └──────────────────────────────      │  ...
│  Op_on_B ≙ b.Op_on_B                  └────────────────────────────────
│  Combined_Op ≙ b.Op_on_B ∧ LocalOp
│  ...
└────────────────────────────────
```

Applying the Flatten pattern, we redefine *InteractorA* as follows:

```
┌─ InteractorA flattened ─────────────────────────────────────────────────
│
│  ┌──────────────────────────────────────────────────────────────────┐
│  │ attribute_of_b : Type                                            │
│  │ ...                                                              │
│  └──────────────────────────────────────────────────────────────────┘
│  ┌─ LocalOp ─────────────────────       ┌─ Op_on_B ────────────────────
│  │ ...                                  │ ...
│  └──────────────────────────────        └──────────────────────────────
│  Combined_Op ≙ Op_on_B ∧ LocalOp
│  ...
└─────────────────────────────────────────────────────────────────────────
```

Renaming may be required to avoid clashes between names used in *InteractorA* and *InteractorB*.

The Flatten pattern is depicted in Figure 2(a). The upper circle in the diagram represents the original specification interactor, with an enclosed sub-interactor, while the lower circle represents the augmented interactor after applying the Flatten pattern. The operations of the resultant interactor remain identical to those of the original interactor.

Example We apply the Flatten pattern to *FileSelector*, replacing the *directory* agent with its constituent attributes, predicates and operations. We remove the secondary attribute *files* and define operations directly in terms of the sequence of files for the directory. There is a data-transformation of *files* : $\mathbb{P}{\downarrow}File$ to *fileSeq* : $iseq{\downarrow}File$. Because the *View* operation is unaffected, it is elided.

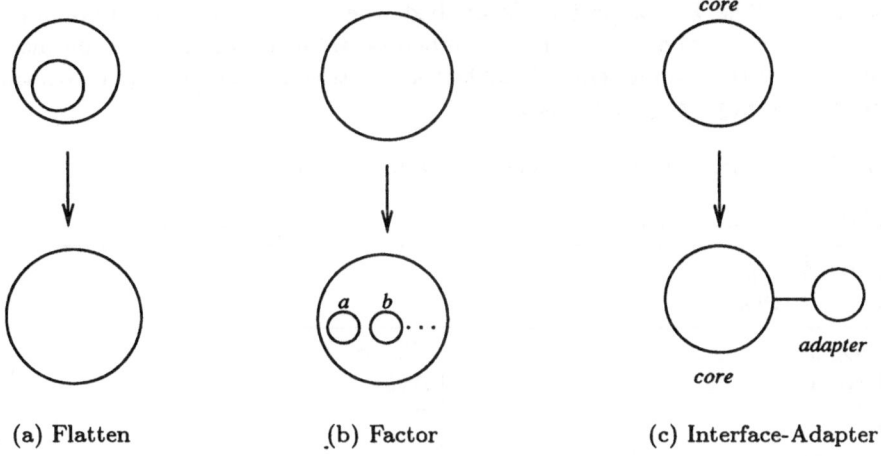

Fig. 2. Transformation patterns for interactors

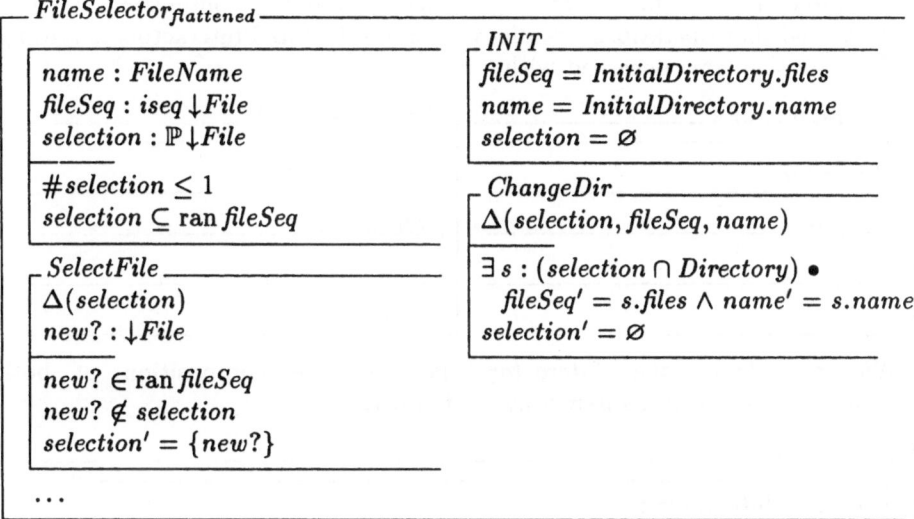

4.2 Factor

Intent The Factor pattern partitions an interactor to produce two or more sub-interactors.

Motivation To simplify user-interface design, we partition an interactor into two or more new interactors. Ideally each such new interactor can be redefined using a library interactor. The Factor pattern is effectively the inverse of applying the Flatten pattern.

Applicability The **Factor** pattern is applied when a specification interactor is effectively a union of several library interactors. Information may be communicated between the components of the factored interactor and/or the invocation of operations may be synchronised.

Form We commence from an interactor class, *Interactor*:

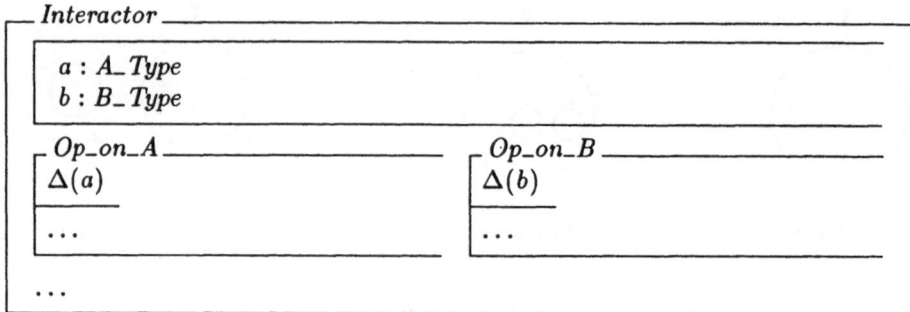

Applying the **Factor** pattern introduces one or more new interactor classes. For example, the class *Interactor* may be factored into two components. We factor state and that operations are allocated to the factored interactors according to the state they are concerned with:

```
┌─ NewInteractorA ──────────────    ┌─ NewInteractorB ──────────────
│  a : A_Type                       │  b : B_Type
│  ┌─ Op_on_A ─────────────         │  ┌─ Op_on_B ─────────────
│  │  ...                           │  │  ...
│  ...                              │  ...
```

We reconstruct the *Interactor* class as the composition of both *NewInteractorA* and *NewInteractorB* as follows:

```
┌─ Interactor ──────────────────────────────
│  a : NewInteractorA
│  b : NewInteractorB
│  OponA ≙ a.Op_on_A
│  OponB ≙ b.Op_on_B
│  ...
```

The operations of the resultant interactor remain identical to those of the original interactor.

The **Factor** pattern is depicted in Figure 2(b). The upper circle in the figure represents an original interactor, while the lower circles show the resulting interactor with two or more sub-interactors.

Example In the example, we observe that the name of the directory currently viewed can be presented by a label widget and the file sequence by a list widget, i.e., the *FileSelector* class can be represented as a combination of two widgets. We show this by applying the **Factor** pattern to *FileSelector*$_{flattened}$, producing the following new classes.

$\begin{array}{|l}
\hline
\text{\textit{DirectoryName}} \\
\hline
\begin{array}{|l|}
\hline
name : FileName \\
\hline
\begin{array}{|l}
\textit{INIT} \\
\hline
name = InitialDirectory.name \\
\hline
\end{array}
\end{array}
\quad
\begin{array}{|l}
\textit{SetName} \\
\hline
\Delta(name) \\
name? : FileName \\
\hline
name' = name? \\
\hline
\end{array} \\
\hline
\end{array}$

We elide details of the *SelectFile*, *ChangeDir* and *View* operations because they are unaltered from *FileSelector*$_{flattened}$.

$\begin{array}{|l}
\hline
\text{\textit{FileList}} \\
\hline
\begin{array}{|l|}
\hline
fileSeq : iseq \downarrow File \\
selection : \mathbb{P}\downarrow File \\
\hline
\#selection \leq 1 \\
selection \subseteq \operatorname{ran} fileSeq \\
\hline
\end{array}
\quad
\begin{array}{|l}
\textit{INIT} \\
\hline
fileSeq = InitialDirectory.files \\
selection = \varnothing \\
\hline
\ldots \\
\hline
\end{array} \\
\hline
\end{array}$

We define the *DirectoryName* interactor class using the **Label** library widget and the *FileList* interactor class using the **List** widget (see the Appendix). The latter redefinition involves a data-transformation of *selection* : $\mathbb{P}\downarrow File$ to *num_sel* : $\mathbb{P}\mathbb{N}$ with a corresponding transformation of the interface for *SelectFile*.

$\begin{array}{|l}
\hline
\text{\textit{DirectoryName}}_{library} \\
\hline
\textbf{Label}[FileName][name/label] \\
\begin{array}{|l}
\textit{INIT} \\
\hline
name = InitialDirectory.name \\
\hline
\end{array} \\
\hline
\end{array}$

FileList$_{library}$

$\textbf{List}[\downarrow File][SelectFile/Select, num\_sel/selection, fileSeq/elements]$

$\#num\_sel \leq 1$
$\#fileSeq = \#\,\mathrm{ran}\,fileSeq$

___ INIT ___
$fileSeq = InitialDirectory.files$
$num\_sel = \varnothing$

___ ChangeDir ___
$\Delta(num\_sel, fileSeq)$
$new!: FileName$

$\exists s: fileSeq (\!| \; num\_sel \; |\!) \cap Directory \bullet$
$\quad fileSeq' = s.files \wedge new! = s.name$
$num\_sel' = \varnothing$

___ View ___
$contents!: FileContents$

$\exists s: fileSeq (\!| \; num\_sel \; |\!) \cap NonDirectoryFile \bullet$
$\quad contents! = s.contents$

In the original *FileSelector*, invoking *ChangeDir* alters the displayed directory name to the chosen directory. The output, *new!* from *fileList.ChangeDir* is needed to enable definition of the system operation *ChangeDir* in terms of the two factored interactors. We describe *FileSelector* in terms of the new file list and directory label widgets. We expect the operation *ChangeDir* to be invoked by user interaction with the interactor *fileList*, rather than by interaction with the interactor *name*.

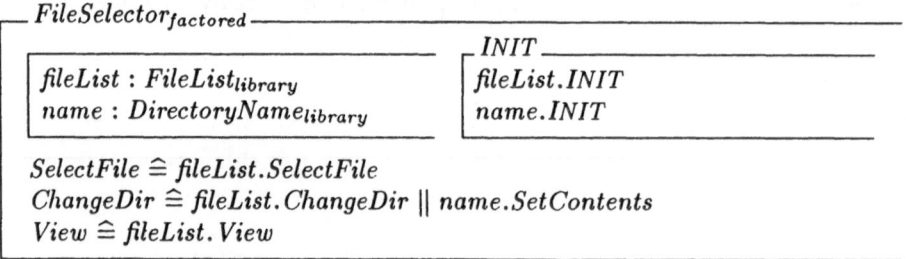

FileSelector$_{factored}$

$fileList: FileList_{library}$
$name: DirectoryName_{library}$

___ INIT ___
$fileList.INIT$
$name.INIT$

$SelectFile \mathrel{\hat{=}} fileList.SelectFile$
$ChangeDir \mathrel{\hat{=}} fileList.ChangeDir \parallel name.SetContents$
$View \mathrel{\hat{=}} fileList.View$

4.3 Interface-Adapter

Intent In the Interface-Adapter pattern, an *adapter* interactor is interposed between the user and a *core* interactor. Input to the core interactor and/or output from the core interactor are handled by the adapter interactor. The Interface-Adapter pattern is similar to the *Adapter* pattern [4], but is expressed in terms of restructuring user-interface specifications. For the Interface-Adapter pattern, the "user" of the adapting interactor may be either a human user or another class in the specification. The Interface-Adapter pattern corresponds to task decomposition. System-level operations of a specification (e.g., in *FileSelector*) are transformed to use the adapter interactor to obtain input (attributes denoted by ?) or to display output (attributes denoted by !).

Motivation Not all user inputs that alter the state of an interactor can be sensibly handled by that interactor. For example, a list interactor has a presentation that accepts user actions such as mouse-button clicks. By clicking the mouse-button over entries in the list, the user can alter the list selection. However it is often the case that we want to perform operations using the list selection as a parameter. The number of such operations can be potentially large and defining several distinct key or mouse actions to invoke such operations may require modification of the list interactor. Instead, we can use *adapter* interactors to obtain user inputs for the *core* list interactor. By separating the input behaviour of the adapter interactor from the core interactor, the reusability of the core interactor is enhanced.

If a core interactor outputs information (in Object-Z this is denoted by operation attributes ending in !) via operations rather than by updating its state, an adapter interactor should be interposed to define the form in which such information is displayed. The adapter is interposed between the core interactor and its original environment so that output is defined in terms of changes to the state of the adapter. Such adapter interactors may be components of a widget library. For example, labels are inactive, i.e., they never directly respond to user input, yet labels are often updated in response to user interaction with other interactors. A label may be an output-adapter for the interactor that it displays (its associated core).

Applicability The Interface-Adapter pattern can be used in the following situations:

- an operation of the core interactor cannot be sensibly effected by user interaction with the core interactor. An adapter interactor performs processing of user input prior to invoking a method of the core;
- the input behaviour of the core interactor should be explicit to the user but there is a requirement not to present this behaviour via the core's presentation;
- an operation of a specification interactor produces output rather than updating the state of an interactor.

Form We consider a *Core* interactor class with an operation, *CoreOperation*, that is the only component of a system operation, *SystemOperation*.

$$\begin{array}{l} \text{\_\_ System _____} \\ \hline \quad core : Core \\ \quad \dots \\ \hline SystemOperation \,\widehat{=}\, core.CoreOperation \\ \dots \end{array}$$

We introduce an *InterfaceAdapter* interactor class with an operation *AdapterOperation*. The core and adapter interactors are related at the system level with the adapter interactor being responsible for receiving user input and presenting results to the user. The symbol $\heartsuit$ indicates that we may use either the $\wedge$ operator (conjunction) or the $\|$ operator (parallel composition, for when information is passed between the core and adapter). If parallel composition is used, one or more input attributes of the core operation should be matched with output attributes of the adapter operation. By convention, where the adapter receives input from the environment, it is placed on the left of the operator, e,g.:

```
┌─ System_new ───────────────────────────────────────────────
│  ┌──────────────────────────────────────────────────────────
│  │  core : Core
│  │  adapter : InterfaceAdapter
│  └──────────────────────────────────────────────────────────
│  ...
│  SystemOperation ≘ adapter.AdapterOperation ♡ core.CoreOperation
│  ...
└─────────────────────────────────────────────────────────────
```

Where the adapter interactor receives output from the core interactor, it is placed on the right of the operator. To apply the Interface-Adapter pattern, there is an additional requirement that the alteration of the system operation is a task decomposition. Usually this requirement will be satisfied because the tasks that can be performed using the original system can also be performed using the modified system by replacing invocations of the original system operation in traces of the original system by a sequence of operations of the modified system.

The Interface-Adapter pattern is depicted in Figure 2(c). The line between the adapter and core interactors in the depiction indicates that the adapter and core co-operate to define one or more system operations e.g., in our example, the operation *SystemOperation*.

Example The Interface-Adapter pattern can be used to introduce a button adapter to invoke the *View* operation of the *fileList* interactor. We introduce a button interactor, *viewbutton*, from the widget library. The effect of invoking the operation *Release* for the button is to invoke *View* operation for *fileList*. Likewise, we introduce a button widget, *chgbutton*, to invoke *ChangeDir*. The labels of both buttons are text. The alteration to the specification is an augmentation of *View* and *ChangeDir* as follows:

```
┌─ FileSelector_augmented ─────────────────────────────────────
│  ┌──────────────────────────────┐ ┌─ INIT ──────────────────
│  │ fileList : FileList_library   │ │ fileList.INIT
│  │ name : DirectoryName_library  │ │ name.INIT
│  │ chgbutton,                    │ │ chgbutton.INIT
│  │     viewbutton : Button[Text] │ │ viewbutton.INIT
│  └──────────────────────────────┘ └─────────────────────────
└─────────────────────────────────────────────────────────────
```

$SelectFile \mathrel{\widehat=} fileList.SelectFile$

$View \mathrel{\widehat=} viewbutton.Click \wedge fileList.View$

$ChangeDir \mathrel{\widehat=} chgbutton.Click \wedge (fileList.ChangeDir \parallel name.SetContents)$

$FastChangeDir \mathrel{\widehat=} fileList.SelectFile \mathbin{\S} fileList.ChangeDir$

We add an operation *FastChangeDir* that enables a user to select a directory and change to that directory in one operation. For example, the lexical action required to invoke *FastChangeDir* could be a double-click of the mouse on a directory name in the file list. Adding operations to a specification is permissible because the added operations can only augment the available traces of the system.

Figure 3 shows a possible display for $FileSelector_{augmented}$ using Tcl/Tk [7].

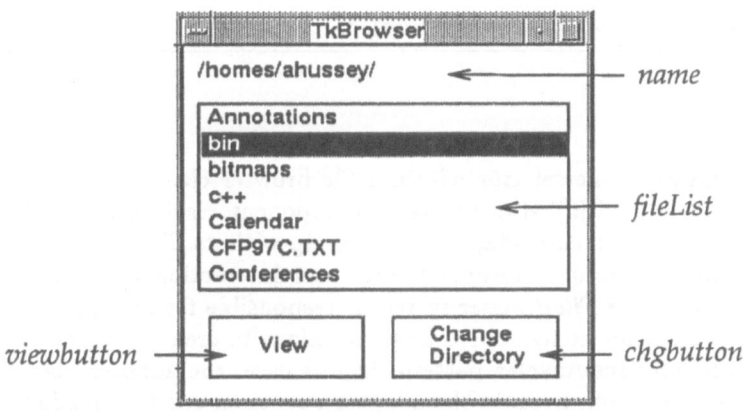

Fig. 3. Tcl/Tk implementation of $FileSelector_{augmented}$

We also apply the Interface-Adapter pattern to specify output for the *View* operation at a lower level of abstraction. We define a file viewer interactor that presents the contents of a file; further development could define the *Viewer* in terms of a text display widget:

Viewer
___

contents : *FileContents*

We define a *FileBrowser* system class, containing a single file selector and multiple viewer instances.

```
┌─ FileBrowser ──────────────────────────────────────────────────────────
│ ⌈(ChangeDir, FastChangeDir, SelectFile, DestroyViewer, View)
│  ┌──────────────────────────────────┌─ INIT ──────────────────────
│  │ fileSelector : FileSelector_augmented │ fileSelector.INIT
│  │ viewers : ℙ Viewer                  │ viewers = ∅
│  └──────────────────────────────────└────────────────────────────
│
│  ChangeDir ≙ fileSelector.ChangeDir
│  FastChangeDir ≙ fileSelector.FastChangeDir
│  SelectFile ≙ fileSelector.SelectFile
│  ┌─ DestroyViewer ──────────────────┌─ NewViewer ──────────────────────
│  │ Δ(viewers)                        │ Δ(viewers)
│  │ viewer? : Viewer                  │ contents? : FileContents
│  ├──────────────────────────────────├──────────────────────────────────
│  │ viewer? ∈ viewers                 │ ∃ viewer : Viewer • viewer ∉ viewers ∧
│  │ viewers' = viewers \ {viewer?}    │    viewer.contents = contents? ∧
│  └──────────────────────────────────│    viewers' = viewers ∪ {viewer}
│                                      └──────────────────────────────────
│  View ≙ fileSelector.View ∥ NewViewer
└────────────────────────────────────────────────────────────────────────
```

Encapsulating a file selector within a file browser class is an application of the Factor pattern, with just one factored component. Each instance of the *File-Browser* system is in a core-adapter relationship with its *fileSelector* component. The instance *fileSelector* is responsible for user interaction with respect to the operation *View*. The *FileBrowser* system is responsible for creating instances of *Viewer* to present file contents. Adding operations to create viewers is an application of the Interface-Adapter pattern. In this case, the adapter operation is a system class operation, because the adapter operation creates an adapter interactor dynamically and adds it to the system. The operation *NewViewer* creates a new instance of the class *Viewer*, the contents of which are supplied by the *fileSelector* interactor's *View* operation. The destroy operation allows a selected viewing interactor to be destroyed.

The change to the *View* operation at the system level (as defined by *File-Browser*) is a task decomposition because the additional pre-conditions (from the *NewViewer* operation) are trivially satisfied and so the traces for the original system (which is an instance of $FileSelector_{augmented}$) are simply a subset of those for the new system (in the new system there is the additional operation *DestroyViewer*). Further, the effect on the state of the system arising from the original *View* operation (as defined by the class *FileSelector*) is a subset of the effect for the augmented system (as defined by the class *FileBrowser*).

Figure 4 summarises the transformations described in Sections 4.1 to 4.3. For clarity, we omit operations and only trace the state arising from the original abstract specification.

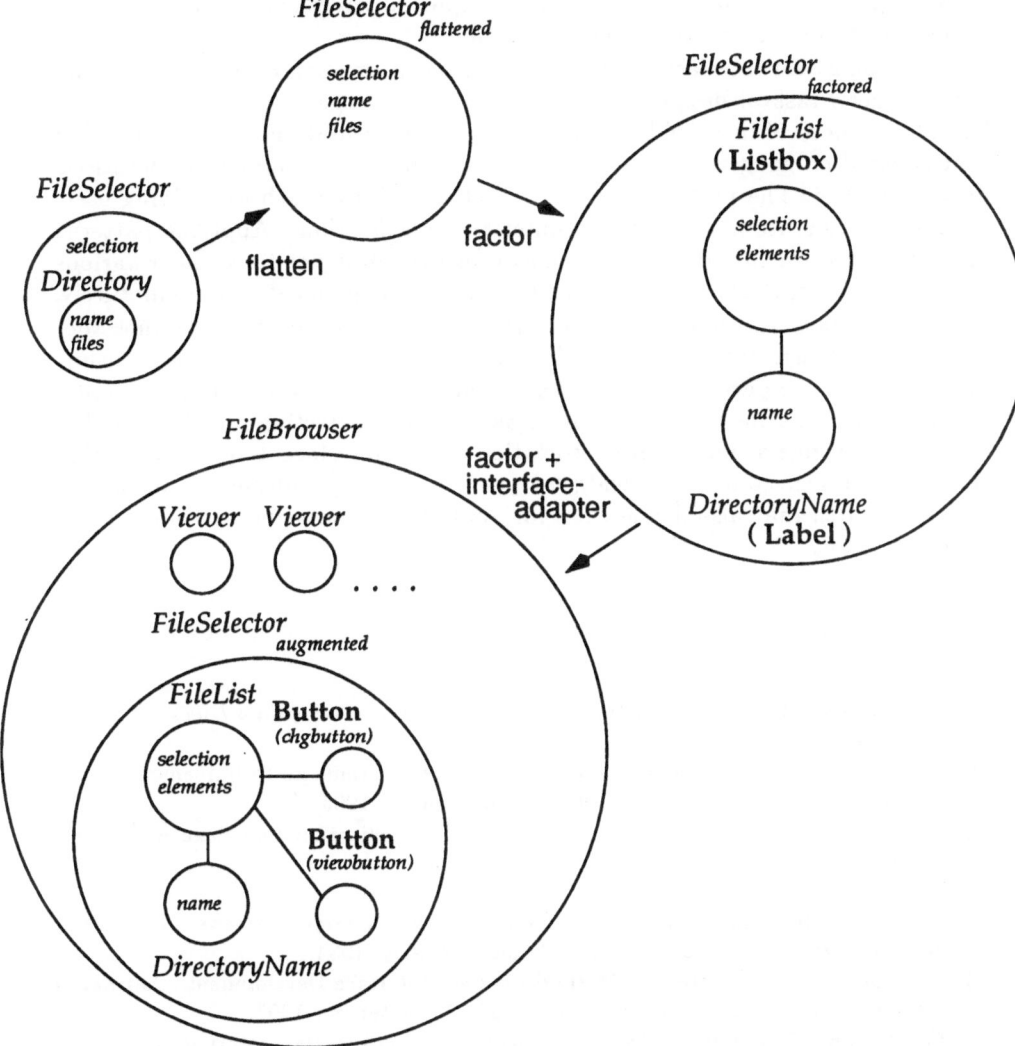

Fig. 4. Transforming a file browser specification

5 Summary

Our patterns do not automate the process of user-interface development: the designer needs to perceive whether a pattern can be applied, and whether an interactor in the specification can be re-defined in terms of one or more library widgets. That is, the patterns are not algorithms for transforming specifications. Where several widgets are applicable (e.g., listboxes and comboboxes), the designer must choose between widgets. The designer needs to have some notion of the direction that they intend the transformation to take; applying the patterns to develop a user-interface design from a complex abstract specification requires some expectation of possible transformations.

Describing user-interface specifications in terms of library widgets simplifies the designer's task of designing the presentation because the presentation and lexical behaviour of these widgets is defined. The presentation for a specification that is based on widgets is easily deduced from the corresponding presentations for each widget. The patterns provide a methodical approach to deriving user-interface designs from abstract user-interface specifications. Applying patterns to a user-interface specification may encourage the designer to consider various design options for the user-interface rather than settling on a design prematurely.

We anticipate future research will produce additional patterns to those defined in this paper. Future work involves developing a tool to assist the transformation process; in particular we envisage that such a tool would simplify applying the transformation patterns, provide assistance in detecting possible matches with library widgets, and permit association of user-interface design information (presentation aspects such as widget layout) with the resulting specifications. Future research may also define rules for applying the patterns to achieve more usable systems.

References

1. G. D. Abowd. Formal Descriptions of User Interfaces. *Colloquium Digest*, 192:7/1–7/3, 1991.
2. D. J. Duke and M. D. Harrison. Mapping User Requirements to Implementations. *Software Engineering Journal*, 10(1):13–20, January 1995.
3. R. Duke, G. Rose, and G. Smith. Object-Z: A Specification Language Advocated for the Description of Standards. *Computer Standards and Interfaces*, 17:511–533, 1995.
4. E. Gamma, R. Helm, R. Johnson, and J. Vlissides. *Design Patterns: Elements of Reusable Object-Oriented Software*. Addison-Wesley, 1994.
5. F. Losavio and A. Matteo. A Method for User-Interface Development. *Journal of Object-Oriented Programming*, pages 22–27,75, September 1997.
6. C. Morgan. *Programming from Specifications*. Prentice-Hall International Series in Computer Science. Prentice Hall, 2nd edition, 1994.
7. J. K. Ousterhout. *Tcl and the Tk Toolkit*. Addison-Wesley, 1994.
8. ParcPlace Systems Inc. *VisualWorks User's Guide*. ParcPlace, 1994.
9. F. Paterno. A Methodology for a Task-driven Modelling of Interactive Systems Architectures. In *Critical Issues in User Interface Systems Engineering*, chapter 6, pages 93–108. Springer, 1996.
10. A. Puerta. A Model-Based Interface Development Environment. *IEEE Software*, 14(4):40–47, July/August 1997.
11. J. M. Spivey. *The Z notation: a Reference Manual*. Prentice-Hall, 2nd edition, 1992.
12. P. Szekely. Retrospective and Challenges for Model-Based Interface Development. In F. Paterno, editor, *Interactive Systems: Design, Specification and Verification – 1st Eurographics Workshop*, pages 1–27. Springer-Verlag, 1994.

13. M. van Harmelen. Object-Oriented Modelling and Specification for User-interface Design. In F. Paterno, editor, *Interactive Systems: Design, Specification and Verification – 1st Eurographics Workshop*, pages 199–232. Springer-Verlag, 1994.

14. P. Viljamaa. The Patterns Business: Impressions from PLoP-94. *Software Engineering Notes*, 20(1):74–78, January 1995.

15. S. Wilson and P. Johnson. Empowering Users in a Task-Based Approach to Design. In *DIS'95 Symposium on Designing Interactive Systems: Processes, Practices, Methods and Techniques*, pages 25–31. ACM Press, 1995.

16. S. Wilson, P. Johnson, C. Kelly, J. Cunningham, and P. Markopoulos. Beyond Hacking: A Model Based Approach to User Interface Design. In *Proceedings of HCI'93*, pages 215–231. Cambridge University Press, 1993.

Appendix: Widget Library

In this appendix, we describe an abstract widget library that expresses the behaviour of three widgets (label, button and list), without committing to a particular concrete (extant) toolkit. We use Object-Z to specify the widgets and we also provide informal descriptions of the widgets' lexical behaviour. Because we do not commit to a particular toolkit, we do not give examples of each widget's appearance, relying instead on the reader's understanding of similar widgets in toolkits such as Tk [7].

Label

A label is an inactive widget, i.e., it has state but it does not respond to input. The inactive status of a label widget means that operations on a label should never be directly available to the user.

$$
\begin{array}{l}
\underline{\text{Label}[X]}\\[4pt]
\begin{array}{|l|}\hline
label : X \\\hline
\end{array}
\qquad
\begin{array}{|l|}\hline
\_SetContents\_ \\
\Delta(label) \\
new? : X \\\hline
label' = new? \\\hline
\end{array}
\end{array}
$$

Button

A button offers operations to:

set the text *label* on the button;

press the button so that it is *engaged*;

release the button following a *press* (causing the button to return to its initial state, i.e., not *engaged*);

click the button, effectively a *press* followed by a *release*.

Each button has a label that characterises the button. The button agent is generic to allow the class of object defining the label to vary.

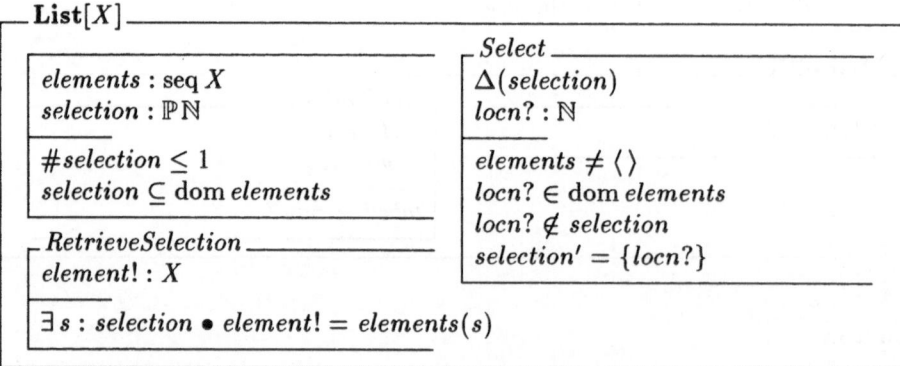

```
┌─ Button[X] ─────────────────────────────────────────────────────────────
│  Label[X]
│  ┌────────────────────────────────┐   ┌─ INIT ──────────────────────┐
│  │ engaged : 𝔹                    │   │ ¬ engaged                    │
│  └────────────────────────────────┘   └──────────────────────────────┘
│  ┌─ Press ────────────────────────┐   ┌─ Release ───────────────────┐
│  │ Δ(engaged)                     │   │ Δ(engaged)                   │
│  │ ───────────────────────────    │   │ ─────────────────────────    │
│  │ ¬ engaged                      │   │ engaged                      │
│  │ engaged'                       │   │ ¬ engaged'                   │
│  └────────────────────────────────┘   └──────────────────────────────┘
│  Click ≙ Press ⨾ Release
└──────────────────────────────────────────────────────────────────────────
```

The *Press* operation is effected by the user moving the mouse cursor inside the button and pressing a mouse-button[2] while the *Release* operation defines the situation in which the user releases the mouse-button with the mouse cursor inside the button and with *engaged* true.

List

A list is a selectable sequence of objects. A single element in the list can be selected. Selecting a new element replaces the previous selection. The selection is defined by the position of the element within the list because the list may have duplicate elements.

```
┌─ List[X] ───────────────────────────────────────────────────────────────
│  ┌────────────────────────────────┐   ┌─ Select ────────────────────┐
│  │ elements : seq X               │   │ Δ(selection)                 │
│  │ selection : ℙℕ                 │   │ locn? : ℕ                    │
│  │ ───────────────────────────    │   │ ─────────────────────────    │
│  │ #selection ≤ 1                 │   │ elements ≠ ⟨ ⟩               │
│  │ selection ⊆ dom elements       │   │ locn? ∈ dom elements         │
│  └────────────────────────────────┘   │ locn? ∉ selection            │
│  ┌─ RetrieveSelection ────────────┐   │ selection' = {locn?}         │
│  │ element! : X                   │   └──────────────────────────────┘
│  │ ───────────────────────────    │
│  │ ∃ s : selection • element! = elements(s)
│  └────────────────────────────────┘
└──────────────────────────────────────────────────────────────────────────
```

The selection is altered by the user pressing a mouse-button with the mouse cursor over an item in the list. A list therefore must differentiate between the different regions of the list within which the user may press the mouse-button. The regions in the presentation of the list and the elements in the list correspond on a one-to-one basis.

[2] The precise button is toolkit dependent.

A framework for generating spatial configurations in user interfaces

Markus Fischer

Information Technology Research Institute, University of Brighton
Brighton, BN2 4GJ, UK – www.itri.brighton.ac.uk

Abstract. This paper describes an approach to the problem of designing and implementing visual presentations in direct-manipulative user interfaces. Such presentations are often complex and their construction requires in-depth design knowledge. A framework is proposed that includes declarative models and inference mechanisms, aimed to significantly reduce the demands on the interface developer. Models of application characteristics form the input for a generation system which is parameterised by the interface developer. The inferred layout is produced both as a declarative model and executable code, which, integrated with the rest of the application, produces the presentation at application run-time.

1 Introduction

Graphical user interfaces have become the most popular way to interact with computers. The paradigm of Direct Manipulation (DM) [23] has paved the way of success for desktop operating systems and applications. However, this wide-spread use also brings along the problem of appropriately constructing such interfaces. Choosing an interaction paradigm for the interface that is highly cognitively plausible in principle is no guarantee for the quality of the final interface. Adequate design knowledge and implementation skills are necessary to develop a user interface that is not only cognitively plausible but appropriate for the task at hand. The World Wide Web gives an indication of the problems that can arise when interfaces or documents are designed by inexperienced developers.

The design knowledge which is contributing to a good interface has to be made easily accessible to interface developers, for example, by means of guidelines, styles and rules. A recently developed approach is to apply design heuristics automatically. However, this calls for the formalisation of not only the design knowledge, but also of the domain and application characteristics to which it is applied, such as concept structures, tasks and required system functionality. These models can be used to form the input for inference systems which produce interface models and ultimately, the interface code. This approach is called *Model-Based User Interface Development (MB-UID)* [19] [25]. The software engineering community has for some time demonstrated that explicit modelling can be an invaluable aid for analytical and constructive purposes [32] [20].

2 Motivation and problem

The MB-UID approach can be seen as an attempt to formalise significant portions of HCI knowledge. Traditionally, MB-UID has focused on the functional design aspects of an application and its interface. This includes analysing and modelling the tasks and dialogues that are found in the application domain. These phenomena are then reflected in the user interface by widgets, message sequences, animated help and similar constructs.

The problem of producing adequate visual presentations from models has received less attention than the functional aspects, although awareness exists [29]. Obviously, there is a virtually infinite number of different application domains. However, design knowledge should be domain-independent so that it can be stated once and applied to many different domains. It is difficult to strike a balance, as rules and guidelines must not be too general, as is often the case in the HCI literature. In particular, there is a lack in guidelines for the design of spatial configurations (or layout) of visual elements. Rather more attention has been focused on the design of icons and similar self-containing constructs than identifying how elements in a larger visual structure work together to form a meaningful whole.

There is a need for clear rules that indicate the use of layout techniques, such as justification, indentation, or the choice of tabular versus graphical presentation of data structures, depending on their type and the purpose of the presentation. Ideally, a formalisation of such rules could be implemented in a MB-UID framework to make the construction of application presentation code a semi-automatic process – one of generation – relieving the developers from the need to obtain in-depth design and implementation knowledge themselves. It would also allow them to try out different designs easily and quickly.

3 Related work

There is a tendency in HCI research to focus on the role of functional aspects of an interface, such as the implementation of domain tasks. The work presented in [8] and [9] is a notable exception that also gives indications of how to construct a suitable visual presentation for domain objects. This problem of construction is also addressed by the document and graphic design community, traditionally coming from paper-based and textually oriented documents ([12] [30]) but now increasingly acknowledging the importance of on-line publishing and interactive documents [13]. Another example of document design guidelines is [22], pointing out the relevance of the Gestalt theory and other aspects of Cognitive Psychology [1]. Understanding human visual perception of visual item arrangements is the key to conveying the right meaning to the reader of the document – or, in the case of HCI, the user of the application. Awareness of the problem has long been raised, for example in [27], [28] and [4]. However, few examples exist that take a less philosophical and analytical but a more practical and constructive view on the matter. For example, [15] is an attempt to develop a rule system for designing pictures which is based on the concept of grammar for languages. A comprehensive list of layout techniques is presented in [29], largely based on the philosophy of graphic design. However, such recommendations for graphic layout are aimed to be a knowledge resource for the more experienced interface designers.

Modelling Approaches. Formalised methods to produce presentations have been developed since the late 1980s as part of automatic document synthesis systems [7] [17] [2]. These algorithms plan a presentation by employing modelled semantic information about the involved objects and their interrelationships, as well as rhetorical information – in this context mostly referred to as communicative goals. However, the driving force in this area has been the exploitation of different presentation modes – that is, choosing the appropriate mode (text, graphics, video, etc.) for individual objects and combining them effectively. Complex presentations within one mode, such as nested tables and sequences are generally not supported.

The aim of the research in the MB-UID context is aimed at interactive systems rather than static presentations. Although significant efforts are made to model tasks and actions, using state transition networks, Petri nets and similar event-chaining mechanisms, models for complex presentations have not enjoyed the same level of attention [11].

The systems AME [18] and JANUS [3] employ object-oriented models as the base for the interface construction. The data structures and their associated tasks are used to generate windows (which are often a reflection of a certain task) and their contents, such as menus, scrolling lists, dialogue buttons (OK, Cancel etc.), text fields and labels. The resulting interface is principally a form-based interface, with only little structure within the presentations.

The approach described in [11] considers subtle display phenomena, but as it is based on a background of relational databases, their queries and management, the visualisation is again form-based.

4 Goal and approach

Current direct-manipulative interfaces demand complex presentations, particularly, because the presentation does not only serve an informative purpose, but also forms an action potential – the user will perform gestures on the presented objects, the predominant interaction style of such interfaces. As an example of interactive presentations consider popular diary management systems, like the Sun Calendar Manager (Figure 1) where each small box represents a day. The user can click on such day presentations to perform operations, such as scheduling appointments.

This is a typical scenario for direct-manipulative interfaces. Firstly, the display contains two-dimensional as well as hierarchical structures. In this example, there is the matrix of days; each day presentation contains the number of the day as well as a list of appointments, which is again a structured display of appointment start time and description. The entire presentation is very much text-based but even so, the layout is a result

Fig. 1. A sample direct-manipulative interface

of many design decisions. In fact, the appearance of individual items in DM interfaces is less often graphical or iconic than is commonly assumed. It is the construction of a meaningful layout that can form the thread of visual design for DM interfaces. This observation leads to the question of how to find the right construction *method* on the one hand and the influential *factors* for a layout that is suitable (for a given application) on the other hand.

Rudimentary factors which the user interface designer could modify include sequence orientation (horizontal/vertical), justification, and border lines (yes/no). Choosing values for these parameters and others yields a particular spatial configuration. The goal of the research presented in this paper is to obtain (semi-automatically) a configuration that reflects the semantics of the application and the intentions of the developer so that the end-user will have little difficulties understanding what the presentation is about. The interface developer need not to be an expert in visual design and is also freed from the daunting implementation task.

4.1 The theoretical approach

Spatial configurations are hierarchical structures formed by (usually binary) relations between elements. For example, one object is presented to the left of another; one object presentation surrounds another one, etc. These spatial relations must find part of their motivation from semantic relations from the application domain. The object-oriented paradigm is a suitable basis to formally describe the application structure. Given that it is a popular and well regarded paradigm in software engineering, it is reasonable to assume the existence of such a model which can form the starting point of the interface development.

It is a crucial part of the approach to focus on the relations between data objects on the one hand and visual elements on the other hand. Just as all data relations form a structure, the spatial relations form a configuration. However, current user interface management systems (UIMS) do not provide sufficient support for a relation-based visualisation. Instead, atomic interface concepts such as icons and buttons are often the central repository of functionality of such systems. A set of spatial configuration phenomena has to be identified and integrated into the modelling framework.

The mapping of data structures into spatial configurations involves factors that are not part of the application data model, including the purpose of the presentation. That is, the application objects should be presented in a way that makes the interpretation by the user as simple as possible. This, of course, depends on the given task, such as contrasting two pieces of information, getting an overview of a group of items or searching through a list. Note that the notion of presentation purpose is different to that of communicative goal (commonly used by many of the presentation systems described in the previous section) which is a concept partly derived from Speech Act Theory [21] in the field of pragmatics [16], and other considerations of how pictures represent intentions, as outlined in [14]. Systems that follow the DM paradigm present themselves as a tool with a set of associated objects, and therefore are in themselves not engaged in communication – application objects are *presented* by the system as an extension to the set of objects from the real world and *manipulated* by the user.[1]

Once the relevant information (such as application semantics and presentation purpose) is explicitly modelled, it can be used by an inference system to plan suitable presentations.

Such an inference mechanism stores visualisation heuristics and constructs a spatial configuration according to the criteria specified by the interface developer. This task of producing a surface realisation for an abstract description is called generation. This process can be seen analogous to the task of natural language generation [10], a research field within computational linguistics, where a grammar governs the mapping between information stored in a language-independent formalism into text in a natural language like Italian or English.

The generation of spatial configurations, or indeed any visualisation, can in principle follow two different paths: 1) a visualisation engine is used at application run-time; 2) a visualisation engine operates purely on the class model rather than the actual objects (this can be seen as a compile-time phenomenon). The approach taken here is based on the second path, which compromises to some extent on dynamic behaviour but leads to interfaces with shorter response time, as the visualisation does not have to be inferred at run-time. There is also no need to bind the inference mechanism (the generator) into the application code. Instead, the inference mechanism will produce native code (with respect to a particular UIMS) that will be integrated with the non-interface-oriented core of the application.

---

1. Obviously, applications might also include dialogue structures if these occur in the domain. This is, however, another interaction technique and does not involve issues of graphic design in the same sense as direct-manipulation systems.

5 The framework

Figure 2 summarises the different models and processes of the development framework. The object-oriented application class model is used as the starting point for the design. As stated above, the emphasis will be on the relations that hold between classes, for example, part-of or subsumption relations. To be able to infer a spatial realisation for any configuration of interrelated classes, more information is needed. This is given by the interface developer – whose familiarity with the nature and functioning of the application and its domain is assumed – and is predominantly of a non-visual, application-centred nature. This means that in this scenario the interface developer should be an expert of the application domain, but not necessarily an expert of cognitive psychology or graphic design. Many application programmers are in exactly this position.

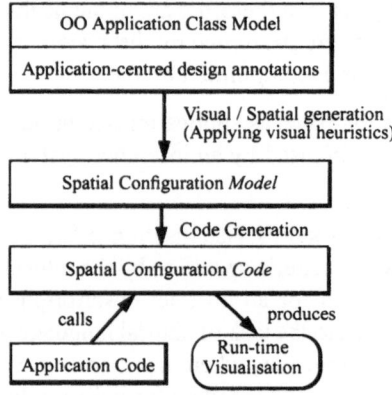

Fig. 2. Overview of the framework

The system provides the design knowledge in the form of a rule base which is applied at the request of the developer. It is important to note that the research presented here is not primarily concerned with the development of new visualisation heuristics, but the storing and application of such rules in a semi-automatic way – the generation process and the associated knowledge resources.

Instead of generating code directly, it is advantageous to produce a declarative representation of the spatial configurations first. This gives the developer the opportunity to easily modify the generated result. Then, the amended declarative model is transformed into executable code (of a specific UIMS language). Running this code in conjunction with the application core and the interface code that takes care of the functional aspects will produce the desired presentations in the user interface.

5.1 Overview of the interface development steps in the generation framework

To be able to generate executable interface code, several modelling steps and inference processes have to take place. The following sections describe the sequence of steps, us-

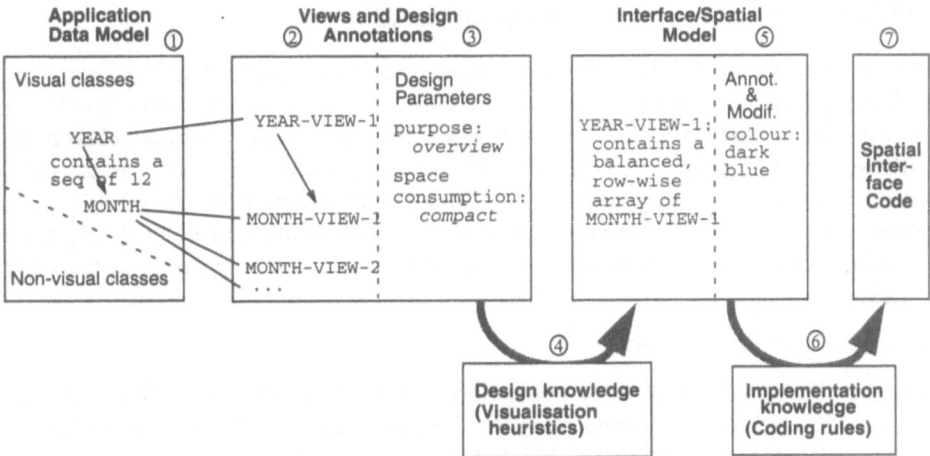

Fig. 3. A graphical summary of the design steps and the involved modules

ing the diary management domain as an example throughout. Figure 3 illustrates the design process graphically.

A substantial part of the theoretical work carried out – the declarative modelling of spatial configurations, the heuristics and their parameters that map application data relations into spatial relations – has been implemented as a prototype to which references are occasionally made.

5.2 Application modelling ①

In most modern software engineering projects, some form of model of the domain concepts that are to be included in a computer system is constructed. The object-oriented paradigm is an expressive way to reflect relevant portions of reality in a natural fashion. These models include classes and their interrelationships. To use these models in the spatial configuration design process, they have to be computationally available. One possibility is to import code written in an object-oriented programming language and extract the necessary information, so that modelling task has only to be performed once. The prototype system imports class descriptions written in the CLOS language [24].

The developers can indicate to the system which classes they wish to be part of the interface, that is, which contain objects that are to be visualised on the screen at run-time of the application.

Result of the modelling step: A model of classes for which appropriate visualisation is to be developed.

Example: Every object of class YEAR contains a sequence of twelve objects of class MONTH. The developer indicated that year objects as well as month objects will have to be displayed on the interface (this decision is made based on task requirements, which are not modelled in this framework).

5.3 Identification of application configurations ②

The goal is to put the developer in the position to be able to construct an interface without having to know visualisation rules. Nevertheless, the developer will have to indicate those portions of the class model that are to be visualised together. For each class to be visualised the developer assigns one or more *views*. A view defines a set of relations to other classes (programming languages use terms like 'attributes' or 'slots'). It is conceivable to have several different views for a class. The reason is that objects might be visualised for different purposes and the visualisation should be appropriate for each context.

Result: A list of logical views.

Example: The YEAR-VIEW-1 for year objects will include the presentation of the sequence of month objects connected with the year, each month being presented in month-view-1 (which in turn might involve objects of type day – not included in the figure).

5.4 Setting parameters for the spatial realisation ③

The visual presentation of application data cannot be planned based on the description of application classes and relations alone. Firstly, the application relations that will be turned into spatial relations are domain-specific and will as such be meaningless to any generalised rule system. For this reason, the relations have to be characterised in terms of domain-independent relations representing more abstract semantics.

Secondly, the developer must indicate which purpose the visualisation will serve. Different purposes need different types of spatial configuration.

Finally, the developer might set semi-visual or stylistic parameters which will trigger the use of specific visual techniques.

A variety of parameters can be set by the developer, which – as the focus lies on spatial *relations* – describe the application relation in various terms. Examples are given below.

Semantic relations. An application relation which connects application objects is domain-specific and has to be characterised in more general terms which are used in the visualisation heuristics of the spatial configuration generator. A number of such semantic relations exist, including among others:

- Identification – the string "September" identifies the sequence of its days
- Constituency – (often referred to as *part-of*) a form of context particularly applicable to material objects such as cars and wheels, but also used metaphorically: a month is part of a year
- Subordination – a relation found between abstract objects, for example, concept hierarchies. It also refers to the notion of hierarchies in which one object exerts influence over another.
- Extension – the relation between one object and an addition to that object, contain-

ing further functionality or properties that extends the main object (but cannot exist on its own).

The semantic relations serve a vital function in the generation framework. They allow the interface developer to express facts about the application domain – information with which particularly software engineers are familiar with. At the same time, in-depth visualisation knowledge (here: spatial configuration knowledge) is no longer required from the interface-developing person. It is the responsibility of the rule base in the generation system (discussed later in this section) to map the specification of the application domain in terms of the abstract, semantic relations into concrete spatial configurations. The current framework contains 13 semantic relations, divided into three groups. They are based on an analysis of around 30 graphical presentations in commercial graphical user interfaces. Crucially, the framework allows the extension of this set of relations – the architecture of the generation system is only based on the concept of using semantic information, not which particular semantic relations are actually employed.

Presentation purpose. A presentation can serve one of several different purposes, i.e., what the user will do with the presented items. The purposes currently considered in the framework are cognitive processes, such as:

- Overview – the user will take the presented information to gain the big picture rather than detailed insight
- Search – the user will look for a particular item in the presentation
- Contrast – two or more objects are compared, with emphasis on the differences

By indicating the purpose of the presentation on an abstract level, the interface developer implicitly makes a decision for a particular spatial configuration to be used for these items. The exact implication of the presentation purpose is handled, just as for the semantic relations, by the rule base in the generator.

Stylistic parameters. Other influential factors, which are more of a stylistic, semi-visual nature include: *space consumption* (compact vs. distributed); *relation coding by graphical elements* (very graphical, medium, low), for example, using lines; *coding by colour* (yes, no); *coding by font* (yes, no). *Reading order* is also considered.

A significant number of aspects of a presentation are, of course, not of a spatial nature, such as text font and colour. The research carried out does include these aspects to some extent. In fact, space, shape or colour often form a set of alternatives for visualising the same underlying semantic relationship. It is also possible, in principle, to redundantly code a single relation by employing more than one visual technique, such as colour and font together.

The set of influential factors can be easily extended, along with the introduction of new visualisation heuristics (in the generator, discussed below) that use them. As it is necessary to keep the list of employed semantic relations domain-independent, the extension of the list of relations has to be well-founded. The WordNet system [31] is one possible source for abstract relations.

Result: Each relation between application objects is described in domain-independent, predominantly non-visual terms.

Example: The relation between YEAR and MONTH is characterised as *constituency*, the purpose of the presentation of the list of months has been characterised by the developer as *overview*.

5.5 Applying the design knowledge ④ – the process of generation (phase 1)

This is the central module of the framework. Its function is to map the non-visual, application-centered specification provided in the earlier stages into a model of a suitable layout. Here, spatial configurations will be assigned to configurations of application classes and relations. Note that this mapping is a design step, based on the application structure, not the actual run-time data.

The process of generating a spatial model is one that applies design knowledge or heuristics. One could also speak of visual rhetoric – the ability to use visual techniques effectively. This formal knowledge, covering the fields of cognitive psychology, graphic design and, to some extent, linguistics, has to be provided by experts. The implemented prototype provides a number of heuristics but is open for future extensions.

The aim of the research described here is to provide a generation mechanism; this is made extensible so that experts of the above-mentioned fields can amend the set of heuristics.

A taxonomy of spatial relations. Figure 4 presents the hierarchy of spatial constructs that form the resources for the types of layout that covers a substantial part of the graphical presentations that were analysed during the course of the research programme. Each construct has several parameters, but for simplicity purposes these are not discussed here.

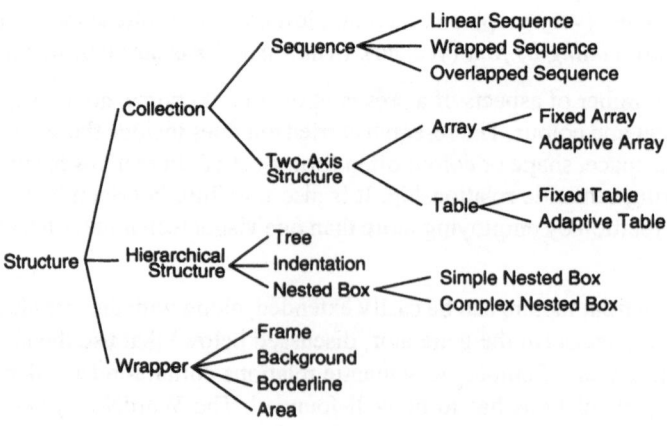

Fig. 4. Extracts of a spatial constructs taxonomy

The following examples clarify the meaning and the typical purpose of these constructs.

- Sequence – probably the most versatile construct. It exists as a special case for two objects and as a generalisation for a larger number of objects. Two objects might be contrasted or compared by juxtaposing them – a special case of a sequence – or an association relation can be visualised by a (usually horizontal) sequence.
A larger number of objects appearing in a sequence are often presented for the purposes of overview or searching. A wrapped sequence produces a table like appearance for a sequential data structure, like text can be wrapped across several lines.

- Table – a construct to display two-dimensional data structures, such as the array of days in a month, with one dimension being the weeks in the month and the other the days in the week.

- Indentation – an essential technique to visualise hierarchies and embedded structures. Traditionally used in document design, some graphical user interfaces employ it to reflect the hierarchical nature of file and similar systems

- Area – white space around an object. This is a vital method to group visual elements together and separate them from others. Its use is often to be preferred over lines and borders [22].

The difference between design- and run-time visualisation decisions. It is important to note an essential difference between two kinds of relations that occur within object-oriented modelling which have a significant impact on the way visual, spatial configuration is modelled and implemented.

Firstly, there are static relations which do not change at run-time of the application because they occur between fixed parts of the class model. For example, in the diary management domain, there will be always exactly one name for a month and there will be a list of days for each month – no matter what month it is. The spatial relation in the visualisation of a month object that exists between the name of the months (for example, as the header) and the list of days (for example, being placed underneath the name) is static.

Secondly, there are spatial relations that hold between objects of sequences, arrays and hierarchies. The number of objects in a sequence is most often not predictable at compile-time, i.e. design-time. For example, each object of type day is related to a list of appointments, yet the number of appointments will vary for each day. The exact spatial configuration can therefore not be designed beforehand. Instead, a general spatial configuration pattern is assigned as surface realisation to the application relation. The executable code that will handle this visualisation will have to be able to adapt to any number of involved objects. A similar phenomenon can be observed for arrays and hierarchies.

The generation mechanism. Mapping one type of data onto another one can be done in various ways. In computational linguistics, there are many different grammar and lexicon formalisms that attempt to bridge the gap between an abstract specification of the contents of a sentence and its surface realisation in a natural language. The spatial configuration generator described here uses some of the constructs employed in computational linguistics.

236

The approach taken here is similar to unification-based grammars (UBG) [6]. The formalism uses rules that infer feature values in one object based on feature values in another object. In linguistics, such rules are used to build up a larger structure from smaller components. For this, feature-value pairs are matched across several different objects. But valid combinations of feature-value pairs can also be stated within one single object. This is the case for the rule in Figure 5. It can be read as "IF the object type is *Application Relation* and, among others, its feature *purpose* is set to *overview* THEN the feature realisation must be wrapped-sequence". Of course it is conceivable to have several applicable rules (matching patterns), which means that there are multiple solutions to the visualisation task.

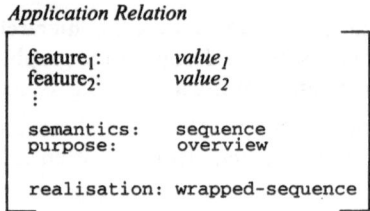

Fig. 5. A simplified generation rule

Unlike procedural *if-then* rules, unification works in a bidirectional way, as the combination is simply defined as valid and not one feature is stated as condition and the other as consequence. This means that, in natural language processing, unification-based grammars can be used both to retrieve the abstract description for a natural language sentence (*parsing*) and to produce a sentence starting from its abstract description (*generation*). Another implementation-oriented advantage of the unification approach is the fact that it is a built-in mechanism in the Prolog programming language, which, in conjunction with back-tracking, forms an ideal basis for the implementation of UBGs.

Result: The generator produces a declarative model of spatial configurations (using the concepts as presented in Figure 4).

5.6 Amendment of the spatial configuration model ⑤

Instead of generating the visualisation code directly, the developer is given a declarative model as the outcome of the design inference stage. This has the enormous advantage of easy modification and maintenance. Some MB-UID projects are in fact concentrating on the design of comprehensive modelling languages [26]. It is highly desirable that the developer can modify the spatial configuration model, in order to override or correct the design decisions made by the automatic generator. In the prototype, these modifications can be performed via a graphical editor. The developer can either override the automatically produced design suggestions or simply add detailed, not inferred visualisation elements, such as colour or type face information.

Result: An edited model of spatial configurations

Example: The colour of the month presentation was decided to be dark blue.

5.7 Generation of the interface code ⑥

This step transforms the declarative, language-independent model into code suitable for a particular UIMS, such as Java/AWT or C/Motif. The choice of language is independent from the presented framework, but should obviously be the same as the core of the application for which the interface is being developed.

The prototype system is coded in Lisp and uses a conventional recursive list construction mechanism to generate code in the CLIM UIMS language [5].

The generated code will produce presentations of application data once executed. It does not cover the entire interface behaviour. Interactive elements such as commands (available through menus or buttons) are not provided. The reason lies in the focus on presentation issues in the generator, usually neglected by other MB-UID systems.

Result: Executable code for data presentation

5.8 Integration and execution of the interface code ⑦

The generated code must be connected with the application core which will provide the actual data that is to be presented, see Figure 2. Since the design decisions were already taken before the execution of the application, the result is fast interface behaviour.

5.9 A prototype for the generation framework

In order to demonstrate the practical viability of the theoretical approach using abstract design information to guide an interface generator, a prototype system has been implemented. The system contains all necessary components to support the interface developers in their task to create the spatial configuration for a particular set of application data structures. An object-oriented modelling language and a corresponding direct-manipulative user interface is provided. The interaction is characterised by pop-up menus and drag-and-drop mouse actions. It is important to note that the system is still a prototype without suitable guidance and support for the designer. In order to give an impression of the model editor – we will not elaborate on it here – a snapshot is shown in Figure 6.

The system also contains a full implementation of the generation mechanism, with an easily extendable rule base. A spatial configuration for some data following a model of the diary management domain and that has been generated with the system is given in Figure 7. It contains various spatial configurations following the constructs of indentation, table and sequence.

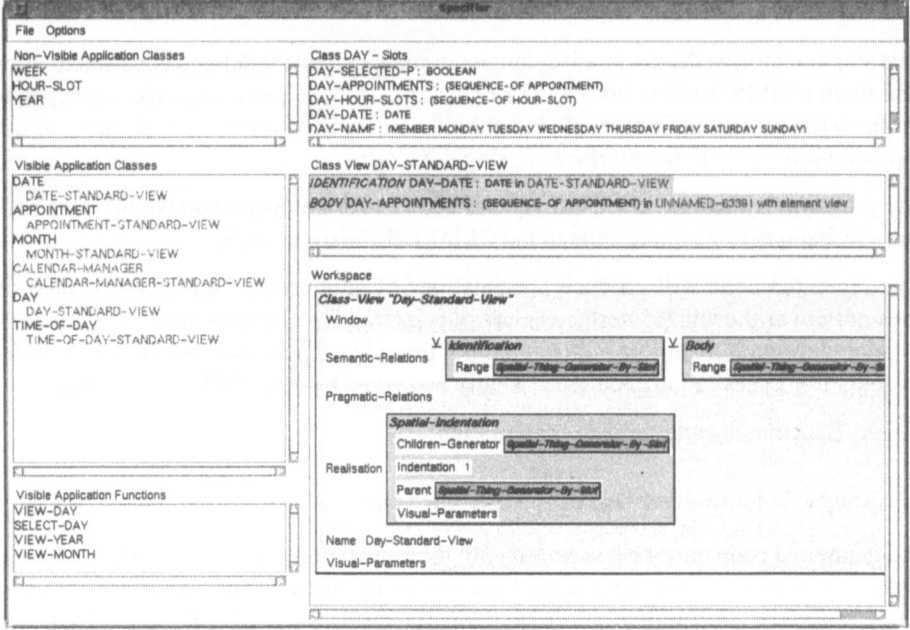

Fig. 6. A snapshot from the prototype modelling editor

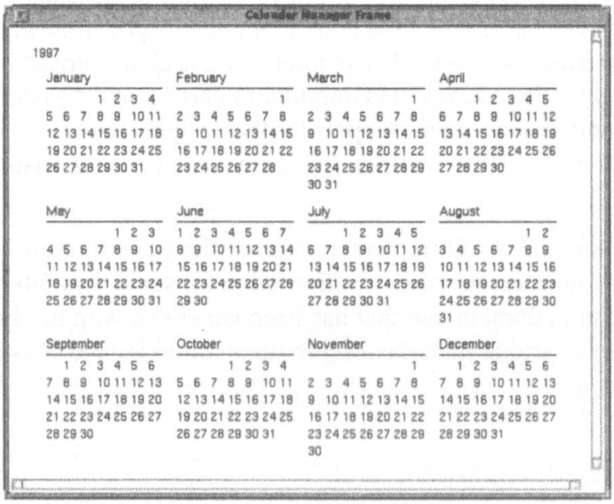

Fig. 7. A generated display for some randomly produced data in the diary management domain

6 Conclusion

As the number of people writing interfaces (this includes, in effect, interactive WWW documents) is getting larger, the ratio of people with the necessary in-depth design knowledge cannot be assumed to increase. The model-based approach has the potential to be a significant support for interface (and document) development in such circumstances.

One aspect of interface design that is often neglected in the MB-UID paradigm is that of spatial configuration of interface elements. The right layout has a great impact on the usefulness of any application interface and its design requires great care. The framework we presented in this paper is designed to support and guide the interface developer in this difficult design task. The perspective on the design task is that of generation, that is, the (semi-) automatic design of the spatial configuration. This automatic process requires substantial formalisation of the interface requirements as well as the formalisation of the design knowledge, that is, visualisation heuristics. In our approach, this formal specification of the requirements is analogous to that of natural language generation and the constructs used are partially based on concepts from computational linguistics.

Even though the developer can be supported to a large extent by automatic generation, it is nevertheless important to maintain the possibility for manual intervention. The framework accounts for this fact, in particular by using a two-step generation process.

Acknowledgements

The many discussions with Donia Scott, Richard Power and, early on, Cécile Paris, have been very useful and are gratefully acknowledged.

References

1. Anderson, J.R. *Cognitive Psychology and its Implications, 3rd Edition.* W.H. Freeman & Company, 1990

2. André, E., Rist, T. The Design of Illustrated Documents as a Planning Task. In: Maybury, M. (ed), *Intelligent Multimedia Interfaces.* AAAI Press, 1992

3. Balzert, H. From OOA to GUI - The JANUS System. In: *Proceedings of the 5th Conference on Human-Computer Interaction (INTERACT'95).* Chapman & Hall, 1995

4. Bertin, J. *Semiology of Graphics.* University of Wisconsin Press, 1989

5. *Common Lisp Interface Manager, User Manual.* Web: http://www.harlequin.co.uk/education/books/CLIM-2.0/

6. Covington, M.A. *Natural Language Processing for Prolog Programmers.* Prentice-Hall, 1994

7. Feiner, S.K. and McKeown, K.R. Coordinating text and Graphics in Explanation Generation. In: *Proceedings of AAAI'90. Boston, MA,* 1990

8. Galitz, W.O. *User-interface screen design.* QED Publishing Group, 1993

9. Galitz, W.O. *The essential guide to user interface design.* John Wiley & Sons, 1997

10. Gazdar, G. and Mellish, C. *Natural Language Processing in LISP.* Addison-Wesley, 1989. (also available for Prolog and Pop-11)

11. Harning, M.B. An Approach to Structured Display Design – Coping with Conceptual Complexity. In: Vanderdonckt (ed) *Computer-Aided Design of User Interfaces.* Presses Universitaires de Namur, Belgium, 1996

12. Hartley, J. *Designing instructional text, third edition.* Kogan Page, 1994

13. Horton, W.K. *Designing and writing online documentation: hypermedia for self-supporting products.* John Wiley & Sons, 1994

14. Kjørup, S. Pictorial Speech Acts. In: *Erkenntnis 12*, pp. 55-71, 1978

15. Kress, G. and van Leeuwen, T. *Reading Images: The grammar of visual design.* Routledge, 1996

16. Leech, G. *Pragmatics.* Longman, 1983

17. Maybury, M. Planning Multimedia Explanations Using Communicative Acts. In: *Proceedings of AAAI '91*, Anaheim, CA, 1991

18. Märtin, C. Software Life Cycle Automation for Interactive Applications: The AME Design Environment. In: Vanderdonckt (ed) *Computer-Aided Design of User Interfaces.* Presses Universitaires de Namur, Belgium, 1996

19. Puerta, A. and Szekely, P. *Model-based Interface Development.* Tutorial notes for CHI'94, 1994. Web: http://WWW-SMI.Stanford.EDU/projects/mecano/model-based.html

20. Rumbaugh, J., Blaja, M., Premerlani, W., Eddy, F., Lorensen, W. *Object-Oriented Modeling and Design.* Prentice Hall, 1991

21. Searle, J.R. *Speech Acts.* Cambridge, UK: Cambridge University Press, 1969

22. Schriver, K.A. *Dynamics in Document Design.* John Wiley & Sons, 1997

23. Shneiderman, B. (1983)
    Direct Manipulation: A step beyond programming languages. In: *IEEE Computer*, 16(8), 57-69

24. Steele, G. *Common Lisp, The Language, 2nd Edition.* Digital Press, 1990

25. Szekely, P. Retrospective and Challanges for Model-based Interface Development. In: Vanderdonckt (ed) *Computer-Aided Design of User Interfaces.* Presses Universitaires de Namur, Belgium, 1996

26. Szekely, P., Sukaviriya, P., Castells, P., Muthukumarasamy, J., Salcher, E. Declarative interface models for user interface construction tools: the MASTERMIND approach. In: *Proceedings of the 6th Working Conference on Engineering for Human-Computer Interaction (EHCI'95)*. Chapman & Hall, 1995

27. Tufte, E.R. *The Visual Display of Quantitative Information*. Graphics Press, 1983

28. Tufte, E.R. *Envisioning Information*. Graphics Press, 1990

29. Vanderdonckt, J. and Gillo, X. Visual Techniques for Traditional and Multimedia Layouts. In: *Proceedings of the 2nd Workshop on Advanced Visual Interfaces (AVI'94)*. ACM Press, 1994

30. Williams, T.R. (1993) What is so different about visuals? In: *Technical Communications*, Vol. 40, No 4, 1993

31. Wordnet Project at Princeton University. Web: http://www.cogsci.princeton.edu/~wn/

32. Yourdon, E. *Modern Structured Analysis*. Prentice-Hall, 1989

Using Model Checking for the Automatic Validation of User Interfaces Systems

Bruno d'Ausbourg

ONERA-CERT
2, Avenue Edouard Belin
B.P. 4025, 31055 Toulouse Cedex 4
France
+33 (0)5 62 25 26 48
ausbourg@cert.fr

Abstract. This paper describes the prototype of a software environment devised for assisting the formal validation of user interfaces systems (UIS). It suggests an approach to include such formal operations in the design process. It explains why the UIS can be modelled properly by a dataflow system, how this model can be expressed by using equations of flows in the language Lustre and how techniques of model checking can be used to check properties on it and to generate tests. It describes then how these functions are integrated in a software environment prototype.

1 Introduction

User interface systems(UIS) are becoming a quite important part of applications. They ensure the well understanding of their internal state by the user. They make communications between users and such applications easier. So, this increasing part must behave as intended. What is intended can be considered as behaviouring laws. This point is particularly important when those interactive systems drive critical applications or general public applications. As an example, the following sentences can be viewed as such constraints:

- "the UIS must react and present a feedback to each action of the user; so, the user is always aware of what he has done";
- "the UIS must reflect every change of the internal state of the application; so, the user is always aware of what happens";
- "the user can never be blocked by the UIS; the user is always given an opportunity to perform any action";
- "screens X or Y are always displayed before screen Z that never appears when screen T is displayed";
- "it takes always less than x actions to go from screen X to screen Z";
- "there are always less than n screens displayed at the same time";

The problem is to define properly those behaviouring constraints and to verify that systems run in accordance with them. These constraints have to

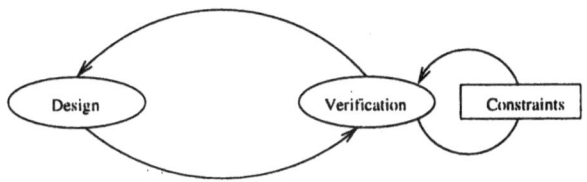

Fig. 1. An iterative design process

be defined in the first stages of the process development in order to get final systems that satisfy them. The problem resumes then to define properly these constraints during the specification process. But in practice, there is no really such a specification process for UIS. Designers use rather mockups or prototypes of the UIS than usual written specifications. So, in this case, taking account of these behaviour constraints consists in producing mockups and prototypes that integrate them and behave in full accordance with them.

Techniques for automated verification are very useful in this context. By using them, designers can enforce an iterative process for designing and devising user interfaces. This process, depicted on figure 1 links design stages with verification steps. A first mockup is devised and then submitted to verification steps: properties that express the behaviour requirements are then checked. If the designed mockup does not meet these requirements, a new design step is necessary that will produce a new mockup. This mockup will be checked also. This process continues until the produced mockup satisfies the requirements, and therefore is verified successfully because it implements the expected behaviouring laws.

These techniques for an automated verification process make an explicit use of formal languages. These languages permit to describe and to perform computations on formal models of UIS. Writing those models must be done in a rapid and efficient way; otherwise, the process would not be interactive enough and it would be not realistic to implement the process depicted in figure 1. Semantic analysis techniques are described in [3] ; they are used to build mechanically the formal model of a UIS from the description that is produced by an interface generator. This formal description can be used also to build test cases that permit to compare the final system with the requirements and, by this way, that help to validate it. So this leads to achieve a development process as depicted by figure 2.

The paper describes the prototype of a validation environment that implements the whole process of figure 2. Section 2 describes an example of an interactive application. Section 3 details how the environment permits to build a formal model for this application by using the formal language Lustre used to denote models of UIS. Section 4 describes the prototyped environment and the main tools necessary to implement the suggested approach.

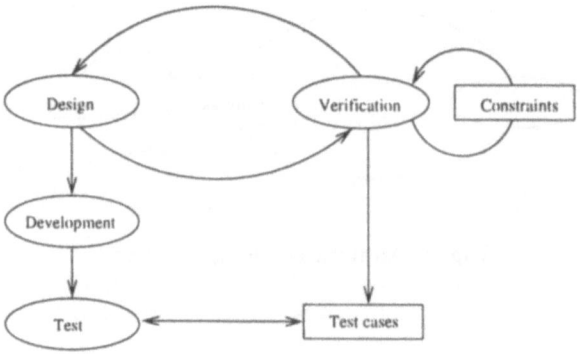

Fig. 2. The whole development process

2 A small interactive application

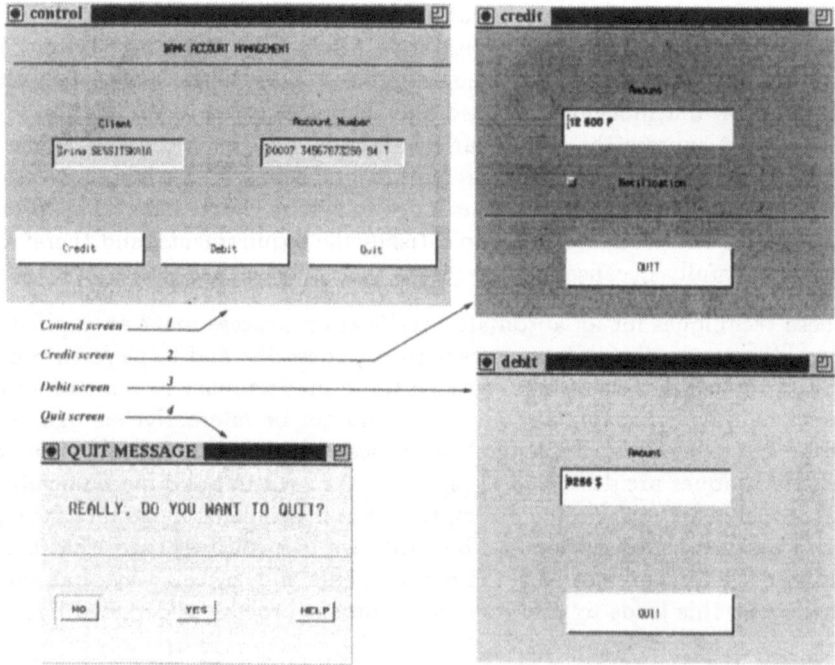

Fig. 3. A bank account management application

The figure 3 shows four screens, that make up the mockup of an interactive application. They were produced by using the *UIM/X* interface generator. The application is intended to manage bank accounts. The main display is the *Control* screen. The textfield *Client* is used to enter the identity of a particular client of the bank. The textfield *Account Number* permits to enter the account number of the client. Three pushbuttons are available to activate three other screens that correspond to particular operations.

The *Credit* pushbutton activates the *credit* display. This display shows a textfield *Amount* that accepts the value to credit on the selected bank account. The *Notification* togglebutton indicates, when set, that the credit operation must be notified to the client by surface mail. The pushbutton *QUIT* validates the credit operation and erases the display. Similarly, the the *Debit* pushbutton activates the *debit* display. This display shows a textfield *Amount* that accepts the value to debit on the selected bank account. The pushbutton *QUIT* validates this debit operation and erases this display. The *QUIT* pushbutton on the *control* screen activates the *Quit* message box to confirm the user wants to quit. The message box presents three options. The *YES* pushbutton confirms that the application must be leaved. The *NO* pushbutton returns to the control screen. The *HELP* pushbutton does no operation: this function is not implemented inside the mockup.

Of course, the application functionalities are not quite well devised. A more realistic application would proceed quite differently. Our purpose, here, is not to devise a proper application but to use the existing mockup (or prototype) of an application as an input for our verification environment.

```
module controle_uil


procedureactivateCB_pushButton1;
procedureactivateCB_pushButton2;
procedureactivateCB_Client;
procedureactivateCB_pushButton3;
                                            controls
                                            {
object controle : XmDrawingArea             XmLabel label1;
{                                           XmPushButton pushButton1;
arguments                                   XmPushButton pushButton2;
{                                           XmTextField Client;
XmNresizePolicy = XmRESIZE_NONE;            XmPushButton pushButton3;
XmNwidth = 485;                             XmLabel label4;
XmNheight = 300;                            XmSeparator separator1;
XmNx = 481;                                 XmTextField numero;
XmNy = 408;                                 XmLabel label5;
XmNunitType = XmPIXELS;                     };
XmNbackground = color( 'pink' );            };
};
```

Fig. 4. The UIL text

The figure 4 depicts a piece of the UIL [16] code that was produced by the interface generator. The UIL text describes the hierarchical architecture of the interface (see the *controls* part) and links the callback function names to the related widgets. Each display is declared in a UIL module as an object: in particular, the three first displays are *XmDrawingArea* objects and the fourth is a *XmMessageBox* object. Each of them includes the declarations of the elementary primitive widgets: labels, textfields, pushbuttons, togglebuttons, ...

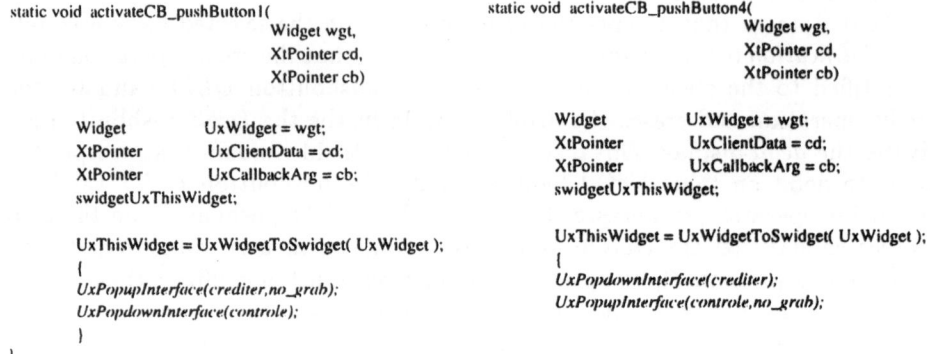

Fig. 5. The C Callback functions

.The behaviour of the application is defined by using the editing features of the interface generator. In particular, callbacks, that are linked to the widgets resources, can be defined and programmed.

For instance, figure 5 depicts two callbacks. The designer writes the C program lines in *italic*. The other lines are produced automatically by the interface generator. The function *activateCB_pushButton1* depicts the behaviour of the interface when the pushButton 1 (the button *Credit* of the *control* display) is activated. Typically, this function pops up the *credit* display (instruction *UxPopupInterface*) and pops down the *control* screen (instruction *UxPopdownInterface*). The function *activateCB_pushButton4* depicts the behaviour of the interface when the pushButton 4 (the button *Quit* of the *credit* display) is activated. This function pops down the *credit* screen and pops up again the *control* display. The other callback functions program the interactive behaviour of the application in the same way.

Reasonning on the structure of the programmed behaviour is possible if a formal model of this behaviour can be produced. Next section describes how this can be achieved.

3 Building a formal model of the interactive application

3.1 Interactors and flows

Previous works in the field of interactive systems describe the interface of a system in terms of a collection of interactors. A formal model of interactor was developped at Cnuce in Pisa, Italy, using process oriented formalisms such as *Lotos* and *CSP* [11,13,17,18]. The interactor model developed at York [9–11] consists of an internal state which is reflected by a presentation relation onto some perceivable representation *P*. The interface between an interactor and its environment consists of a set of events. Some events are caused by agents within the environment and bring about state changes, and some other events are responses generated by the interactor.

Authors in [10,12] concluded by observing that specifying the behaviour of interactive systems in accordance with this model requires to have at one's disposal a formal language to describe events and states. Indeed, events are atomic, non-persistent occurences in the world. States refer to things that persist and have a measurable value. This requirement is largely discussed and developed in [1,8]. We feel that the dichotomy between event and status phenomena can be taken into account by describing interactor as a dataflow system.

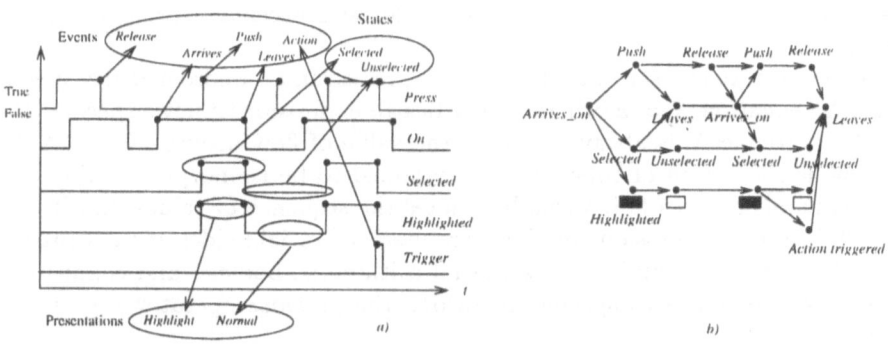

Fig. 6. Boolean flows of a pushButton interactor and structure of events

Informally, a flow is a sequence of values. Figure 6*a)* depicts boolean flows that describe the behaviour of a pushbutton interactor. The flows *On* and *Press* take a value *true* (high) while the pointing device (a cursor) is put *On* the interactor, and while the mouse button is *Pressed* by the user. The flow *Selected* reflects the internal state of the interactor. The flow *Trigger* takes a value *true* when an action is triggered by the interactor.

Events can be depicted by leading or trailing edges of flows. A leading edge of the flow *Press* expresses that an event *Push* occurred: the user pushes the mouse button in order to get it pressed. A trailing edge of this flow depicts the occurrence of the event *Release*, and indicates that the user released the mouse button. Events are depicted on figure 6*a)* by bold dots. The configuration of these flows shows that this pushbutton is selected only if the mouse button is pressed as the pointing device was already on the interactor. So, the sequence of events [*Arrives, Push*] in the interaction structure of this interactor leads to the state *Selected*. Moreover, the interactor triggers a specific action when the mouse button is released as the interactor was in the internal state *Selected*.

These events are time ordered as depicted on figure 6*b*). Dots are events and arrows illustrate the time precedence relation. This relation structures the set of events as a partially ordered set. Reasonning about the behaviour of the interface resumes to reasonning on those poset of events. For instance the logical formula *Highlighted* $\Rightarrow$ *Selected* that expresses that the button is highlighted only if it is selected or the logical formula *Action* $\Rightarrow$ ($\neg$*Selected* $\wedge$ *preSelected*) that expresses that an action is triggered only on a trailing edge of the flow *Selected* can be evaluated as *true* on the poset of figure 6*b*. The language Lustre denotes such flows and permits therefore to reason on posets of events embedded in these flows.

3.2 Describing interactors using the language Lustre

The reader will find in [5, 14, 15] a full description of the language Lustre. The presentation herein is restricted to the only elements necessary for understanding the paper.

A Lustre text is a set of declarations expressed in an unordered list of equations. An equation $X = E$ where E is a Lustre expression of flows specifies that the flow variable X is always equal to the value of flow denoted by E. A flow variable is a function of time which is assumed to be isomorphic to the set of natural numbers. So a flow variable denotes the sequence of values that it takes at each instant. Expressions on flows are made of variable identifiers, constants (considered as constant functions), usual arithmetic, boolean and conditionnal operators, and only two specific operators: the *previous* operator *pre* and the *followed_by* operator $\rightarrow$

If the Lustre epxression E denotes the sequence of values $(e_0, e_1, \ldots e_n, \ldots)$, then $pre\,E$ denotes the sequence $(nil, e_0, e_1, \ldots e_n, \ldots)$ where nil is an undefined value.

If E and F are Lustre expressions of the same type, denoting the sequences $(e_0, e_1, \ldots e_n, \ldots)$ and $(f_0, f_1, \ldots f_n, \ldots)$, then $E \rightarrow F$ denotes the sequence $(e_0, f_1, \ldots f_n, \ldots)$.

```
node edge(s:bool) returns (e:bool);
let e = false -> s and not pre s; tel
```

Fig. 7. A Lustre node

Lustre equations can be structured in *nodes*. A node is in fact the declaration of a particular function of input flow variables onto output flow variables. These variables are declared within input and output signatures of the node. The functionnal part of the node is declared by a set of equations that involve possibly local flow variables. Once declared, a node can be used as a functionnal operator inside any Lustre expression. The very useful node *edge* depicted on figure 7 returns a value *true* of its output flow *E* on each leading edge of its input flow *X*.

```
node pushButton( ES_pB_display, ES_pB_hide, UDS_pB_on, UAG_push, UAG_release :bool)
returns ( P_pB_highlight, P_pB_change_pres, S_pB_selected, S_pB_change_state, A_pB_activateCallback:bool)
var IS_pB_displayed:bool;
let
IS_pB_displayed = from_to(edge (ES_pB_display),  edge (ES_pB_hide));
S_pB_selected = IS_pB_displayed and  from_to(UDS_pB_on and edge (UAG_push),  not UDS_pB_on or UAG_release);
P_pB_highlight = S_pB_selected;
P_pB_change_pres = edge (P_pB_highlight) or  edge (not P_pB_highlight);
S_pB_change_state = edge (S_pB_selected) or  edge (not S_pB_selected);
A_pB_activateCallback = false -> pre S_pB_selected and UDS_pB_on and UAG_release;
tel
```

Fig. 8. Modelling the behaviour of a pushButton in Lustre

The node *pushButton* in figure 8 describes the behaviour of the pushButton interactor that was depicted on the figure 6. This node includes six equations of flows that assign a boolean value to each output flow. It uses the temporal node *from_to(a,b)* that is *true* from any instant *a* is *true* and *b* is not until *b* becomes *true*. So, the internal flow *IS_pB_displayed* is *true* during the time interval whose bounds are the two events *ES_pB_display* and *ES_pB_hide* that denote, when they are *true*, that the environment displays the interactor or hides it. The *S_pB_selected* flow is *true* to denote that the interactor is selected. That is possible only if the interactor is displayed. And from the instant where the user pushes on the mouse button (flow *UAG_push*) as the cursor is located on this interactor (flow *UDS_pB_on*) until the instant at which the user releases the mouse button (flow *UAG_release*) or leaves the interactor location (*not UDS_pB_on*). The interactor is highlighted as long as it is selected. An action is triggered (flow *A_pB_activateCallback* when the user releases the mouse button (flow *UAG_release*)as he is located on the interactor (*UDS_pB_on*) and as the interactor was previously selected (*pre S_pB_selected*).

3.3 Generating a formal model in Lustre

The generation of the formal representation of the user interface system uses techniques that are more largely explained in [3], [4] . We make the assumption that the UIS is generated by using the UIM/X interface generator: this tool produces the UIL [16] and C texts of the UIS that are the input data of the generating process.

Figure 9 depicts this process. An analysis of the UIL text, that describes the hierarchy of the envolved interactors, permits to produce the structure of nodes inside the text in Lustre.

Each primitive widget in UIM/X is mapped to a Lustre basic node in the Basic Lustre Library. The representation of composite widgets is obtained by

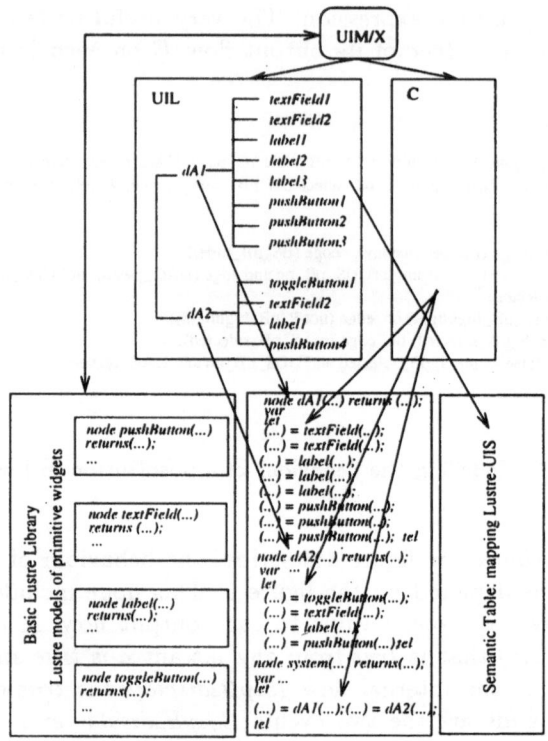

Fig. 9. Generation of a Lustre model

composition of these basic Lustre nodes. So, for example, the UIL text of figure 9 shows that the *drawingArea2* object, that corresponds to the *credit* display, is made of four primitive objects: *label*, *textField*, *toggleButton* and *pushButton*. Then, the corresponding Lustre node *dA2* incorporates the equations defining the output flows of the *label textField*, *toggleButton* and *pushButton* nodes that are used as operators on flows.

The input and output signatures of equations are made by instantiating the signatures of the basic models. The signature of the composite node *dA2* is built by making the union of the input and output flows of its internal basic nodes. The node *system* contains all the interactors and then constitutes a representation of the whole user interface system. A semantic table is produced also. It permits to map objects and events of the user interface system onto Lustre flows, giving them some semantics in the user world.

The analysis of C texts, that contain in particular the instructions of the callback procedures, performs some data flows analysis in order to interconnect flows inside the Lustre model.

Figure 10 illustrates the main principle of this analysis. The function *activateCB_pushButton4* is the callback function associated with the *pushButton*

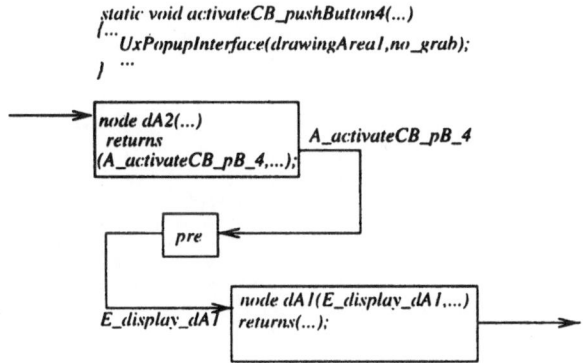

Fig. 10. Data flow analysis and interconnection of Lustre flows

object of the composite object *dA2*. The C program of this function is depicted on figure 5. This program shows that triggering the action linked to this button calls the function *UxPopupInterface* with the *control* object (*drawingArea1*)as first parameter. This function of the UIM/X library displays the object given as first parameter: so, in this case, this function call displays the interactor *dA1*.

So, the flows *A_activateCB_pB_4*, that is an output flow of the node *dA2*, and *E_display_dA1*, that is an input flow of the node *dA1*, are related in the global node *system* by the equation:

$$E\_display\_dA1 = preA\_activateCB\_pB\_4$$

This equation expresses that the *drawingArea1* object (the *control* screen) is displayed at a given instant t if the *pushButton4* (the *QUIT* button of the *credit* screen) was activated at the previous instant $t-1$. Similar connections between flows are obtained by performing the same kind of analysis and by extending this semantic interpretation over the whole C and UIL texts.

4 The prototype of a validation environment

The formal representation in Lustre can be used to verify the full UIS and to produce some tests that will be applied to the completed user interface system once it has been developped.

We implemented the software prototype of an environment that achieves some formal validation operations. This environment,coupled with a user interface generator, permits to realize the iterative design process described in figure 1. This prototype, as depicted in figure 11 offers several tools to the designer that can be activated by navigating inside menus:

- a Lustre model generator;
- a verification and diagnosis tool;

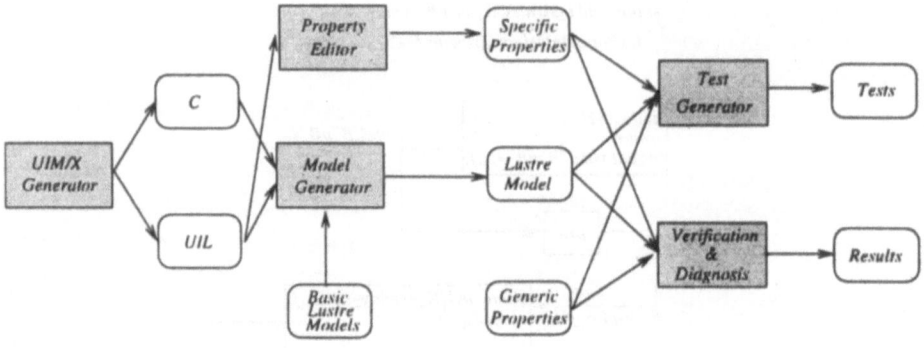

Fig. 11. A prototype environment

- a graphic editor of specific properties;
- a test cases generator for the full completed UIS.

4.1 The model generator

This tool is the heart of the system. It implements the principles discussed in 3.3 and performs the syntactic and semantic analysis of the C and UIL texts produced by the interface generator. The analyzers that perform the automatic generation of these Lustre models were developped within the system *Centaur* [6]. They are coded as programs written in Metal for the syntaxic analysis steps and in Typol for the semantic steps and the model generation.

4.2 Formal verification of properties

Lustre is also a temporal logic [19] and permits to perform verifications by model-checking. The verification techniques require the Lustre model to be transformed into a logical model, for instance a state graph, and the properties to be expressed as logical formulae that are verified to be *true* in the logical model. Roughly speaking, a Lustre observer node is built and is connected to the system to be verified. This observing node has an only output flow P that is defined by the equation $P = E$ where E it he expression associated with the observed property. Examining the values of P in the produced state graph permits to decide if the property is satisfied. When it is the case, the output flow P takes always a *true* value in the state graph. The Lesar tool described in [15] performs automatically these operations in order to verify safety properties on Lustre programs.

Generic properties. These techniques allow to verify properties that characterize the interaction structures and the expected behaviour of the user interface system. Some properties are generic and might be checked on any user interface system. These properties are defined by a generic expression that must be unfolded and instantiated on a particular interactor in order to check the property on it.

Some of these properties describe links between the presentation, the internal state of an interactor, and the user actions. For instance, the *conformity* of an interactor can be defined by the following expression, where the term *implies* denotes a Lustre node that defines the logical implication operator:

```
implies (I#(S_*_change_state_*),I#(P_*_change_pres_*));
```

This expression states that an interactor satisfies the conformity property if its presentation is modified when its internal state has changed. The flow names in the generic expression are partially given: they must be instantiated with the identification of the interactor on which the property is checked. The macro instruction *I#* means that the following pattern between parentheses must be replaced by the flow identifier that matches it inside the signature of the node on which the property is checked. These expression can be viewed as expression schemes.

So, for instance, assume that this property is checked on the *drawinArea3* interactor (*debit* display), whose signature looks like:

```
(...,P_dA_change_pres_3,S_dA_change_state_3,...) =
drawingArea3(...);
```

So, if the conformity property is checked on the interactor *dA2*, the *observer* node that contains the formula to be checked on the model and that is built by the protoype environment is the following.

```
node verify_conformity(...) returns (p:bool);
let
(...,P_dA_change_pres_3,S_dA_change_state_3,...)=
drawingArea3(...);
p = implies(P_dA_change_state_3,P_dA_change_pres_3);
tel
```

In a similar way, *reactivity* of interactors can be verified also. Informally, this property states that the UIS emits a feedback on each user action. More formally this property can be defined by the following generic expression:

```
implies (false IF# [UDS_ ]
            or (edge(UAG_push)
        and (IM#(or {I#(UDS_*_on*-tF*)}) )) @
            IF# [UDS_ _t]
            or ((UAG_enter_c or UAG_enter_cr)
            and (IM#(or{I#(UDS_*_tF*)
        and pre I#(S_*tF_selected*) }))) @,
          I#(P_*_change_pres*));
```

This expresses that the presentation associated to the interactor is changed on each action performed by the user. Capturing the user actions is done by the two conditional terms that are prefixed with the macro instruction *IF#*. The following pattern between brackets indicate that if flows are present in the signature of the node and match the pattern, then, the following conditional expression (endded by @) must be instantiated on the formal Lustre node describing the checked interactor. The *IM#* macro instructions indicate that the following term, between parentheses, that contains a Lustre operator and an instantiation instruction *I#*, must be instantiated as many times the signature contains flows that match the pattern. All these instantiations are linked by the mentionned Lustre operator. Patterns of flows may contain filters: for instance the first pattern in hte above expression (*UDS_*_on*-tF**) contains the subexpression *-tF**. This filter indicates that instantiation is not performed by using flow identifiers that contains this substring.

Assume this property is checked on the *pushButton* interactor of figure 8. The Lustre expression that captures the property instantiated on this interactor is the following:

```
implies (false or (edge(UAG_push) and UDS_pB_on),
         P_pB_change_pres);
```

This expresses that the button is reactive (with respect to the above definition) if the presentation of the button changes when the user pushes the mouse button as he is located on this button. Other definitions for reactivity, as for any property, can be suggested. The difficulty is there to find the formula that captures exactly what is intended from the UIS.

The authors in [2] describe a set of relevant properties to checkon the dialog and interaction structures of UIS. They do not give a formal definition of these properties. But, some of them look like some generic properties defined in our protoype environment.

As an example, the *deadlock freedom* property is informally defined as the impossibility for a user to be in front of a black screen, to get into a state where no actions can be taken. This can be formally defined by the following generic expression. It states that as long as the UIS is running, an interactor is presented to the user who can then perform at least one action; in other words, it is not possible the system is running and there is no interactor displayed.

```
not (I#(S_*_active*) and IM#(and {not(I#(P_*_displayed*))}));
```

An other property may characterize an *unavoidable* interactor. This interactor is said unavoidable because the user must interact with it at least once in any interactive session of the UIS. A generic definition can be found in the following expression where *occur_from_to(a,b,c)* is a temporal operator whose output is *true* when *a* occurs at least once in the time interval [*b..c*], and where *start* and *stop* reflect the start and stop events of the UIS:

```
occur_from_to(P_*_displayed_*,start,stop)
```

The Lustre node *count(n,plus,minus,reset)* acts as a counter: it returns an output value that is *false* as long as the internal value of the counter is less than the threshold value n. This internal value is incremented (resp. decremented) when the input flow *plus* (resp. *minus*) is *true*. A value *true* of the input flow *reset* resets the counter. This operator is used to express the following property. It checks that there is always no more than n interactors displayed on the screen at the same time.

```
not count($1,
          IM#( or {edge (I#(P_*_displayed_*))} ),
          IM#( or {edge (not I#(P_*_displayed_*))} ),
          stop);
```

Schematically, the counter is incremented when an interactor becomes displayed (this corresponds to the leading edge of the associated *P_*_displayed_** flow) and decremented when an interactor is erased (and this corresponds to the leading edge of the (*not P_*_displayed_**) flow). When the internal value reaches the value of the first parameter *$1*, the output flow is set to the value *true*. The property expresses that this value is always *false*.

The same operator can be used to check that an interactor can be accessed at each instant in less than n steps, where n is given by the first parameter (denoted *$1* in the following expression). The property is checked on a given interactor whose name is given as the second parameter (designated as *$2*).

```
not (S_APPLI_active and
     count ($1,
            from_to(S_APPLI_active, IP#$2 (P_*_displayed_*)) and
            (IM#(or{edge (I#(P_*_displayed_*))} ) ),
            false,
            IP#$2 (P_*_displayed_*) or stop);
```

The macro-expression above uses the macro-instruction *IP#* that is followed by a reference to a parameter (*$2* here) and by a pattern to instantiate. This macro-instruction indicates that the pattern must be instantiated on the signature of the interactor node (*$2*). The above expression includes the operator *count*. This counter is incremented when any interactor other than *$2* is displayed while *$2* is not displayed. It is never decremented and a reset occurs when the parameter interactor is displayed or when the application ends. So, the parameter interactor *$2* can always been accessed in less than *$1* steps if the output flow is always false while the application is running.

A light modification can be performed by adding a new parameter *$3* in order to get an other property to check. The property *p($1,$2,$3)* is satisfied if it takes less than *$1* steps to reach the interactor *$3* from the interactor *$2*. The main difference with the previous expression stays in the new definition of the time interval. The *count* operator is activated when the interactor *$2* is displayed and stays active until interactor *$3* is displayed.

```
not (S_APPLI_active and
     count($1,
           from_to(IP#$2 (P_*_displayed_*),
                           IP#$3 (P_*_displayed_*)) and
  (IM#(or {edge (I#(P_*_displayed_*))}))),
           false,
           IP#$3 (P_*_displayed_*) or stop);
```

These instantiation mechanisms can be used to evaluate other kinds of temporal properties. For instance, look at the following macro-expression. This property *p($1,$2,$3)* checks the interactor *$1* always appears on the screen after *$2* has been displayed and before *$3* is displayed.

```
implies (S_APPLI_active,
         occur_from_to(IP#$1(edge(P_*_displayed_*)),
                       IP#$2(edge(P_*_displayed_*)),
                       IP#$3(edge(P_*_displayed_*)))));
```

All these properties are *safety* properties. Their expression E describes a system state that can be viewed as invariant in the behaviouring of the system. In others words, the system satisfies the predicate *always(E)*. The language Lustre permits to build only safety epxressions. In fact properties to check on UIS are mainly safety properties. Nevertheless, it may be interesting to verify reachability properties, in particular properties that express that a particular state characterized by E can be reached. In other words, these properties express that the predicate *eventually(E)* is satisfied. This can be done by demonstrating $\neg(always(\neg E))$. In other words, when E depicts a satisfied reachability property, the verification of the Lustre expression $\neg E$ must fail.

For example, the *rule set connectedness* property defined in [2] may be understood as a reachability property: an interactor is reachable from any initial state. This property can be checked by submitting to the verification process some instance of the following generic expression:

```
p = not ( I#(P_#_displayed#));
```

Assume, the property is checked on the *credit* interactor (*drawingArea2*) of the application example. So, in this case, the verification of the instantiated expression *not (P_displayed_dA2)* leads to a failure because this expression is *false* in some state. This means that the flow *P_displayed_dA2* is *true* in this state. And this fact expresses that the interactor *dA2* is reachable and can be displayed to the user.

Conversely, it may be useful during the design steps to be sure that a mechanism exists in order to hide or erase an interactor. This avoids to block an interactor displayed for ever. The ability to erase a displayed interactor is a reachability property. It can be checked by submitting to the verification process the instantiation of the following generic expression, where the temporal operator *never* returns a *true* value as long as its input parameter is *false*, where the temporal operator *after* returns a *true* value after the first occurence of a *true* value of its parameter, and where the flows *start* and *stop* reflect the start and stop events of the application:

```
implies (after(start) and never(stop),
         not (edge(not I#(P_#_displayed#))));
```

These some examples illustrate how some generic properties may be verified within the environment. However, it may be necessary to check some more specific properties, semantically linked to the UIS under design.

Specific properties These properties deal with how presentations, states and events are dynamically linked into the UIS. A generic definition of these properties is not always available. Sometimes, the user must produce its own definition by himself. In fact, this definition is an expression in Lustre. But a basic requirement for this environment is to hide formalisms to the end user. A graphic editor is being developed in order to build expressions of properties the user wants to check on the UIS. This property editor allows the user to build schemes of logical and temporal relations between the interaction objects that are involved in the UIS. It offers a set of palettes to the user:

- A palette of interactors that contains all the types of interactors that are used in the UIS, a list of the interactors defined in the UIS and captured by the formal model.
- A palette of logical and temporal operators that permit to draw graphically some relations between the basic or composite interactors in the UIS.
- A palette of editing and drawing operators. They allow to describe relations between the objects defined in the UIS and to perform some classical editing operations (cut, paste, copy, delete,...) on graphic objects.

Using these palettes and their operators permits the user to draw a graphical representation of the property he wants to check on the UIS.

The graphical structure of such drawings is constrained by a graphical language that guides the expression of properties. The translation of these graphical representations into a Lustre formal expression is mechanically done by interpreting the produced graphical constructs and by associating Lustre formulae with them.

4.3 Verification diagnosis

The verification process fails when the checked property is a safety property and when a behavioural trace is encountered that assigns to *false* the output flow of the observer node. On the contrary, when the checked expression is associated with a reachability property, a verification failure expresses that this trace describes a behaviour of the system that satisfies the checked property.

The Lustre text associated to the verification process is compiled into a state graph, a finite automaton more precisely. This graph describes states and transitions that assign *true* or *false* values to the output flow of the observer node that checks the P property onto the interactor I. The value of this output flow is the value of the Lustre expression of the property. The state graph is analyzed in order to point out one or several sequences of transitions that invalidate this expression and assign a *false* value to it. We showed in the previous paragraph that a such assignmnent corresponds to the invalidation of a safety property or to the validation of a reachability property. In both cases, these sequences are *diagnosis* sequences of the P property on the interaction structure of I.

These exhibited sequences of transitions in the state graph are associated with sequences of values of input flows that can be mapped to sequences of user actions. The sequences of values of input flows are translated by using the semantic table depicted in figure 9 into actions or data that can be understood by the end user because these actions and these data refer to actions and objects of the UIS perceivable by this user.

4.4   Generating test sequences of the UIS

When the verification process succeeded for a property P onto an interaction structure I, the environment suggests to build an exhaustive set of behavioural traces that lead to particular configurations of the UIS that satisfy P. These traces can be viewed as test sequences that will be used later in order to check that the final interactive system, once developped, satisfies P on I. This may be helpful in order to validate the final system.

Generating tests is then a welcome side effect of verification and diagnosis operations and is also based on observers. The technique used to produce the test observer in Lustre are based on instantiating generic properties and inserting some relevant Lustre expressions associated with the tested properties. However, the Lustre expressions needed in order to generate test sequences are the negations of the expressions that are necessary to process verifications. So, if $e(p)$ is the formal expression of P, two cases may occur.

If P is a safety property, then an expression $\neg e(C)$ is introduced in the Lustre text of the observer node where C describes a particular configuration of flows that satifies P. In other words, all is done in order to check that this configuration C is always unreachable. This checking must fail because P was already checked and its previous verification succeeded. So, for example, in order to test the conformity property, the following generic macro-expression is used:

```
not (I#(S_#_change_state#) and I#(P_#_change_pres#));
```

So, to test conformity of the *control* interactor (*drawingArea1*) of the application, the environment generates the following epxression to be introduced in the test observer node:

```
not (S_change_state_dA1 and P_change_pres_dA1);
```

If P is a reachability property, then the Lustre text of the observer node contains $e(P)$. This expression is already a negative formula, as any reachability formula in this environment. So $e(P) = \neg e'(P)$. And the checking of this expression must fail when P is satisfied.

So, if the example of the reachability property is taken back, in order to test that the *credit* interactor *drawingArea2* is reachable, the environment produces the following expression to introduce in the test observer node:

```
not(P_displayed_dA2)
```

In any case, the verification step leads to a failure. The diagnosis tool is then used to point out sequences of input flow values that lead to configurations C satsifying P in the case of safety properties P or that lead to states that satisfy P if P is a reachability property. In both cases these sequences can be considered as tests.

These test sequences are in fact sequences of input flow values that are associated with user actions. As in the diagnosis case, these sequences are translated by using the semantic table depicted on figure 9 in terms of actions and objects that are related to the UIS ant that are well known by the user.

5 Conclusion

The environment described in this paper is actually under development. We developped a prototype that contains the set of tools demonstrated in the paper. These tools are used with an interface generator. This use permits to associate some formal operations (checking and diagnosis, test generating) to pure design steps as explained if figures 1.

A major advantage of this approach is to keep the usual community that is envolved in the design process while performing formal operations. This is due to the fact that formalisms are hidden to the designer who focuses on the objects and events of the UIS only. We feel that such an approach may be a mean to spread the use of formal methods in the UIS development process.

A lot of work has to be done in order to get a real operationnal system. In particular, generating the Lustre model must be optimized in order to avoid to get huge models that are quite difficult to manage. This can be done by parameterizing the building process with properties for example. Or by performing the analysis of causal dependences one flows in order to keep only flows involved in checking a particular property. Moreover, in order to make performances better, the produced models would have to be submitted ot other more powerful checkers.

Nevertheless, this environment implements an approach we feel helpful for UI designers. It is based on a clear an precise description of the UIS to be validated. The data flow description combines expressiveness and semantic accuracy, with the facilities that are due to the functionnal and declarative style of the language Lustre.

References

1. G.D. Abowd and A.J. Dix. Integrating status and event phenomena in formal specifications of interactive systems. *SIGSOFT'94, ACM Press*, pp. 44–52, 1994.
2. G.D. Abowd, H.M. Wang and A.F. Monk. A formal technique for automated dialogue development. In *Proceddings of the First Symposium on Designing Interactive Systems, DIS'95*,Ann Arbor, MI, *ACM Press*, August 1995.
3. B. d'Ausbourg, G. Durrieu and P. Roché. Deriving a formal model of an interactive system from its UIL description in order to verify and to test its behaviour. In *Proceedings of DSVIS 96*, Namur, Belgium, June 1996.
4. B. d'Ausbourg, C. Seguin, G. Durrieu and P. Roché. Assisting the Automated Validation Process of User Interface Systems In *Proceedings of the 20th International Conference on Software Engineering (ICSE'98)*, Kyoto, Japan, 1998.
5. P. Caspi, D. Pilaud, N. Halbwachs and J. Plaice. Lustre: a declarative language for programming synchronous systems. in *14th ACM Symposium on Principles of Programming Languages*, January 1987.
6. D. Clément, T. Despeyroux, J. Incerpi, G. Kahn, B. Lang and V. Pascual. Centaur: the system. In *Proceedings of SIGSOFT'88. Third Annual Symposium on Software Development Environments (SDE3)*, Boston, 1988.
7. A.J. Dix. Formal methods for interactive systems. *Academic Press*, 1991.
8. A.J. Dix and G.D. Abowd. Modelling status and event behaviour of interactive systems. In *Software Engineering journal*, November 1996.
9. D.J. Duke and M.D. Harrison. Abstract interaction objetcs. *Computer Graphics Forum*,1993, 12, n°3, pp. 25-26.
10. D.J. Duke and M.D. Harrison. Event model of human system interaction. In *Software Engineering journal*, January 1995.
11. D.J. Duke, G. Faconti, M.D. Harrison and F. Paterno. Unifying views of interactors. In *Proceedings of Advance Visual Interface'94 Workshop*, Bari, 1994
12. M.D. Harrison and D.J. Duke. A review of formalisms for describing interactive behaviour. In *Proceedings of the ICSE'94 Workshop*, R.N Taylor and J. Coutaz, editors, *Software Engineering and Human Computer Interaction, LNCS 806*, May 1994.
13. G. Faconti and F. Paterno. An approach to the formal specification of the components of an interaction. In *Eurographics 90*, 1990.
14. N. Halbwachs, P. Caspi, P. Raymond and D. Pilaud. The synchronous dataflow programming language Lustre. In *Proceedings of IEEE*, number 9 in 79, pp. 1305–1320, September 1991.
15. N. Halbwachs, F. Lagnier and C. Ratel. Programming and verifying Real Time Systems by Means of the Synchronous DataFlow Programming Language Lustre. *IEEE Transactions on Software Engineering, Special Issue on the Specification and Analysis of Real Time Systems*, pp 795–793, Spetember 1992.
16. D. Heller, P. Ferguson and D. Brennan. *Motif Programming Manual*. O'Reilly and Associates Inc, February 1994.
17. F. Paterno and G. Faconti. On the use of Lotos to describe graphical interaction. In A. Monk, D.Diaper, and M.D. Harrison, editors, People and Computers VII; HCI'92 Conference, *BCS HCI Specialist Group, Cambridge University Press*, 1992.
18. F. Paterno and M. Mezzanotte. Formal verification of undesired behaviours in the CERD case study. In *Proceeedings EHCI'95 Conference*, Wyoming, August 1995.
19. D. Pilaud and N. Halbwachs. From a synchronous delarative language to a temporal logic dealing with multiform time. In *Symposium on Formal Techniques in Real Time and Fault Tolerant Systems*, Springer Verlag, September 1988.

Specification and Verification of Media Constraints using UPPAAL[*]

Howard Bowman[1], Giorgio P. Faconti[2] and Mieke Massink[3]

[1] Computing Lab., U. of Kent, Canterbury, Kent, CT2 7NF, UK
[2] CNR-Istituto CNUCE, Via S.Maria 36, 56126 - Pisa - Italy
[3] Dept. of Computer Science, U. of York, Heslington, York, YO1 5DD, UK

H.Bowman@ukc.ac.uk, G.Faconti@cnuce.cnr.it and M.Massink@guest.cnuce.cnr.it

Abstract. We present the formal specification and verification of a multimedia stream. The stream is described in a timed automata notation. We verify that the stream satisfies certain quality of service properties, in particular, throughput and end-to-end latency. The verification tool used is the real-time model checker UPPAAL.

1 Introduction

The acceptance and utility of a broad range of application systems is substantially affected by their ability to present information in an effective and appealing way to human users. Rapid progress in the development of multimedia technology promises more efficient forms of man/machine communication. However, the use of multimedia for conveying information does not guarantee effective and intelligible presentations per se. Appropriate design decisions must be drawn that lead to a fine grain coordination of communication media and modalities. This may even become a harder and more complex task than solving the application problem. Furthermore, in the vast majority of non-trivial applications the information needs will vary from user to user and from situation to situation. Consequently, a multimedia system should be able to flexibly generate various presentations for one and the same information content in order to meet individual requirements of users and situations, resource limitations of the computing system, and so forth.

In this respect, technology based techniques and models are just one out of many components contributing to the design of an interactive system. Other disciplines provide complementary views and perspectives on design problems and those contributions need to be related to one another to help support design reasoning and decisions. Different kinds of analysis contribute to augment the

---

[*] The first author is currently on leave at CNUCE under the support of the European Research Consortium for Informatics and Mathematics (ERCIM). The work is partially supported by the TACIT network under the European Union TMR Programme, contract ERB FMRX CT97 0133.

comprehension of a particular design space either by contributing complementary information or by providing criteria addressing equivalent requirements. In addition, some design issues may be raised by one particular kind of analysis from a discipline, but only solved if another kind of analysis is applied from another discipline.

In such a scenario, many system requirements are generated and derived from disciplines distant from technology and computer science such as semiotics and cognitive psychology. With the current state of the art in system design, these requirements cannot be bounded in a straightforward manner to a specific technology but require that system designers be informed both of *why* requirements have been formulated and *how* they can possibly be satisfied. Techniques for representing design decisions, and frameworks for communicating and contextualizing more analytic approaches into the practicalities of design exist already in the literature of both software engineering and human/computer interaction. Although significant conceptual progress has been made in both of these directions, their general application requires us to understand how the basic approaches can actually be used in practical settings; this remains an open issue.

Here, we refer to a particular class of interactive systems, namely Multi-Media Presentation Systems. This class of systems has been characterized in [5] where a Reference Model for Intelligent Multi-Media Presentation Systems is presented, integrating system concerns with the necessary representation of the contextualized knowledge about domain problem, design process, and user modeling. The model is abstract since it identifies the basic components of a presentation system and relates them. The details are addressed by specific models that are located in the abstract model, such as the Presentation Environment for Multimedia Objects [11]. Examples of applications that can be described are teleconferences and automatic generation of multimedia help systems, their distinguishing features being the *continuity* of the involved media, and the kind of *indirect interaction* with the media objects.

Interaction in these systems is indirect since it doesn't concern the manipulation of the media objects themselves (i.e. the video content); rather, it addresses the mechanisms influencing their presentation (i.e. compression/decompression algorithms, allocation of band) and the global quality of service. In [2], for example, it is suggested that audio/video quality of service be controlled by separate sliders each dealing with a specific parameter. The issue is that some parameters reflect perceivable properties of the media objects with no direct link to the underlying technology and it is difficult to predict the demand of computational resources required to achieve the quality of service set by the end-user.

Continuity refers to media streams conveying digital objects with associated time constraints, distinguishing these applications from traditional protocols. Usual techniques such as retransmission of data in case of faults or losses are no longer applicable and the verification of system throughput and latency against the time constraints becomes a must. As an example, Video/Audio streams must satisfy $inter-media\ synchronization$ constraints as in the case of the lip-synchronization. However, continuity plays also an important role in the context of a single media stream since it demands *intra − stream synchronization*, i.e. the relationship between media objects within the same data stream thus adding to throughput and latency a further constraint on jitter.

Consequently, timing plays an important role in multimedia presentation systems. The quality and the usability of those systems is crucially dependent on their performance with respect to timeliness. Often there is a trade-off between the quality of the presentation of multimodal information and the quality of service that can be offered by the medium over which the information is transported. Specification and verification of real-time aspects of (multi)media systems is however a difficult problem. The most common approach to building those systems is to implement new ideas directly in a prototype and to measure the performance. This approach is not always satisfactory. The complexity of the behaviour of the distributed algorithms is often considerable and their correctness is difficult to estimate by mere testing. Furthermore, it is often very hard to find the causes of rare errors and to improve the implementation accordingly. This has been illustrated for example in [10] where an Audio/Video protocol has been analyzed that had been developed in an industrial setting.

In this paper, we restrict our analysis to the investigation of a number of issues for the single data stream case. This allows us to set up a basic framework for further work on multi-(inter-)media synchronization while enabling the investigation of the capabilities and the practical use of formal notations and their associated tools with small size experiments.

2 A Simple Media Stream

The most basic requirement for supporting multimedia is to be able to define continuous flows of data; such structures are typically called *media streams* [4]. In this paper, we will discuss and illustrate a number of aspects related to media constraint modeling using such a multimedia stream.

The basic media stream is as depicted in figure 1. It has three top level components: a *Source*, a *Sink* and a *communication Medium* (which we will from now on simply refer to as the *Medium*). The scenario is that the *Source* process generates a continuous sequence of packets[1] which are relayed by the *Medium* to a *Sink* process which displays the packets. Three basic inter-process communication actions support the flow of data (see figure 1 again), *sourceout*, *sinkin* and *play*, which respectively transfer packets from the *Source* to the *Medium*, from the *Medium* to the *Sink* and display them at the *Sink*.

Formal descriptions of media streams have been given before, e.g. [4] etc. However to our knowledge, no formal verifications have been performed. This is one contribution of this paper.

The following informal description of the behaviour of the stream is kept similar to the LOTOS/QTL specification that appears in [4].

---

[1] These could be video frames, sound samples or any other item in a continuous media transmission. In this way the scenario remains completely generic. However, instantiation of data parameters will specialize the scenario.

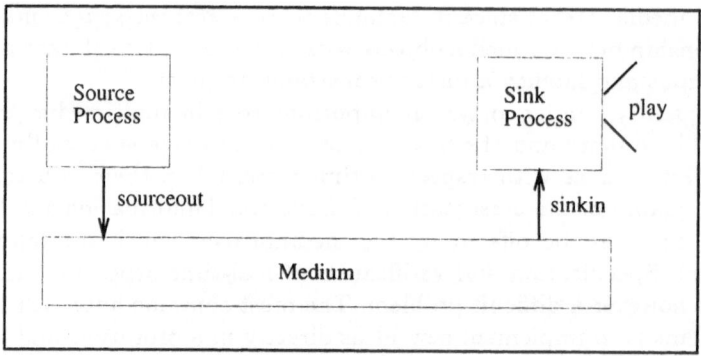

Fig. 1. A Multimedia Stream

- All communication between the *Source* and the *Sink* is asynchronous.
- The *Medium* is unreliable; it may loose and reorder packets.
- The *Source* transmits a packet every 50 ms (i.e. 20 packets per second).
- Packets that do not get lost arrive at the *Sink* between 80 ms and 90 ms after their transmission. This is the latency of the *Medium*.
- Whenever the *Sink* receives a packet, it needs 5 ms to process it, after which it is ready to receive the next packet.

In section 4, we will present an UPPAAL description of this basic behaviour. Then we focus on our main objective: to check that this system satisfies certain quality of service properties. Conceptually, these properties can be viewed as being derived from user presentation requirements. The quality of service properties that we wish to verify are:

1. **Throughput.** We would like to ensure that the *Sink* process receives packets at the rate of between:

    15 and 20 packets per second.

    Clearly, there is a direct link between the rate of loss of the *Medium* and the throughput at the *Sink*. Thus, the flavour of our investigation of this property will be to determine what are the bounds on the rate at which the *Medium* looses messages in order to satisfy this throughput property.
    We will also build into the system the possibility that it can go into an error state and halt, if the throughput property is invalidated.
2. **Latency.** We will check the following latency property:

    The end-to-end delay between a *sourceout* action and its corresponding *sinkin* action cannot be more than 95ms.

    which puts an upper bound on the end-to-end transmission delay.
3. **Jitter.** Jitter is defined as the variance of delay. It ensures that there is not an unacceptable variability around the optimum presentation time, e.g. if one packet is presented quite early and the next is presented relatively late

an unacceptable stutter in the presentation will result. A full analysis of jitter would require stochastic techniques [9] to be employed. This is clearly not possible with the verification technology we have available to us. However, placing both an upper and lower bound on the latency would impose a crude bound on jitter. Apart from noting that we could extend our latency analysis to do this, we do not consider the property any further in this paper.

3 Introduction to UPPAAL

UPPAAL is a tool-suite for the specification and automatic verification of real-time systems. It has been developed at BRICS in Denmark and at Uppsala University in Sweden. In UPPAAL a real-time system is modeled as a network of extended timed automata with global real-valued clocks and integer variables. The behaviour of a network of automata can be analyzed by means of the simulator and reachability properties can be checked by means of the model checker.

In UPPAAL, automata can be specified in two ways. Graphically by using the tool Autograph or textually by means of a normal text editor. The graphical specification can be used by the graphical simulator 'simta' or be automatically translated into textual form and used as input for the model checker 'verifyta' together with a file with requirements to be checked on the model. The requirements are formulas in a simple temporal logic language that allows for the formulation of reachability properties. The model checker indicates whether a property is satisfied or not. It the property is not satisfied a trace is provided that shows a possible violation of the property. This trace can be fed back to the simulator so that it can be analyzed with the help of the graphical presentation.

3.1 The UPPAAL model

UPPAAL automata consist of nodes and edges between the nodes. Both the nodes, which are called locations, and the edges, which are called transitions, are labeled. A network of automata consists of a number of automata and a definition of the configuration of the network. In the configuration the global real-time clocks, the integer variables, the communication channels and the composition of the network are defined.

The labels on edges are composed of three optional components:

- a *guard* on clocks and data variables expressing under which condition the transition can be performed. Absence of a guard is interpreted as the condition *true*.
- a synchronization or internal *action* that is performed when the transition is taken. In case the action is a synchronization action then synchronization with a complementary action in another automaton is enforced following similar synchronization rules as in CCS [14]. Given channel name a, a! and a? denote complementary actions corresponding to *sending* respectively *receiving* on the channel a. Absence of a synchronization action is interpreted as an internal action similar to τ-actions in CCS.

– a number of *clock resets* and *assignments to integer variables*

The label of locations consists also of three parts:

– the *name* of the location which is obligatory.
– an *invariant* expressing constraints on clock values, indicating the period during which control can remain in that particular location.
– an optional marking of the location by putting **c:** in front of its name indicating the location as *committed*. This option is useful to model atomicity of transition-sequences. When control is in a committed location the next transition must be performed (if any) without any delay or interleaving of other actions.

In the configuration, the following aspects of the network are defined:

– declarations of global clock and integer variables
– the channel names that are the names of the actions. Channels can be defined as normal communication channels or *urgent* channels. When a channel is urgent no timing constraints can be defined on the transition labeled by that channel and no invariant can be defined on the location from which that transition leaves. Urgent actions have to happen as soon as possible, i.e. without delay, but interleaving of other actions is allowed if this does not cause delays.
– the list of names of automata the system is composed of.

Formally, the states of an UPPAAL model are of the form $(\bar{l}, v)$, where $\bar{l}$ is a *control vector* and v a *value assignment*. The control vector indicates the current control location for each component of the network. The value assignment gives the current value for each clock and integer variable. All clocks proceed at the same speed. There are three types of transitions in an UPPAAL model:

Internal transitions Such transitions can occur when an automaton in the network is at a location in which it can perform an internal action. The guard of that transition has to be satisfied and there must be no other transitions enabled that start from a committed location.
Synchronization A synchronization transition can occur when there are two automata which are in locations that can perform complementary actions. The guards of both transitions must be satisfied and there must be no other transitions enabled that start from a committed location.
Delay A delay transition can occur when no urgent transitions are enabled, none of the current control locations is a committed location and the delay is allowed by the invariants of the current control locations.

An example of an UPPAAL specification is given in Figure 2. The transition between *s1* and *s2* can only be taken when the value of clock y is greater than or equal to 3. This holds also for the transition between *r1* and *r2* because the automata *A* and *B* are synchronized on channel *a*. The transition *must* happen

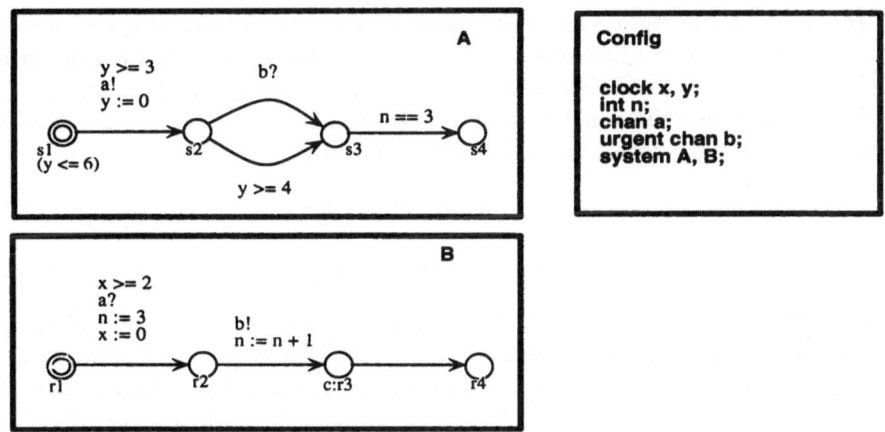

Fig. 2. Example of an UPPAAL specification

before y is equal to 6 because of the invariant at location *s1*. If this invariant would not be there control could have remained in *s1* and in *r1* indefinitely.

When control is in *s2* and *r2* the only transition that is possible is the synchronization on action b. This is because b has been declared as an *urgent* channel in the configuration. Note that if the guard $y >= 4$ would not have been labeling the transition between *s2* and *s3* in A both transitions between those two locations would have been enabled! This is because urgency only prevents the passing of time, but does not prevent the occurrence of other actions that are enabled at the same time. To prevent interleaving actions in this case the location *r2* can be annotated as a committed location. This forces the action b to happen without delay or interference of other actions.

3.2 Simulation and Model Checking

The future behaviour of a network of timed automata is fully determined by its state, i.e. the control vector $\bar{l}$, and the value of all its clocks and data variables. Clearly this leads to a model with infinitely many states. The interesting observation made by Alur and Dill was that states with the same $\bar{l}$ but with slightly different clock values have runs starting from $\bar{l}$ that are "very similar". Alur and Dill described exactly how to derive the sets of clock values for which the model shows "similar" behaviour [1]. The sets of clock values are called *time regions*. Regions can be derived from the guards, the invariants and the reset-sets in the UPPAAL model. Since clock variables in the constraints are always compared with integers and because in every model there is a maximum integer with which a clock is compared the state space of a model can be partitioned into finitely many regions. This makes model checking for dense time decidable.

In UPPAAL the regions are characterized by simple constraint systems which are conjunctions of atomic clock and data constraints. Details on the calculation of these constraint sets for simulation and model checking can be found in [15].

The properties that can be analyzed by the model checker are reachability properties. They are formulas of the following form:

$$\Phi ::= A\,[]\,\beta \mid E <> \beta$$

$$\beta ::= a \mid \beta_1 \text{ and } \beta_2 \mid \beta_1 \text{ or } \beta_2 \mid \beta_1 \text{ implies } \beta_2 \mid \text{ not } \beta$$

where a is an atomic formula of the form: $A_i.l$ where A_i is an automaton and l a location of A_i or $v_i \sim n$ where v_i is a variable, n a natural number and $\sim$ a relation in $\{<, <=, >, >=, ==\}$. The basic temporal logic operators are, $A\,[]$ and $E <>$, where, informally, $A\,[]\,\beta$ requires all reachable states to satisfy β and $E <> \beta$ requires at least one reachable state to satisfy β.

Although the final aim of the developers of UPPAAL is to develop a modeling language that is as close as possible to a high-level real-time programming language with various data types the, current version is rather restrictive. For example it does not allow assignment of variables to other variables and there is no value-passing in the communication.

Despite these restrictions, quite a number of case-studies have been performed in UPPAAL ranging from small examples to real industrial case studies, e.g. [3, 7, 12].

4 Stream example formalized in UPPAAL

4.1 The basic model

Consider the stream example introduced in section 2. The simplest part of the example is the *Source*. In the informal specification it is said that a packet is sent every 50 ms. To make this more precise we assume that the first packet is sent at time equal 0 and all later packets exactly 50 ms one after the other. This behaviour is modeled as an UPPAAL automaton with two locations. The initial location (indicated by a double circle) is annotated as committed to enforce that the first packet (*sourceout!*) is sent immediately. To assure that every following packet is sent exactly 50 ms after the previous one, a clock $t1$ is introduced. The guard $t1 == 50$ enables the sending of *sourceout* at exactly 50 ms after the last one. The invariant at *State*1 enforces that the enabled transition really happens at $t1 == 50$. When the transition is performed $t1$ is reset and the behaviour repeats itself.

The *Sink* is required to always accept a packet, except when it is playing a packet. Whenever it receives a packet it plays it immediately during the next 5 ms. This behaviour is modeled by another automaton with two locations. In the initial location the automaton waits for a packet from the medium. When it arrives a timer $t2$ is set that is used to model the 5 ms delay caused by playing of the packet before control returns to the initial location.

The third part to model is the medium. What is known of the medium is that it acts as an infinite buffer, it has a latency of between 80 ms and 90 ms, it may loose and reorder packets. At first sight we should model the medium as an infinite structure. However, if we are only interested in the throughput of the medium, the order in which packets arrive is irrelevant. What *is* relevant is that we model the medium in such a way that it always allows the *Source* to perform the next *sourceout*. We will show that the medium can be modeled by two independent one-place-buffers. We first model the medium assuming that it does not loose packets. Each buffer is modeled as an automaton with two locations (see Figure 3). At the initial location the buffer can receive a *sourceout* from the *Source*. At that point a timer is started to model the latency of the medium. The *sinkin* action following the *sourceout* is delayed by at least 80 ms and at most 90 ms.

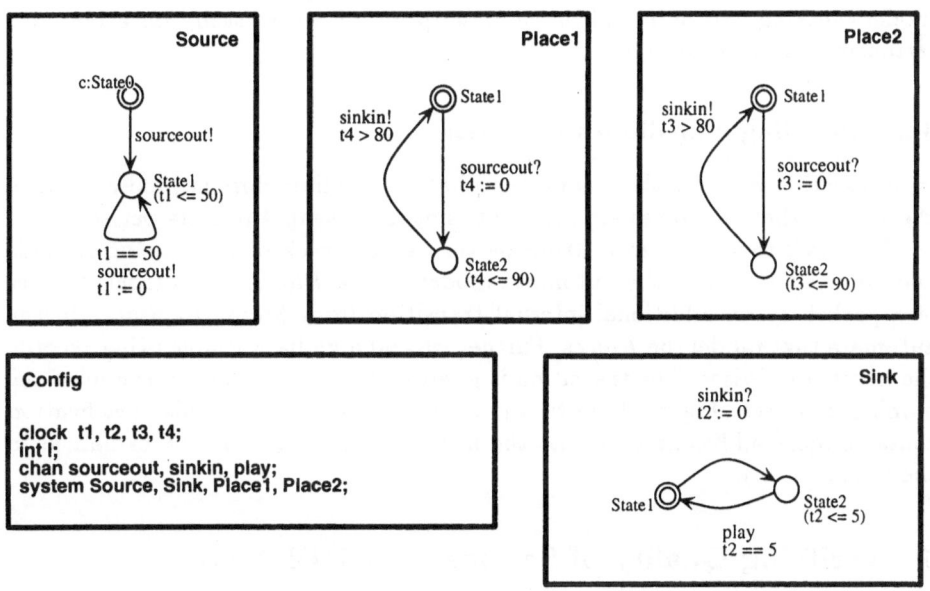

Fig. 3. UPPAAL specification of media stream

To be sure that it was correct to model the medium by only two one-place-buffers, we should prove that it is never the case that when the *Source* wishes to perform a *sourceout*, i.e. when $t1 == 50$, both one-place-buffers are full, i.e. they are in location *State2*. In UPPAAL this situation can be formalized as:

$$E <> (t1 == 50 \text{ and } Place1.State2 \text{ and } Place2.State2)$$

which using the UPPAAL model checker can be shown not to hold.

It is important to note however that the minimal number of *Places* needed to guarantee that the *Source* can always send its packet depends on the time constraints used in the model. If the time between packets at the *Source* would be less than 45 ms there are going to be problems. In our model we can easily verify this by means of the reachability property we formulated before. In this example it is not difficult to find a general formula that gives the minimal number of *Places* needed as a function of the time between the packets and the maximal latency. Let p be the number of *Places*, m the maximal latency and d the interval time between packets sent by the *Source* then:

$$p = \lceil m/d \rceil \qquad (+)$$

In general however, time dependent behaviour can be very hard to predict and a model checker can be helpful to get a good intuition about the relations that hold between parameters of the system. An interesting illustration of this use of model checking can be found in the description of a case study on a bounded retransmission protocol [7].

4.2   Modeling a medium with losses

In this section we relax the assumption that the medium does not loose packets. We assume that the losses are limited to not more than 4 packets per second.

To model this we need a *Monitor* that keeps track of the passing seconds and we need to adapt the automata modeling the *Places*. We model the loss of a packet by an additional internal transition from *State2* to *State1* in the automata that model the *Places*. Further we add a global variable l that records the number of losses. The transition is guarded by a constraint on the maximal number of losses. Figure 4 shows the new medium (in fact, this specification contains more additions than just the new medium; these will be explained in the next section).

5   Verifying Quality of Service with UPPAAL

In this section we investigate how the quality of service properties identified earlier in this paper can be verified using UPPAAL.

5.1   Throughput

Let us assume that the throughput of the medium is checked every second and when it is below the threshold of 15 packets per second an *error* is signaled.

The number of packets that arrive at the *Sink* is counted by a global variable x which is updated every time a *sinkin* action occurs. The *Monitor* checks the variable x every second. If the throughput is sufficient then x is reset and the timer starts again. If the throughput is too low an urgent action *error* is generated. As soon as the *Sink* reaches state *State1* it will synchronize on the *error* action and the media stream will be stopped. In Figure 4 the automata for the *Monitor* and the *Sink* are shown.

The *Monitor* that we present only forces an *error* if too few frames arrive, i.e. if $x < 15$, this is because the possibility of too many frames arriving, i.e. $x > 20$, cannot arise because of the parameters of the system. However, if it was necessary we could easily add an extra branch in the transition system which caters for this situation.

In addition, we can use UPPAAL to determine the parameters that bound our throughput property. Specifically, we can check under what circumstances our specification satisfies the formula:

$$E <> (Sink.Stop)$$

Satisfaction of this formula implies that our throughput requirement does not hold. As suggested earlier, the obvious parameter that affects throughput is the rate of loss in the medium. Using UPPAAL we can show that if the constraint $l < 4$ is associated with the *loss* action in the medium, as it is in figure 4, then the *Stop* state can be reached, and UPPAAL provides a sample trace. However, if we change the constraint to $l < 3$ then the *Stop* state cannot be reached. Thus, this gives us a clear bound on the number of errors that an acceptable medium should allow.

A subtle point that arises from this specification is that since *State*1 in *Sink* has two outgoing transitions, *error* and *sinkin*, if *State*1 is reached at a time point in which both transitions are enabled then even though *error* is an urgent action, either transition may be taken. This would clearly be undesirable as one would like the system to stop as soon as it is in *error*. However, using UPPAAL an analysis can be made that shows that as long as the *Source* is transmitting at a rate of a frame every 50 ms then this situation cannot arise (interestingly, if it was transmitting at the rate of a frame every 53 ms the situation could indeed arise).

5.2 Verifying Latency

Although in fact, upper and lower bounds for latency of the stream can be very easily discerned by inspection from the automata specification given, this will not always be the case. In fact, in real world systems, communication mediums have highly complex real-time behaviour. For example, there may be a number of different potential routes that frames can take, each accumulating very different latency delays. Furthermore, in the presence of congestion, analysis of latency is far from straightforward. Thus, even though analysing latency is rather superfluous in our stream scenario, it is a valuable exercise to determine the suitability of UPPAAL in this respect.

The first thing to note is that in order to express our latency requirement we must relate corresponding *sourceout* and *play* actions. In order to do this some means of identifying corresponding packets, e.g. by means of time stamps or sequence numbers, must be included.

272

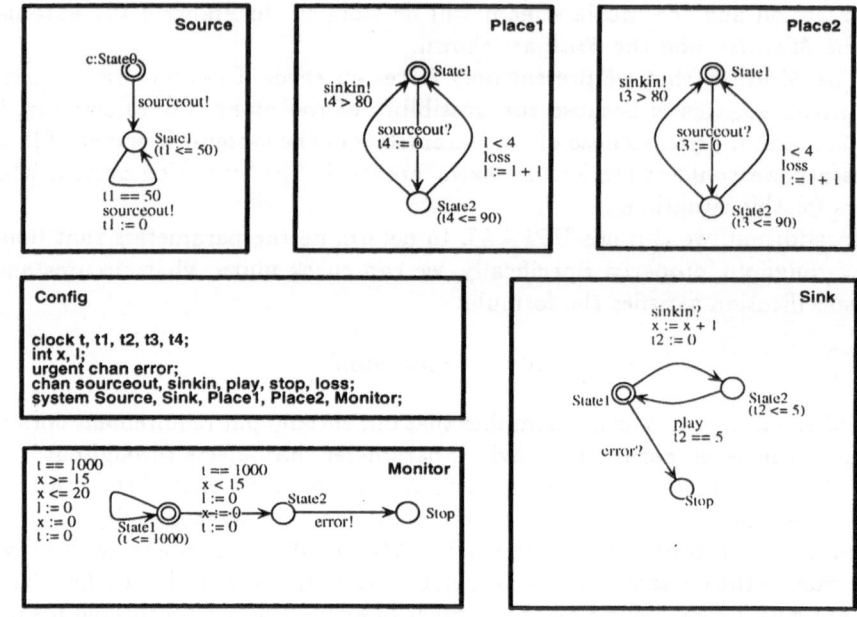

Fig. 4. UPPAAL specification of mediastream with QoS *Monitor*

So, let us formulate our basic latency property with the required sequence numbering. The obvious property that we would like to verify is:

$$\forall x \in \mathbb{N} \,.\, (\Box(play(x) \Rightarrow \Diamond_{\leq 95}\, sourceout(x)))$$

where the operators used are linear time temporal logic operators [13], which contrast with the branching time operators used in UPPAAL. $\Box P$ is the always/henceforth operator (i.e. in the future it is always the case that P holds), $\Rightarrow$ is logical implication and $\Diamond_{\leq t} P$ is a past tense operator stating that, P must hold no more than t time units before the current moment. So, the formula states that it is always the case that, if a *play* occurs then at some point not more than $95ms$ before a *sourceout* must have taken place. The significance of the past operator is that it allows for loss in the system, i.e. it only enforces a timing constraint on the *plays* that arise from successfully received packets.

However, this property cannot be verified using UPPAAL. There are two reasons for this.

1. Infinite data sets, such as the natural numbers; and
2. expressing data passing actions

are not supported at present by UPPAAL.

We will show how to handle the second of these difficulties shortly, but for the moment, let us concentrate on the first. The problem is that we need to bound the set of sequence numbers used and in fact, it will greatly simplify the resulting automaton and the state space explosion problem if we can keep the size of this bound very small.

What we would like to ensure is that we have a sufficient number of sequence numbers that we do not get two packets with the same sequence number in the system at the same time. This is a similar requirement to the bounding of the size of the medium investigated in section 4.1. In fact, we can use formula $(+)$ stated there to derive that two sequence numbers are sufficient in a correctly behaving system. Importantly though, we replace m in the formula with the *desired* latency value rather than the known one.

Having decided that two sequence numbers, i.e. 1 and 0, will be sufficient we have to adapt our automata specification accordingly. Now as already noted, actions in UPPAAL are not data passing however, we can get the effect of data passing actions by including a more discriminating set of actions and including extra transitions[2]. The *Sink* in Figure 5 is a good illustration of the approach. Specifically, rather than refering to actions *sinkin* and *play* as was the case in our earlier formulations of the stream, now it refers to actions *sinkin0?*, *sinkin1?*, *play0?* and *play1?*. Thus, we have flattened out our data type into a more discriminating set of action names.

The formula that we would like to verify over this automata is:

$$\forall x \in \{0, 1\} . (\Box(play(x) \Rightarrow \Diamond_{\leq 95} sourceout(x)))   \quad (*)$$

Unfortunately a further problem remains: UPPAAL does not support past operators[3]. We could though reformulate the property as:

$$\forall x \in \{0, 1\} . (\Box(sourceout(x) \Rightarrow \Diamond_{\leq 95} (play(x) \lor loss(x))))   \quad (*)$$

which avoids the past operator. However we prefer an alternative approach that avoids the reference to *loss*. This is because latency is an end-to-end property and formulating in terms of actions local to components of the communication path seems conceptually unsatisfactory. Thus, we would like to view the medium as a black box and formulate our property purely in terms of the "end-point" actions *sourceout* and *play*.

In order to do this, let us consider the interplay between loss and latency. In the presence of congestion, loss will relieve congestion and thus allowing loss will implicitly reduce latency values. Thus, a reasonable strategy is to determine upper bounds on latency on a stream specification which does not allow loss, knowing that if it is added, this bound will still be valid. This is the strategy that we adopt.

---

[2] This is in fact a standard approach in process algebras for getting from a data passing calculus to a basic calculus, see for example [14].

[3] Actually, there is in any case a rather subtle problem with this formula, to do with the interplay between the possibility to loose messages and not knowing the end-to-end latency.

So, let us work with a basic medium which does not contain the possibility to loose packets. The medium is as shown in Figure 5.

Now the property that we have to check is:

$$\forall x \in \{0, 1\} . (\Box(sourceout(x) \Rightarrow \Diamond_{\leq 95} play(x)))$$

which can, in the standard way, be expanded out to avoid the universal quantifier, which is not supported in UPPAAL (note: we write $a(n)$ as an in order to match action denotations in the automaton).

$$\Box(sourceout0 \Rightarrow \Diamond_{\leq 95} play0) \ \wedge \ \Box(sourceout1 \Rightarrow \Diamond_{\leq 95} play1)$$

However, this is not a reachability property and can thus, not be directly verified using UPPAAL. A strategy outlined in [12] can though be used to verify such a "bounded liveness" property using reachability analysis. The approach is to derive a testing automaton from the property using a form of tableau algorithm, compose the testing automaton in parallel with the system and verify a simple reachability property. This strategy is not yet implemented in the UPPAAL tool, so the automaton has been derived by hand using the informal algorithms to be found in the literature [12].

The bounded liveness properties accepted by the testing automaton approach are expressed in a different logic to any that we have seen so far: STL, a timed modal logic. Our property can, with relative ease, be expressed in this logic however, rather than introduce another logic, we will go straight to the testing automaton that is derived from the formula. It is shown in Figure 5 along with the full revised stream specification. In fact, this is the scenario used to check that *sourceout0*s and *play0*s are correctly matched. A similar approach can be used to check *sourceout1*'s and *play1*'s.

Note that *sgout0* is a probe action that has been inserted at appropriate places in the system. It is inserted (using a committed state) to signal the occurrence of *sourceout*s to the test automaton.

The property that we check is:

$$E <> (Tester.bad)$$

which, when checked with UPPAAL does, as would be hoped, fail to hold. However as indicated earlier, this is not a very interesting result because it is directly deducible by inspection of the system. Thus, the contribution of this section is not this verification, but rather the investigation of a general strategy for checking latency which can be applied to systems that are not so easily interpreted. It is clear that the strategy we have documented is indeed generally applicable.

6 Concluding Remarks

We have investigated the suitability of UPPAAL for the verification of multimedia systems. The specification and analysis of a simple multimedia stream

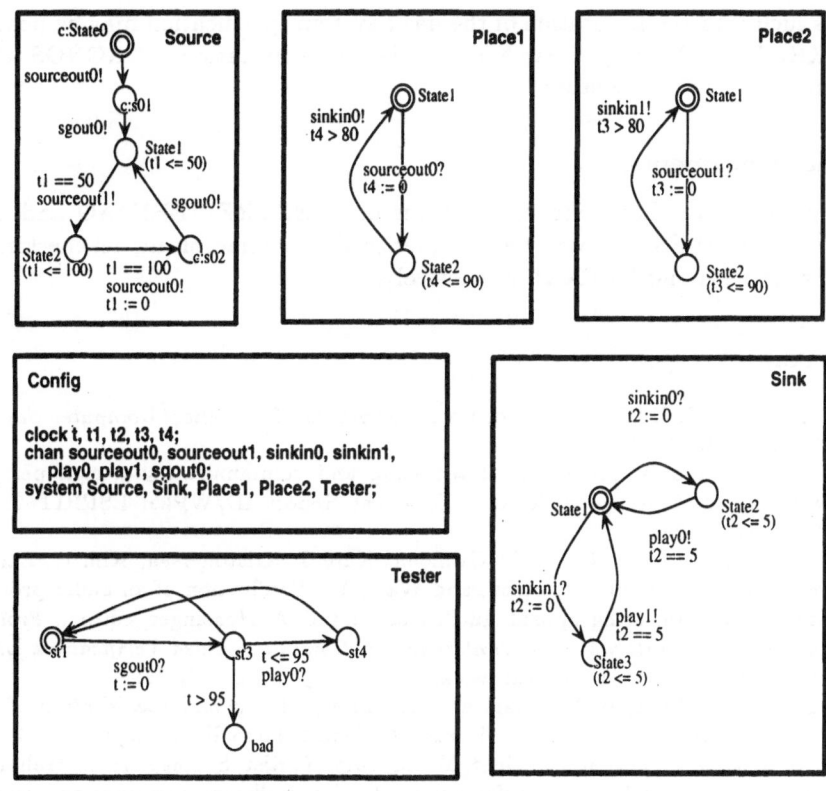

Fig. 5. The Stream with Testing Automata

was presented for this purpose. The main results of this paper are the identification of generally applicable strategies for checking real-time quality of service properties, specifically, checking throughput and latency.

Although our experiences with UPPAAL have generally been favourable, some criticisms of the approach can be highlighted. [6] considers a number of such criticisms. One criticism is though particularly worth considering here as it arises directly from our case study. It is that due to expressiveness limitations of the temporal logic accepted by the UPPAAL model checker it is difficult to directly verify the standard temporal logic formulations of quality of service, rather the basic system specification has to be adapted in order that checking the property can be reduced to checking a reachability property. This can most noticeably be seen in the latency verification where the basic system specification has to be adapted through composition of a test automata and addition of probe actions. Consequently the verification is not "transparent" to the behavioural specification.

Other real-time model checking tools, in particular KRONOS [8], support a richer set of temporal logic properties. Thus, we hope that verification that avoids such invasive adaptation of the basic system specification may be possible with KRONOS. Ongoing research is investigating application of KRONOS to the multimedia stream case study.

Acknowledgements

We would like to thank Stavros Tripakis of SPECTRE-VERIMAG and Paul Pettersson of UPPSALA who fielded queries that we had on model checking of timed automata and UPPAAL respectively.

References

1. R. Alur and D. Dill. A theory of timed automata. *Theoretical Computer Science*, (126):183–235, 1994.
2. V. Bellotti and A. MacLean. Integrating and communicating design perspectives with QOC design rationale. Technical Report ID/WP29, ESPRIT 7040 - AMODEUS, 1994.
3. Johan Bengtsson, W. O. David Griffioen, Kåre J. Kristoffersen, Kim G. Larsen, Fredrik Larsson, Paul Pettersson, and Wang Yi. Verification of an audio protocol with bus collision using uppaal. In R. Alur and T. A. Henzinger, editors, *Proceedings of the 8th International Conference on Computer-Aided Verification*, LNCS 1102, pages 244–256, New Brunswick, New Jersey, USA, July 1996.
4. G.S. Blair, L. Blair, H. Bowman, and A. Chetwynd. *Formal Specification of Distributed Multimedia Systems*. University College London Press, September 1997.
5. M. Bordegoni, G. Faconti, S.Feiner, M.Maybury, T. Rist, S. Ruggieri, P. Trahanias, and M. Wilson. A standard reference model for intelligent presentation systems. *Computer Standards and Interfaces*, 1998.
6. H. Bowman, G. Faconti, J-P. Katoen, D. Latella, and M. Massink. Automatic verification of a lip synchronisation algorithm using UPPAAL. *Accepted at FMICS'98*, Amsterdam, The Netherlands, May 1998.
7. P.R. D'Argenio, J.-P. Katoen, T.C. Ruys, and J. Tretmans. The bounded retransmission protocol must be on time! In *Proceedings of the 3rd International Workshop on Tools and Algorithms for the Construction and Analysis of Systems*, LNCS 1217, pages 416–431, Enschede, The Netherlands, April 1997.
8. C. Daws, A. Olivero, S. Tripakis, and S. Yovine. The tool KRONOS. In *Hybrid Systems III, LNCS 1066*. Springer-Verlag, 1996.
9. P.G. Harrison and N.M. Patel. *Performance Modelling of Communication Networks and Computer Architectures*. Addison-Wesley, 1993.
10. Klaus Havelund, Arne Skou, Kim G. Larsen, and Kristian Lund. Formal modelling and analysis of an audio/video protocol: An industrial case study using uppaal. In *Proceedings of the 18th IEEE Real-Time Systems Symposium*, pages 2–13, San Francisco, California, USA, 3-5 December 1997.
11. I. Herman, G. Reynolds, and J. Van Loo. PREMO: An emerging standard for multimedia. part i: Overview and framework. *IEEE MultiMedia*, 3:83–89, 1996.
12. Henrik Ejersbo Jensen, Kim G. Larsen, and Arne Skou. Modelling and analysis of a collision avoidance protocol using spin and uppaal. In *Proceedings of the 2nd SPIN Workshop*, Rutgers University, New Jersey, USA, August 1996.
13. Z. Manna and A. Pnueli. *The Temporal Logic of Reactive and Concurrent Systems*. Springer-Verlag, 1992.

14. R. Milner. *Communication and Concurrency*. Prentice-Hall, 1989.
15. Wang Yi, Paul Pettersson, and Mats Daniels. Automatic verification of real-time communicating systems by constraint solving. In *Proceedings of the 7th International Conference on Formal Description Techniques*, Berne, Switzerland, 4-7 October 1994.

Modelling direct manipulation
with
Referent and Statecharts[1]

Hallvard Trætteberg

Department of Computer and Information Sciences
The Norwegian University of Science and Technology
Trondheim, 7034 NTNU - Trondheim, Norway

Abstract. An approach to modelling mouse gestures in direct manipulation interfaces is presented. The Referent and Statechart languages are used for modelling structure and behaviour, respectively. A gesture is divided into a series of steps, driven by user action and aided by feedback, all modelled as Statechart states. The Referent describes dynamic relations between these states. The states and transitions determine the gesture syntax and the actual relations established and changed during recognition. We discuss how reasoning about these models can support the design of composite gesture recognisers and provide consistency checking and design critique.

1. Introduction

Direct manipulation interfaces are characterised by providing a more natural way of interacting with computers than command line, forms and menu interfaces [1]. The desktop interface of the Macintosh Finder™ and Windows 95™, with files, folders and windows give direct manipulation access to the most commonly used functionality of the file system, including moving, copying and renaming files. Similarly, applications for drawing pictures and charts, like TopDown Flowcharter™ and Visio™ provides direct manipulation modes for the most common editing tasks, including creating, moving and resizing objects. These are all mass-market products with hand-coded user interfaces. However, most applications built with visual development tools still use menus, forms and buttons for interaction.

Several reasons can be suggested for this difference:
- Most applications cannot gain from providing direct manipulation interaction techniques.
- Programming direct manipulation interfaces is too time-consuming and costly for low volume applications and is left to mass-market products like the ones mentioned.
- Development tools do not provide practical means for building direct manipulation interfaces.
- There is a lack of developer-friendly models for describing such interfaces.

Although true for some applications, we generally object to the first of these. The other three are valid reasons for the lack of direct manipulation in most applications and the high cost of implementing direct manipulation interaction techniques. User interface modelling [2] can provide the necessary tools for making such interfaces easier to de-

---

[1] This work is part of project 116388/410, funded by the Norwegian Research Council.

sign and implement. However, most of the current modelling efforts concentrate on dialogues and presentation, few of them focus on the gesture recognition aspect of user interfaces.

In this paper we describe an approach for mouse gesture recognition modelling, based on the Referent [3] and Statechart [4] modelling languages. Although we focus on mouse gestures, the approach is general enough to handle combinations of mice and other devices. Besides presenting the specific approach, we also hope to illustrate the general advantage of using formal modelling languages for user interface development.

The following section will introduce an example mouse gesture, and some initial reflections about mouse gesture recognition will be presented. In section 3, a simple application architecture will be introduced, to establish a context for the gesture recogniser. Then, a classification of elements of a generic gesture recogniser and its structure will be modelled in the Referent language and its behaviour in a dialect of Statechart, that is integrated with Referent. In section 4, the advantage of using such formal languages will be illustrated by exemplifying how design support can be provided by reasoning about models. The paper will conclude with a comparison to similar work and some suggestions for further work with the approach.

2. A mouse gesture example

To introduce the various aspects of mouse gesture recognition, this section presents a mouse gesture example. This kind of mouse gesture is found in most desktop interfaces to file systems, and this particular variant is found in Microsoft's Active Desktop™. The table below illustrates and explains the main steps of the gesture.

This example reveals several important points about gesture recognition in general:
- The gesture was sensitive to the file and folder icons, i.e.a gesture can depend on the set of *displayed elements*.
- The gesture recognised the relation between mouse pointer position and icon area, i.e. a gesture must be able to detect display element *hits*.
- The feedback included *changing* the cursor, *highlighting* displayed elements and *displaying* copies of displayed elements, i.e. a gesture must have access to the display system.
- The gesture is completed by issuing a command to the operating system, i.e. the gesture must have an interface to a command executing facility.

The Active Desktop™ interface support two related gestures used for opening files and applications and moving file icons. The relation between these three gestures, identify some further points:
- If the mouse button was released outside of the folder icon, the file *icon* would move and not the file itself, suggesting that a *different* command was issued.
- If the mouse button was released before having moved the file icon at all, a third command would be executed, suggesting that not only the release *target* mattered, but also the release *timing*.

At this point the reader will have noticed that we have adopted a command oriented execution model as used in CLIM [5], as opposed to a side-effect oriented one, as used in Garnet [6]. In the former model the meaning of the gesture is only *suggested* by the feedback, the *actual* semantic interpretation is implemented by an executor outside the gesture recogniser, which is activated when the gesture (recognition) is completed. This gives a cleaner separation of user interface functionality, and provides better support for e.g., macro recording and scripting.

Step	User action	Feedback
file folder	The mouse pointer starts outside both icons.	The mouse pointer is an arrow and no icon is highlighted.
file folder	The user moves the mouse pointer over the file icon.	The mouse pointer changes from an arrow to a hand and the file icon is highlighted.
file file folder	The user presses the left mouse button and moves the mouse pointer towards the folder icon	The mouse pointer changes to an arrow and a dimmed (copy of the) file icon follows the mouse pointer.
file file folder	The user moves the mouse pointer over the folder icon.	The folder icon is highlighted.
folder	The user releases the left mouse button.	The feedback is removed, the Move file to folder command is executed and the desktop is updated.

Table 1: Move file to folder gesture

The gesture example and the two variants described above, demonstrate three important points:
- The actual command that is issued is not necessarily determined until it is issued, i.e. after the last gesture step.
- The command parameters can be a function of several aspects of the gesture, e.g., mouse position of button release, display elements that are hit when pressing or releasing the button or the objects that these represent.
- The actual gesture aspects that are used as command parameters, can be determined both at the same time as the command and not before.

The next section will introduce our approach to modelling the identified aspects and its role within an application and its user interface.

3. Modelling of gesture recognition

In this section, gesture recognition is discussed in the context of an application and its user interface. A simple model representing (one way of structuring) an application's structure and its execution model will be presented. Much can be said and argued about this specific model (see [7] for a general discussion of architectures). Since the main purpose is to provide a context for the gesture recogniser, we leave this discussion to the concluding section.

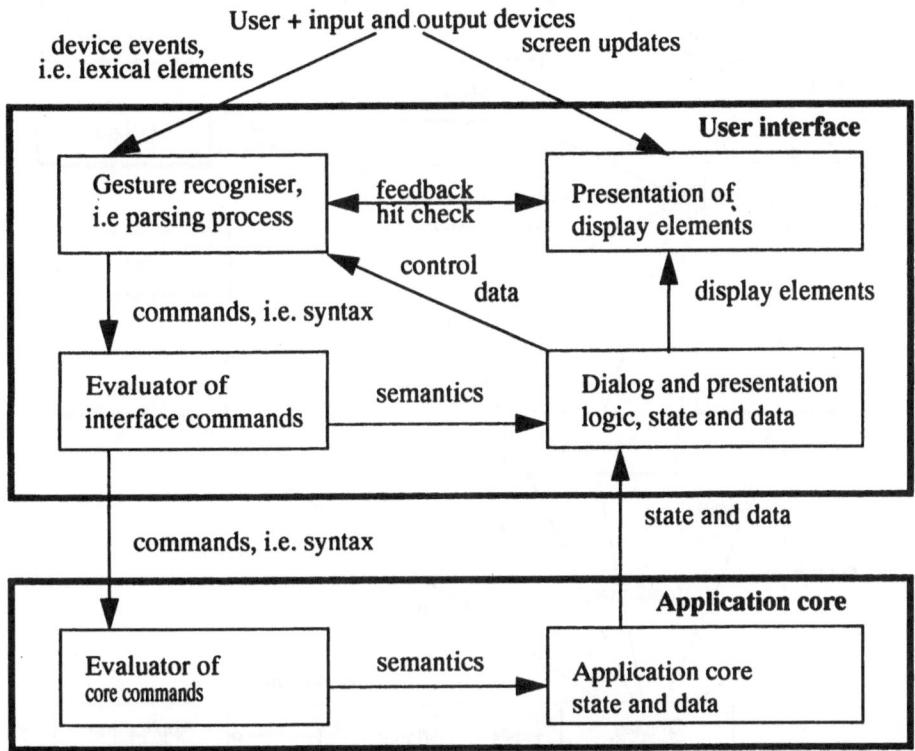

Fig. 1. Application architecture

3.1 Gestures in user interfaces

A *user interface* can be thought of as a mediator of information and actions between an *application core* and a *user*. Together the interface and the core constitutes the application. The user and application has to their disposal a set of devices, e.g., display, keyboard and mouse, to support communication. The display contains a *presentation* of *display elements* to indicate the application's state and information content. The user generates a stream of *events* by manipulating the *input devices* to indicate her intentions. Gesture *recognition* can be thought of as a *parsing* process, where the events as *lexical* elements are assembled and interpreted according to a *syntax*. The intention of each parsed gesture is represented by a *command*, the *semantics* of which is defined by a set of *evaluators*. Figure 1 illustrates the gesture recognition process and surrounding elements.

As indicated, the gesture recogniser communicates with several other components:
• The dialogue component has overall control, e.g., the set of commands that are legal

282

in the current context, current mode etc.
- The presentation unit can be queried to detect object hits and requested to give feedback during recognition.
- The evaluators receive commands and provide their semantics by executing them.

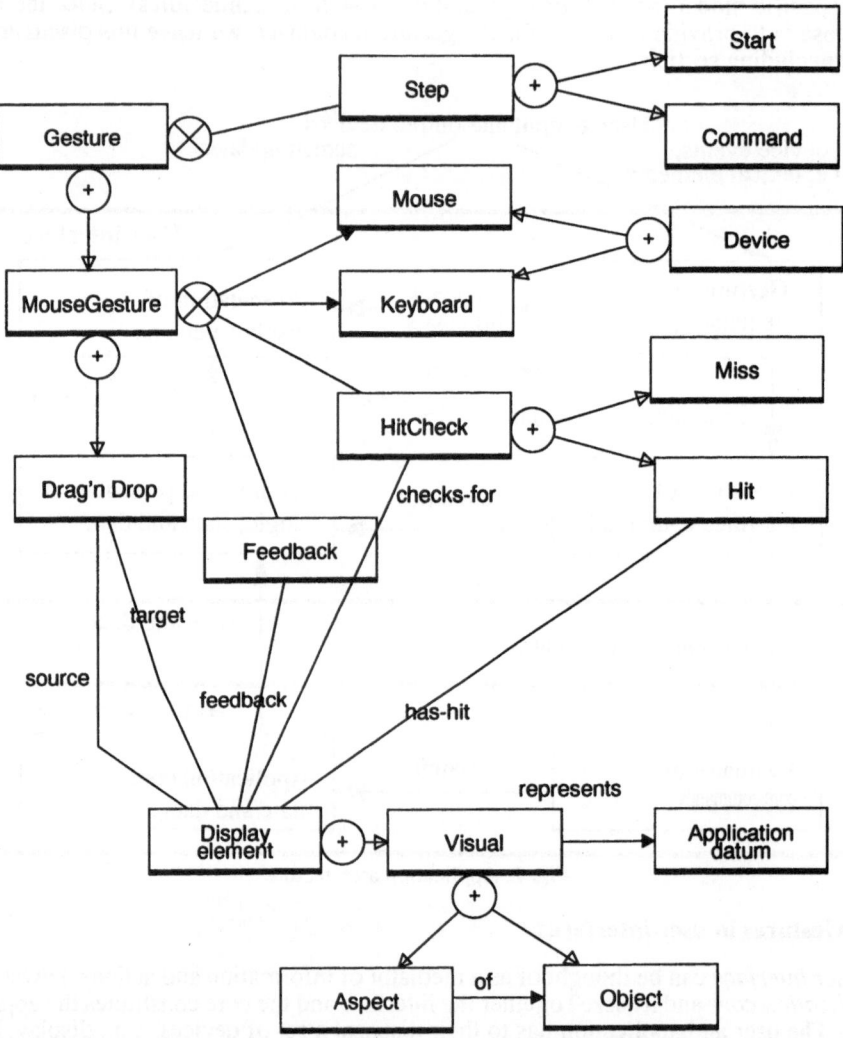

Fig. 2. Aspects and elements of gesture recognisers

Using the Referent and Statechart languages, the structure and behaviour of the gesture recogniser will be detailed in the next sections. We will see that Referent is used for modelling structure, as well as relating the gesture to other models, e.g., domain and user interface models. It will also be an aid when modelling the dynamic behaviour with Statechart.

3.2 Structure of recognisers

The previous section identified several important features needed in a gesture recogniser, e.g., cursor feedback and highlighting, hit checks, commands and their parameters, mouse handling, presentation and display elements. Figure 2 shows a Referent model of these aspects and elements.

Since few are familiar with the Referent language and notation, it will be briefly introduced in this section.For more comprehensive introduction, see the Referent Model homepage at http://www.idi.ntnu.no/~ppp/referent/. The language was developed for conceptual modelling and is based on concepts as sets (rectangles with thick baseline) of elements (rounded rectangle) and relations (segmented lines) between them. Figure 2 among others, defines the concepts GESTURE, MOUSEGESTURE and DRAG'NDROP. These concepts are related through specialisation, i.e. the set of MOUSEGESTURES is a subset of the set of GESTURES. By grouping several subset relations using a circle, we can express that the subsets are disjoint (+) or overlapping (⊆). Hence, the DEVICE set is a *superset*, i.e. generalisation, of MOUSE and KEYBOARD and a device *element* must be *either* of these. The part-of and element-of relations are similarly grouped, using (×) and (∈), respectively. The end of relations indicates cardinality; a filled arrow indicates one and no arrow many. Hence a MOUSEGESTURE, which is a specialisation of GESTURE, has one MOUSE, one KEYBOARD, and several HITCHECKs and FEEDBACKs.

The main features of figure 2 are the hierarchy of GESTURES, the set of GESTURE parts and their relation to DISPLAYELEMENTs. A generic GESTURE has a set of STEPs and is a superset of MOUSEGESTURE. DRAG'NDROP is a MOUSEGESTURE, for dragging from a source DISPLAYELEMENT to a target DISPLAYELEMENT. Our example gesture, Move File to Folder, is an element of the DRAG'NDROP set. The FEEDBACK part can use DISPLAYELEMENTs for feedback, while HITCHECK will indicate which of the checks-for DISPLAYELEMENTs that have been hit.

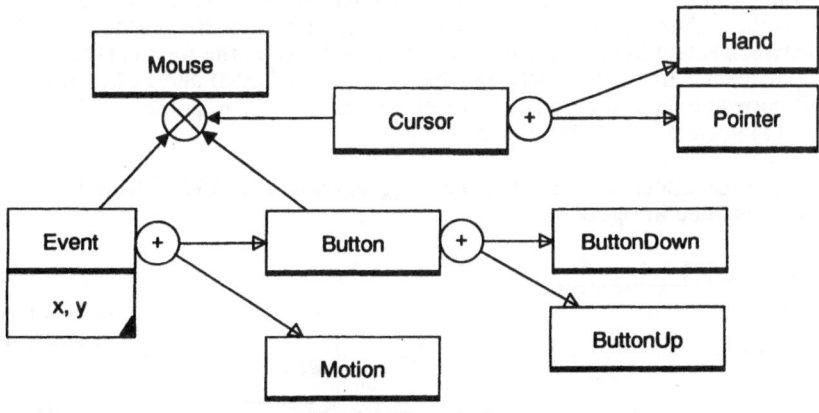

Fig. 3. Mouse device

The VISUAL concept represents DISPLAYELEMENTs that are related to application data. The represents relation is tracked by the presentation component of figure 1.

The MOUSE and KEYBOARD concepts refer to devices generating the lexical elements, that are parsed by the gesture recogniser. Figure 3 details the definition of MOUSE, since it will be used later when modelling the gesture recognisers' dynamic behaviour as Statecharts. MOUSE contains BUTTONs, which can be either up or down, two kinds of CURSORs, and finally EVENTs, which have x and y attributes for recording mouse coordinates. EVENTs are of two kinds, BUTTON and MOTION.

3.3 Referent's sets vs. Statechart's states

When turning from the *static* structure of the gesture recognisers to their *dynamic* behaviour, we will need to reinterpret the concepts already modelled as Referent sets, in terms of Statechart state machine concepts. To ease the transition (pun intended) we will use a variant of Statecharts, that we have designed as a natural extension of the Referent language. According to this integration, elements of Referent sets corresponds to Statechart states, *disjoint* specialisation correspond to *XOR*-decomposition and *aggregation* to *AND*-decomposition The presentation below will use the already introduced gesture recogniser model as example.

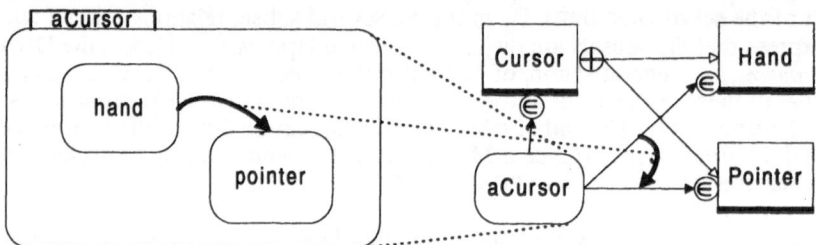

Fig. 4. Disjoint sets and XOR-decomposition

The Referent model of the MOUSE device expresses that a CURSOR must be either a POINTER or a HAND cursor. More precisely stated, the model expresses that a member of the CURSOR *set*, e.g., the aCursor *element* in figure 4, must be member of either the POINTER or HAND sets. Imagine that this set membership can vary, i.e. that aCursor can move back and forth between the POINTER and HAND sets, as illustrated by the arrow. At any time aCursor will be a member of either set. Reformulated in Statechart terms, we can say that aCursor is in a *state* of being a member of a specific CURSOR set. Movements between sets will correspond to *transitions* between the membership *states*. In figure 4, aCursor's movement between the *disjoint* sets HAND and POINTER ($\in$ = element-of) corresponds to the transition from state hand to state pointer in the *XOR*-decomposed Statechart labelled aCursor.

A similar correspondence exists between *aggregation* and *AND*-decomposed Statecharts, as illustrated in figure 5.

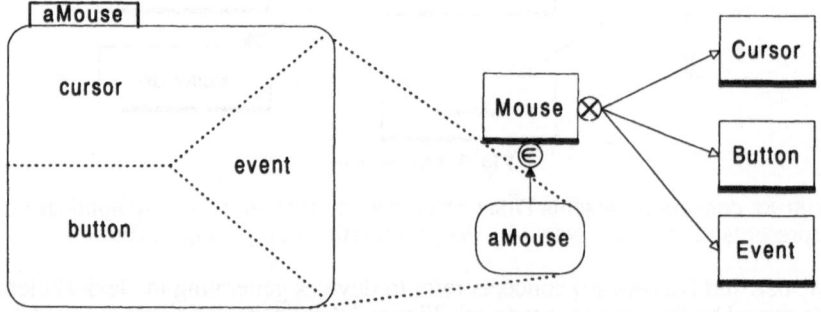

Fig. 5. Aggregation and AND-decomposition

Note that these Statecharts states represent *typical* elements, not sets, as identified by the references to aCursor and aMouse. Note also that even though they are interpreted as states, they still have relations and properties like ordinary elements. This represents an extension to Statecharts in the spirit of Objectcharts [8], but unlike UML [9], and will come to great use later. Normally, Statechart states will represent generic or *typical* set elements and will be identified by the lowercased set name, like for hand and pointer in figure 4.

Based on the described relation between Referent sets and elements and Statechart states, where disjoint sets correspond to XOR-decomposed Statecharts and aggregation to AND-decomposed Statecharts, we can now move on to the behaviour of gesture recognisers.

3.4 Behaviour of recognisers

For a user, the behaviour of a gesture recogniser is visible through the feedback generated during parsing of lexical device events. In the table describing the gesture example, we listed a sequence of steps that were identified by observing the relation between user action and feedback. When modelling the behaviour of recognisers it seems *natural* to represent these visible steps as states of a Statechart machine. This is in accordance with the discussion in the previous section. For our example, this amounts to five states, one for each step, including the initial start state and the command issuing step completing the gesture. The relation between user actions and feedback, i.e. feedback to the user actions, is modelled by adding transitions that are triggered and controlled by appropriate (device) events and conditions, respectively. A Referent model and a preliminary Statechart model of the main steps are shown in figures 6 and 7.

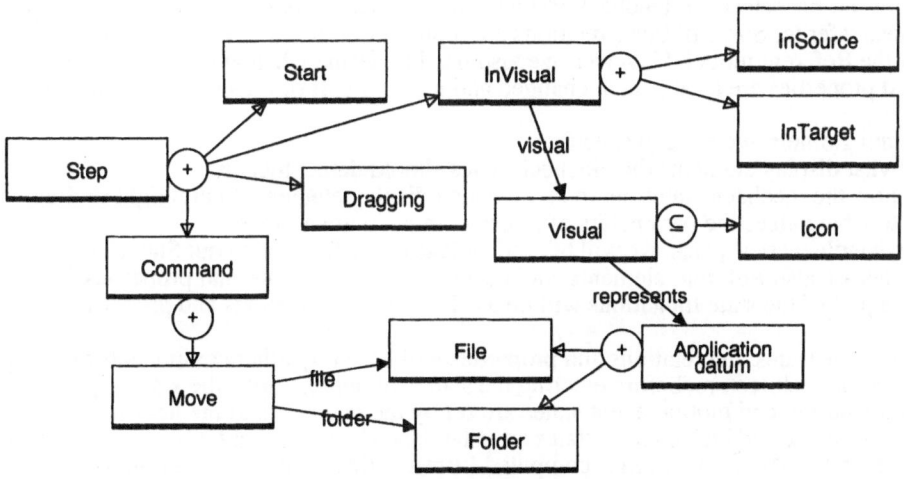

Fig. 6. The structure of the five gesture steps

In the Referent model, several special kinds of steps including the final move command are shown, in addition to part of the file system domain. In the statechart, the user actions performed with the mouse are only illustrated by the transitions. However, according to the previous section, the MOUSE referent and its events can be modelled as Statechart states and transitions, and similarly for of hit checks and feedback. This will let us provide a more formal and complete representation of the behaviour, as shown in figure 8.(The notation ">state" and "<state" is short for "entering state" and "leaving state", respectively. The "hit" condition is short for a check for if the mouse cursor is in/on one of the display elements that the hit state is related to through the checks-for relation.)

The states in the top row are concerned with user actions, the unconditional double transition illustrating that these are controlled from outside the Statechart machinery. These top four states drive the transitions in the main Statechart in the middle, which contains states for the steps of the gesture. The four states at the bottom are concerned with feedback, with one state for the cursor, two for highlighting and one for dragging icons. All these are driven by the main Statechart, hence ensuring that the steps are clearly visible for the user.

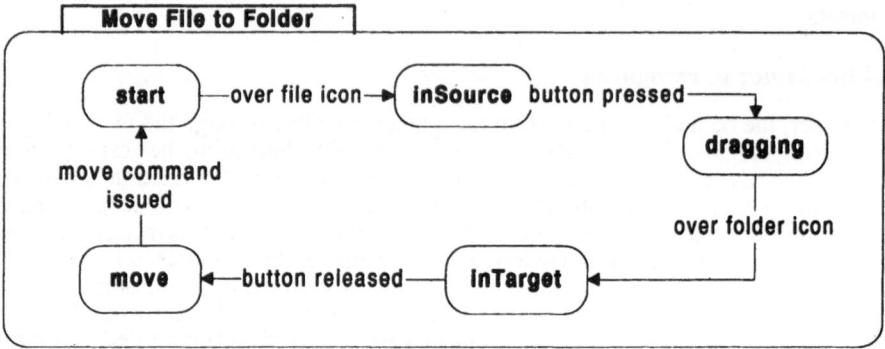

Fig. 7. The behavior of the five gesture steps

An important aspect of the dynamic behaviour still remains to be specified, the relations between hit detection, feedback issued commands and the visual and domain objects these refer to. Some of these relations are represented as static relations and properties in the Referent model. However, we also need to define when and how these relations and properties are established, changed and used, as part of the dynamic behaviour.

Among others, we need to specify:
• what display elements the hitCheck states should detect hits on
• how the feedback states get to know which display elements to highlight or drag
• to what values the parameters of issued command are assigned
To handle these aspects, we will take advantage of the fact that in our Statechart dialect, states are also Referent elements, and hence can have relations and properties. The action part of the state transitions will be used to set these relations and properties.

For some states, the relations and properties will be set by other components of the application architecture, before entering the states. In our example, the x and y properties of the button and motion event states are set by the devices, and the has-hit relation of the hitSource and hitTarget hit states are established by the presentation component. For other states, the information is computed from existing relations and properties, as part of the transitions' action part, as shown in table 2

As mentioned before, the flow of values is from the upper states in figure 8 to the lower ones. The actions in the table will ensure that the relations and properties of the states are set to appropriate values at appropriate times.

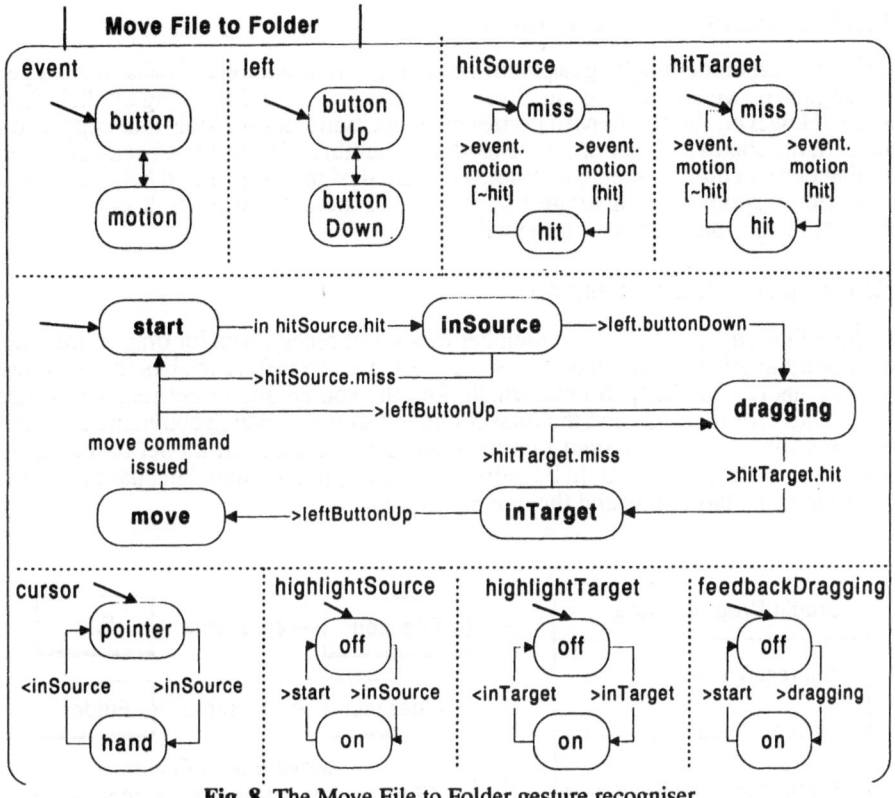

Fig. 8. The Move File to Folder gesture recogniser

State	Relation/Property	Value
hitSource	checks-for	Move File To Folder.source
hitTarget	checks-for	Move File To Folder.target
inSource	visual	hitSource.hit.has-hit
highlightSource.on	feedback	inSource.visual
feedbackDragging.on	feedback	inSource.visual
inTarget	visual	hitTarget.hit.has-hit
highlightTarget.on	feedback	inTarget.visual
move	file	inSource.visual.represents
move	folder	inTarget.visual.represents

Table 2: Transition actions

4. Gesture recognition and tools

By using formal modelling languages for describing the structure and behaviour of gesture recognisers, we are helping ourselves in understanding and agreeing on their functionality. However, the full benefit comes when we build design tools that support our models. In the context of user interface models, a number of tools have been suggested, including design editors, (semi-)automated design, design critiques and help generators [11]. In this section, we will suggest how some of these could be built upon our approach for the gesture recognition modelling.

4.1 Creating models from templates

The Move File To Folder model is member of a set of recognisers for drag'n drop gestures. The structure of these recognisers are the same, the difference lies in which display elements can be dragged onto which, i.e., the source and target relations of the DRAG'N DROP Referent set, and the final command step, i.e., which command is issued. This similarity could be captured in a template, i.e., a Statechart model based on the Move File To Folder model could be defined as a Drag'n Drop template, parameterised by the source and target sets and the command step.

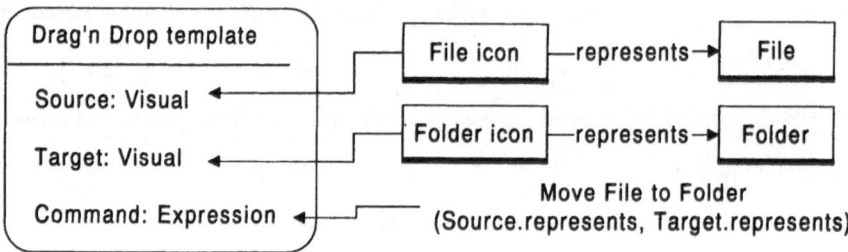

Fig. 9. Move File to Folder as instance of template

Defining our Move File To Folder model based on this template would be done by choosing two VISUALS representing the FILE and FOLDER domain concepts, from our model, and formulating an expression for creating a Move File To Folder command based on these, as illustrated in figure 9. The Drag'n Drop template and other templates for standard gestures could be part of a library of models, from which the designer could choose.

The Drag'n Drop template supports the Move File To Folder command, since the latter requires two parameters and the former provides them. This *supports* relation, illustrated in figure 10, can be represented in a tool and provide design support. The template example above, is based on the observation that a class/set of gestures supports a certain set of commands. Providing the designer with a template library, corresponds to focusing on the right hand side of the supports relation. The opposite approach, i.e., focusing on the left hand side, could also be helpful. The designer could select a command and, based on the supports relation, the tool could suggest suitable gestures templates and provide the template parameters automatically. E.g., upon selecting the Move File To Folder command, the tool could suggest the Drag'n Drop template since the former is supported by the latter.

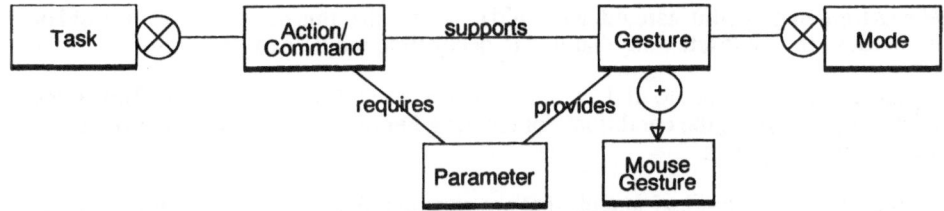

Fig. 10. The supports relation

4.2 Creating composite models from simple models

In section 2 we mentioned a variant of the example gesture; one where the target area was the desktop surface and the command was Move File Icon. These two gestures were both recognised and differentiated, without the user having to choose a specific mode for disambiguating them. It is easy to see that this composite model would need two hitTarget states, two inTarget states and two command states, i.e. one for each gesture. There are two ways of building such a composite recogniser: a model for recognising one of these gestures, could be augmented by the additional states, or models for each gesture could be combined.

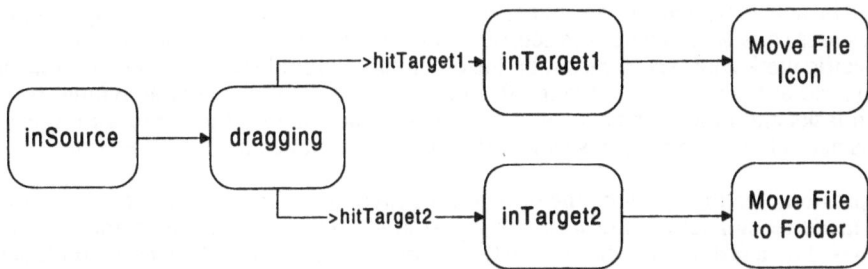

Fig. 11. Composing Move File Icon and Move File to Folder

The second of these is interesting, since in principle, it can be automated. The idea is to combine the two sets of states using AND-decomposition, giving a new and valid state machine. However, often many states will be duplicated, so a merging step can be added where equivalent states are merged, leaving a much simpler machine. Figure 11 illustrates that the two pairs of inSource and dragging states have been merged, while the pairs of inTarget and the commands states are retained. Given the formal nature of Statecharts, the equivalence of states normally can be proven by starting at the initial states, analysing the possible transitions and noting which states are always active simultaneously. Of course, the states must also be equivalent in other respects, e.g., their actions and interactions with the other application components, like the command executor and presentation components.

4.3 Analysing the usability of gestures

In the context of user interfaces and gesture recognition, evaluation of models could detect several kinds of usability problems.

A gesture can be defined as *invalid* if some STEP states never can be entered. Such a case could be detected by analysis, since the transitions represent explicit constraints on state sequences. Hence, if in our example gesture, the transition from dragging to inTarget was triggered by >hitState.hit, we could conclude that this transition never could occur, because the >hitState.miss that had to occur first, would exit dragging.

A gesture can be difficult to understand if some STEP states lack feedback. This is easy to detect by analysing the conditions for entering FEEDBACK states and their relation to entry of the STEP states.

When combining individual models that are considered *usable*, there is little guarantee that the result represents a recogniser for a usable gesture. For instance, if two gestures for creating rectangles and ovals are combined, the resulting gesture will allow the creation of both kinds of objects at the same time! Although such a state machine will be valid, the gesture is ambiguous from the user's point of view. This ambiguity is due to the parallel nature of the recogniser, and may result from overlapping hit regions. A detection algorithm could look for different STEP states that can be entered at the same time, by analysing the transitions' events and conditions. A different strategy would be to check for feedback states originating from different gestures, that can be active simultaneously.

4.4 Composing modes from commands

Within a user interface modelling environment supporting other design models, we should be able to take advantage of previous design decisions, when designing composite gestures. A *task model* defines sets of actions that make sense for the user to perform in specific work contexts. A *mode*, on the other hand, provides a set of gestures that are recognised at the same time. Figure 10 illustrates that there is a similar symmetry between tasks and modes as between actions/commands and gestures. For a designer it seems natural to try exploit this symmetry, i.e. design modes for identified tasks.

The previous sections provide the basis for a generic tool for designing modes, where each mode recognises a set of gestures supporting a set of commands. A mode design tool based on a task model, could take the commands in a task and generate mode suggestions from gestures corresponding to these commands. However, the gestures supporting for an arbitrary set of commands cannot normally be combined directly. As suggested in the previous section, the tool could check for ambiguities to prevent unusable modes.

Some kinds of ambiguity are due to overlapping hit regions. Many applications, although not based on formal analysis like the one suggested here, disambiguates gestures by providing distinct hit regions, like resize and move handles. A *presentation model* may be helpful for detecting where such handles could be useful and perhaps suggest where to add them.

An interesting extension is to allow the composition of modes to be done by the end-user. Many applications already allow the user to define keyboard short-cuts to commands, assign commands to tool bar buttons and edit the set of buttons in a tool palettes. Based on the techniques suggested above, such end-user tailoring could be extended by allowing the user to define new mouse gestures for invoking commands.

5. Comparison and future work

This paper has presented an approach to gesture recognition using the set based Referent language for structure and the state based Statecharts for behaviour. State transition networks (STNs) has been previously been used for dialogue modelling, and was early suggested as a model for drag and drop [13]. Section 12.3 of [14] discusses various

STNs and concludes that they are easier to understand and use than grammars, though formally equivalent.

Statecharts extends STN with concurrency, to better handle orthogonal state spaces, which naturally appear in multi-modal user interfaces. Statemaster [15] makes use of this feature for dialogue modelling, and a similar usage is suggested in [16]. Although the main steps of our example gesture do not use concurrency, we take advantage of it for modelling input devices, hit detection and feedback. We take the ease with which other devices and extra feedback can be added as evidence that Statecharts is more suited for this domain than standard STNs. The need for concurrency is even more evident when considering two-handed gestures, like the See-Through Tools described in [17].

However, the real advantage is demonstrated when designing recognisers for composite gestures, as discussed in the previous section. Tool support based on the reasoning power of Statecharts should greatly ease the design of e.g., diagram model editors, where complex editing modes are used.

The mouse gesture example, although found in many variants in modern desktops, represents only one of many gesture interaction techniques. Palmtop computers supporting (and making sense of) freehand drawing and writing are becoming widespread, and 3D pointing devices is a hot research topic. We believe our approach can be extended to handle gestures in the general sense. By analysing other gestures the way we analysed the example, we can complete our Referent model of the structure of recognisers. Based on the described relationships between constructs in the Referent and Statechart languages, we can explore different behavioural models. Currently, we are investigating ways of recognising structured freehand drawing, by adding mouse movement classifiers.

Although presented in the context of a particular application architecture, we believe the approach is not dependent on it. The Statechart machinery may fill the role of the Controller in the MVC architecture. The Garnet Interactors [18] use an implicit state machine that we are able to model by our approach, with the additional possibility of extending it. An interesting possibility that we are looking into, is encapsulating the gesture recognisers in Interactor abstractions, like the ones presented in [7]. This will make it easier to integrate our low-level approach with higher-level dialogue models.

We have validated the approach by implementing the application architecture, Statechart machinery and models in Java. Although the models are translated by hand, we have used an approach suitable for code generation. This is planned implemented as part of a graphical tool based on the already implemented architecture and machinery. Hopefully, using the approach for designing a tool for itself, will provide a real validation of it.

References

1. "Direct Manipulation: A Step Beyond Programming Languages". Ben Shneiderman. IEEE Computer, August 1983.
2. "Retrospective and Challenges for Model-Based Interface Development". Pedro Szekely. Computer-Aided Design of User Interfaces. Proceedings of CADUI'96. Edited by Jean Vanderdonckt. Presses Universitaires de Namur.
3. "The Referent Model Language". Arne Sølvberg, Terje Brasethvik. Supplement to chapter 14 in Sølvberg, Kung "Information Systems Engineering".
4. "Statecharts: A Visual Formalism for Complex Systems." David Harel. Science of Computer Programming 8, 1987.

5. "A Guided Tour of the Common Lisp Interface Manager". Rao, R., York, W. M., Doughty, D. In Lisp Pointers, 4. 1991.
6. "Comprehensive Support for Graphical, Highly-Interactive User Interfaces: The Garnet User Interface Development Environment". Myers, B.A., Guise, D.A., Dannenberg, R.B., Vander Zanden, B., Kosbie, D.S., Pervin, E., Mickish, A., Marchal, P. IEEE Computer 23, 11. November 1990.
7. "A compositional model for the formal specification of user interface software". Markopoulos, P. PhD thesis at Department of Computer Science, Queen Mary and Westfield College, University of London.
8. "Introducing Objectcharts or How to Use Statecharts in Object-Oriented Design". Derek coleman et.al. IEEE Transactions on Software Engineering, vol. 18, no. 1, January 1992.
9. UML Summary, Version 1.1 http://www.rational.com/uml/html/summary/ and Statechart notation, http://www.rational.com/uml/html/notation/notation9a.html
10. "Readings in Human-Computer Interaction: Toward the Year 2000". Baecker, R.M., Grudin, J., Buxton, W.A.S., Greenberg, S. Second Edition. 1995
11. "State of the Art in User Interface Software Tools". Brad Myers, CMU. In [10], pp 323-343.
12. "Embedding Computer-Based Critics in the Context of Design", Fischer, G., Nakakoji, K., Ostwald, J., Stahl, G., Sumner, T. Proceedings of the Conference on Human Factors in Computing Systems, INTERCHI'93, pp. 157-164. ACM Press.
13. "A Three-State Model of Graphical Input". Buxton, W. In Human-Computer Interaction - INTERACT'90, pp. 449-456.
14. "Modelling User Interface Software". Part I of dissertation of Niels Vejrup Carlsen. Technical University of Denmark. 1991.
15. "Statemaster: A UIMS based on Statecharts for Prototyping and Target Implementation". Wellner, P.D. In Proceedings of CHI'89 Conference on Human Factors in Computing Systems, May 1989.
16. "Integration of User Interface and Conceptual Modelling". Farshchian, B., Krogstie, J., Sølvberg, A. In Workshop Proceedings for ERCIM Workshop "Towards User Interfaces for All: Current efforts and future trends". 1995
17. "A Taxonomy of See-Through Tools". Bier, E.A., Stone, M.C., Fishkin, K., Buxton, W., Baudel, T. In [10].
18. "A New Model for Handling Input". Myers, B.A. ACM Transactions on Information Systems 8. 1990.

Integrating Joint Behaviour and Dialogue Description

Gavin Doherty and Michael D. Harrison

Human Computer Interaction Group,
University of York
Email:{gavin,mdh}@cs.york.ac.uk

Abstract. Agents are becoming increasingly common as a means of structuring interactive systems, due to the highly complex and concurrent nature of modern systems. The manner in which interaction between these agents is specified is of fundamental importance, and must pay heed to expressivity and reuse concerns. There are also concerns specific to interactive systems, and in particular the need to specify and reason about user-system dialogue. We have shown previously that the standard model of object interaction is inadequate with respect to these concerns, and that the action model performs better with respect to these criteria. In this paper these results are drawn together with approaches previously taken in interactive systems. From this basis a schema calculus with interleaving semantics is proposed, which better addresses the concerns of expressivity and reuse in the interactive systems context.

1 Introduction

Modern interactive systems are large, complex entities comprising a number of components with the capability of handling multiple simultaneous threads of dialogue. In this environment, the concept of *object* and the concept of *agent*, an independent active object, has become crucial, as it affords us an ability to manage this complexity.

By specifying the system as a collection of co-operating agents operating concurrently, further expressive power has been gained. Defining the manner in which the agents co-operate and communicate is of fundamental significance in harnessing this power. When choosing a specific model for concurrency and co-operation, there are two issues of particular importance, namely those of *expressive power* and of *reuse*.

Furthermore, there is a need to consider the goodness of fit in relation to the concerns of the domain of the system under consideration. Our own interest is in *interactive systems* and hence issues of *behaviour* are of importance. For example, the order in which operations can be invoked (the user input syntax) is of particular relevance, as this must relate to the user's tasks and goals, and its structure affects issues such as the likelihood and consequences of user errors.

We have previously illustrated the failings of the standard model for object interaction, the event model, with regard to reuse and expressive power [5]. We have explored an alternative to the traditional event model, based on the concept of *actions*, in a general software engineering context, and shown how it copes with the reuse aspect.

The next challenge is to apply this knowledge in an interactive systems context in a practical fashion, keeping in mind our commitment to specification reuse and to tractable usability reasoning. In the following sections we shall consider in turn the concerns of interactive systems, reuse, and the concept of enhancement, and show how these concerns may be addressed by means of a new schema calculus.

1.1 Interactive System Concerns

In the domain of Interactive Systems, we are naturally concerned with the interaction between the user and system. In this context state, which is visible in the presentation or which affects the actions which may be taken by the user, is of particular importance.

The difficulty which arises is the interdependence between this **dialogue description**, and the **behaviour**, and functional dependencies of the system. If the two are separated then **consistency problems** arise, also the **separation of concerns** between the components of such a specification can be problematic. Yet if we seek to use a single notation, then it must be one expressive enough to encompass both dialogue and behaviour. We consider three previous hybrid approaches [1,14,2] in the domain of interactive systems which attempt to cover both dialogue and function description. These provide a concrete basis for the discussion and exemplify interactive systems concerns.

Behaviour and Dialogue The behaviour of an interactive system generally concerns when and under what conditions certain events can happen. Those events which directly involve the user (user input and system output, ie. the *dialogue*) are of most concern. The means by which this dialogue is specified determines the ease with which usability reasoning can be carried out.

In a scheme designed to allow designers to *"specify formally the structure of complex and concurrent dialogues"*, Alexander [2] uses CSP [13] behavioural definitions to describe user input syntax, linking operations to each event. CSP provides a rich set of operators for combining events and processes, the main operators being prefix, choice, sequence and parallel composition. User inputs and system responses are represented as atomic events, but causation of events and the communication between components are unspecified. The system model consists of an association between events and a specification in *me too* (a lisp-like executable specification language based on VDM [15]). The events themselves are specified with eventISL (interaction specification language for events). An event describes only one interaction with the user, an interaction consisting of one input from the user and one output from the system. Thus no real model of the system is provided apart from the fact that functionality is structured via events with a single input and single output.

Alexander's CSP approach covers only the dialogue structure aspect of the interactive system specification, and is not sufficient for the task in hand in unaugmented form. Nevertheless, the interleaving semantics of CSP provides a powerful means for specifying and reasoning about concurrent operations without the complexity overhead of computation based models of parallelism.

Hybrid Specification As CSP does not provide support for describing either the structuring of the system as a collection of objects, nor for defining the behaviour of these objects, an obvious step is to combine it with a mechanism for defining an object's state and behaviour. There are a number of difficulties with the use of hybrid notations:

- the problem of maintaining consistency between the two components of each specification,
- no overall meaning can be given to a specification unless there is a semantic link between the two components,
- there can be ambiguity in the *separation of concerns* between the two components (explored below),

– using two notations adds to the complexity of construction, analysis and refinement, and also makes automated support for these more difficult to realise.

This criticism of hybrid notations is not to be confused with the construction of multiple (partial) models of a system as advocated in [9]. As the specifications under discussion define the joint behaviour of a set of interactors, it is desirable that a single specification be constructed for this purpose.

The agent language of Abowd [1] is illustrative of a move towards object based specification, in the form of independent agents. Abowd pays particular attention to the composition of agents to form complete systems, and provides a means of specifying interleaving of agents. Agents include internal and external components, the internal component detailing the operations and state changes of the object, and the external specification (a CSP behavioural specification) detailing interactions with other agents. Although there is a semantic link between the components of the specification, the notation is a hybrid with the attendant problems thereof. Also, as pointed out by Hussey [14], the composition operations deal only with entire agents rather than with individual operations, severely limiting the opportunities for reuse.

Hussey [14] harnesses the expressiveness of the formalism for dialogue description within a more complete specification process through the application of interactor style specifications: using CSP for user input syntax and Object-Z[8] for state and operations. The events (alphabet) in the CSP dialogue description each correspond to a single Z schema. Additionally, each interactor[6] has a behavioural description (alphabet and trace definition) associated with it. In addition to the lack of a semantic link between the components, the lack of integration of the external specification into the object model means that the standard object mechanisms for reuse cannot be applied to external behaviour. There is also the problem of consistency. Whereas the CSP specification gives the sequence of allowable user actions, the object definition could disallow all such sequences completely through the precondition on the operation schemas.

Separation of Concerns With hybrid notations, a difficulty is encountered in obtaining a clear separation of concerns between the two components of the specification. For example, it is possible to express the same behaviour using different combinations of CSP and schema definitions. Consider a simple system which can be either locked or unlocked, with an initial state of unlocked, and two corresponding operations:

$lockstate = \{locked, unlocked\}$

```
┌─ lock₁ ────────────────        ┌─ unlock₁ ──────────────
│ s : lockstate                  │ s : lockstate
│────────────                    │────────────
│ s' = locked                    │ s' = unlocked
```

$SYS_1 \cong lock_1 \rightarrow unlock_1 \rightarrow SYS_1$

```
┌─ lock₂ ────────────────        ┌─ unlock₂ ──────────────
│ s : lockstate                  │ s : lockstate
│────────────                    │────────────
│ s = unlocked                   │ s = locked
│ s' = locked                    │ s' = unlocked
```

$$SYS_2 \cong (lock_2 \to SYS_2)[](unlock \to SYS_2)$$

Clearly the same set of possible traces of behaviour is described by the two definitions, but whereas the first uses the external CSP expression to ensure legal behaviour, the second uses a combination of CSP and precondition schemas.

Summary While all three approaches use CSP as the basis for describing joint behaviour, there are significant differences in the mode of application. Abowd includes communication and a higher level notation of agent interleaving, while Hussey relies on a one-to-one mapping between user input events and operation schemas. Object-Z provides extensive object support, whereas Abowd is limited to structuring only, and Alexander provides none at all. A table summarising the three approaches is given below: Hussey's work effectively illustrates that the expressive power of this combination

Approach	Alexander	Hussey	Abowd
Joint Behaviour	. CSP	CSP	CSP+Agent language
System Behaviour	meToo (VDM based)	Object-Z	Agent language
Object Support	none	good	weak
Semantic Link	no	no	yes

Table 1. Comparison of approaches

is very good and that the size of specifications, including both these components, is not unwieldy. A notation which afforded us this degree of expressive power within a consistent semantic framework, would contribute significantly to the development of a pragmatic approach.

1.2 Reuse Concerns

Elaborating on the reuse aspect, we are concerned with reuse in the presence of inter-object (multi-agent) behaviour. Specifically, a serious reuse problem emerges when inter-object behaviour is specified in an event style. As we are concerned with systems comprised of multiple objects, we are interested in the ways in which better performance might be achieved with respect to reuse, as is the case with action based systems.

Reuse Criteria To help structure our analysis of the reuse problem, three views on the reuse problem are utilised, labelled:

- **contextualisation** as observed by Mili [17], in the object model all behaviour must be attached to an object or class, and hence all interaction between two objects must be specified as an operation on one of the two, thus decreasing the reusability of that object.
- **viscosity** pertains to the fact that although changes to inter-object behaviour are very likely to be needed so that the object can be reused, such changes are difficult to carry out in the standard model.
- **dependency** concerns the degree of unnecessary dependency introduced into an interaction by the model of inter-object behaviour, for example the need to specify explicit interaction trajectories in components whose behaviour does not depend on them.

Evaluating the approaches in section 1.1 above with respect to these criteria, we see that the agent language fares badly, concentrating as it does on entire agents as the main unit of specification, and the lack of provision for *alterations* of inter-object behaviour. Hussey's approach performs better as a large class of changes can be encompassed by rewriting the CSP syntax definition, but there is little scope for reuse of inter-object behaviour.

Action Models In contrast to the event model, action based systems suffer relatively little from the above problems. In the action model, a specification consists of a collection of objects and actions. A number of objects can participate in an action, and actions may place preconditions on these participants. All state changes are effected by means of actions. A comprehensive survey in [16] shows the action model to have a high degree of expressive power according to a broad range of criteria. Summarising the work in [5], there a number of features of systems such as DisCo [11] (an object oriented action based language) which contribute towards resolution of the above problems.

- **contextualisation:** the separation of object definition and interaction in a semantically consistent way through the use of actions moves us away from a purely object based system. Hence the context dependence of objects including inter-object behaviour is addressed, at the price of a very different specification architecture.
- **viscosity:** the ability to alter inter-object behaviour through strengthening of guards and extension of states. Although again not unique to action based systems, the use of action style specification makes this type of change more likely to encompass a larger proportion of desired changes to inter-object behaviour.
- **dependency:** the environmental selection of actions based on the availability of appropriate objects satisfying the preconditions. This is the basis of the action style, and allows specifications to be written in such a way that we need not define the sequence of operations which put the system into a certain state in order to define an operation which is enabled in that state.

The key concepts then, are the environmental selection of actions, the ability to strengthen and alter action guards, and the shift in focus away from the objects alone.

1.3 Enhancement

The concept of enhancement is of particular interest. For our purposes we can define enhancement as adding *observable behaviour* to a system specification in a manner which preserves properties of the original system. Following Bramwell [3] we agree that the designer often works by *enhancing* a previous specification, and with this in mind, we will take enhancement as our mode of reuse. Such an incremental mode of development is of particular importance in the interactive systems context, given the modern emphasis on rapid prototyping and fast feedback into the design process over many iterations of the development cycle.

Past approaches to enhancement have generally focussed on data refinement and state [3]. While there is a relationship between refinement and enhancement, as noted by Bramwell, refinement can include simplification or elimination of observables and hence not all refinements are enhancements. We are also interested in *behavioural* enhancements which concern the *trace* of a composite operation. The notion of trace allows us to formulate definitions of enhancement which are meaningful in an interactive systems context. This focus can also be used to resolve the distinction between *composition refinement* and *enhancement*. Bramwells' definition, based on He [12], requires that the traces of the refined interactor yield a subset of those of the original interactor when projected onto the alphabet of the original (a formal definition is given in section 2.4). This can involve the loss of observable behaviour, so we introduce the notion of *composition enhancement* in which the traces of the enhanced interactor yield *exactly* those of the original when projected onto the alphabet of the original.

A challenge posed by this is to revisit such formalisations of enhancement in the context of object oriented specification, for which we need a framework in which inter-object behaviour is defined in such a way that we can reason about traces of behaviour.

1.4 Other Concerns

Action systems have the ability to express multiple object participation in composite operations. This is a powerful model for object interaction, and satisfies the concerns in the object-oriented literature regarding the **expressive power** of the event model. We do not advocate direct use of action models for a number of reasons; on a practical level, use of such models for specification is not widespread at the present time. Also, within the field of interactive systems specification, the impact of the use of such formalisms on usability reasoning is not known.

Model based specification languages such as Z[18] and VDM[15] are a more practical alternative as they are widely used and supported. Although they are not based on the event model, event style specifications using them have been common [7]. As they model the state and operations of the system we can usefully reason about modes, goal achievement, functional invariants and information to be presented to the user. We are particularly interested in object based variants of these mainstream specification languages for the reasons previously discussed (namely, object reuse and ease of implementation). A pragmatic approach would be to incorporate action concepts into a framework based on a conventional specification language, taking into account the concerns of interactive systems.

Above, the examination of interactive system concerns has suggested that an expressiveness similar to CSP behavioural definitions is desirable (particularly for concurrent dialogues), but must be augmented to describe joint behaviour. Previous approaches to this have involved hybrid specifications, which cause consistency and tractability problems. Likewise the reuse concerns mitigate against purely event based specification of joint behaviour, favouring more action based approaches. Our goal is to factor both of these sets of concerns into any proposed approach.

2 A New Schema Calculus

Motivated by the analysis above, we take Object Z [8] and the schema calculus as the basis for our approach, and demonstrate that this approach satisfies the above concerns. Examination of these concerns also allows us to justify the differences between our approach and previous approaches such as that of Hussey [14]. Object Z is a natural choice as it incorporates many object oriented concepts and is based on a widely used model-based formalism (Z). Operations may be declared in much the same way as schemas in Z or as composites of operations. A class encapsulates both state and operations.

2.1 Defining joint behaviour with the schema calculus

As Hussey notes [14], Object Z classes provide a convenient means for structuring a system as a collection of interactors. The attributes of the class correspond to the state of the interactor, with state transitions effected by means of operations. Rather than relying on an external description of the allowable traces of such operations, as was the case in the approaches examined earlier, we define these traces using the schema calculus.

Taking the basic schema calculus operators of choice ([]) and sequential composition (⨟), inter-object behaviour and syntax can be defined simultaneously, as the schema calculus expression determines both the flow of data and sequencing of operations. For example the CSP definition:

MENU = (display → selection → (MENU [] SKIP))

will have an equivalent effect to the schema calculus expression:

$menu \,\hat{=}\, display \fatsemi selection \fatsemi (menu[]skip)$

2.2 Separation of Concerns

One aspect of the action model which must be considered carefully concerns the need for moding state to sequence internal operations. This state is neither visible nor meaningful to the user. However an opportunity is present to resolve both this problem and the difficulty in obtaining a clean separation of concerns identified above.

Essentially, the problem of separation of concerns is that moding can be expressed either by means of schema preconditions (guards) or the schema calculus. Given that user visible moding is of particular interest, we formulate the rule that user-visible moding be expressed through the use of guards, and that where possible 'internal' modes be expressed by means of the schema calculus. This allows us to achieve a more distinct separation of concerns and should also yield more structured specifications.

For example, a paste command in an editor might be specified as the following:

$$paste \,\hat{=}\, File.isWritable \fatsemi Clipboard.getContents \fatsemi File.Insert$$

Where *File.isWritable* is a precondition on the mode of the file (essentially a guard on the command), *Clipboard.getContents* returns the contents of the clipboard and *File.Insert* inserts the text returned by the clipboard.

2.3 Defining Behaviour

Under the semantics of Object Z, sequentially composed schemas are equivalent to atomic schemas. The existing 'parallel' operator is actually a form of conjunction with communication, with no concept of visible intermediate states or interleaving.

This is entirely suitable when describing functionality. In the interactive systems context, however, the specific *behaviour* is of interest, and the lack of parallel operations is a problem. As all operations are effectively atomic, we cannot meaningfully discuss intermediate states or simultaneous operations. At best, the possibility of simultaneous operations can be encoded by introducing state variables for each operation, storing the current point in the operation. The operations are then split into sub-operations with preconditions over this state to sequence each sub-operation. This is obviously not an ideal solution. Firstly the abstraction for operations no longer matches that provided by the notation, secondly we have had to encode the execution model explicitly, and thirdly the granularity has been forced to the lowest level.

What is needed is an expressiveness akin to the interleaving parallel semantics of CSP. With such an approach, the schema calculus could be used to define composite behaviour in a way which allows us to define and reason about intermediate states and concurrent operations, without having to resort to hybrid specifications.

In order to achieve an interleaving semantics, there must be a notion of atomicity of sequentially composed schemas. Thus the meaning of a given schema expression can be given in terms of the meaning of a set of sequentially composed schemas, with simple operations defined as sequences of length one. With this we can have a notion of intermediate states within a schema expression, that is, the state at a point in time determines the simple or 'atomic' schemas (within a sequential composition) which may occur next. In our semantics, we allow either an incomplete operation to be continued, or an operation (possibly the same one) to be invoked. Specific concurrency constraints can easily be added to this general framework. To elaborate on the interleaving behaviour we would wish to define, we see two particular cases, namely interleaving of sequences at the top level, and an interleaving parallel operator ($\|$). Thus if we have two objects obj_1 and obj_2 and operation definitions: [1]

$$obj_1.op_1 \mathrel{\widehat{=}} a \mathbin{\text{\textschwa}} b \mathbin{\text{\textschwa}} c$$
$$obj_2.op_2 \mathrel{\widehat{=}} x \mathbin{\text{\textschwa}} y \mathbin{\text{\textschwa}} z$$

then interleaving of the sequence $a \mathbin{\text{\textschwa}} b \mathbin{\text{\textschwa}} c$ with the sequence $x \mathbin{\text{\textschwa}} y \mathbin{\text{\textschwa}} z$ is possible. Within a sequence we might also define a parallel sequence: $a \mathbin{\text{\textschwa}} (x \mathbin{\text{\textschwa}} y \parallel w \mathbin{\text{\textschwa}} z) \mathbin{\text{\textschwa}} b$ Where $x \mathbin{\text{\textschwa}} y$ and $w \mathbin{\text{\textschwa}} z$ can be interleaved with each other (and also with other sequences at the top level). This semantics allows us to talk about traces of behaviour, which can be used to relate actions to tasks [4] and to reason about the likelihood and consequences of sequencing errors [19].

2.4 Enhancement

An interesting result of this semantics, in relation to reasoning about systems is that it allows us to develop a more formal notation of enhancement. We can talk about possible traces of an operation, where the alphabet is the set of sequentially composed schemas. Consider the notion of *composition refinement* [13]; the definition of which states that one action is a composition refinement of another if its alphabet is a superset of the other, and if it is a subset of the other when projected onto its alphabet.

$$I \sqsubseteq_C J \Leftrightarrow (\alpha(I) \subseteq \alpha(J)) \wedge (traces(J) \restriction \alpha(I) \subseteq traces(I))$$

Formalising the notion of *composition enhancement* introduced earlier:

$$I \sqsubseteq_{CE} J \Leftrightarrow (\alpha(I) \subseteq \alpha(J)) \wedge (traces(J) \restriction \alpha(I) = traces(I))$$

---

[1] For consistency we use the symbols "$\mathbin{\text{\textschwa}}$" and "$\|$" for interleaved sequential and parallel composition.

We can define object based versions of the above, saying that an action is an enhancement of another if the set of objects which participate in it (denoted ω) are a superset of the other and if it is trace equivalent when projected onto the object set of the other (operator $\lceil_{obj}$). A behavioural enhancement is necessarily a composition enhancement.

$$X \sqsubseteq_{be} Y \Leftrightarrow (\omega(X) \subseteq \omega(Y)) \land ((traces(Y) \lceil_{obj} \omega(X) = traces(X))$$

These forms of enhancement help us to reason intuitively about changes to behaviour and dialogue of interactive systems specified as a collection of objects.

2.5 Reuse

The schema calculus and the evaluation model of Z can be applied in a straightforward fashion to arrive at a semantics similar to the action model. In Object Z, operations are 'selected' (by the environment) from the set of currently enabled operations, and data (input parameters) may be provided by the environment. This is similar to the action model, where both the action and the objects it executes with are selected by the environment. Hence a schema at the top level, which has a precondition or guard, selectable by the environment, and whose inputs are provided by the environment, can be thought of as an action. Operations defined at the top level may also be defined with schema expressions (expressions in the schema calculus), and in fact this must be done where inputs are provided by other schemas in the system. Since choice and selection are possible within schema expressions we can view a component schema as a form of action. This is strengthened by the interleaving semantics which allows interaction between schemas through the state transitions they perform.

The fact that operations can themselves be constructed from other schemas, by means of the schema calculus, makes it possible to deal with the composition of behaviour and communication/interconnection. Environment enrichment can be used to denote explicitly (possibly nondeterministic) selection by the environment.

Let us now consider the reuse criteria. This style can be criticised from the *contextualisation* viewpoint as being another form of a meta-method approach. In such an approach, higher level methods are used to call methods in given objects and define the manner in which they interact. However there are differences:

- the top level is still selected by the environment and as such the unit can be reasoned about as an action.
- the combination of interconnection and enablement allows the schemas themselves to be written with a relatively low degree of dependency. Thus even if the inputs are supplied by other schemas in the expression, we still write schemas as if they were being produced by the environment (ie. in the action style).
- there is a difference between a schema expression and what may appear in the body of a schema, particularly in the context of an interleaving semantics.

Looking at the other reuse criteria, the *dependency* aspect is good. This is because the source and destination of communication is entirely dependent on the context in which the schema appears, and hence unnecessary dependency has not been introduced to the communication. Also, schemas have preconditions allowing dependencies to be encoded at a relatively high level of abstraction. Likewise for the *viscosity* issue, precondition schemas allow us to alter inter-object behaviour without modifying schema bodies.

302

3 Example

A small case study of a web browser is presented below to illustrate the style of specification we envision. We start by noting the main components of functionality the application is to provide. File access and markup form the functional core, file presentation, hyperlinks and navigation form the user interface component. We have a number of requirements on the interaction the system is to support. The user must be able to: (1) move within the text (2) resize text (3) select hyperlinks (4) type in a URL. We opt to distinguish interaction with text (especially hyperlinks) (requirements 1-3) from rest of front end (requirement 4). The interface is defined with two interactors (HText and Location) and the system with a single *Core* class, each of which is specified as an Object-Z class. The *HText* interactor represents the component displaying the page, and so includes operations to move within the page[2], resize the page display and to display a new page.

```
┌─ HText ──────────────────────────────────────────────────┐
│ ┌──────────────────────────┐  ┌─ move_up ──────────────┐ │
│ │ contents : tagged;       │  │ Δ(position)            │ │
│ │ links : ℙ linktype;      │  └────────────────────────┘ │
│ │ position : ℕ;            │  ┌─ move_down ────────────┐ │
│ │ size : sizetype          │  │ Δ(position)            │ │
│ ├──────────────────────────┤  └────────────────────────┘ │
│ │ position ∈ dom contents  │  ┌─ resize ───────────────┐ │
│ └──────────────────────────┘  │ Δ(size)                │ │
│ ┌─ new_text ───────────────┐  │ newsize? : sizetype    │ │
│ │ Δ(contents)              │  └────────────────────────┘ │
│ │ text? : tagged           │                             │
│ └──────────────────────────┘                             │
└──────────────────────────────────────────────────────────┘
```

The *location* interactor simply displays the address of the page currently being displayed:

```
┌─ Location ───────────────────────────────────────────────┐
│ ┌──────────────────────────┐  ┌─ new_loc ──────────────┐ │
│ │ loc : URL                │  │ Δ(loc)                 │ │
│ └──────────────────────────┘  │ url? : URL             │ │
│                               └────────────────────────┘ │
└──────────────────────────────────────────────────────────┘
```

We must also identify the operations which the functional core will provide, namely the retrieval of files (from a URL) and markup of HTML files into tagged text.

```
┌─ Core ───────────────────────────────────────────────────┐
│ ┌─ getfile ────────────────┐  ┌─ markupfile ───────────┐ │
│ │ url? : URL;              │  │ file? : HTML;          │ │
│ │ url! : URL;              │  │ text! : tagged         │ │
│ │ file! : HTML             │  └────────────────────────┘ │
│ └──────────────────────────┘                             │
└──────────────────────────────────────────────────────────┘
```

---

[2] Schema bodies are omitted for brevity.

We use a higher level class to tie the specification together [3], and to contain joint behaviour:

$$
\begin{array}{|l|}
\hline
\textit{System} \\
\hline
\lceil(hlink, type\_url, move\_up, move\_down, resize) \\
\hline
text : HText; \\
site : Location; \\
fcore : Core \\
\hline
\text{[Composite operations to be defined here]} \\
\hline
\end{array}
$$

The first item of joint behaviour performs file fetching, markup and display, taking a URL as input, and takes the form of a sequential composition.

$$new\_url_0 \cong fcore.getfile \,\S\, fcore.markupfile \,\S\, text.new\_text$$

Then we can specify the actions to handle clicking on hyperlinks and typing locations directly using nondeterministic selection (by the user), from the set of links within the current page (*text.links*), with the joint behaviour defined above (see fig. 1):

$$hlink \cong \big[\, url? : text.links \,\big] \bullet new\_url_0 \,\S\, site.new\_loc$$
$$type\_url \cong \big[\, url? : URL \,\big] \bullet new\_url_0$$

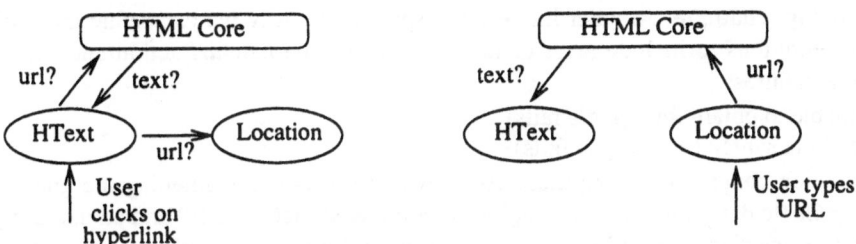

Fig. 1. *hlink* and *type-url* behaviours

Enhancing behaviour We will develop our specification by means of two enhancements, the first of which is a simple history mechanism, by means of which the user can move through the list of previously visited sites. In terms of our dialogue, we can allow for this by means of buttons which move the user either one step forwards or backwards in the list of previously visited sites. A single interactor should suffice for this purpose.

$$
\begin{array}{|l|l|}
\hline
\textit{History} & \\
\hline
fw : seq\ URL; & \begin{array}{l} \textit{new\_site} \\ \Delta(fw, bw) \\ url? : URL \end{array} \\
bw : seq\ URL & \\
\hline
\begin{array}{l}\textit{fwpress}\\ url! : URL\end{array} \Big| \begin{array}{l}\textit{bwpress}\\ url! : URL\end{array} & \begin{array}{l}\textit{fwhist}\\ \Delta(fw,bw)\end{array} \Big| \begin{array}{l}\textit{bwhist}\\ \Delta(fw,bw)\end{array} \\
\hline
\end{array}
$$

---

[3] The $\lceil$ expression lists the visible operations of the class.

304

Selecting a new site from a previously visited site will discard sites in the history after the current one. An instance of the history must obviously be defined[4]:

$$hist : History$$

The *new-site* action must be invoked whenever a new site is visited and so we must define a new joint behaviour:

$$new\_url_1 \mathrel{\hat=} fcore.getfile \mathbin{\S} fcore.markupfile \mathbin{\S} text.new\_text \mathbin{\S} hist.new\_site$$

The new_url_1 operation is a behavioural enhancement of new_url_0, as the same set of possible traces are yielded when the traces of new_url_1 are projected onto the object set of new_url_0:

$$new\_url_0 \sqsubseteq_{be} new\_url_1$$

Note that with the event model we would have had to alter one of the interactors themselves with this configuration specific detail. We also see that Griffiths' [10] composition semantics (described later), which does not hide matching inputs and outputs allows us to make such additions without altering the other schemas to 'preserve' the *url* input. The action specifications for *forward* and *backward* are quite straightforward.

$$forward \mathrel{\hat=} hist.fwpress \mathbin{\S} new\_url_0 \mathbin{\S} hist.fwhist$$
$$backward \mathrel{\hat=} hist.bwpress \mathbin{\S} new\_url_0 \mathbin{\S} hist.bwhist$$

Enhancing Dialogue Another interesting aspect is the way we can refine these dialogue definitions to include error handling. Consider the *new-url* action and the two possible failures:

1. unable to obtain file (*getfile* fails)
2. bad file syntax (*markupfile* fails)

In an action context, handling these errors would involve strengthening the guard on *markupfile* (to determine whether *getfile* has completed successfully) and on *new_txt* (to determine whether *markupfile* has completed successfully). In the schema calculus, this corresponds to adding a "precondition schema" which constrains it's input variables (and does not manipulate state) through sequential composition (or conjunction), for example: $ok \mathrel{\hat=} [\, status? : \mathbb{B} \mid status? \,]$. Expressions including *markupfile* and *new_text* can then be prefixed with this precondition schema. This allows us to deal with these failures quite cleanly in the behaviour definition, which uses the choice operator:

$$new\_url_2 \mathrel{\hat=} fcore.getfile \mathbin{\S}$$
$$((ok \mathbin{\S} fcore.markupfile \mathbin{\S}$$
$$((ok \mathbin{\S} text.new\_text \mathbin{\S} hist.new\_site)$$
$$[] (notok \mathbin{\S} markup\_error)))$$
$$[] (notok \mathbin{\S} getfile\_error))$$

It can be seen that the new_url_2 operation is a compositional enhancement of new_url_1 due to the prefix closure property of the *traces* function. The capabilities of the interleaving semantics can be exploited when dealing with concurrent operations the specification includes the possibility of performing operations such as *resize* while a *new-url*

---

[4] In fact, we could use mechanisms such as inheritance to perform such state extensions.

action is in progress. Furthermore, the effects of the resize can be taken into account in the markup;

$$new\_url_3 \cong fcore.getfile \, \S \, [\, dsize! : sizetype \mid dsize! = text.size \,] \, \S fcore.markupfile$$

Other examples could include specification of behaviour for an 'abort' function which would halt a *new-url* operation already in progress.

Discussion A number of the issues discussed earlier may be seen in the above examples. Returning first to our characterisation of the reuse problem:

- Precondition schemas such as *ok* have been used in a manner similar to the strengthening of guards in the action model. This has allowed us to make changes to inter-object behaviour (such as the conditions under which *markupfile* can occur) without altering the operation schemas.
- The schema calculus has also allowed resolution of the *dependency* issue, since the inputs and outputs of an operation are not associated with a particular source or destination. Thus in the case of *markupfile* the operations output can determine the next operation, but this is not encoded into the operation itself.
- *Contextualisation* remains something of a problem, but is alleviated by concepts such as environmental selection and the behaviour of the choice operator within the interleaving semantics.

The atomicity of sequentially composed schemas also allows us to talk of traces of such schemas within composite operations, making a more rigorous treatment of enhancement of behaviour and dialogue possible.

4   An Overview of the Formal Semantics

In this section we shall summarise a semantics embodying interleaving behaviour. Our semantics is based on that given by Griffiths [10]. Only those aspects of the semantics which differ from the original are detailed, and we shall endeavour to communicate how each component relates to the overall semantic architecture. A diagram of the relationship between components of the semantics is given in figure 2. The aim of the

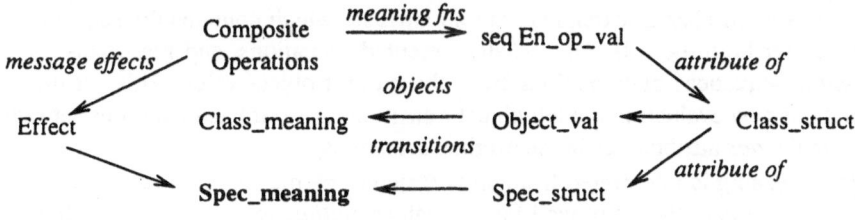

Fig. 2. Semantic Architecture

semantics is to formalise the notion of interleaving and interleaving parallel detailed earlier.

Two-part model The basic premise of Griffiths' semantics [10] is that all operations can be reduced to a simple two-part form, consisting of an internal transition and an external message. Griffiths defines a syntactic translation from 'full' Object-Z to this sub-language; since we use the same sub-language we need not include the details here. The two-part simple operation is the basic building block of the sub-language. Each operation is represented by a set of *enabled operation values* or *En_op_val*, which consist of a single state in which the operation is defined, and a set of *transactions*. A transaction is a relation between an $(in, post, out)$ triple describing the **internal transition**, and a *message* describing **external interaction**. The pairs in the transaction relation capture the behaviour under different inputs and the possibility of non-determinism. Each *En_op_val* thus encodes all the possible transitions from a given state.

Composition Operators The first level of the semantics relates simple operations to composite operations. Since the meaning of an operation is represented by a set of *En_op_val*, the composition operators are defined by a set of meaning functions mapping sets of *En_op_val* representing the composed schemas to a single set of *En_op_val* representing the composite operation:

$$\mathcal{M}_{sequence} : (\mathbb{P} \, En\_op\_val \times \mathbb{P} \, En\_op\_val) \rightarrow \mathbb{P} \, En\_op\_val$$

This must be altered to accommodate the notion of interleaving; particularly we must keep the components of sequences distinct in order to allow an interleaving semantics. In our semantics, all these functions manipulate sets of *sequences* of *En_op_val*. A simple operation is represented by a set of sequences of length 1. In this way, the meaning of any schema expression is defined by a set of sequences of *En_op_val*. We also introduce a meaning function for the interleaving parallel operator:

$$\mathcal{M}_{parallel} : (\mathbb{P} \, \text{seq} \, En\_op\_val \times \mathbb{P} \, \text{seq} \, En\_op\_val) \rightarrow \mathbb{P} \, \text{seq} \, En\_op\_val$$

Class, Object and Specification Meaning The next level of the semantics relates operation definitions in the form of sets of sequences of *En_op_val* to the meanings of classes and hence to the meaning of a specification. With the redefinition of the meaning of an operation as a sequence, the class and object meanings must be altered. In the definition of *Class_struct*, the *ops* attribute containing the operations of the class now maps names to sequences of *En_op_val*; *ops* : *Name* $\nrightarrow$ ($\mathbb{P}$ seq *En_op_val*). The state of an object at a particular point in time is represented by an *Object_val*, which is extended to encompass the state *between* steps of a sequence. This is critical since the meaning of a class is defined in terms of object values and transitions between them. So the *Object_val* class is extended with an attribute which contains the sequences of *En_op_val* for both the full and partially executed operations, and represents the set of possible sequences of transitions from the current object value. This set directly supports our new evaluation model; object transitions are extracted from this set rather than from the *ops* attribute (as in the original semantics).

Class meaning is interpreted from class structure by means of three functions: *objects* which produces the set of well formed values, *initial_objects* which does likewise for the initial states, and *OT*, which produces the set of object transitions defined by the class. These functions are rewritten to incorporate the new definition of object value, and the representation of operations by sets of sequences of *En_op_val*. Both the objects and transition map may include unreachable values, so the functions *reachable_objects* and *poss_ob_behavs* are defined as those reachable from the initial states. Since *OT* now includes all "internal" transitions, *reachable_objects* and *poss_ob_behavs* are as in [10].

Relating Messages to Effects The final level of the semantics concerns the *effect* of a given message on an object map under a particular set of inputs. This aspect is closely related to the first (compositional) component of the semantics. Both are required to fully define the behaviour of a specification. The *Effect* structure comprises two object mappings (before and after), a message, and valuations for the input and output parameters [10].

$$Map == O \nrightarrow Object\_val$$
$$Effect == Map \times Map \times Message\_val \times Valuation \times Valuation$$

The effect of composite messages are constructed from the "known" effects of the component messages. An interleaving parallel message type is introduced which denotes that the messages composed are to be combined in an interleaved parallel fashion. This must be done since we wish to define an effect set for operations which are occuring at the same time, a concept not previously defined in the schema calculus. The effect set is then used to determine the system transitions, and hence the *meaning* of a specification (see [10] for more details).

5 Discussion

To discuss this approach to the specification of joint behaviour, it is appropriate to return to our original concerns. The interactive systems issues have been addressed through the use of a single consistent notation, which allows us to reason about behaviour and dialogue. This has allowed us to avoid the attendant problems of hybrid notations. We have done this within the framework of a model based object oriented specification language (Object-Z) and thus are in a position to apply object oriented techniques to specification and reuse.

We have seen that performance of the schema calculus with respect to the reuse problem was good. When specifying an operation with a certain precondition and input parameters, no assumptions are made about how these preconditions are met and parameters supplied, which helps reduce *dependency*. The schema calculus allows us to conjoin schemas with existing schemas to achieve strengthening of guards and state extension as is the case with the action model. This allows us to reuse schemas which include object interaction, without modification, in a range of different contexts, and is a significant step towards addressing the *viscosity* issue. *Contextualisation* is more problematic, although there are similarities between the evaluation model of Z and the action model. It is still an object only system, albeit one in which action definitions are easily constructed within a given object by means of the schema calculus. So in this case one might say that the problem has been reduced in scale and severity, but not completely eliminated.

In summary, our aim has been to integrate descriptions of joint behaviour and dialogue in the context of object oriented specification of interactive systems. Our approach has been to use a single notation, taking into account interactive systems concerns such as the analysis of enhancements and more general concerns such as reuse and expressive power.

308

References

1. G. D. Abowd. *Formal Aspects of Human-Computer Interaction*. DPhil Thesis, University of Oxford Computing Laboratory: Programming Research Group. 1991. Available as Technical Monograph PRG-97.
2. H. Alexander. Structuring dialogues using CSP. In M. D. Harrison and H. W. Thimbleby, editors, *Formal Methods in Human Computer Interaction*, pages 273–295. Cambridge University Press, 1990.
3. C.J. Bramwell. *Formal aspects of the Design Rationale of Interactive Systems*. DPhil Thesis, Department of Computer Science, University of York. 1995.
4. A.M. Dearden and M.D. Harrison. Formalising human error resistance and human error tolerance. In *Proceedings of the Fifth International Conference on Human-Machine Interaction and Artificial Intelligence in Aerospace*. EURISCO, 1995.
5. G. Doherty and M.D. Harrison. Reuse in action and event based object oriented systems. Department of Computer Science, University of York, 1998.
6. D. J. Duke and M.D. Harrison. Abstract interaction objects. *Proceedings of Eurographics '93*, Computer Graphics Forum, 12(3), 1993.
7. D.J. Duke and M.D. Harrison. Event model of human-system interaction. *Software Engineering Journal*, 10(1):3–12, 1995.
8. R. Duke, G. Rose, and G. Smith. Object-Z: A specification language advocated for the description of standards. *Computer Standards & Interfaces*, 17:511–533, 1995.
9. B. Fields, N. Merriam, and A. Dearden. DMVIS: Design, Modelling and Validation of Interactive Systems. In M.D. Harrison and J.C. Torres, editors, *Proceedings, 4th Eurographics Workshop on Design, Specification, and Verification of Interactive Systems*, Springer Computer Science. Springer Wien, 1997.
10. A. Griffiths. Object-oriented operations have two parts. In D.J. Duke and A.S. Evans, editors, *Proceedings of BCS-FACS Northern Formal Methods Workshop, Ilkley*, 1997.
11. H-M. Järvinen. *The design of a specification language for reactive systems*. Doctor of technology, Tampere University of Technology, 1992. Available as Tampere University of Technology Report 95.
12. Jifeng He. Various simulations and refinements. In *Volume 430 of Lecture Notes in Computer Science*, pages 340–360. Springer Verlag, 1989.
13. C.A.R. Hoare. *Communicating Sequential Processes*. Prentice-Hall International, 1985.
14. A. Hussey and D. Carrington. Using Object-Z to specify a web browser interface. In J. Grundy and M. Apperley, editors, *OzCHI '96 – The Sixth Australian Conference on Computer-Human Interaction*, pages 236–243. IEEE Computer Society Press, 1996.
15. C. B. Jones. *Systematic Software Development Using VDM*. Prentice-Hall, 1986.
16. Y. Joung and S. Smolka. A comprehensive study of the complexity of multiparty interaction. *Journal of the ACM*, 43(1):75–115, January 1996.
17. H. Mili, F. Mili, and A. Mili. Reusing software: Issues and research directions. *IEEE Transactions on Software Engineering*, 21(6), June 1995.
18. J.M. Spivey. *Understanding Z: A Specification Language and its Formal Semantics*, volume 3 of *Cambridge Tracts in Theoretical Computer Science*. Cambridge University Press, 1988.
19. P. Wright, B. Fields, and M. Harrison. Deriving human-error tolerance requirements from task analysis. In *Proceedings, ICRE'94 The First International Conference on Requirements Engineering, Colorado Springs*, pages 135–142. IEEE, April 1994.

Discussion topics for the DSV-IS '98 working groups

Panos Markopoulos and Peter Johnson

Department of Computer Science
Queen Mary and Westfield College, University of London
Mile End Road, London E1 4NS, UK
email: {markop, pete} @dcs.qmw.ac.uk

On the first day of the DSV-IS'98 workshop, the participants were split randomly into three working groups. The groups were given three design problems to work on. The intention was that these design problems should provide the focal point for discussions. This document presents the three design problems put up for discussion. The next chapters of this book present the reports of the three working groups.

The problems presented in this document were chosen from the current research literature. It was intended that they should depart from the well-studied desk-top computer applications. A design solution was not anticipated or solicited. Rather, our intention was that these design problems should prompt participants to reflect on the role of models (of users, tasks, devices, contexts) in supporting the design of interactive systems, how they are recruited for a particular design problem and who are their envisaged users. Also, working groups were invited to work on their own problems if this would help highlight the issues they considered as interesting for the workshop.

1   A hand-held context-sensitive multi-media city-tourist guide

This design problem was inspired by the 'Guide' project of Nigel Davies, of the University of Lancaster. This project experiments with the design and implementation of hand-held devices, which provide tourist information in video and audio media. The following description of the concept is taken from an EPSRC publication [1]:

> "Imagine yourself as a tourist in an unfamiliar city. But instead of thumbling desperately through a thick guidebook as you try to figure out where you are, you carry a slim grey pad about the size of a large paperback. It tells you where to look and when to turn off the beaten track. Turn around, and the information it displays changes to reflect what you are looking at."

Some of the problems: informing the user and adapting interaction to the different bandwith available at different areas, visitors can be in groups or independent, the device must be used outdoors at all conditions, it should adapt to situations like queues in the museum, it should manage an itinerary with unpredictable delays, the tourist may want to add their own information to that supported by the system. The task of using the device is embedded within multiple activities of the user outside its scope, e.g., crossing the road, ordering food, etc.

2   An interactive reading/writing device

This design problem is inspired by the comparison of reading paper and on-line documents by O'Hara and Sellen, reported in CHI'97 [2]. They report significant advantages of paper over digital devices for reading, which pertain to: supporting annotation, quick navigation, flexibility of spatial layout. These features of paper enable readers to extract a sense of its structure, plan for writing their own documents, cross-refer to other documents, and interleave reading and writing. [2] report design requirements for the technology to assist 'reading to support writing':

• Annotation is an integral part of reading which must be supported. Notes are not necessarily used verbatim for writing, but they support the process of extracting structure from a document and to speed second reading. The reader might want to write on one document while writing on another.

• Quick effortless navigation. Input and feedback should be designed to aid 'navigation within a document'.

• The need to support more flexibility and control in spatial layout. Electronic displays have limited dimensions. How can a 'virtual space' be created which can match/improve upon the flexibility of laying out paper in space?

These are the requirements that followed the empirical studies of [2]. The groups were asked to report on how they thought modelling could help develop such an innovative device. The groups were given a copy of [2,3] to gain a deeper understanding of the problem and [4] to see a design solution presented at the CHI'98 conference.

3   Modelling for mode-awareness

This final problem was the narrowest in scope but not necessarily the simplest. It concerns the notion of modes in human computer interaction. The following narrative is by Andre and Degani [5] who use it to motivate their analysis of 'mode error'.

"The incident occurred while the second author was driving on a highway during a rainy night. The traffic was slow at about 40 mph. Bored and tired, the driver engaged the cruise control by turning it ON and pressing the SET_SPEED button. The cruise control engaged, and the car cruised at 40 mph. Several minutes later the rain stopped and the traffic speed increased; subsequently, the driver depressed the gas pedal to manually override the cruise control and increase the speed to 60 mph. He drove in this configuration for some 10 miles until coming to his planned exit from the highway.

At this point he had completely forgotten that the cruise control was previously engaged (there was no indication in this type of car that the cruise control was on and engaged). The exit ramp was initially sloped downhill and then extended uphill ending with a curve into a busy intersection. Aware of this landscape, the driver planned to release the gas pedal and let the car glide downhill (lifting the foot from the gas pedal) and maintain a slow speed during the turn into the intersection. Initially it all worked as planned. However, once the car reached a speed of just below 40 mph the cruise control "kicked in". Not expecting such a jolt, the driver lost control of the car as it sped into the intersection. Luckily, no other cars where present at this late-night hour."

Participants were asked to reflect on whether modelling could help anticipate, analyse this mode error and/or help design the device to prevent it.

References

[1]   Bacon, M. (1997) Guide in Hand, EPSRC-Newsline Special Issue, March 1997.

[2]   O'Hara K., & Sellen, A. (1997) A comparison of reading paper and on-line documents, Proceedings, CHI'97 Conference Proceedings, ACM Press, 335-341.

[3]   Adler, A, Gujar A, Harrison B.L., O'Hara K, Sellen, A., (1998) A diary study of work related reading: design implications for digital reading devices. CHI'98 Proceedings, ACM-Press, 241-248.

[4]   Schillt B.N., Golovchinsky G., Price M.N (1998) Beyond Paper: Supporting Active Reading with Free Form Digital Ink Annotations. CHI'98 Proceedings, 249-256.

[5]   Andre, A. & Degani, A.(1997) Do you know what mode you're in? Analysis of Mode Error in everyday things, In M. Mouloua & Koonce, J.M., (Eds.) Human-Automation Interaction: Research and Practice, Mahwah, Lawrence Erlbaum, 19-28.

Working Group 1 Report

M.D. Harrison

Department of Computer Science, University of York, Heslington, York, YO10 5DD, U.K.
Email: Michael.Harrison@cs.york.ac.uk

1 Participants

Keith Butler
Anke Dittmar
Gavin Doherty
Giorgio Faconti
Reinder Haakma
Michael Harrison (rapporteur)
Sarah Jones (chair)
Panos Markopoulos
Chris Roast
Meurig Sage
Fco Luis Gutierrez Vela
Martijn van Welie
Michael Wilson

2 Problem 1

2.1 Orientation

The working group chose problem 1, the portable guidebook for the City of Lancaster, and remained with this problem for the duration of the working group. Although the group came to the problem with knowledge of a diversity of techniques ranging from data modelling, object oriented design to product management, there was an inevitable specific interest in DSVIS subject matter: model based interface design; specification of interactive systems; expressing and checking properties of interactive systems. Some of these interests were relevant at specific stages of the design process. Their "irrelevance" during discussion in the early stages was a source of frustration to some of the more commercially minded members of the group.

A diversity of views of the problem was further complicated by the nature of the problem description itself. The form of the description led to the assumption that the problem concerned evaluation of the particular technical solution created by Lancaster University. The description indicated that the device had already been chosen and much of the functionality had been defined. However, the organisers of the workshop suggested that a contextual approach to the problem should be taken. Given the background of the group, this approach seemed at odds with the fact that many of the design questions that a contextual account would raise were fixed already.

2.2 Early Lifecycle Issues

As a result of this initial confusion, the early discussion was somewhat unfocussed. The initial process of orientation involved some discussion of how the artefact would be used. Hence, for example, unrelated and unsystematic discussions of features such as how physical location might affect communications with the device, or how the system might modify the itinerary to adapt to queues, made little progress towards a common group view of the activity.

Without a clear statement of the design and evaluation process, different participants were proposing approaches that might be taken to various aspects of the design process. These approaches were as follows:

- To take a collection of *use cases* [5] relating to the device and to use claims analysis as a means of assessing how well the device, as characterised by the Lancaster group, would fare. This discussion also included a comparison between the role of use cases on the one hand and use case instances or *scenarios* [7] as a means of drawing a contextual understanding into the analysis. One proposal was that low fidelity prototypes (possibly using "Wizard of Oz" techniques) might be used as a way of exploring the role that the proposed technology would play as part of the claims analysis.

- To understand the work that the device was intended to perform by taking a task analysis, including a knowledge analysis, as a means of assessing the range of activities and the ease with which the proposed device would support these activities [6].

- To establish the requirements for the proposed system. Here discussion revolved around the agents and goals of the system (for similar approach, see [1]). It was noted that different requirements and constraints would need resolving depending on viewpoint (see, for example [2]). Hence the city council might be interested in supporting and stimulating the key activities of the City while aiming to reduce traffic. On the other hand telecommunications providers might wish to maximise electronic communication and the Board of Trade might wish to ensure that the small businesses of the City would derive maximum benefit from the arrangement. One of the points that was made here was that part of this requirements process would involve the setting of a vocabulary so that the different parties to the design process could communicate.

Significantly, the last viewpoint to be considered was that of the user. Here the group discussed again the user goals and the means by which they were to be achieved and the information needs that were a consequence of these goals. It discussed the problem of representing tasks where multi-agent activity was involved as might be necessary if the system supported communication between members of tour groups. It was decided that the main purpose of the device was to set an itinerary and to provide dynamic guidance for the user.

2.3 Representation Issues

Having discussed these front-end phases of the design process, the group then explored representations that might be used to support these analyses. As already stated, very few members of the working group were currently engaged at this stage of the design or analysis life-cycle. However, some members of the group produced the following list, and indeed one member (Keith Butler) produced data descriptions as representations of use cases:

- *modelling information or data*: This could be done using entity relationship diagrams or alternatively something more orientated towards interactive systems, for example ERMIA [3].

- *modelling dialogues*: This could be done using data flow diagrams.

- *context — impact on interaction*: Here no formalism was discussed but it was decided that information was required to capture information from the environment (for example that would influence whether sound or display is appropriate), information that relates to location that may affect the nature of the communications link or the type of interaction.

- *mental model of the system*: One example where this might be useful was suggested as communicating concepts about signal strength.

- *interaction styles*: This involves characterising information about interaction styles and representation format that are appropriate to these different situations of use. No representations were discussed.

- *architectural descriptions*: In this context some initial analysis was proposed concerned with communications behaviour, and in particular deadlock behaviour.

2.4 Design Issues

In the final stages of the discussion the group decided that the down-stream techniques which were most represented within the group and, for that matter, at the workshop had not been addressed at all in the discussion. The group therefore decided on a scenario. The scenario was as follows:

one person, a foreign visitor, wants a half day walking tour including a visit inside at least one historic attraction and requires a plan.

The group then provided a short list of "what ifs" associated with this scenario. For example,

- what happens if too long is spent at a particular location?

- what happens if a break for refreshments is required?

A sketch design was required that included information: a list of places, map, information about places, time constraints as well as a definition of the itinerary. The design must then be analysed in the context of the scenario:

– by superimposing a goal decomposition based on a task analysis onto the scenarios and thereby checking how the system helps to achieve the goals and plans and actions;

– by refining the sketch using User Action Notation [4], using a component based architecture, an information model and a prototype.

The properties based on the scenario would then be reduced to checking that:

– goals are supported;

– information is presented;

– actions are accessible over time.

Here the group discussed the role that component based models supported by model checkers might play and what an appropriate user model might be. Time expired before getting to the real grit of analysis. The whole process of the working group raised a number of questions about why the analytic techniques that were the basis for discussion at DSVIS were not more applicable in the context of this problem. The superficial answer is that many of these techniques apply at a more advanced stage of the design process when the initial requirements have been established. However, this does not really answer the question because representatives from the task analysis community and people concerned with the role of sketch models were also in the group. It seems more likely that in this particular case the problem was relatively undefined, there were too many viewpoints amongst the group and too little time to resolve them.

References

1. A. Dardenne, A. van Lamsweerde, and S. Fickas. Goal-directed requirements acquisition. *Science of Computer Programming*, 20:3–50, 1993.

2. S. Easterbrook and B. Nuseibeh. Managing inconsistencies in an evolving specification. In *Proceedings of IEEE Symposium RE'95*, pages 48–55, 1995.

3. T.R.G. Green and D.R. Benyon. The skull beneath the skin; entity-relationship modelling of information artefacts. *International Journal of Human-Computer Studies*, 44(6):801–828, 1996.

4. H.R. Hartson, A.C. Siochi, and D. Hix. The UAN: a user-oriented representation for direct manipulation interface designs. *ACM Transactions on Information Systems*, 8(3):191–203.

5. I. Jacobson. The use-case construct in object-oriented software engineering. In J.M. Carroll, editor, *Scenario based design: envisioning work and technology in system development*, pages 309–336. Wiley, 1995.

6. P. Johnson. *Human Computer Interaction: psychology, task analysis and software engineering*. McGraw Hill, 1992.

7. K. Kuutti. Work processes: Scenarios as a preliminary vocabulary. In J.M. Carroll, editor, *Scenario based design: envisioning work and technology in system development*, pages 19–36. Wiley, 1995.

This article was processed using the LaTeX macro package with LLNCS style

Working Group 2 Report

Issues in the design of a writing-for-reading device

J. Rowson

Department of Computer Science,
Queen Mary and Westfield College, University of London
London E1 4NS, UK
email: jon@dcs.qmw.ac.u*k*

1   Participants

Jose Campos
Bob Fields
Patrick Girard
Richard Guedj
William Hudson
Andrew Hussey
Mieke Massink
John McCarthy
Dan Olsen
Jon Rowson (Rapporteur)
Carmelina Santoro
Hallvard Traetteberg

2   Introduction

This report is a summary of the discussions of Working Group 2 that took place over three working group sessions.

The group had been given the brief to consider the role of models, representations and formality in the design of interactive systems. In order to focus the subsequent discussion the group decided to choose as their example application the reading-writing program that had been given to us for earlier consideration. The basic idea of this program as suggested to us was to try to provide an alternative to pen and paper for the reading of documents (such as research papers). It was quickly realized that this was a very challenging application that raised difficult and deep questions about an extremely complex human activity. In order to allow the example to be useful in subsequent discussion the group narrowed down the problem to the two basic requirements of providing fast navigation in a document and allowing a means for creating and attaching annotations to the text. This envisaged program was called the 'writing-for-reading' device.

3   Formality

The group contained both experts in the use of formal methods in interactive systems design as well as critics (in the sense of being of careful observers) of their practical advantages in an application such as this. Consequently, many of the well-rehearsed debates concerning the use of formal methods in interactive systems were briefly replayed. These included (a) the question of whether or not formal specifications were useful other than for proving formal properties and (b) the replies that formal descriptions provide an abstract view of system and a stable, though not necessarily precise, shared understanding of it.

We were reminded of the semi-formal method students are sometimes taught in order to make an information processing analysis of an activity as part of the design process. First, analyze the information used and the forms in which this appears. Then, in a similar way, examine the information produced by the activity and describe the information processing activities that have been performed.

In terms of the given application, the group asked themselves 'What questions would we want to be able to ask of any formal specification of such a device?'. Two answers to this were (a) 'can the user access any part of the document within a minimum number of button presses?' and (b) 'can the system unambiguously determine from the input which of the many possible activities the user is performing?'. We can see that these two questions are formulations of a different nature for the first relates to the explicitly stated requirement of fast navigation, whereas the second concerns a more generally desirable user requirement.

4   Representations

The group returned to considering the requirements of the writing-for-reading device for the purpose of generating and comparing alternative representations for the problem.

Two alternative paradigms for discussing the design of the device were suggested. The first consisted of viewing the document as a structured text consisting of sections, paragraphs, words etc., with the annotations being integrated into this structure in some form. The second view, prompted by a deep consideration of the properties of working with pencil and paper, was of a sheet with ink marks that provided a space in which the user could add further ink marks of a different kind (the annotations).

In order to compare how each of these two options might be represented in a design some sample tasks were analyzed. One example was the way in which a user might, given a very reduced view of the entire document, be able to make immediate, expanded access to a part of it. The operations involved were described in terms of a 'rubber-sheet' metaphor, in which the user would be able to stretch the sheet at the point of interest. This was appropriate to either paradigm previously mentioned.

5   Models and the design process

The group also focused on the issue of the use of models in the design process by asking what models could be produced and what would they be models of? These were asked in conjunction with Richard Guedj's important observation that one can only model what one has previously understood.

Various aspects of the design process were discussed. Dan Olsen contrasted two phases of design: fan-out (when all ideas are welcome, discuss what's possible) and refinement/focusing (when we concentrate attention on what's actually wanted).

For the purpose of discussion we then considered a conventional software engineering design process involving user needs analysis, task analysis, conceptual models and the standard UML approach ending with the generation of program code. It was emphasized that this process is more concerned with producing documentation and code and, perhaps, with satisfying clients rather than specifically addressing interface issues. For example, it does not address 'the gulf of evaluation' (e.g. do I understand the state of the interface from looking at the screen?) or 'the gulf of execution' (e.g. do I understand what I have to do to achieve my goal?). In order really to consider users in design there must be another process of interface development and refinement running in parallel alongside this software engineering design process. This additional process might, for example, involve conventional prototyping, contextual enquiry and non-functional requirements as well as more nebulous matters such as 'ideas' and 'things I've seen elsewhere' .

This dichotomy in the design process was of particular interest to the group. Whereas the conventional software development process captures nothing of user experiences user interface designers refine user experiences in a progressive way and stick entirely to this. It should be noted that whereas there are plenty of modelling techniques available for use in the software engineering process there were none available for the refinement of the interface. Just as importantly there is no way of systematically linking the two processes in order to allow ideas to flow back and forth between them.

6   Discussion

It is interesting here, perhaps, to reflect on the roles the group played during its discussions and the way in which it both consciously and unconsciously moved from one to another.

Initially, the group put themselves in the place of the users of the proposed application. This was natural and easy as all members of the group are themselves involved in the activity of writing-for-reading on a daily basis. But a shared reaction within the group to the proposal for the creation of such a program was to question the need for such a device at all ('why not just use pen and paper?'). This, of course, can be seen to be the common and wide-spread reaction of many users to any proposed change to their working practices. In this case, however, there was an obvious solution to the discomfort caused by this perceived loss of control over our own established working practice. What better way was there to re-assert our control than by making a subtle side-step to becoming the designers of the proposed device? No longer were we users threatened with change but instead were the designers instigating it.

As designers the group proceeded to analyze, if only briefly due to the time constraints, some aspects of the requirements of the system, introducing as it did so alternative models for understanding the problem and tentative solutions to it. From here the group then started to reflect on this process and to consider its deficiencies and flaws. At this point, we may say that the group turned to the role of 'scientist', reflecting on the processes used in design. Another important question was posed by Richard Guedj during this reflection. He asked 'How will a designer know they have identified the user's needs?' - a question which neatly brought us back full circle!

Working Group 3 Report

D.A. Duce

Rutherford Appleton Laboratory, Chilton, Didcot, OX11 0QX, UK
Email: D.A.Duce@rl.ac.uk

1 Participants

Richard Butterworth
David Duce (Rapporteur)
David Duke
Miguel Gea Megias
Tony Griffiths
Sheila Guilford
Roelof Hamberg
Francis Neelamkavil
Philippe Palanque
Fabio Paternó
Mark Springett
Kurt Stirewalt
Jean Vanderdonckt

2 Problem 3

The working group started by considering problem 3, the cruise control problem. Initially the discussion focused on how the problem could be described within conceptual frameworks known to members of the group, which led to the generation of some plausible explanations of why the problem arose. Two approaches were considered. David Duke sketched out a mapping of the problem onto Barnard's Interacting Cognitive Subsystems (ICS) model [1]; Richard Butterworth suggested that the problem might be an example of the trailing sub-goals phenomenon.

A simple block diagram showing the information flows between device and user is given in Figure 1.

The content of the cognitive resources box is provided by psychology, for example by ICS. This model describes human information processing in terms of information flows between nine cognitive subsystems. A high level representation of the ICS model is shown in Figure 2.

Information is transformed between different mental codes by transformation processes. The integration box models blending between information flows of different types. Transformation processes can also call on memory in certain ways.

The car driving problem can be approximated by the flow diagram in Figure 3. Here information from the display is received by the visual system and transformed

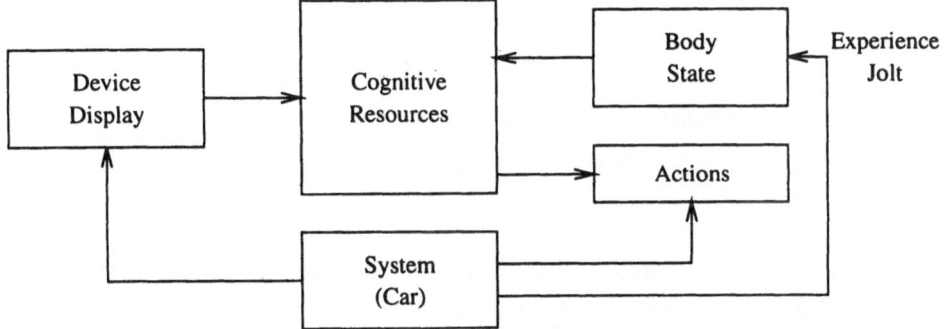

Fig. 1. Block diagram showing key information flows

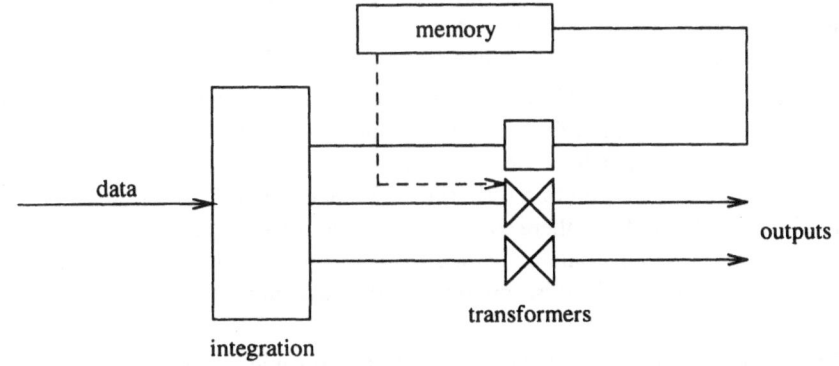

Fig. 2. High level description of the ICS model

into representations dealing with spatial awareness, then into representations that deal with how the limbs are controlled in order to control the car. With experience of driving, such proceduralization leads to a direct channel between display and limb subsystems, which does not involve higher level cognitive subsystems in decision making. To make decisions requires the use of memory as well. If the processing is highly proceduralized, it is unlikely that memory will be deployed. When the driver has to cope with the rainy conditions, PROP-OBJ-LIM processing may be involved, and as a result awareness of cruise control mode then becomes unavailable. When cruise control engages, the car jolts, the driver receives body state input and the processing configuration collapses, resulting in loss of control.

Semiformal arguments can be made about how cognitive resources are expected to be deployed in such situations, and some experiments have been carried out using formal reasoning. Proceduralization seems to be a clue to understanding this problem, thus the model can have something to say about mode awareness failure.

There is a pattern of actions inherent in the use of cruise control; when a driver enters a freeway, cruise control is turned on, when leaving the freeway, cruise control is turned off. One can posit that driver tiredness, coupled with adverse driving conditions and the consequent need to make manual adjustments (i.e. accelerating), provided a

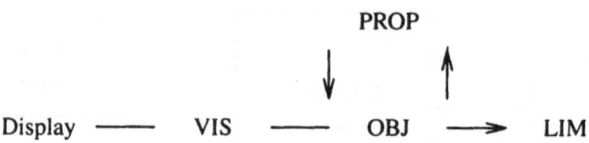

Fig. 3. Flow diagram for the cruise control problem

distraction from the rehearsed pattern of cruise control use, and consequently the goal of disengaging cruise control when leaving the freeway was lost. This is the trailing subgoals problem referred to by Richard Butterworth.

During the course of the discussion it was realized that the effects of accelerator and brake on cruise control mode are different. Hitting the brake causes the car to leave cruise control mode, whilst hitting the accelerator does not. This led into discussion of how the problem identified in the example could be avoided.

Should the driver be made aware of the cruise control mode at all times, or when some action is taken by the driver, or when some action is taken by the car? Is there a possibility that such indications themselves become proceduralized and hence ignored at critical moments? This led to a discussion of what is essential in cruise control and what is incidental, and from there to a discussion of what requirements cruise control should satisfy. The group contained at least two people who do not drive and only one person who regularly uses cruise control, so this was not an ideal group to identify requirements!

The suggestion was made that cruise control is in some way secondary to the basic driving skills. The use of accelerator and brake, especially in emergency situations, is somehow more deeply rooted than their side effects on cruise control, and it seemed that cruise control might not be proceduralized in the same way, or to such an extent, as these basic functions. This led to thoughts about how cruise control is or might be covered during driver training. Is there an approach to training that would proceduralize the behaviour of cruise control modes in the same way as behaviour under control by the brake and accelerator?

Some state machine diagrams were drawn to show the behaviour of user and device. Using state information retrieved from accident analysis reports, it is in principle possible to address, and engineer out, identified, known, problems.

The session concluded with a general discussion of design trade-offs. What catches the designer out is not what is known, but what isn't. Bridge designers know about stress analysis and over engineer bridges accordingly, but still occasionally something goes wrong, or some new combination of circumstances arises and a design fails, for example as seen in the torsion problems that led to the collapse of the Tacoma Narrows bridge.

In the one hour devoted to this problem, it was felt that modelling was being applied to offer explanations of a problem, but was not really generating alternatives or solutions. Peter Johnson joined the group at one stage and managed very effectively to produce counter examples for every bright idea we had, which rather left the group (of mainly Europeans) feeling that cruise control is fundamentally a not very good idea, even in a country as large as the USA!

3 Problem 1

In the second session, the group looked at the first problem on the sheet, designing an interface to a mobile guide book. After some initial discussion it was suggested that there ought to be a set of requirements, distilled from discussions with potential users. So the next step was to consult some potential users, i.e. ourselves! This led to the following list.

1. map showing where you are;
2. information about restaurants;
3. opening times of activities;
4. directions to nearest facilities;
5. panic button in case the user gets mugged;
6. access to other information services:
    (a) railway timetable;
    (b) active warnings (train departs in 5 minutes)
    (c) support for decision making if alternatives are possible, e.g. information about queue lengths at attractions;
    (d) ability to annotate information sources;
    (e) ability to annotate the map, so the user can return another day
7. track of where the user has been
8. display of information from central repositories:
    (a) support for local annotation;
    (b) searching on categories.

The potential for displaying dynamic information about queue lengths led to some amusing discussion about possible consequences. On the way to one attraction the user might be informed that a party of 100 had just arrived, then decide to change direction towards another attraction only to be told that same thing had just happened there, meanwhile the queue at the first attraction had now disappeared, so the user changes course for the first, only to be told minutes later that .... Thus oscillatory behaviour could be induced in the user.

This working group session took place after John McCarthy's talk and so discussion widened to consideration of group and social issues. How would the device be used by a group of people? Would the group as a whole have one device or would each member have their own? We explored the latter scenario. Should it be possible to track the locations of group members through the device? This raises privacy issues and the answers might well be different for a group of children and a group of adults. Does the group have a leader, a structure? How should the social structure be taken into account by the device? Should the leader be able to see where everyone is, even if other members cannot see where everyone is, except possibly the leader? We realized that if there were privacy modes, mode awareness problems could arise as in the first problem.

In the design brief given, it was clear that the device would be a walk up and use device. The functionality should be directly accessible, leading to a criterion that if some functionality could not be supported in this way, it should be omitted.

Adaptability was discussed. Several dimensions were identified: user abilities, frequency of use (use for first visit and for subsequent visits may impose different requirements), environment (in a library, beside a busy road, in daylight, in a cinema, ...). This led to discussion of whether adaptation should be static or dynamic. Should user abilities be specified at the start of a session or incrementally as the session proceeds? Should the user indicate when the device is being taken into a library or should the device sense this from the environment in some way? Should there be one universal device or many specific devices tailored to different user abilities, environments, etc?

The session concluded with a discussion of how modelling could be used to support design. Given some level of agreement on functionality, classes of users could be identified and knowledge analysis techniques and models such as PUM could be used to assess interface designs. This line of thought led to the question of when decisions should be made about binding information to specific modalities such as screen display, audio or even tactile feedback.

This led to further discussion of adaptation and mode awareness issues. If you are in a library, it is not helpful to use a loudspeaker for information presentation, yet if your train is leaving in 10 minutes and you are 8 minutes walk from the station, should the device issue an auditory warning? Is catching the train higher priority than avoiding the social consequences of sound in a quiet place? How should the design change from silent to non-silent mode, say? What should be the triggers? How should the user be made aware of mode changes? As noted earlier, there are ample opportunities for engineering mode awareness problems into the system; but in this design context there are many social issues, the "messy stuff" of John McCarthy's talk, that need to be taken into account during the design process.

4 Problem 2

The final one hour working group session was spent discussing problem 2.

First thoughts on the problem were that a small screen workstation will not enhance paper and so we started to think about environments such as the "digital desk" (Cambridge University/ Xerox) which combines a physical desk, paper, video projection and image analysis techniques to create a mixed paper/electronic working environment [2].

Consideration of our own working practices led us to realize the importance of spatial layout as a way to classify the sources one is working with and the ease of browsing and retrieval that comes through sensitive use of spatial layout. Techniques such as the use of coloured pens, coloured folders, were also discussed.

Technology such as hand tracking and gaze tracking could be used to support a virtual version of a 3D space.

Speed of interaction with physical paper is high and one can perform other operations such as folding or even tearing up - a useful way to control emotion!

There is a need to be able to replicate the qualities of the manipulations that can be done with paper and also the qualities of the instruments used to make marks on paper

- for example, the use of coloured inks and expressions of mood and emotion that can be made with a pen (the giant exclamation mark gouged into the surface of the paper).

We concluded the session with a discussion of the cognitive significance of a page in understanding the structure of a paper-based document. Paper gives a sense of progress when reading a document. Print width on the page is chosen for ease of scanning and reading. References to pages give a "fuzzy" reference to information - saying something is on page 10 does not give a precise location, but does give a pointer to the context in which a particular reference is to be found. Pages are also keys for retrieval and the feature structure of a page, position within the book, location of diagrams, headings, length of paragraphs, etc. give useful spatial clues by which information is classified and retrieved from memory.

References

1. P. Barnard and J. May. Interactions with Advanced Graphical Interfaces and the Deployment of Latent Human Knowkedge. In F. Paternó, editor, *Interactive Systems: Design, Specification and Verification*. Springer, 1995.
2. P. Wellner. Interacting with Paper on the Digital Desk. *Communications of the ACM*, 36(7):87–96, 1993.

SpringerEurographics

George Drettakis,

Nelson Max (eds.)

Rendering Techniques '98

Proceedings of the Eurographics
Workshop in Vienna, Austria,
June 29–July 1, 1998

1998. 231 partly coloured figures. XI, 339 pages.
Soft cover DM 118,–, öS 826,–
ISBN 3-211-83213-0. Eurographics

Some of the best current research on realistic rendering is included in this volume. It emphasizes the current "hot topics" in this field: image based rendering, and efficient local and global-illumination calculations. In the first of these areas, there are several contributions on real-world model acquisition and display, on using image-based techniques for illumination and on efficient ways to parameterize and compress images or light fields, as well as on clever uses of texture and compositing hardware to achieve image warping and 3D surface textures. In global and local illumination, there are contributions on extending the techniques beyond diffuse reflections, to include specular and more general angle dependent reflection functions, on efficiently representing and approximating these reflection functions, on representing light sources and on approximating visibility and shadows. Finally, there are two contributions on how to use knowledge about human perception to concentrate the work of accurate rendering only where it will be noticed, and a survey of computer graphics techniques used in the production of a feature length computer-animated film with full 3D characters.

Dirk Bartz (ed.)

Visualization in Scientific Computing '98

Proceedings of the Eurographics
Workshop in Blaubeuren, Germany,
April 20–22, 1998

1998. 82 figures. VII, 151 pages.
Soft cover DM 85,–, öS 595,–
ISBN 3-211-83209-2. Eurographics

In twelve selected papers common problems in scientific visualization are discussed: adaptive and multi-resolution methods, feature extraction, flow visualization, and visualization quality. Four papers focus on aspects of mesh reduction, mesh compression, and increasing the quality of the resulting mesh. Two extentions on particle tracing are presented as well as a paper on the simulation of material transport. Two papers are on feature extraction in dynamics systems and on the accuracy of algorithmic extracted features. Three papers focus on stereoscopic volume rendering, on the visualization of atomic collision cascades and of quality of visualization systems in general.

 SpringerWienNewYork

Sachsenplatz 4-6, P.O.Box 89, A-1201 Wien, Fax +43-1-330 24 26
e-mail: order@springer.at, Internet: http://www.springer.at
New York, NY 10010, 175 Fifth Avenue • D-14197 Berlin, Heidelberger Platz 3
Tokyo 113, 3-13, Hongo 3-chome, Bunkyo-ku